Luther, Barth, and Movements of Theological Renewal (1918–1933)

Theologische Bibliothek
Töpelmann

―――
Herausgegeben von
Bruce McCormack, Friederike Nüssel
and Christoph Schwöbel

Volume 188

Luther, Barth, and Movements of Theological Renewal (1918–1933)

Edited by
Heinrich Assel and Bruce McCormack

DE GRUYTER

ISBN 978-3-11-099155-0
e-ISBN (PDF) 978-3-11-061206-6
e-ISBN (EPUB) 978-3-11-061266-0
ISSN 0563-4288

Library of Congress Control Number: 2020933285

Bibliographic information published by the Deutsche Nationalbibliothek
The Deutsche Nationalbibliothek lists this publication in the Deutsche Nationalbibliografie;
Detailed bibliographic data are available in the Internet at http://dnb.dnb.de.

© 2022 Walter de Gruyter GmbH, Berlin/Boston
This volume is text- and page-identical with the hardback published in 2020.
Druck und Bindung: CPI books GmbH, Leck

www.degruyter.com

Preface

The essays contained in this volume are revised versions of papers delivered at a trans-atlantic, interdisciplinary conference held at Princeton Seminary, June 18–21, 2017. The goal of this conference was to place the "dialectical theology" of Karl Barth and his friends in conversation with other movements of renewal taking place in the Weimar era (1918–1933). I should note that, although the Weimar Republic itself came to an end in early 1930, we extended our *terminus ad quem* to the 1933, in order to consider as well the break-up of the dialectical theologians.

2017 being a year of Luther celebrations, a proposed focal-point of the research leading to the conference was to examine whether and to what extent Luther provided stimulus for the theologians treated in this volume. Our thought was to say something about divergent interpretations of Luther that accompanied and, in some cases, informed the work of the theologians and philosophers treated here. In the end, the cohesiveness of the volume did not require Luther-reception as a red-thread through all of the essays, but our hope was realized by some in a thoroughly natural way through concentration on theological renewal.

We are especially pleased that this volume could contain a hitherto unpublished work from the pen of Rudolf Bultmann – his review of Friedrich Gogarten's *Ich glaube an den dreieinigen Gott*. Appearing in the Appendix, it is the discovery of Prof. Dr. Heinrich Assel, my co-editor who also served as its editor.

Funding for this project was provide by the German Academic Exchange Service (DAAD). We were able to workshop the papers of European contributors at the University of Greifswald in March 2017 with further financial assistance from the Alfried Krupp Wissenschaftskolleg at that University. Our sincere thanks go to Michael Thomanek of DAAD in New York City and Dr. Christian Suhm at the Krupp *Stiftung* in Greifswald. And finally, a big word of thanks to doctoral candidate Chelsea Williams at Princeton Theological Seminary who edited all of the papers in this volume for English style and did the formatting. Dr. Knud Henrik Boysen, Lena Eke and Florian Pataki at Greifswald Theological Faculty revised the proof batches and prepared the index of names.

Prof. Dr. Bruce L. McCormack
Director of the Center for Karl Barth Studies
Princeton Theological Seminary

Table of Contents

Heinrich Assel
Introduction
    Luther Renaissance and Dialectical Theology – A tour d'horizon 1906–1935 —— 1

Part I: Anticipations

Hartwig Wiedebach
Karl Barth on Kant's "Biblical Theology" A Reading with Hermann Cohen —— 19

Jacqueline Mariña
The Religious *A Priori* in Otto and its Kantian Origins —— 39

Christine Svinth-Værge Põder
Luther's Lectures on Romans in the Work of Karl Holl, Rudolf Hermann, and Karl Barth —— 57

Part II: Parallel Movements

Henning Theißen
Barth's Explicit Reception of Luther
    An Auxiliary Tool for the Study of Karl Barth —— 77

Claire E. Sufrin
Martin Buber between Revelation and Scripture —— 93

Volker Leppin
Luther and Mysticism
    The Case of the Seebergs and Vogelsang —— 109

David W. Congdon
Desperatio Fiducialis
   Barth and Bultmann on the Anthropological Significance of
   Revelation —— 125

Part III: **Disruption**

Hent de Vries
Theologia paradoxa, theologia crucis
   Heidegger's Luther —— 149

Bruce L. McCormack
The Man who became God or the God who became Man?
   The Concept of Revelation in the Theologies of Karl Barth and Friedrich
   Gogarten —— 171

Heinrich Assel
Trinity, Incarnation, Political Theology
   Gogarten's Luther between Luther Renaissance and Rudolf
   Bultmann —— 193

Christian Neddens
Werner Elert and Hans Joachim Iwand – Political Theology and Theology of the Cross —— 213

Appendix
   Rudolf Bultmanns unpublizierter Kommentar (1928)
   zu Friedrich Gogartens „Ich glaube an den dreieinigen Gott" (1926).
   Ediert von Heinrich Assel —— 233

Contributors —— 261

Index of Names —— 263

Heinrich Assel
Introduction

Luther Renaissance and Dialectical Theology – A tour d'horizon 1906–1935

1 Illusions and Origins of a Luther Renaissance 1932

1.1 State of Emergency

A reviewer of the noteworthy new publications on Martin Luther in 1932 and 1933, the period leading up to the election of Hitler as Reich's Chancellor and the 450th Anniversary of the birth of the Wittenberg Reformer in November 1933, would scarcely be able to avoid the impression that the leading academic voices in Lutheran theology were proclaiming a state of emergency: a worsening crisis in and of the organs of state regarding the republican constitution and the democratic sovereignty of the German people. They intensified the crisis with their rhetoric of "judgment" and "fateful plight"[1] and they responded by producing drafts of "an emerging new Protestant doctrine of the state."

Three prominent authors formed the triumvirate of an illusion called *A new Protestant doctrine of the state*[2]: Friedrich Gogarten's *Political Ethics*, Werner Elert's *Morphology of Lutheranism*, and Emanuel Hirsch's treatise, *On the Hidden Sovereign*. This Protestant doctrine of the state turned into a controversy about the content and the validity of Martin Luther's legacy. They wanted to renew the basic structures of Luther's political theology in a relevant way for their time. In particular, they wanted to distinguish a worldly political realm from a spiritual realm: that is, the distinction between a "worldly kingdom of God" as the created realm of worldly authority and "natural law," and a "spiritual kingdom of God in Christ" as the "priesthood and kingdom of the baptized" and "Christianity."

---

[1] Emanuel Hirsch, "Vom verborgenen Suverän," *Glaube und Volk* 2 (1933): 4–13, 5.
[2] Friedrich Gogarten, *Politische Ethic: Versuch einer Grundlegung* (Jena: Diederichs, 1932); Werner Elert, *Morphologie des Luthertums* Bd. 2, Sozialllehren und Sozialwirkungen des Luthertums (Munich: Beck, 1932); Hirsch, "Vom verborgenen Suverän," s. fn. 1.

1.2 Looking Back: Origins

In 1932, the politicized Lutherans were reacting to the global economic crisis, the mass suffering, and the insurgence of terrorism on the streets. But the concept of viewing the political as the hermeneutical location for the law and the gospel of God had been in preparation for years. We must turn, for a moment, our attention from 1932 back to 1921. At the end of 1921, Karl Holl's famous book *Luther*[3] and the second edition of Karl Barth's *Commentary on Romans*[4] were published. Holl's *Luther* and Barth's *Romans Commentary* became the best-selling theological books in the Weimar Republic. The impact of both books from 1923 on can be explained by their rivalry, since Holl's *Luther* became the catalyst for the Luther Renaissance while Barth's *Romans Commentary* was the catalyst for dialectical theology. However, in 1921, it would be erroneous to understand the origin of both books primarily in terms of this rivalry. For Holl's interpretation of *Luther*, the rivalry with Max Weber and Ernst Troeltsch was the guiding factor, and what was at stake was the definition of the significance of Protestantism – and thus of Luther – in the emergence of the modern world.[5]

This was a struggle about the final (e)valuation (Werturteil) of Luther's and Calvin's political theology, their social doctrine, and the relationship of their vocational ethos to the "spirit of capitalism." This debate continued from 1906 onwards and reached its peak in 1920.

For Holl "Luther" and "Calvin", taken together, generated a certain Ethos of Responsibility springing from early Reformation religion. In 1921, Holl introduced the programmatic formula "Luther's Religion of Conscience." It was pio-

---

[3] Karl Holl, *Gesammelte Aufsätze zur Kirchengeschichte*, Luther Bd. I. (Tübingen: Mohr Siebeck, 1921, extended and revised 1923^{2+3}, 1927^{4+5}, 1932^6, 1948^7).
[4] Karl Barth, *Der Römerbrief* (München: Kaiser, 1922^2).
[5] Heinrich Assel, "Karl Holl als Zeitgenosse Max Webers und Ernst Troeltschs: Ethikhistorische Grundprobleme einer prominenten Reformationstheorie," *ZKG* 127 (2016): 211–248. Troeltsch measured the importance of Protestantism for the modern world not in terms of Luther's early reformation, but of those Calvinist churchdoms and Puritan and radical reformatory sects that Max Weber addressed in his famous studies. In view of the "madness" of the lost World War, Troeltsch called for the "development" of Germany towards a republican and mass-democratic, free-market capitalist constitution and to a demilitarized neutrality under international law. Cf. Ernst Troeltsch, "Die Bedeutung des Protestantismus für die Entstehung der modernen Welt (1906/1911)," in *Kritische Gesamtausgabe: Schriften zur Bedeutung des Protestantismus für die moderne Welt (1906–1913)*, ed. Trutz Rendtorff, Stefan Pautler, Ernst Troeltsch (KGA) 8 (Berlin/New York: De Gruyter, 2001), 183–198, 199–316; Ernst Troeltsch, and "Wahnsinn oder Entwicklung? Die Entscheidung der Weltgeschichte (1917/1919)," in *Schriften zur Politik und Kulturphilosophie 1918–1923*, ed. Gangolf Hübinger, KGA 15 (Berlin/New York: De Gruyter, 2002), 70–94.

neering because Holl expounded it using Luther's texts extensively and comprehensively. At the same time, he developed it into a multi-dimensional theory of long-term changes to all dimensions of religion, morality, and society that take the name Reformation. The Religion of Conscience originates in the experience of sacred wrath, of God's judgment as the gift of divine love, and the purification of the conscience. This is a "non-experiential experience" of conflict with God, resulting in the person's passivity as God makes the human person his "instrument". In this experience, an ethos of responsibility is born, to be carried out in worldly vocation. The intention of Holl's book about Luther was to illuminate the contemporary situation after the Great War. In 1921, Luther's Religion of Conscience and Ethos of Responsibility shaped the "spirit" of a Reformation theory that was critically equivalent to an economic ethic of western Christianity – one which Max Weber had announced for 1920, but which was never published because of Weber's unanticipated early death.

The Weber/Troeltsch/Holl debate was exemplary of the "new construction" of a Protestant morality and a socio-political ordering of society after the imperial monarchy, as well as for the scientific standard of Reformation theory after historicism. This debate formed the horizon of Karl Holl's book about Luther, rather than the contrast with early dialectical theology. Sadly, the premature deaths of the three protagonists, Max Weber in 1920, Ernst Troeltsch in 1921, and Karl Holl in 1926, deprived the Luther debate of its leading scientific and politically "republic-minded" thinkers.

That was a great misfortune!

In the year of Holl's death, 1926, the Luther Renaissance went through a mutation.

1.3 Illusion and Ideology

During the "state of emergency" in 1932, there emerged concepts of an authoritarian state or a totalitarian dictatorship in the name of the people's sovereignty, that is, new Protestant doctrines of the state. These doctrines of the state linked up with another reform program: the program of a Protestant national church. This national church was supposed to be developed as a "church of the *Volk*" and established from the royal priesthood of all baptized Christians. That priesthood was defined by Holl as the heart of Luther's concept of the church, and as the source of "charismatic" authority in a Weberian sense. A synodal and episcopal reform of the German provincial churches rooted in this principle. A merging of the the Reformed, United, and Lutheran confessional churches into the German Protestant Church was to replace the bureaucratic ruins of the former state churches. These two reform programs, the "authoritarian state" and the "church of the *Volk*" were confronted in 1933 by the violent impositions of the Nazi state. The enforced conformity of the Nazi state to its party line confronted the "church of the *Volk*"-program with its internal illusions. The injustice of the Nazi state made evident that the new doctrines of the state were an ideology. The critical voices of the opposition, who also appealed to Luther and who, upon closer inspection, were already influential by 1932, gained more and more substance and attention.

2 The Struggle for Luther's Legacy in 1933: Shifting Fronts

2.1 Three Controversies

The struggle for the content and validity of Luther's legacy took shape during three great controversies in the year of his 450th birthday.

(1) The controversy over the church's reception of the so-called "Aryan Paragraphs" in the spring of 1933, and the formation of the Confessing Church in opposition to them. This controversy made visible within Lutheranism, the irreconcilable opposition between nationalistic and racist orders of creation theologies and the voices against this racist legislation. These voices laid claim to Luther's concept of natural law in order to adopt the superior rule of "God's natural justice" in the sense of the "legal equality" of all citizens.

(2) The controversy about the violent construction of a national church which included the option that the *Führer* should himself be the highest bishop.

(3) The controversy over the legal requirement of an oath of allegiance to the Führer in both state *and church* in the fall of 1934. This was the occasion for the final collision within the Protestant doctrines of the state; between the option for a *Führer*-state versus the option for a republican constitutional state.

Where was Luther's "church believed in" truthfully to be found?

The question of Luther's "church believed in" was resolved in 1934 amid the June murders, the new oath of allegiance to the *Führer* in August, the fall of the German Christians in October, and the oath of allegiance case prosecuted against Karl Barth in December.

The controversy concerning the Protestant doctrines of the state and Lutheran political theologies resulted in frozen irreconcilable fronts being formed. It was only after a long period of stagnation that, beginning in 1938, theologians of a younger generation revised Luther's 'doctrine of the two kingdoms'[6] into a "doctrine of *preaching in* the two kingdoms."[7] Luther's legacy should not be a political theology, but a doctrine of how to preach the divine word as law and gospel and gospel and law in both kingdoms.

2.2 Looking Back: Positions within Luther Research

Three programs of Luther research in the Weimar Republic generated a Renaissance of Luther study. Dialectical Theology, Lutheran confessionalism, and the Luther Renaissance in the narrower sense encountered each other in a threefold controversy. These three networks dissolved in 1933, but re-grouped anew along the boundaries between the Confessing Church and the German Christians, the "middle parties of the united churches of the *Volk*" and the so called intact Lutheran confessional churches. The fronts had shifted. Gogarten, who was Hirsch's most bitter opponent around 1930, suddenly became a German Christian. Hirsch brought him to Göttingen in 1935. Conservative exponents of the Luther Renaissance such as Anders Nygren and Rudolf Hermann became the pioneers of the Confessing Church and unflinching critics of racial politics. Whoever wants to assess the scientific Luther research during the Weimar Republic cannot totally ignore the public "use" of Luther after 1933. But one should also not let oneself be bewitched by that "use".

(a) The most important research network in Luther studies was the German and Scandinavian Luther Renaissance.[8] It was an ecumenical reform movement

---

[6] Harald Diem, "Luthers Lehre von den zwei Reichen untersucht von seinem Verständnis der Bergpredigt aus. Ein Beitrag zum Problem 'Gesetz und Evangelium'" reprinted in *Zur Zwei-Reiche-Lehre Luthers*, ed. Gerhard Sauter, TB 49 (Munich: Kaiser, 1973), 1–173.

[7] Hermann Diem, "Luthers Predigt in den zwei Reichen (1947)," reprinted in *Zur Zwei-Reiche-Lehre Luthers*, ed. Gerhard Sauter, TB 49 (Munich: Kaiser, 1973), 175–214.

[8] Heinrich Assel, "The Luther Renaissance," *The Oxford Encyclopedia of Martin Luther*, ed. D. Nelson, P. Hinlicky (Oxford: Oxford University Press, 2017); Heinrich. Assel, *Der andere Aufbruch. Die Lutherrenaissance – Ursprünge, Aporien und Wege: Karl Holl, Emanuel Hirsch, Rudolf Hermann (1910–1935)*, Forschungen zur Systematischen und Ökumenischen Theologie 72 (Göttingen: Vandenhoeck & Ruprecht, 1994); Dietz Lange, "Eine andere Luther-Renaissance," *Luthers Erben: Studien zur Rezeptionsgeschichte der reformatorischen Theologie Luthers*, Festschrift für Jörg Baur zum 75. Geburtstag, ed. Notger Slenczka and Walter Sparn (Tübingen: Mohr Siebeck, 2005), 245–274.

which made its impact on the national confessional cultures in diverse ways. The Swedish Lutherans were characterized by being republican, democratic, and adherents to the welfare state. As the nationalistic, political theologians in the German Luther Renaissance became ever louder after 1933, the international shape of Luther studies entered into a crisis. One after another, the Danish and Swedish Luther scholars withdrew; a process which we have only now begun to investigate. The German Luther Renaissance continued to remain under the influence of Karl Holl's *Luther* in one particular point: Holl had moved the "young Luther" into the center of Luther research. These included certain topoi of Luther's *Romans Commentary* which, in their boldness, never became part of the general content of the Lutheran confessional documents: the thesis that the baptized are *simul justus et peccator*, the theology of election, and the church as the "royal priesthood of all the baptized."[9] Holl anchored the community's Christian conscience and its charismatic authority in the "young Luther's experience of justification."

After Karl Holl's early death, his students, the "Holl School," held important professorates in the 1930s. Notably, Holl's oldest student, Emanuel Hirsch (1888–1972), Erich Vogelsang (1904–1944), Hanns Rückert (1902–1974), and Heinrich Bornkamm (1901–1977).[10] In 1933, the Holl students enthusiastically supported the so called "German Christians" as the church party which brought the provincial churches into political subordination. After the church elections of July 1933, the German Christians generally dominated the church synods and presbyteries. They assigned a new function to Holl's rediscovery that the general priesthood of "all the baptized" is the charismatic source of authority: it now served to neutralize the churches via plebiscite. Holl's rediscovery was no longer a source of spiritual authority but a principle of pseudo-democratic domination.

The pioneering thinker was Emanuel Hirsch. He was well known for his extraordinary intellectual brilliance, but of a "negative-critical" bent and not "pro-

---

9 With the general priesthood, Holl formulated not a principle of authority, but the legal autonomy of church and *Volk* church from a principle of spiritual-charismatic authority.
10 Thomas Kaufmann and Harry Oelke, eds., *Evangelische Kirchenhistoriker im "Dritten Reich,"* VWGTh 21 (Gütersloh: Bertelsmann, 2002); in this volume: Berndt Hamm, "Hanns Rückert als Schüler Karl Holls: Das Paradigma einer theologischen Anfälligkeit für den Nationalsozialismus," 273–309; Hartmut Lehmann, "Heinrich Bornkamm im Spiegel seiner Lutherstudien von 1933 bis 1947," 367–380; see also Volker Leppin, "In Rosenbergs Schatten: Zur Lutherdeutung Erich Vogelsangs," *ThZ* 61 (2005): 132–142.

ductive-originality."¹¹ Together with the Nazi Reich's Bishop Müller, Hirsch rose to the zenith of his theological and church power in 1933. He used that power for focused denunciations. In October 1934, his power collapsed along with that of the Bishop. In December 1934, as his influence was declining he nevertheless pursued his most effective denunciation – that of Karl Barth and Paul Tillich. His "success" is well known. After 1938, Hirsch became a radical anti-Semite, and an apologist of the *Shoa* and the East European war of annihilation.

Alongside the Holl School, and of equal standing, was the Luther Renaissance carried out by the German-Swedish network linked to Rudolf Hermann (1887–1862) and Anders Nygren (1890–1978), who was the best known Luther scholar of the so-called Lund School. From the spring of 1933 onward – earlier than Karl Barth! – this group stood by the side of the harsh, public critics of Nazi church politics, and by the side of the Confessing Church in 1934. Going beyond the issues of church politics, they criticized the racist and anti-Semitic Nazi ideology from the very beginning.¹²

Finally, there was a group of younger theologians who belonged to the network of the Luther Renaissance, people like Hans Joachim Iwand, Ernst Wolf, in his early work Dietrich Bonhoeffer¹³, and later Harald Diem, as well as the writer Jochen Klepper, and not forgetting Christa Müller (and Katharina Staritz). As students, they were under the influence of Karl Holl or Rudolf Hermann. They advocated for a substantial revision of the Lutheran theology of the law and of political ethics.¹⁴ After 1934, the Barmen Theological Declaration served as their basis.

(b) Lutheran confessionalism was virulent in the homogenous Lutheran provincial churches and regions. Its spokesmen were the Erlangen theologian Werner Elert (1885–1954) and Paul Althaus (1888–1966). In contrast with Karl Holl, they smoothly integrated Luther's theology and political ethics into the confes-

---

11 Bultmann about Hirsch, "Letter to Friedrich Gogarten, 15 March 1928," in *R. Bultmann, F. Gogarten, Briefwechsel 1921–1967*, ed. H. G. Göckeritz (Tübingen: Mohr Siebeck, 2002), 117.
12 Cf. Anders Nygren, *The Church Controversy in Germany: The Position of the Evangelical Church in the Third Empire* (London: Student Christian Movement Press, 1934). Nygren commented publicly on the German situation from October 1933, at first in Swedish publications, then in September 1934 in a book in English. This promoted initiatives such as the visit of the Archbishop of Uppsala, Erling Eidem, to Hitler on 2 May 1934.
13 Michael P. deJonge, *Bonhoeffer's Reception of Luther* (Oxford: Oxford University Press 2017).
14 This took place in the "Young Reformational Movement," which formed in March 1933 during the course of the constitutional reform debate in the Deutschen Evangelischen Kirchenbund against the plans of the radical German Christians for enforced conformity. The main representatives were W. Künneth, H. Lilje and M. Niemöller. The Berlin Circle around M. Niemöller, G. Jacobi, D. Bonhoeffer, F. Hildebrandt, and H. Sasse became increasingly important.

sional traditions of the diverse Lutheranisms. In order to do that, they constructed "Lutheranism" as a unified confession. This was already signaled by the title of Elert's major work, *The Morphology of Lutheranism*. Accordingly, Luther's primal religious experience was supposed to be formative for the confession: the fateful hiddenness of the holy, full of terror and fascination. Luther's justification experience of saving grace in the midst of jealous holiness is not deducible, because it is irrational. Out of that, Elert generated an anti-Calvinist, "anti-western" Lutheran world view and an ethno-nationalistic doctrine of the orders of creation.

Paul Althaus was one of the most widely read theologians of German Lutheranism and the president of the German Luther Society for almost four decades (1926–1964).[15] He was adaptable and so his theological concepts shaped by *Volk*-centered (ethnocentric) thought were often vague. However, he is especially representative for certain milieus and mentalities within German Lutheranism.[16]

(c) Friedrich Gogarten (1887–1967) was of an entirely different makeup; he was *the* acknowledged Luther researcher of dialectical theology. Rudolf Bultmann supported the call of Gogarten as successor to Rudolf Otto in Marburg. He ranked Gogarten above Barth on his list. He wrote in his confidential recommendation that Gogarten was the only one "who worked with the insights gained from Luther that legitimate, basic theological concepts can only arise from the faith's self-reflection on Christian existence." "Above all, he is a thinker of the highest power and distinctiveness."[17] With a clear insight for distinctiveness, but also for incorruptibility, Bultmann considered Friedrich Gogarten and Rudolf Hermann to be *the* pioneering Luther scholars of his generation.[18] And he was right! Consequently, it was all the more confusing for Bultmann when Gogarten cast his lot with the German Christians in 1933.[19]

---

[15] By 1927, Althaus was teaching that in the "hour" of the German *Volk*, the judgment and the calling of God were to be heard. This could be read in his frequently reprinted lecture at the Second German Protestant Church Rally [Kirchentag] in Königsberg under the theme, "Church and *Volk*": "The Will of the *Volk* in the Light of the Gospel." (Paul Althaus, *Kirche und Volkstum: Der völkische Wille im Lichte des Evangeliums* [Gütersloh 1928]).

[16] Paul Althaus, *Die deutsche Stunde der Kirche* (Göttingen: Vandenhoeck & Ruprecht, 1933–1934); idem, *Obrigkeit und Führertum: Wandlungen des evangelischen Staatsethos* (Gütersloh: Bertelsmann 1936); further idem, "Juxta vocationem. Zur lutherischen Lehre von Ordnung und Beruf," *Luthertum* 48 (1937), 129–141. Althaus, who moved closer to Elert from 1933 onwards, adopted in 1936 the state ethos that Hirsch had already expressed in 1932/33.

[17] Bultmann about Gogarten in his "Sondervotum" to the faculty of theology in Marburg, 27.1. 1929, in: Bultmann, Gogarten, *Briefwechsel*, 294–295.

[18] *Briefwechsel*, 124.134.

[19] *Briefwechsel*, 209–213.

2.3 Gospel and Law, Law and Gospel

Karl Barth's fundamental critique of contemporary Lutheran theology is, in my judgment, provoked by Hirsch's, Elert's, and Gogarten's nationalistic political self-disclosure. His critique misses the mark when it is directed toward figures like Karl Holl, Rudolf Hermann, or Anders Nygren. When he was forcibly banished from Germany in 1935, Barth criticized the theory that equates the law of the *Volk* with God's law in his essay *Gospel and Law*.[20] He sharply attacked the *Volk*-centered political realignment of "law and gospel" that had occurred since the death of Karl Holl in 1926. It proved to be a great *aporia* that the issue with "law and gospel" was the *preaching of the word in both kingdoms* and thus the orientation of conscience in Christianity. Barth's critique received a productive hearing among the younger theologians of the Luther Renaissance, with Wolf, Iwand, Bonhoeffer and Diem. They understood Holl, Hermann and Nygren, for whom law and gospel were the Word of God in *conscientia*, *assertio* and *agape*, within Barth's critical horizon. They also continued to think in further, highly original ways.

3 Decisions and Breakdowns 1934

The new doctrines of the state failed as they confronted the reality of the Nazi state, although they did so in (characteristically) different ways. They were, however, remarkably of one mind, in that all three withdrew legitimation from the Weimar Republic. Gogarten and Elert did so in favor of an authoritarian or a fascist state, while Hirsch was in favor of a totalitarian Nazi party dictatorship.

3.1 *Führer* State or Constitutional State

In Gogarten's *Political Ethic*, the "political" becomes concrete in a doctrine of the authoritarian state.[21] "Obedience and Bondage" form the core of the *ethical*, and "the sovereignty of the state [...], its 'holy right' to the life and property of its sub-

---

[20] Karl Barth, *Evangelium und Gesetz*, TEH 32 (Munich: Kaiser, 1935).
[21] Friedrich Gogarten, *Politische Ethik* (subsequently cited in text as *PE*). On the antagonism between an "authoritarian" orientation and a *voelkisch* option for the 'total state,' cf. Christoph Strohm, *Theologische Ethik im Kampf gegen den Nationalsozialismus: Der Weg Dietrich Bonhoeffers mit den Juristen Hans von Dohnanyi und Gerhard Leibholz in den Widerstand* (Munich: Kaiser, 1989), 78–83.

jects" (*PE*, 124) form the core of the *political*. The *Lutheran* approach to the political is demonstrated in the concept of divine law: political sovereignty works under the authority of the state and its coercive rights. The state's authority is a coding of the law which upholds and realizes the divine creation order against the wicked. The problem of the state and of its authority is "the first and most important political problem," and it is "solely from the political problem [i.e., the authority of the state] that all other ethical questions derive their relevance." (*PE*, 118) Gogarten politicizes contemporary personalism with its supposedly more morally substantial, concrete communities of honor, nation, and *Volk*.[22] "Church" denotes the realm of the gospel and should be something beyond the authoritarian state and coercive law.[23] Gogarten's authoritarian state has control over the property and life of its citizens but not over their faith and their neighborly relationships. This boundary between state and church defines the political dimension and empowers its legitimate worldliness and secularity. The Nazi appeal to *Volk*-centered sovereignty as absolutely creative of the law is, by contrast, an attack upon the divine right of the authoritarian state. It crosses over this boundary and becomes an illegitimate secularity. Gogarten's statist political ethic confronted the *Volk*-centered political religion of radical Nazis, which could under no circumstances acknowledge the boundary he drew between state and church. Nazi students and faculty colleagues even tried to burn Gogarten's book in Breslau in May 1933, but they failed.[24] Gogarten claimed to be the disciple and heir of Luther's dialectical theology of God's word. In fact, this illusion, which nourished Gogarten's *Political Ethic*, signified the collapse of dialectical theology, not just with Karl Barth, but also with Rudolf Bultmann.

Karl Barth's departure from the program of a dialectical theology made this public by the end of 1933. The theological work on basic concepts of Trinitarian doctrine and Christology; the Word of God and the existence of faith; the legitimate secularity and the mystery of the worldliness of the world, that is, the entire fruitful controversy between Barth and Gogarten, now ended forever.

This was a misfortune of another kind!

The decision became crystal clear when Barth, in November 1934, refused to take the personal oath of allegiance to "the *Führer and Reichskanzler* Adolf Hit-

---

22 Gogarten, *Politische Ethik*, 57–64, 108–132, 133–208.
23 Gogarten, 208–220.
24 Incited by Karl Bornhausen. Cf. Hermann Götz Göckeritz, "Friedrich Gogarten," in *Profile des Luthertums: Biographien zum 20. Jahrhundert*, ed. Wolf-Dieter Hauschild (Gütersloh: Gütersloher Verlagshaus, 1998), 215–258, 244. Concerning Gogarten's criticism of Bornhausen cf. Friedrich Gogarten, *Glaube und Wirklichkeit* (Jena: Diederichs, 1928), 26–30.

ler."²⁵ In the logic of a political ethic like that of Gogarten, the personal oath of allegiance to the *Führer* applied the model of military loyalty to all vocational relationships in the university, the bureaucracy, and the church (!). The oath of allegiance to the *Führer* was a model example of authoritarian citizenship. The fact that the Nazi State in November 1934 had become a totalitarian regime destroying the rule of law itself, was not provided for in the categories of Gogarten's political ethics. Barth's refusal to take the oath of allegiance was the political climax of his doctrine of state sovereignty which could not be reconciled with Gogarten and Hirsch.²⁶

3.2 A *Volk*-centered Order of Creation or the Rule of "Natural Law"

In 1932, Werner Elert published the second volume of his *Morphology of Lutheranism*,²⁷ entitled *Social Doctrines and Social Implications of Lutheranism*.²⁸ It offered a worldview of *Führer*-ship, recommending such a *Führer*-ship for all social classes, strata, and occupations. Featuring titles such as "creation order and the three-fold class doctrine," "occupation and *Führer*-ship," "Ethnic *Volkstum* and the peoples [*Völker*]," "Luther's view of the state," and, "the welfare state and socialism," Elert projected a Lutheran doctrine of the state.²⁹ Elert's state is a fas-

---

25 The oath of allegiance was: "I will be faithful and obedient to the *Führer* of the German Empire and people Adolf Hitler, to observe the law, and to conscientiously fulfil my official duties, so help me God."
26 Michael Beintker, "Barths Abschied von 'Zwischen den Zeiten': Recherchen und Beobachtungen zum Ende einer Zeitschrift," *ZThK* 106 (2009): 201–222. Heinrich Assel, "Grundlose Souveränität und göttliche Freiheit: Karl Barths Rechtsethik im Konflikt mit Emanuel Hirschs Souveränitätslehre," *Karl Barth in Deutschland (1921–1935)*, Aufbruch – Klärung – Widerstand, Beiträge zum Internationalen Symposium vom 1.–4. Mai 2003 in der Johannes-a-Lasco-Bibliothek Emden, eds. Michael Beintker, Christian Link, Michael Trowitzsch (Zurich: Theologischer Verlag, 2005), 205–222; Heinrich Assel, "'Barth ist entlassen ...': Emanuel Hirschs Rolle im Fall Barth und seine Briefe an Wilhelm Stapel," *ZThK* 91 (1994): 445–475.
27 Werner Elert, *Morphologie des Luthertums* Bd. 1, Theologie und Weltanschauung des Luthertums hauptsächlich im 16. und 17. Jahrhundert (Munich: Beck, 1931).
28 Elert, *Morphologie* Bd. 2 (page numbers only in the text). The subtitle "Social doctrine of Lutheranism" is clearly in opposition to Ernst Troeltsch (Ernst Troeltsch, *Die Soziallehren der christlichen Kirchen und Gruppen* [Tübingen: Mohr Siebeck, 1994], reprint of the 1912 edition).
29 Cf. Elert, *Morphologie* Bd. 2, 37–64, 65–80, 125–158, 291–302, 313–334, 409–428.

cist *Führer*-state, with the elements of welfare, culture, education, militarism, civil service bureaucracy, and state economics.[30]

In September 1933, Elert opened his theology to *Volk*-centered racism. The ethnocentric system was to be the comprehensive order of creation which should be authoritative in state and church. This should also apply to the visible church in the worldly realm. Together with Paul Althaus, he published a "theological report on the admission of Christians of Jewish origin to church offices in the German Protestant Church." This report argued for the church to adopt the state's Aryan Laws.

"The church must require that its Jewish Christians refrain from holding clerical offices."[31]

The doctrine of a "*Volk*-centered destiny" distorted the reality of this special racist legislation.

The heretical teaching of the Erlangen Lutherans about the implementation of the Aryan Laws in the church was energetically opposed.[32] Back in April 1933, ten days *before* the promulgation of the state's "Law on the Restoration of the Professional Civil Service" and months before the discussion in the church, Rudolf Hermann authored an open letter. It was a letter of solidarity with the philosopher Richard Hönigswald and addressed to the Bavarian Ministry of Education. He protested against the firing of Hönigswald based on the "Aryan Laws."[33] The state's right to have special racist laws was by no means the consensus within the Lutheran doctrines of the state in early 1933. Rudolf Hermann was a constant critic of such special legislation in state and church from April 1933 onward. This protest led him, as a consequence, into the Confessing Church. He participated in the decisive confessional synods of the German Protestant Church. Hermann saw soberly the reality of the unjust Nazi state. He assessed that this totalitarian form of the state was against "God's commandment and commission". In terms of the topos of God's just rule as a constituent of Luther's doctrine of the worldly kingdom that is:

---

30 Cf. Elert, *Morphologie* Bd. 2, 301 f., 331–333. Lacking are market ventures, media, associations and unions, parliament and political parties, supreme courts, and constitutions.

31 Heinz Liebing, ed., *Die Marburger Theologen und der Arierparagraph in der Kirche: Eine Sammlung von Texten aus den Jahren 1933 und 1934*, Aus Anlaß des 450-jährigen Bestehens der Philipps-Universität Marburg (Marburg: Elwert, 1977), 20–23, 22; on the basis of the report, 9; Siegfried Hermle and Jörg Thierfelder, eds., *Herausgefordert. Dokumente zur Geschichte der Evangelischen Kirche in der Zeit des Nationalsozialismus* (Stuttgart: Calwer, 2008), 164–167.

32 E.g., in a report of the Marburg Theological Faculty, for which Rudolf Bultmann and Hans von Soden were responsible.

33 Saul Friedländer, *Das Dritte Reich und die Juden* Bd. 1, Die Jahre der Verfolgung 1933–1939 (Munich: Beck, 1998), 65.

Identifying which form of the state is the right one for a particular nation, a community of nations, or a world empire, is an historical and political task. But every form of the state which becomes a reality stands under God's commission *to serve the just and the good, to resist the unjust and the wicked*, and to strive to be of a proper order for the people who are linked together by it and submit to it.[34]

The totalitarian state, which claims to secure the right to life of the German nation, must know that it is "summoned before the divine forum to which it is held accountable."[35]

Whoever appeals to one's *right* to life must also live *rightly*. To make this claim is simultaneously to accept this obligation. However, this includes the expectation that *all* persons who accept the responsibility of a state and want it to depend upon them, are assured of the validity of the *justice* achieved through its rule.[36]

In 1935, the same year in which the Nuremberg Race Laws were enacted, Hermann was insistent on the fundamental principle of the equality of all before man-made laws and the courts.[37]

3.3 *Führer* Church or Confessing Church

Emanuel Hirsch was the pioneer of a political theology.[38] Of key significance for his break with the doctrine of the authoritarian state was his doctrine of *Volk*-centered sovereignty, for which there was no precedent in Lutheranism. It was no longer the worldly authority, but rather the "*Volk*," in its sending and self-assertion, who were the divinely established sovereign, and to whom obedience was due.[39] The Germanic "Volksnomos,"[40] the "law of the *Volk*," which can-

---

34 Rudolf Hermann, "Zur Frage der 'christlichen' Geschichtsdeutung," *Wort und Tat* 12 (1936): 69–75, 227–235, 234 (my italics, HA).
35 Rudolf Hermann in the essay published in 1935, "Christlicher Glaube und politisches Handeln," in *Gesammelte und nachgelassene Werke VI: Theologische Fragen nach der Kirche*, ed., Gerhard Krause (Göttingen: Vandenhoeck & Ruprecht, 1977), 113–122, 115.
36 Hermann, "Christlicher Glaube und politisches Handeln," 115 (in part my italics, HA).
37 Hermann, "Christlicher Glaube und politisches Handeln," 119.
38 Heinrich Assel, "Emanuel Hirsch: Völkisch-politischer Theologe der Lutherrenaissance," *Für ein artgemäßes Christentum der Tat: Völkische Theologen im "Dritten Reich*,*"* eds., Manfred Gailus and Clemens Vollnhals (Göttingen: Vandenhoeck & Ruprecht, 2016), 43–67.
39 Hirsch, "Vom verborgenen Suverän," 5.
40 Emanuel Hirsch, *Christliche Freiheit und politische Bindung. Ein Brief an Dr. Stapel und anderes* (Hamburg: Hanseatische Verlagsanstalt, 1935), 17. Cf.: Wilhelm Stapel, *Der christliche*

not be discerned in democratic processes, becomes the standard of political loyalty.[41] As a consequence of this doctrine of sovereignty, Hirsch affirms the revolutionary empowerment of the Nazi party. Later he defends a permanent provision against the rule of law. Hirsch legitimates special laws and People's Courts not only in exceptional cases, but as a matter of principle.[42]

As advisor to the German-Christian Church government, Hirsch applied his doctrine to church-politics. In effect, this neutralized the clergy. In August 1934, this led to a third and final controversy regarding Luther's legacy that proved to be Hirsch's downfall. He formulated a law regulating the clerical oath of allegiance for the National Synod that obligated all clergy and church officials to take the oath of allegiance to Hitler. The enforced integration of all clergy into the National Church was to be celebrated with this oath.[43] This attempt to arrive at a final neutralization of all pastors by means of a personal oath of allegiance to Hitler failed in the early fall of 1934. The church's oath of allegiance to the *Führer* was nothing less than the attempt to make Hitler the "highest bishop" of a national church. In light of such an unprecedented act of coercion, even the members of the Holl School refused to follow Hirsch.

Staatsmann. Eine Theologie des Nationalismus (Hamburg: Hanseatische Verlagsanstalt, 1932), 174 et pass.

41 Hirsch, "Vom verborgenen Suverän," 7.

42 After January 30, 1933, Hirsch could erroneously consider his version of a new Protestant doctrine of the church to be confirmed. "According to the unambiguous declarations of the *Führer,* what must now be regarded as the distinctive thing about the new German structuring of life, is that the state and the political are subservient to *Volk*-centeredness, and that they should be seen as the indispensable means to the end of *Volk*-centeredness." Emanuel Hirsch, *Die gegenwärtige geistige Lage im Spiegel philosophischer und theologischer Besinnung* (Göttingen: Vandenhoeck & Ruprecht, 1934), 60, cf. 62f.

43 The written formulation of the oath betrayed Hirsch's hand. Since, however, the *Führer* alone was the proper interpreter of the laws of the *Volk*, the vow of allegiance encompassed every possible sacrifice (including the sacrifice of one's own conscience), the readiness to be obedient over against terrorist actions, special laws, and a policy of war and annihilation. The text was (expressions that indicate Hirsch's theology are in italics): "The clergy shall swear the following oath: I, (name), swear an oath *to God the All-knowing and Holy,* that I, as a vocational servant in the office of the proclamation, both in my current office and in every other clerical office, as befits a servant of the gospel in the German Evangelical Church, shall be faithful and obedient to the Führer of the German *Volk and State,* Adolf Hitler, and shall employ myself for the German Volk with *every sacrifice* and every service that befits a German evangelical man." Hermle and Thierfelder, eds., *Herausgefordert,* 217–218.

4 The Barmen Declaration and the Luther Renaissance

The spectrum of Lutheran theology at the end of 1934 looked like this:
- More than a few theologians of the Luther Renaissance, such as R. Hermann, A. Nygren, and the Young Reformation Movement, had adopted the Barmen Theological Declaration in May 1934. They rejected a doctrine of a double revelation of God: in the Law of the *Volk* and in Jesus Christ as the gospel.
- Those Lutherans who rejected the first and second theses of the Barmen Theological Declaration by appealing to Luther – this includes almost the entire Holl School, Elert and Althaus, as well as Gogarten – could now scarcely make any plausible arguments against the third and fourth theses of the Declaration.[44]
- The church's witness to Christ had to take place not only in the church's doctrine, but also in its order and institutions. There could be no offices in the church which validated the rule of some over others. There could not be any "special leaders vested with ruling powers" in the Church (Barmen IV). That had been crystal clear ever since Holl's rediscovery of the "royal priesthood of all the baptized."
- At this point, the temporary consensus stretched from some Holl students, through Althaus, and up to Hermann, as well as Bonhoeffer, who had begun his Berlin dissertation as a result of Holl's encouragement.[45]
- The temporary consensus on Barmen III and IV may not have concealed the fact that there were irreconcilable differences in political ethics and in the stances on anti-Semitism. The other side of the consensus on the understanding of the church was that a Protestant doctrine of the state was only hinted at in the fifth thesis of the Barmen Theological Declaration. It was only after 1938 that Lutherans made some suggestions in this direction.

---

44 Nevertheless, they tried to. [Werner Elert, *Bekenntnis, Blut und Boden: Drei theologische Vorträge* (Leipzig: Dörffling & Franke, 1934), dated 31 August 1934.]
45 Dietrich Bonhoeffer, *Sanctorum Communio: Eine dogmatische Untersuchung zur Soziologie der Kirche*, eds. Joachim von Soosten and Eberhard Bethge, DBW 1 (Munich: Kaiser, 1986).

5 Looking Ahead: Unresolvedness – Stagnation – Re-Education

The irreconcilable conflicts about political theology and the withdrawal of the Scandinavian Lutherans resulted in stagnation. Luther's legacy after 1935 seems to be an unresolved problem. The theologians of a younger generation revised Lutheran political theology and ethics after 1938. It was symptomatic that they worked outside the theological faculties, for instance, Harald Diem and Gerhard Ebeling or Christa Müller and Katharina Staritz. Or, as in the case of Hans Iwand and Dietrich Bonhoeffer, they had lost their academic teaching positions.[46]

The re-education of the Lutherans after 1945 can be connected not only with Karl Barth, but also with these voices, as well as with the voices of the Scandinavian Lutherans. It should be noted that many of the most gifted younger theologians were victims of the war, such as Harald Diem. Or they became victims of National-Socialism, as in the case of Dietrich Bonhoeffer and Jochen Klepper.

This is the third misfortune, which should not be forgotten.[47]

---

[46] Ernst Wolf, "Zur Frage des Naturrechts bei Thomas von Aquin und bei Luther (1935)," in *Peregrinatio: Studien zur reformatorischen Theologie und zum Kirchenproblem* (Munich: Kaiser, 1954), 183–213; H. J. Iwand, "Gesetz und Evangelium I (1937)," in *Nachgelassene Werke* Bd. 4, Gesetz und Evangelium (Munich: Kaiser 1964), 13–230 (Lecture to the seminar of the East Prussian Confessing Church); D. Bonhoeffer, *Nachfolge* (Munich: Kaiser, 1937), drawn from courses in the seminar of the Berlin-Brandenburg Confessing Church, 1935–1937 [Martin Kuske and Ilse Tödt, eds., DBW 4 (Munich: Kaiser 1989)]; Gerhard Ebeling, *Evangelische Evangelienauslegung: Eine Untersuchung zu Luthers Hermeneutik* (Munich: Kaiser, 1942) (Thesis Zurich 1938).

[47] Funded by *Theoria*, Kurt von Fritz-Wissenschaftsprogramm zur Förderung der Geistes- und Sozialwissenschaften Mecklenburg-Vorpommern. – Translated from German by Prof. Dr. Darrell L. Guder and Dietrich Wenzel.

Part I: **Anticipations**

Hartwig Wiedebach
Karl Barth on Kant's "Biblical Theology" A Reading with Hermann Cohen

1 The Freedom for Evil

Immanuel Kant (1724–1804) pondered questions of "biblical theology" in several of his writings in his later years, and indeed drafted such a "theology." However, he was not motivated in this by any genuine theological interest. Here too he remained the philosopher and regarded biblical theology as something else, indeed something alien, different. Nonetheless, he approached and drafted this alien element employing philosophical means. What unites biblical theology and philosophy is Reason. For Kant, to deal with Reason was primarily and indivisibly a task of philosophy. But biblical theology is also shaped by Reason. What distinguishes it from philosophy is the role of the question of purity. Kant as a philosopher seeks out the critique of *pure* Reason in all spheres of systematic foundation: in knowledge, in ethics and aesthetics. He looks for a strictly general and necessary procedure that makes it possible for us to arrive at valid determinations. All kind of accidental being there, no matter how important it may appear at the moment, blurs philosophical purity. Purity is Kant's basis for valid knowledge, proofs and above all the consciousness of precisely determined, unsurpassable limits of the human spirit. Yet he does not separate Reason from sensuality, inclinations, natural drives or historical experience. Central for him is the hierarchy: Kant wants to make sure that the principles of order derived from the critique of Reason are made a condition for every order in the sphere of sensuality, inclination, drives and the like, and to maintain that in this position. In no case must the opposite be allowed to occur. In knowing, desiring and in general any act of judgment, allowing the sense data, inclinations and historical situations to be the predominant shaping force, perverts the order of Reason and is therefore false.

Yet it would appear that biblical theology works differently. It accepts (we shall later see more precisely how) principles of order "based on the teachings of history and revelation,"[1] from personal witness, indeed grounded on feeling.

---

[1] Immanuel Kant, *The Metaphysics of Morals* [1797/98], "Akademie-Ausgabe": *Kants Gesammelte Schriften* (Berlin: Reimer/De Gruyter, 1900 ff., hereafter *AA)*, VI 488. Page references from the AA are given in English standard translations. With some exceptions I will quote from: 1) *Critique of Pure Reason* [A 1781/B 1787], trans. Werner S. Pluhar (Indianapolis: Hackett,

Does this not contradict Reason? Not per se and in every respect, but its procedure can only be valid with restrictions. Consequently, Kant's most important work on biblical theology is titled *Religion within the Boundaries of Mere Reason* (Rlg., A 1793/B 1794). Its object thus "is not *pure*; it is rather religion *applied* to a history handed down to us, and there is no place for it in an *ethics* that is pure practical philosophy."² Not without personal reservations, indeed a touch of irony, although nonetheless with scientific respect, Kant correspondingly discusses the "distinctive characteristic of the Theology Faculty" in his university-political tractate *The Conflict of the Faculties*.³ The first sentence in this section reads: "The biblical theologian proves the existence of God on the grounds that He spoke in the Bible."⁴ But proof in the strict sense belong in another faculty, namely the "Faculty of Philosophy." Thus, the biblical theologian, treating his certainty "as a matter of faith, he will therefore base it – even for the scholar – on a certain (indemonstrable and inexplicable) *feeling* of its divine character" ("Gefühl *der Göttlichkeit derselben*").⁵ Karl Barth is interested in particular in the first sentence. He quotes it twice in his chapter on Kant in his *Protestant Theology in the Nineteenth Century. Its Background & History* from 1947 (*PT*),⁶ the second time printing it in bold as his crowning conclusion.⁷ The book derives from lectures he gave for the final time in the academic year 1932/33 in Bonn. His chapter on Kant is Barth's most extensive expression of his position on Kant's importance for modern theology.⁸ It is my point of departure.

1996); 2) *Critique of Practical Reason* [*KpV* 1788], trans. Werner S. Pluhar (Indianapolis: Hackett, 2002); 3) *Religion within the Boundaries of Mere Reason and Other Writings* [*Rlg* A 1793/B 1794], trans. Allen Wood and George di Giovanni (Cambridge Univ. Press, 1998); 4) *The Metaphysics of Morals* [1797/98], trans. Mary J. Gregor (Cambridge Univ. Press, 1996); 5) *The Conflict of the Faculties* [*CFac* 1798], trans. Mary J. Gregor (New York: Abaris, 1979).
2 Kant, *The Metaphysics of Morals*, AA VI, 488.
3 Kant, *CFac*, 1798.
4 Kant, *CFac*, AA VII, 24.
5 Kant, *CFac*, AA VII, 23.
6 Engl. publ.: Valley Forge: Judson Press, ²1976; German original: *Die protestantische Theologie im 19. Jahrhundert. Ihre Vorgeschichte und ihre Geschichte* [1947] (Zürich: Theologischer Verlag, 1981). Page references hereafter from the German and the English editions (*PT* German/English). Cf. as a short introduction Dietrich Korsch, "Theologiegeschichte," in *Barth Handbuch*, ed. Michael Beintker (Tübingen: Mohr Siebeck, 2016), 257–261, esp. 258–59.
7 Barth, *PT*, 277, 278/311, 312.
8 See Michael Beintker, "Grenzbewusstsein. Eine Erinnerung an Karl Barths Kant-Deutung [2004]," in idem *Krisis und Gnade. Gesammelte Studien zu Karl Barth*, ed. Stefan Holtmann and Peter Zocher (Tübingen: Mohr Siebeck, 2013), 122–135, esp. 132ff.; Kenneth Oakes, *Karl Barth on Theology and Philosophy* (Oxford: Oxford Univ. Press, 2012), 140–149. Barth here goes far beyond the lectures on ethics 1928/29 in his theological appraisal of Kant (Barth,

Let me briefly summarize. Kant for Barth is the "awe-inspiring" thinker,[9] in whose person "the eighteenth century saw, understood, and affirmed itself in its own limitations."[10] In particular, the self-"affirmation" will become important for us. Kant enunciates this in a theological form with a modest, self-aware Enlightenment consciousness: "Should one now ask, Which period of the entire church history in our ken up to now is the best? I reply without hesitation: *The present.*"[11] But what actually prompted him, from his view of limitations, not only to recognize biblical theology but even to sketch an extensive outline of it? The initial spark was the problem of so-called "radical evil." Kant addressed that for the first time in the *Berlinische Monatsschrift* in 1792 and then included the essay with a few additions one year later in his book *Die Religion innerhalb ...* (*Religion with the Boundaries ...*). We will have to be satisfied with a compromised brief glance. I will mainly quote Kant's own words (in a standard translation), but consistently in the sense of Barth's expositions.[12]

It concerns ethics. Ethics is the teaching of *practical* Reason, i.e. not just how we "determine" what is reasonable (as in theoretical episteme), but how we "make it actual" by doing ("*wirklich machen*").[13] So it has to do with action. But to act from a basis of Reason involves will, and will is different from a biological impulse. It springs from our *Self* and follows its own laws. But from this a problem arises. Because in actual doing we remain bound to nature. Our body with its emotions, including physics, biography, general contemporary history, in short: the givens of our respective situation, shape our action. What we in very concrete terms "make actual" by doing it is a kind of mixture. Neither in keeping with the law of will nor the laws of nature will it be able to be 'strictly general' and 'necessarily' reasonable. Two different orders of law collide here which, for the sake of purity, must be strictly distinguished one from the other. Consequently, here the pure science of Reason reaches its end. It can say what we in an ideal case *ought to* do, but never what we actually in fact do. Only where it is merely a matter of our personal intentions, the "maxims" of our desire, the pure science of Reason is on solid ground. Thus, Kant formulates for our Self a law of pure im-

---

Ethik, 2 Vols. [Zürich: Theol. Verlag, 1973/1978]). Central there is Kant's categorical imperative, Kant's "biblical theology" is not discussed.
9 Barth, *PT*, 239/269.
10 Barth, *PT*, 237/266.
11 Kant, *Rlg*. B, 197, AA VI, 131; cf. Barth, *PT*, 239, 261/268, 293. Karl Barth quotes Kant's *Religion within the Boundaries [...]* according to the second printing (B, 1794).
12 Barth, *PT*, 260 ff./292 ff.
13 Kant, *Critique of Pure Reason* B, X.

perative obligation, the "categorical imperative." It underpins and grounds our autonomy.

But once more: when we act, even with the best will, we remain inevitably bound to inclinations, moods, situations. Which means: it is never certain that we actually subject ourselves to the categorical imperative. It is precisely a careful self-critical attitude that proves that the ultimate bases of our concrete will and action can never be known. Here we are unrecognizable, and in positive terms that means: we are free, both in regard to the good and to the bad. That is decisive: freedom for Kant is *not* identical with autonomy. It lies deeper. Freedom is how we deal with the *possible* autonomy open to us. We can of course know, and the pure science of Reason proves this: our Self *has* a law of its own. And we have no choice but to wish to preserve this source of Reason of our own. But it is precisely here where Reason itself becomes a pitfall for us. Because when we really take the ethical will seriously, then we can note that autonomy never functions mechanically – that would be a direct contradiction. Our will is always also acting "for autonomy" or "against autonomy." As Kant says: "even what pleases [us to do or not to do something], lies within the subject's reason" ("selbst das Belieben [wird] in der Vernunft des Subjekts angetroffen").[14] If in reality we have to admit that we inevitably are dependent on laws that are not those of autonomy, the necessary conclusion is: we have freely decided *against* autonomy. We have put ourselves in a position subject to the heteronomy of factors determined by nature. But that decision was freely made. We thus apportion to ourselves our own rootedness in nature itself as something freely chosen. This means to say: we have betrayed the moral law, and we constantly do that again and again.

A strange demonism in our being as humans becomes visible here. Kant calls it the "indwelling of the evil principle" – Barth finds the expression striking.[15] It is "radical evil."[16] "Radical" thus does not mean "especially drastic" but rather, from lat. *radix*, "rooted" in our being as humans.[17] And once again it is a matter of hierarchy. Malevolence is the impure "inclination" to make "the driving forces [of our rootedness in nature, i.e.:] self-love and its inclinations the conditioning ground of our adherence to the moral law"[18] – instead, on the contrary, to make the moral law the conditioning ground of our self-love and its inclinations. And because here our own Reason becomes for us a pitfall and we are

---

14 Kant, *Metaphysics of Morals*, AA VI, 213.
15 cf. Barth, *PT*, 262/294.
16 Kant, *Rlg.* B, 3, AA VI, 19.
17 Kant, *Rlg.* B, 27, AA VI, 32.
18 Kant, *Rlg.* B, 35, AA VI, 36.

unable to recognize the reasons for this freely chosen "perversion" of Reason into evil, all that remains for us is to accept it as a fact.

Despite this, Kant is not a pessimist. As Karl Barth says: Kant "affirms" the limitations of our Reason, also *this* limitation! Because he relies on that: it is precisely the borderline knowledge or insight that proves what is nonetheless valid. Man as rational being remains determined by the pure ethical law. His essence is: he is supposed to determine and obligate his will to do good. And because he is free to follow this obligation (naturally just as free to follow evil), he must also actually *be able to do* what he is supposed to do. Kant repeats that for several times especially in the treatise on religion. However, the science of *pure* Reason does not go any further. It cannot positively provide the *hope* that we not only *can* reverse the perverted hierarchy of our motives for action, but that we really will also do it. It can only make the hope "*negatively* palpable" ("negativ *fühlbar*") through that consciousness of being able to, as Heinrich Assel has subtly exposited.[19] That is the reason why Kant drafted a second research work on foundations. This second science, a science of hope of reversal, of turnabout so to speak, seeks, strangely enough, supernatural, transcendent effective forces. And now testimonies from the factual, individual and collective history of humankind become as such sources for basic concepts. We are talking here about grace, divine justification, providence and the church, as the draft design of a community corresponding to this order of reversal. These basic concepts are the subject of "biblical theology."

2 Hermann Cohen

Is this still the Kant whom we are familiar with? Or are these symptoms of old age in a philosopher who is losing control over his concepts? Karl Barth affirms the former: it is still the critical Kant, no weaker. But as Barth says, we need an independent "total survey" (*Gesamtanschauung*)[20] in order to see how this philosopher could become capable of attracting to himself "what is on the other side," juxtaposed to his core endeavor. I will not expatiate here on the multitude of details. I will look solely at the manner in which Barth constructs his "total survey." A brief detour is helpful in that regard. I am referring to his Marburg teacher Hermann Cohen.

---

19 Heinrich Assel, *Geheimnis und Sakrament. Die Theologie des göttlichen Namens bei Kant, Cohen und Rosenzweig* (Göttingen: Vandenhoeck und Ruprecht, 2001), 99.
20 Barth, *PT*, 264/296.

Briefly something on Cohen's biography. Along with Franz Rosenzweig, Hermann Cohen was *the* authoritative German-Jewish thinker of the 20th century. He was born July 4, 1842 in the small town of Coswig in the Duchy Anhalt-Bernburg and died on April 4, 1918 in Berlin, shortly before the end of WW I. His father was a teacher in the Jewish school and prayer leader (*chazan*) in the Jewish Community. Hermann Cohen grew up in the synagogue world of prayer. He began studying at the age of 15 at the later famous rabbinical seminary Fraenckel'sche Stiftung in Breslau. But he discontinued that training and instead switched to study philosophy. He made a name for himself from the early 1870s by publishing several books on Immanuel Kant. In 1876, the Prussian King and German Emperor appointed him Full Professor of Philosophy in Marburg, the first Jew to achieve such an honor. Between 1902 and 1912 he presented three parts of a system of philosophy: *Logic of Pure Knowledge* (*Logik der reinen Erkenntnis*, LrE A 1902/B 1914), *Ethics of Pure Will* (*Ethik des reinen Willens*, ErW A 1904/B 1907) and *Aesthetics of Pure Feeling* (*Ästhetik des reinen Gefühls*, ÄrG I/II 1912). Important sidesteps later on were his two books *The Concept of Religion within the System of Philosophy* (*Der Begriff der Religion im System der Philosophie*, BR 1915) and the *Religion of Reason Out of the Sources of Judaism* (RoR; *Religion der Vernunft aus den Quellen des Judentums*, RV A 1919/B 1929), published after his death. When in mid-1917 he had completed the manuscript of *Religion of Reason*, he wanted to return to his philosophical system and write a fourth part: "The Unity of Cultural Consciousness in Psychology" ("Die Einheit des Kulturbewußtseins in der Psychologie").[21] Another possible title – if we are looking at Cohen's course announcements in Marburg – could have been: "Psychology as an Encyclopedia of Philosophy" ("Psychologie als Enzyklopädie der Philosophie"). He had already given a lecture series using that title.[22] But before he could write the book he passed away.

Karl Barth attended one of these lecture courses on psychology in Marburg in the Winter Semester 1908/09, and of the five works by Cohen stored in the Karl Barth Archive in Basle, he studied two in particular with special attention: *Ethics of Pure Will* (*ErW*, 1st ed. 1904) and *The Concept of Religion within the System of Philosophy* (*BR*, 1915).[23] This had great significance for Barth's theological interpretation of Kant. I wish to advance two theses:

---

[21] Cohen, *Logik der reinen Erkenntnis* [²1914], *Werke*, (Hildesheim: Olms, 1977 ff.), vol. 6, 609, 611, where Cohen is reflecting on the "title of the new Psychology."
[22] Winter Sem. 1905/06; Winter Sem. 1908/09 and Summer Sem. 1916; see Cohen, "Appendix" in *Briefe an August Stadler* (Basel: Schwabe, 2015), 143–157.
[23] The *Ethics of Pure Will* contains the notation: "Geneva June 1910"; *The Concept of Religion [...]* has the notation (another handwriting): "Gift from his mother-in-law Hoffmann, Christmas

1) Where *pure* Reason is concerned (esp. in regard to Kant's *Critique of the Practical Reason*), Karl Barth was directly influenced by Hermann Cohen's *Ethics of Pure Will* (*ErW* A 1904).
2) By contrast, where *religious* Reason or "biblical theology" is central, Barth's thinking moves in striking similarity to Cohen's later religious thought, which he knew through his book *The Concept of Religion within the System of Philosophy* (*BR* 1915) and, as we may assume, through the lecture course mentioned.

However, caution is necessary: in his book *Protestant Theology of the 19th century*, nowhere does Barth quote Cohen. Nonetheless, I think the first thesis can be strictly proven by terminological evidence. However, the second thesis, for me the more important one, is based solely on Karl Barth's fundamental decision in favor of a "total survey" of Kant more generally, and on emphases in content in its exposition. In both cases, I will limit myself to only a few details.

3 Barth's Reinterpretation of Kant's Postulate of God

For my first thesis, I will choose as example Kant's Postulate of God in the *Critique of Practical Reason* (KpV). I do not ask here whether this postulate is valid but only examine how Barth presents it.

According to Kant, "the existence of God, as a postulate of pure practical Reason"[24] is a necessary consequence flowing from the categorical imperative.

1917." – Also by Cohen: *Religion und Sittlichkeit* (1907, notation: "Marburg Winter Sem. 1908/09"); *Die Bedeutung des Judentums für den religiösen Fortschritt der Menschheit* (1910); *Kommentar zu Immanuel Kants Kritik der reinen Vernunft* (²1917). Significant remarks and marginal notes can be found esp. in the *Ethics* (until p. 441) and in *The Concept of Religion*. – There are several smaller works also by Paul Natorp, and his *Die Religion innerhalb der Grenzen der Humanität* (1908, notation: "Winter Sem. 1908/09"). The latter contains numerous remarks and marginal notes, esp. in chap. 4 (with reflections on "feeling"), as well as toward the end (pp. 99–126, chap. "Der Transzendenzanspruch [...]"). Then Barth thoroughly studied Natorp's short *Philosophische Propädeutik [...] in Leitsätzen* (1905). In both texts by Natorp, the spontaneous impression one has is that a student still learning was working on the texts here, not the independent thinker. I am grateful to the director of the archive, Dr. Peter Zocher, for his detailed consultation (Feb. 2017). – My citations of Cohen are translated from: *Werke* (Hildesheim: Olms, 1977 ff.); his opus postumum is quoted from: *Religion of Reason Out of the Sources of Judaism*, transl. Simon Kaplan (New York: Fr. Ungar, 1972 [hereafter *RoR*]).

24 Kant, *KpV*, AA V, 124.

Because we need, in order to orient our will in factual terms to this imperative, the subjective "certainty" of, as Barth summarizes, an "ultimate unity of nature and freedom, of that which is with that which must be, and thus of duty and desire."[25] I will leave open whether each single one of these concepts exactly corresponds to the Kantian usage. More important is that Barth thinks that the concept "postulate" is "not a very happy choice linguistically"; better would be the expression "*Pre-Supposition*" (*Voraus-Setzung*).[26] In German language the writing of this word with a hyphen makes clear that what Barth means by this is more than just a logical linkage. He speaks evidently of a "setting," a "positioning," but in the sense of something "pre-," prior to: the idea of God becomes the setting or postulation of a ground lying prior to the moral law. That is thus not only a hypothesis in the purely formal sense of "if the moral law is valid, then it requires the idea of God." Rather it is an onto-logical hypothesis in the sense of Plato: God is then an idea which first and foremost bestows validity on the moral law. That is why Barth designates Kant's Postulate of God a "presupposition of the truth of the idea of *God*."[27]

Now Kant developed his own idea in order to justify the concept of the postulate. According to that, a postulate in ethics is specifically *not* such a pre-supposition, i.e. a concept that at the core is theoretical. In contrast with mathematical-theoretical postulates, for example, the "certainty" of the *practical* postulates (inter alia of the existence of God) is "not apodictic, i.e., a necessity cognized in regard to the object, but is, rather, an assumption necessary, with regard to the subject, for complying with practical reason's objective but practical laws."[28] And only in this subjective sense of a necessary certainty does Kant also speak here once of "presupposition." Nonetheless, he prefers expressly the concept "postulate" and concludes by noting: "I could not find a better expression for this subjective but nonetheless unconditioned necessity."[29]

In regard to his two other concepts employed with reference to God, namely "truth" and "idea," "truth" fails to appear in Kant's discussion of the Postulate of God, nor does the concept "idea," at least not literally. In particular countering the assumption that Kant meant here after all the "*idea* of God" is that he postulates the "*existence* of God." An "idea" can never have "existence," even if it conceptualized as an "individual thing," i.e. when it is thought as an

---

25 Barth, *PT*, 246/277.
26 Barth, *PT*, 246/277.
27 Barth, *PT*, 246/277.
28 Kant, *Critique of Practical Reason*, AA V, 11.
29 Kant, *Critique of Practical Reason*, AA V, 11.

"ideal."³⁰ Ideas in Kant's thought not only do not contain any "creative power" ("like the Platonic ones"); rather, even in pure theory, their effect is exclusively "practical," i.e. as guidelines (regulative principles) for research.³¹ But pure guidelines have no "existence."

Now let us turn to Hermann Cohen. In his *Ethics of Pure Will*, he oriented himself in many points to Kant, including the fact that God in the book becomes at all a topic. Yet what came of it was a totally different sketch. God for Cohen is, *first of all*, indispensable for the foundation of pure will itself. For that reason, God is actually a "Pre-Supposition," i.e. a hypothesis in a "Platonic-creative" sense, as Kant states. As such a hypothesis, God is, *second*, a necessary "idea" for the basis of an ethics. And this idea of God in turn corresponds, *third*, directly to the "fundamental law of truth" formulated several chapters earlier. Central here is the "connection and harmony between the theoretical and the ethical problem,"³² because "in logic alone there was no truth. But also in ethics alone there can be no truth."³³ Thus, a special "fundamental law of truth" is needed in order to link knowledge of nature and ethics. And the idea of God is the final keystone of this linkage, because it secures "for the eternity of the [moral] ideal the analogous eternity of nature."³⁴

All that is not Kantian. Rather, Cohen rejected Kant's doctrine of postulates, mainly because in his eyes its mere subjective meaning as "certainty" was insufficient. Therefore in his *Ethics* he is *not* concerned with an "existence of God" (as Kant is). But he is explicitly concerned 1) about the "idea of God" and 2) about "truth." From this we can deduce: Karl Barth's reading of the purported Kantian Postulate of God – namely "pre-supposition of the truth of the idea of God" – fits consistently in with the thinking of Cohen, however not at all when it comes to Kant. Barth here read his teacher Cohen into Kant. There is also other evidence from 1910 on that he was influenced by Cohen's ethical doctrine of God (1910 was the year in which he acquired a copy of *Ethics of Pure Will*). I need but mention his book on *Romans* (2ⁿᵈ ed. 1922). There he quotes in connection with Romans 1:19 (Barth: "Der Gottesgedanke ist ihnen bekannt"; "the concept of God is known to them") from Cohen's chapter "The Idea of God" in *Ethics of Pure Will*. He is impressed by Cohen's exposition on the "despairing humility" and the "self-ironization of reason" in Plato, who states in his *Politics* that no foundation can be given for the idea of the good, i.e. for what Cohen

---

30 Kant, *Critique of Pure Reason*, A 568/B 596.
31 Kant, *Critique of Pure Reason*, A 569/B 597.
32 Kant, *ErW* A, 85.
33 Kant, *ErW* A, 85.
34 Kant, *ErW* A, 416.

calls the "Absolute." For that reason, this highest idea can only be grasped by a "self-ironization" lying within Reason itself. It is a waiving of the laying of a foundation in order to be able to see the deepest of all foundations itself.[35] Incidentally, Barth reads Cohen's *Ethics*, as the marginal notes show, generally strongly oriented to the aspects of religion, faith, etc. It is interesting that all marks of reading in the book cease on page 441. There are no notes in the following doctrine of virtue, drafted by Cohen as an "application" of his laying of foundations.[36]

---

[35] Karl Barth, *Der Römerbrief* [II 1922] (Zürich: Theol. Verlag, 1984), 21 (already alluding in this direction: "Der Glaube an den persönlichen Gott [1913]," in *Vorträge und kleinere Arbeiten 1909 – 1914*, K. B. Gesamtausgabe, vol. III, [Zürich: Theol. Verlag, 1993] 529 f.). – See Cohen, *Ethik des reinen Willens* [1st ed.!] (Berlin: Cassirer, 1904), 406 on Plato's *Politeia* 509b-510b; cf. Johann Friedrich Lohmann, *Karl Barth und der Neukantianismus* (Berlin: De Gruyter, 1995) 312. – It would probably prove fruitful to analyse the often discussed difference between Barth's *Römerbrief I* and *II* concerning Paul's letter 1:19 in particular with regard to Cohen's "self-ironization" (without immediately bringing up his concept of "origin"!). Potential points of departure: Michael Beintker's discussion of the "unintuitable" ("Das Unanschauliche," in *Die Dialektik in der 'dialektischen Theologie' Karl Barths* [Munich: Chr. Kaiser, 1987], 89 – 96, 225); along with Bruce McCormack's formulation: "If the unintuitable God is truly to be known, God must make Godself intuitable. [...] But God must do so in such a way that the unintuitability proper to God is not set aside" (*Orthodox and modern. Studies in the theology of Karl Barth* [Grand Rapids: Baker Academics, 2008], 28). – Cf. also D. Paul la Montagne, *Barth and Rationality* (Eugene: Cascade Book, 2012), esp. 89 – 103, 160 – 166; Georg Pfleiderer, "Werk, Liberale Phase," in *Barth Handbuch*, 184 – 189, esp. 187.

[36] For reconstructing Barth's relation to Marburg, it is important to note that he appears to only have been familiar with the first edition of Cohen's *Ethics of Pure Will* (1904). Wilhelm Herrmann had commented on this book ("Hermann Cohens Ethik [1907]," in *Schriften zur Grundlegung der Theologie*, vol. 2, ed. Peter Fischer-Appelt [Munich: Chr. Kaiser, 1967], 88 – 117. See McCormack, *Karl Barth's Critically Realistic Dialectical Theology. Its Genesis and Development 1909 – 1936* [Oxford: Clarendon, 1995], 56 – 61; Kenneth Oakes, *Karl Barth on Theology and Philosophy* [Oxford Univ. Press, 2012], 55 – 58). Cohen, for his part, re-responded to Herrmann's comments by means of several supplements in the second edition of his *Ethics* (²1907). Barth (based on the sources available to me) apparently did not know that or did not take it seriously. He instead refers to Herrmann's later publication: "Die Auffassung der Religion in Cohens und Natorps Ethik [1909]," in *Schriften zur Grundlegung*, vol. 2, 206 – 232, perhaps also indirectly in his sketch "Ideen und Einfälle zur Religionsphilosophie [1910]," in *Vorträge und kleinere Arbeiten 1909 – 1914* (Zürich: Theol. Verlag, 1993), 126 – 138. He also stresses the "canonical" significance of Cohen's *Ethics* (cf. Barth's letter from 3 July 1910, fn. by the editor, ibid. 126). Cf. Oakes, 36 f.; in greater detail see Lohmann, *Karl Barth und der Neukantianismus*, 208. – By the way, it should not be overlooked that Barth, despite his high opinion of thinking *individuals*, clearly distanced himself from the general phenomenon "Neo-Kantianism," see *PT*, 343, 364 (German)/384, 407 (English).

4 Particularity of Religious Reason

Now let us turn to the second thesis on the similarity between Barth's description of Kant's "biblical theology" and Cohen's religious thought. Here, as noted, more important than terminological correspondences are thematic weightings. I will limit myself to two aspects. First, regarding the attachment of biblical theology to the pure science of Reason in general.

Kant's doctrine of radical evil was since its inception the target of many attacks. Barth reacts in a pleasantly humorous manner: To call this doctrine of radical evil "a 'foreign body' in the Kantian teaching is a possibility so obvious in interpreting his work, and one which has been presented so often, that simply for this reason one is unwilling to concur in it. It would perhaps *not* be a foreign body at all if it were part of a total survey given from the Kantian point of view, a survey which we must say Kant neglected to give, both to his own time and to us, and which, considering his position, he was bound to refrain from giving."[37] Such a total survey, Barth comments, would also unavoidably have embraced "the horizon of the neighbouring fields [adjoining pure Reason] upon its borders, and not merely regarding these as marking its limits."[38] Then Kant would have been able not only to summarize biblical theology as the Other over against the pure science of Reason, he would also have had to expand and fill it out in a positive way. However, that was not a possibility at hand for the man in which the 18th century "saw, understood and affirmed" itself in its limitations.

Yet it is worth noting that a limitation gives contour to what it limits, both internally and to the outside.[39] A border, a limit both negates and determines at one and the same time. That is why Kant speaks of grace, miracle, the mysteries of the call to faith in a quite specific way. Such things thus remain "*Parerga* [accessories, H.W.] of religion within the limits of pure reason; *they do not belong within it yet are adjacent to it.* Reason, in the awareness of its incapacity to satisfy its moral requirements, expands itself to extravagant ideas, which could supply this need, without, however, appropriating them as its own extended possession [!]. Reason does not deny the possibility or reality of the objects of these ideas; it is just that it cannot include them in its maxims for thought and action."[40] This expansion of reason should be philosophically rejected. By con-

---

37 Kant, *PT*, 264/296.
38 Kant, *PT*, 264/296.
39 See Beintker: "Grenzbewusstsein," 130–132.
40 Kant, *Rlg.* B, 63, fn., AA VI, 52; cf. the quotation in Barth, *PT*, 268 f./301.

trast, in terms of biblical theology, it evinces – one almost might say: it reveals "positively palpable"[41] "mysteries of the highest wisdom."[42] Because, as Kant stated in a concluding "general note" to his *Religion within the Boundaries of Reason alone*, the "impossibility" of such mysteries "cannot be proven either, since freedom itself [...] remains just as incomprehensible to us according to its possibility as the Supernatural we might want to assume as surrogate for the independent yet deficient determination of freedom."[43] Consequently, Reason "calculates" "with a faith [...] we might call *reflective*."[44] For Karl Barth, Kant's mention of the "Parerga" is a "methodically very illuminating expression."[45] And in this fundamental recognition of Kant's reaching out to a biblical theology I see the analogy to Hermann Cohen's determination of *Religion within the System of Philosophy*.

As mentioned, Barth read Cohen's book of this title carefully. It develops what Cohen calls the "particularity" or "special feature" (*Eigenart*) of religion. As in Kant, as Cohen says, religion must not impair the "autonomy" (*Selbständigkeit*) of the principal philosophical questions regarding pure knowledge, pure will and a pure feeling. Cohen's "*Eigenart*" makes of religion a "secondary order" (*Nebenordnung*), a *parergon* or accessory to philosophy. This "secondary order," he states in *The Concept of Religion*, "must function to *attach* [*angliedern*] the peculiarity to the autonomous elements, attaching it *to all three elements. None must be excluded if the particular feature of religion is to be brought to full clarity and unambiguity.*"[46] But Cohen goes further than Kant. He sees religion not only as something not-impossible but as a positive confession. All spheres of philosophical purity are run through a second time with the faith in God. The special mode of reason with which that occurs is that of a "correlation between man and God."[47] That will never be a "possession" of pure reason, too, but rather, as Kant had said, an "expansion" of Reason. But this expansion

---

[41] Assel, *Geheimnis und Sakrament*, 147 f.
[42] Kant, *Rlg.* B, 261, AA VI, 171; Barth, *PT*, 267/300.
[43] Kant, *Rlg.* B, 297, AA VI, 191).
[44] Kant, *Rlg.* B, 63, Anm., AA VI, 52. See Hans Martin Dober, *Reflektierender Glaube. Die Vernunft der Religion in klassischen Positionen* (Würzburg: Königshausen und Neumann, 2011), 33–48, here 35; on Kant and Cohen see several articles in Dober and Matthias Morgenstern, eds., *Religion aus den Quellen der Vernunft. Hermann Cohen und das evangelische Christentum* (Tübingen: Mohr Siebeck, 2012), esp. Jörg Dierken (131–146), Assel (162–175), Dober (207–222).
[45] Barth, *PT*, 268/301. See Oakes, *Karl Barth on Theology and Philosophy*, 140.
[46] Cohen, *BR*, 110 f.
[47] Cohen, *BR*, 110. Not to be mixed up with Paul Tillich's "correlation" between utterances of faith and human existential situations, see Michael Moxter, "Barth und Tillich," in *Barth Handbuch*, 106–111, here: 110.

shows a positive revelation, a continuous "giving [of the Torah]," as Cohen translates the Hebrew *matan tora*.⁴⁸

For my examination here of Barth, it is important that this "secondary order" is considered precisely where Cohen speaks about the fourth great topic of philosophy: "psychology as an encyclopedia of philosophy." As mentioned, he did not write the book that would deal with this. But in the systematic-philosophical books available to us, he alludes to something, most detailed in exposition in *The Concept of Religion*. Chapter Five is titled: "The Relation of Religion to Psychology."⁴⁹ And it is specifically this relation that Cohen thinks would be instructive, because: "It is precisely the problem of religion in total consciousness that might at least make vividly clear, without a precise exposition, the distinction and synopsis of the events in consciousness, as psychology must demand."⁵⁰ What Kant no longer succeeded in developing, indeed what in Barth's view he was unable to achieve, namely a description of his own "total survey," Cohen seeks to attain in the psychology of a "total consciousness" that includes and encompasses religion. Barth was thus able to feel fully confirmed in his intention to venture a Kantian 'total survey.'

For this reason, it is very significant that in Winter Semester 1908/09 he attended Cohen's lectures on an encyclopedic psychology. In Karl Barth's student's record of courses attended at Marburg University, it is the only course in philosophy; it bears Cohen's own confirmation of Barth's registration and completion, along with a notation about the necessary sum paid for the course.⁵¹

Unfortunately, to date we have no knowledge of any extant lecture notes by Barth or any other students who attended the lectures. That is striking in Barth's case. The impressive series of his other lecture notes housed in Karl Barth's home in Basle, in part very meticulous in their execution, even suggests that in the case of Cohen, he intentionally did not take copious notes.⁵² However, we can proceed from the assumption that Cohen's personality also had a powerful impact on Barth, as it did on every other person who reported their impressions of Cohen. Barth himself wrote: "The fact that once there was an almost priestlike serious philosophy [...], in Marburg that was made impressively clear to us

---

48 Cohen, "Einheit und Einzigkeit Gottes III: Offenbarung [1918]," in *Werke*, 17, 640.
49 Cohen, *BR*, 108–140.
50 Cohen, *BR*, 108.
51 Cf. Barth's "Anmeldungs-Buch" Marburg, Karl Barth Archive, Basel. See picture.
52 The archivist Dr. Zocher does not think there is any serious reason to assume the loss of a previous extant set of lecture notes.

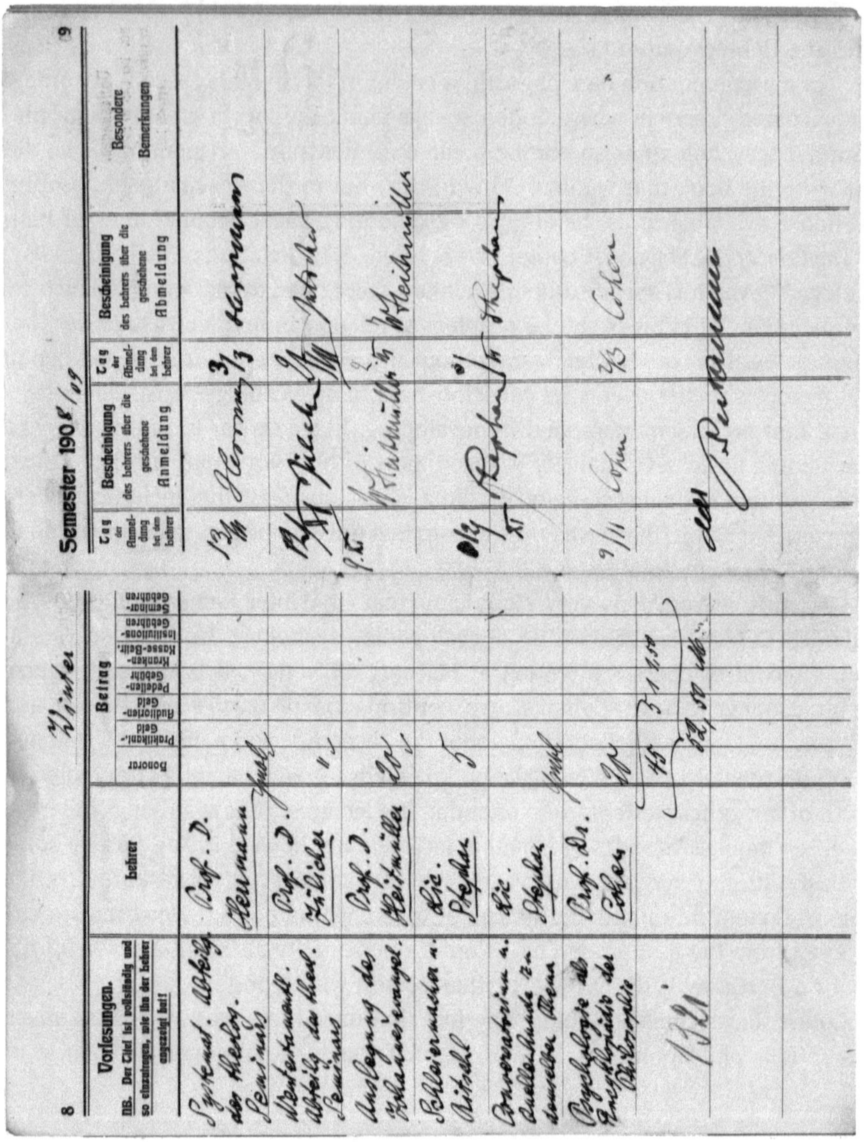

Fig. 1: Barth's "Anmeldungs-Buch" (by courtesy of the Karl Barth Archives, Basel).

[…] in the person of Cohen and Natorp."[53] Given Cohen's power of rhetorical expression, often commented on, it was not necessary to take notes in order to take away a lasting impression.

Here too I will limit myself to but a few points. Initially a methodical detail: in the "new psychology," Cohen writes already in his *Logic of Pure Knowledge* (in an addition to the 2nd ed. 1914), "*unity* would replace *purity.*"[54] Reference is to the "unity of the consciousness of culture as a foundation."[55] However, as Cohen himself noted, that entailed a certain "danger."[56] Because the three previous parts of the philosophical system bore in their title the term "purity" and not "unity" as a methodological guiding concept: pure knowledge, pure will, pure feeling. The transition to "unity" thus appears as a rupture. Cohen does note that the new unity is also a key methodological "guiding concept," and thus "a major sense of purity in unity would be preserved."[57] But it is precisely the guiding principle that changes. Purity, previously the encompassing whole, is now only a part. Psychology encompasses more than what the philosopher of logical, ethical or aesthetic purity presents and describes. It endeavors to find the "systematic-genetic development of all manifestations of consciousness."[58] And this "all" has to be taken seriously, because Cohen means actually all phenomena of consciousness "in the light and the dark, in maturity and in the bud, in the complexion and in the elements."[59]

This unavoidably means chaos, and Cohen realizes that. But he writes: "If however the goal for this total chaos is development from the focal point of the system, then unity must be the goal."[60] This idea of the goal becomes predominant. The previous parts of the system had their point of departure in already ordered facts (science and art). By contrast, a chaos shows no "given primal ground of consciousness" whatsoever. "Fiction supplants the desired fact."[61] But "fiction" here means: 'target design' of a "genetic development."[62]

---

53 Karl Barth, "Die dogmatische Prinzipienlehre bei Wilhelm Herrmann [1925]," in *Vorträge und kleinere Arbeiten 1922–1925* (Zürich: Theol. Verlag, 1990), 545–603, here 585; see Eberhard Busch, *Karl Barths Lebenslauf. Nach seinen Briefen und autobiografischen Texten* (Zürich: Theologischer Verlag, 2005), 56.
54 Cohen, *LrE* B, 611.
55 Cohen, *LrE* B, 610.
56 Cohen, *LrE* B, 611.
57 Cohen, *LrE* B, 611.
58 Cohen, *LrE* B, 611.
59 Cohen, *LrE* B, 611.
60 Cohen, *LrE* B, 611.
61 Cohen, *LrE* B, 611.
62 Cohen, *LrE* B, 612.

Cohen's fourth systematic part was thus to be a set of instructions leading to a goal, as he says, a "hodegetic [i.e. a path-leading] encyclopedia."[63] That is what he calls his psychology in his *Aesthetics of Pure Feeling* (1912). He drafted this work around 1909, and thus precisely at the time when Karl Barth was attending his lectures. Barth experienced directly what we can only surmise from hints: before his eyes a total survey in vital discourse grounded on a soil marked by Kantian elements. Without denying the limitations and without any mixing of objective content, Cohen included in a positive manner the religious "particularity" within the parts of the philosophical system. Psychology is generally such an attachment or inclusion of particularity despite methodological dangers, a moving on and beyond into an open system of human communal consciousness based on Reason.

Something additional is part of that: Cohen's concern for the "naive consciousness of the human being."[64] To be sure, naïveté is for him not a value per se. The goal is to educate that inchoate consciousness, moving toward a philosophical consciousness. But fully valid remains the fact "that the unscholarly, uneducated individual, the person in a sense devoid of any culture, nonetheless has longing for a God. Religion consists in the desire for God. It consists in the yearning for a being outside of man, but for man."[65] Nonetheless, caution is advised: "Outside of man, but for man" does not mean that God appears somewhere 'in the image of Man' or might be thought of as such. The "correlation between man and God" is the opposite of anthropomorphism and myth. "Religion only emerges with the one and only God, with God without a likeness and image."[66] And as a result of this "uniqueness of God [...], the popular consciousness" – and reading Cohen, we must add: the *Jewish* popular consciousness – was unambigiously clear about "the incomparability of the content and treasure of religion over against all allurements of the culture."[67] To be sure, "popular consciousness" has no place in a logic of purity. Yet by contrast, dealing with the "giving" of the Torah, that consciousness has a participating voice in its way, even in the laying of the foundations. That can be shown in multifaceted ways looking at Cohen's conceptions of creation, holiness, freedom of the will for good or evil, liturgy, the community, reconciliation, Messianism, the resurrection and religious virtues. This leads to my second example concerning the analogy between Barth and Cohen: the church.

---

63 Cohen, *ÄrG* II, 432.
64 Cohen, *BR*, 137.
65 Cohen, *BR*, 138.
66 Cohen, *BR*, 138.
67 Cohen, *BR*, 138.

5 Church and Jewish Community

According to Kant the church is an "ethical common entity," a "people of God under ethical laws."[68] To "create" such a people can "only be expected by God himself."[69] Nevertheless, the human being remains morally responsible. In ecclesiastical matters, man must "act in such a manner as if everything depends on himself, and only under this condition he may hope that higher wisdom will grant completion and success to his well-meaning efforts."[70] For that reason, Kant writes, "God himself is in the last instance the author of the *constitution* as founder, whereas human beings are nonetheless as members and free citizens of this realm in all instances the authors of its *organization*."[71]

What exactly does 'as if everything depends on man himself' mean? The church – Barth is detailed here in his discussion – is also for Kant the place of common prayer, baptism, communion. Seen from the perspective of the problem of radical evil, all these are "means of grace" for a real hope for genuine change and turnaround. But Kant suffices with designating their success as a "mystery of satisfaction."[72] He avoids any confession of having experienced their effect. He sticks to stipulating that the "required goodness," i.e. turning back from evil, for a person on the soil of Reason "must stem from a human being himself [...]. Therefore, no one can stand in for another by virtue of the superabundance of his own good conduct and his merit; and if we must *assume* any such thing, this can be only for moral purposes, since for ratiocination it is an unfathomable mystery."[73]

In Cohen, the place of the church is taken by the Jewish Community. It is the place where despite the free will to do bad (Hebrew: *shegaga*) with its unrecognizable reasons, justified hope for a turnabout nonetheless sprouts. Cohen, likewise only late in life, formulates the problem of a free decision contra pure practical reason: "How [in the face of the historical experience of humankind] can the assumption of a mediating will that can choose bad and good come about? How can free will mean the free will to commit sin?"[74] And he refers to the same biblical verse, Genesis 8:21, which Kant (indirectly) also alluded to:

---

[68] Kant, *Rlg.* B, 137, AA VI, 98.
[69] Kant, *Rlg.* B, 141, AA VI, 100.
[70] Kant, *Rlg.* B, 141, AA VI, 101.
[71] Kant, *Rlg.* B, 227, AA VI, 152; English translation, 152.
[72] Kant, *Rlg.* B, 216, AA VI, 143; English translation, 144.
[73] Kant, *Rlg.* B, 216f., AA VI, 143. See Assel, *Geheimnis und Sakrament*, esp. 167–192.
[74] Cohen, *RV* B, 212; cf. *RoR*, 181.

"The *yezer* of man's heart is evil from his youth."[75] He intentionally uses the Hebrew word *yezer* in order to avoid the common translation of "instinct, drive [of the heart]." He wants (like Kant) to repel any biologistic interpretation. In support he mentions the second verse, from Genesis 6:5, *kol yezer machshavot libo rak ra' kol ha-yom*; "every *formation*" (here the translation of *yezer*) "of the thoughts of his heart was only evil the whole day." And he interprets this "formation of the heart" together with the medieval commentator Abraham Ibn Esra (12th cent.) as a "product, which is imitated after it."[76] An 'imitating production' is only superficially an inborn drive. In truth the *yezer* of the evil is an errant free will.

All that fits quite well with Kant – and with Karl Barth's discussion. But from here on the paths separate, those of Kant and Cohen but those of Barth and Cohen as well. Cohen formulates his doctrine regarding the Community as a practical liturgy of the Day of Atonement, Yom Kippur. The few paragraphs where he sketches this in his book *The Concept of Religion* (p. 64), even without a precise exposition, were noticeably marked in Barth's personal copy, and vertically in the margin he wrote the word "synagogue!"

The reason is clear. According to Cohen, the *Jewish* religious service has its core in a "standing before God." A person's reconciliation with being endangered by one's own freedom occurs in a likewise free, public confession of sins, uttered in fixed liturgical formulae. The individual 'relinquishes himself,' merging totally into the we-form of the Community: in the confession of the "sin we have sinned" ('*al chet' she-chata'nu*). His longing for reconciliation is completely absorbed within the linguistic figure of the Community. But in Cohen's eyes, the linguistic form of longing is lyrical, and the longing, when uttered lyrically, experiences its own satisfaction, its being reconciled. Thus the Community praying in Hebrew realizes simultaneously a confession of sins committed and reconciliation. Only the human being speaks here, everywhere. God speaks nowhere. "God," as stated in *The Concept of Religion*, "*who is not participating in this work*," – printed with emphasis! – "is conceived as a symbol, an emblem that brings about liberation from sin."[77] God never intervenes in this economy. Cohen bears witness to the faith of reason that brings forth a power that can drive and shape reconciliation. That is a 'reason out of the sources of Judaism': "The mediator [more precisely: the messenger] between God and Man is reason" (*ha-mal'ach ben 'adam u-ben 'elohav hu' sichlo*), thus Cohen quotes Ibn Esra once

---

[75] Cohen, *RV*, B 212; *RoR* 181; see Kant, *Rlg.* B, 7, 13; AA VI, 22, 25.
[76] Cohen, *RV* B, 212; *RoR*, 181. Ibn Esra reads the word *yezer* as *toldah*, 'result,' 'consequence': *hi' ha-toldah ha-nozrah lo* (Commentary on Gen 8:21).
[77] Cohen, *BR*, 64.

64   H. Cohen,

So muß, so kann allein die Korrelation von Mensch und Gott hier aushelfen, wo Gott erdacht wird, aber nicht anders als in der Korrelation zum Menschen; wo er also bei dem Problem der Erlösung nicht als ein ebenbürtiger Faktor mitwirken kann. In sittlicher Tätigkeit, in der Verwirklichung des Sittlichen, steht der Mensch allein da. Der Gott, der in dieser Verwirklichung, in dieser Befreiung dem Menschen helfen soll, kann und darf den Menschen nicht von seiner Menschenwürde ablösen; dies geschähe aber, wenn er von der Gewissensarbeit entbunden oder sie ihm auch nur erleichtert werden könnte. Gott macht dem Menschen seine eigene Gewissensqual nicht überflüssig; er stellt sich ihm nicht zur Seite und hilft ihm nicht bei dem Geschäfte der Reue und der Buße.

Aber diese hat zur Voraussetzung, daß ein Gott da sei, auf den die Korrelation in dieser Form der Sünde sich richtet; und der die Korrelation zu dem neuen Sinne bringt, daß die Befreiung, die der Mensch selbst nicht vollbringen kann, in dieser neuen Korrelation zu Gott in Vollzug trete. Der neue Sinn Gottes entspricht dem neuen Begriffe des sündigen Menschen. Und dazu entsteht zuvörderst die Korrelation des zur Seligkeit befreiten Menschen.

64. Das ist der neue Gott, der Gott der Religion, im Unterschiede von dem Gotte der Menschheit in der Ethik. Die Erlösung befreit von der Sünde. Und im Hinblick auf diesen Gott der Erlösung breitet der Mensch die Sündenfülle seines Herzens vor sich aus, weil dieser Hinblick ihm zugleich die Gewißheit bringt, daß diese seine sittliche Bußarbeit nicht verlorene Liebesmühe sei, sondern daß sie das Ziel erreichen kann, das ihr ohne Gott unerreichbar bliebe. Der Mensch bleibt in der Arbeit, aber Gott, der an dieser Arbeit selbst nicht teilnimmt, wird als das Wahrzeichen gedacht, das die Befreiung von der Sünde bewirkt.

65. Wie der Begriff des Menschen eine andere Bedeutung erlangt hat als in der Ethik, so auch der Begriff Gottes. Aber wie der religiöse Begriff des Menschen trotz der Differenz zwischen Individuum und Menschheit, und trotz der Differenz zwischen unaufhörlicher sittlicher Arbeit und dem Ziel der Befreiung von der Angst des Gewissens, dennoch in der selbständig bleibenden sittlichen Arbeit auch bei dieser Befreiung in Zusammenhang mit der Aufgabe der Sittlichkeit verbleibt, so verhält es sich auch mit Gott. Wie er in der Ethik für die Menschheit die Verwirklichung des Guten gewährleistet,

[margin annotation: Synagoge!]

Fig. 2: From Karl Barth's copy of Cohen's "Begriff der Religion..." (by courtesy of the Karl Barth Archives, Basel).

again.[78] To make a historical event or a person the grounding for trust in God is excluded. That is why Barth wrote in the margin "synagogue!"[79]

Faith in Jesus Christ marks the barrier between Karl Barth and his Jewish teacher. But Barth also remains clearly separated from Kant. As great as his veneration was for the man in whom "the 18th century saw, understood, and affirmed itself in its own limitations," in content, Kant could never be more than a provocation, the highly emphatic call to a fundamentally different path of Christian self-reflection. Methodologically, however, he remained the model for a critical scientific attitude, one that knew its limitations but also was able to play with them; thus, the model for what Barth – in his very different pathway to the sources – in his *Romans II* (1922) had called a "*critical* theology."[80]

translated from the German by William Templer

---

78 See Ibn Esra's introduction to the commentary on Genesis (reprinted in trad. Jewish Bible editions, *mikra'oth gedoloth*); quoted in Cohen, "Liebe und Gerechtigkeit in den Begriffen Gott und Mensch [1900]," in *Jüdische Schriften* (Berlin: Schwetschke, 1924), vol. III, 65; "Deutschtum und Judentum [1915/16]," in *Werke* 16, 480; see also: Cohen, *Reflexionen und Notizen, Werke*, Suppl. 1, 59; Myriam Bienenstock, "'Von Angesicht zu Angesicht', d.h. 'ohne einen Mittler'," in Dober/Morgenstern, *Religion aus den Quellen der Vernunft*, esp. 57–62.

79 Cohen's negation of Divine intervention was also met with contradiction by several Jewish thinkers, e.g., Franz Rosenzweig, Martin Buber and Leo Strauß.

80 Karl Barth, *Der Römerbrief* (^{2}1922/1984), "Preface to the 2nd ed.," XIII. Along similar lines, see Michael Beintker, "Grenzbewusstsein," esp. 128–132; Bent Flemming Nielsen, "Theologie als kritische Wissenschaft," in: *Barth Handbuch*, 410–416.

Jacqueline Mariña
The Religious *A Priori* in Otto and its Kantian Origins

This paper provides an analysis of Rudolph Otto's understanding of the structures of human consciousness making possible the appropriation of revelation. Already in his dissertation on Luther's understanding of the Holy Spirit, Otto was preoccupied with how the "outer" of revelation could be united to these inner structures. Later, in his groundbreaking *Idea of the Holy*, Otto would explore the category of the numinous, an element of religious experience tied to the irrational element of the holy. This paper first provides a brief account of Otto's account of the holy, especially its numinous, irrational elements. Second, the paper analyzes Otto's understanding of the structures of consciousness grounding the experience of the numinous and allowing the irrational element to be "schematized" by the rational element. Otto's exposition of these structures is heavily influenced by his reception of Kant's analysis of the two stems of human cognition, namely understanding and sensibility, and their possible relation to a common root, which Otto identified with what the mystics called the ground of the soul. Yet it is in Otto's reception of Kant's *Critique of Judgment* that all of these ideas find their completion, and it is here where we must look to understand the relation between the religious *a priori* and Otto's category of the numinous. Kant's aesthetic idea is a singular representation given in intuition; it is infinitely saturated and as such intimates the ideas of God, the soul, and the world as a whole. I show how Otto appropriates Kant's aesthetic idea and its relation to ideas of reason in order to make sense of how an empirically given revelation, for instance, an experience of the numinous, can connect with the inner structures of consciousness and thereby have the singular import that it does.

1 Introduction

How can revelation be interpreted and interiorized? This was Otto's burning question at the heart of his dissertation on Luther's understanding of the Holy Spirit. There he had, among other things, reflected on two propositions from the Lutheran catechism: "The Holy Spirit does not work without means; he is bound to the Word and works through the Word."[1] Otto struggled with the validity and intelligibility of the propositions on several fronts. First, of itself the Word is not a *sufficient* condition of faith; it is only opened up through the Spirit, remaining dead to the natural human being. But insofar as the work of the Holy Spirit precedes, accompanies, and makes possible the understanding of the Word, this is a "work of the Spirit *before* the Word," and is, as such, an action of the Spirit "without means,"[2] contradicting the first part of the formula. Second, Otto questions the intelligibility of the notion that the Holy Spirit works *through* the Word. This amounts to the claim that one energy works through another, and is just as nonsensical as the claim that light gives out its light *through* warmth.[3] A close analysis of Luther's claims leaves the question of the efficacy of the Word shrouded in mystery. Why is it received here in one way, and there in another? The Word is not a magical formula that immediately arouses faith; it has, instead, a significant content that must be interpreted and appropriated before it can give rise to a life-altering faith. This content can be variously received, and can even fail to have an impact altogether if the mind is altogether too preoccupied with other things, or if the individual has no sense for religion.[4]

Already in the dissertation Otto was preoccupied with the human structures of consciousness that make *appropriation* of revelation possible, as well as the conditions of the possibility of genuine religious experience, concerns central to his oeuvre as a whole. This question, of how the "outer" of revelation could be united with the inner structures of consciousness was the basis of what he called a "science of religion," one founded on the groundbreaking philosophy of Immanuel Kant. By 1909 Otto had published two books stamped by his reception of Kantian philosophy: the first, *Naturalism and Religion* argued that Kant's transcendental idealism was uniquely suited to assign religion its proper place given the success of modern science.[5] Kant posited two distinct domains, phenomena and noumena. The first is the realm of appearances or empirical realities. Here nature is presented as the measurable and quantifiable – and as subject to strict causal laws. It is a closed system, for every natural event must have a cause that is itself an appearance. As *appearance*, the realm of phenomena is

---

1 Rudolf Otto, *Die Anschauung vom Heiligen Geiste bei Luther*, Göttingen: Dandenhoeck und Ruprecht, 1898, 45.
2 Otto, *Die Anschauung vom Heiligen*, 45.
3 Otto, 46.
4 Otto, 48.
5 Rudolf Otto, *Naturalistische und religiöse Weltansicht*, Tübingen, 1904; English translation: *Naturalism and Religion*, trans. J. Arthur Thomson and Margaret R. Thomson, New York: G. P. Putnam's Sons, 1907, 68 ff.

not fully real, and Otto continually reminds his readers that this is something that the mystics were already aware of. On the other hand, according to Kant, phenomenal realities are grounded in the realm of noumena or things in themselves, which *as such*, make no appearance and remain unknown and unknowable. These are, Otto argued, the true realities that are the genuine subject matter of religion. One would search in vain, argued Otto, to find God among the real of the phenomena, all of which were subject to scientific explanation. To think of God as a God of the gaps in our knowledge of phenomena was a losing proposition. We must rather turn our attention to the intelligible world grounding the phenomena if we are to ground a science of religion.[6] How this was to be possible was further expanded and contextualized in his second 1909 book, *The Philosophy of Religion Based on Kant and Fries*, in which he presents Kant's philosophy (as received by Fries) in broad strokes.[7] Most significant in this work is his emphasis on Kant's *Critique of Judgment* as containing the key to the science of religion.

In 1911, however, Otto embarked on a journey through North Africa, the Middle East, and India, and in these travels had several remarkable experiences, one, especially, in a Jewish synagogue in Morocco where he heard the *Trisagion* of Isaiah.[8] These experiences, rupturing all rationalistic accounts of religion, gave rise to the phenomenology of religious experience described in the *Idea of the Holy*. There Otto describes the holy as containing non-rational elements that can only be apprehended through feeling. These feeling elements are, as he notes, "*sui generis* and irreducible" to any other mental states.[9] Considered from the point of view of the phenomenology of the history of religions, they are what first appear in religious life, and they do so devoid of any properly ethical content. Only later are they gradually filled in with the ethical, what Otto calls the "schematization" of this primary datum.

Concerns similar to those found in his analysis of Luther are fundamental to his analysis in *Idea*, namely, those having to do with the structures of consciousness making these experiences possible. And while Kant's division of existence into phenomena and noumena, as well as his exposition of the holy in purely

---

6 Otto, *Naturalistische und religiöse*, 69.
7 Rudolf Otto, *Kantisch-Fries'sische Religionsphilosophie und ihre Anwendung auf die Teologie*, Tübingen, 1909. English translation: *The Philosophy of Religion Based on Kant and Fries*, trans. E. B. Dicker, London 1931.
8 On this point see Robin Minney, "The Development of Otto's Thought 1898–1917: From 'Luther's View of the Holy Spirit' to 'The Holy'," *Religious Studies*, Vol. 26, No. 4, 507.
9 Rudolf Otto, *The Idea of the Holy*, translated by John W. Harvey, Oxford: Oxford University Press, 1923, 7. Henceforward this work will be cited as *Idea*, with the page number following.

moral terms, could not *by themselves* accommodate Otto's remarkable insights regarding the holy's irrational aspects, Otto still believed Kant's philosophy singularly suited to illuminating the possibility of the religious experience, its ground in the structures of the soul, and the relationship between its rational and irrational elements. In this paper I first provide a brief description of Otto's analysis of the holy, in particular its irrational elements. I then move to discuss how Otto understood the structures of consciousness both grounding the experience of the numinous as well as allowing the irrational element to be "schematized" by the rational element. This analysis will take us deep into Kant's analysis of the two stems of human cognition and their possible relation to a common root, which Otto links to what the mystics called the ground of the soul.

2 Analysis of the Holy

According to Otto, what we understand as the holy contains two elements. The first is the rational element. It is amenable to the human understanding, can be apprehended through concepts, and is especially associated with the ethical sphere. The note is especially sounded in the prophets of the Hebrew Bible. Amos, for instance, preaches, "Take away from me the noise of your songs; I will not listen to the melody of your harps; But let justice roll down like waters, and righteousness like an ever-flowing stream."[10] Immanuel Kant, famously, identified the holy with morality; in his *Lectures on the Philosophical Doctrine of Religion,* he defines holiness as "the absolute or unlimited moral perfection of the will. A holy being must not be affected with the least inclination contrary to morality. It must be impossible for it to will something which is contrary to moral laws."[11] According to Otto, however, this rational element of the holy is to be contrasted with its non-rational element. Two features are particularly significant about this contrast. First, the non-rational element in the holy is first and foremost apprehended through *feelings* and intuitions, and not through concepts. Moreover, *what* is apprehended – what Otto calls the numinous – is felt to have a sheer overplus of meaning that cannot be adequately expressed through concepts; at best the experience can be suggested by what Otto calls

---

10 All biblical quotations are from the *New Revised Standard Version* (New York: Oxford University Press, 1991), Amos: 5:23–24.
11 Immanuel Kant, "Lectures on the Philosophical Doctrine of Religion" in *Religion and Rational Theology,* translated and edited by Allen W. Wood and George di Giovanni (Cambridge: Cambridge University Press), 409; AA, 28: 1075.

"ideograms," metaphors and analogies that point to the experience and that help to evoke it. Second, the idea of the holy is *synthetic*. Rational and non-rational aspects of the holy are not contained in one another, that is, one cannot, through an analysis of one element, derive or unfold the other. Otto dubs the rational elements of the holy "*synthetic* essential attributes." While we are certainly justified in predicating rational attributes to the holy, "we have to predicate them of a subject which they qualify, but which in its deeper essence is not, nor indeed can be, comprehended in them; which rather requires comprehension of a quite different kind" (2). Now, it is important to note that the rational and non-rational elements of the holy are not two distinct *concepts* that we can simply predicate of the holy. To think of them in this way would be to treat both aspects of the holy as elements that can be comprehended in concepts, and while this may work well enough with the rational side of the holy, it would completely inadequate to picking out the numinous quality of the holy. This, as Otto notes, can only be apprehended through *feeling*, which, as I will show in section two, is that faculty through which something that stands outside the self is *directly* and immediately apprehended. The feeling elements through which the numinous is apprehended are simply the direct effects, so to speak, of the numinous itself on our psychological constitution. The numinous is not to be confused with these feeling elements themselves, but is, rather that which evokes such feelings to begin with. Key expressions associated with it in Western literature are the Hebrew *qadosh*, the Greek *alios*, and the Latin *sacer*.

A large part of Otto's oeuvre consists of a compelling phenomenological analysis of the feelings presaging the numinous. He identifies three principle moments in its apprehension, which is experienced as a *mysterium tremendum et fascinans*. He first begins by providing an analysis of "*tremendum*," which can be further analyzed into three distinct moments. These are a) that of awefulness, b) that of overpoweringness, and c) that of energy or urgency. The three moments are intrinsically related and can easily pass over into one another. Otto describes the element of awefulness as the sense of the absolute *unapproachability* of the numinous. This is well illustrated in the story of the burning bush in the Hebrew Bible. When God calls Moses from the burning bush, God adjures him "Come no closer! Remove the sandals from your feet, for the place on which you are standing is holy ground," and Moses is afraid (Exod 3:5). This sense of the unapproachability of the holy brings with it a peculiar dread of a completely different nature from the fear that can be experienced of objects in the natural world. To mark something off as hallowed is to mark it off by this feeling of peculiar dread, which recognizes its numinous character. For instance, after Jacob receives the promise in a dream at Bethel he is afraid and exclaims, "How awesome is this place! This is none other than the house of God, and this is the gate of heaven" (Gen 28:17). Significantly, the story marks the origin of the northern sanctuary at Bethel.

Otto notes that this feeling of dread is the starting point in the evolution of religion. It first begins as the experience of something 'uncanny' or 'weird.' The feeling can take "wild and demonic forms and can sink to an almost grisly horror and shuddering."[12] Examples from the Bible include the *emah* of Yahweh (Fear of God), which Yahweh can pour forth to paralyzing effect. In the New Testament we find the strange idea of the wrath (ὀργή) of God, analogous to the *ira deorum* of the Indian pantheon. As Otto notes, this *orgé* "is nothing but the *tremendum* itself, apprehended and expressed by the aid of a naïve analogy."[13] The analogy is naïve because the notion of 'wrath' implies purpose and emotion. But a closer analysis of the *tremendum* shows that no such purpose or emotion is involved, for the element of awefulness has two other features worthy of note. First, this *orgé* is devoid of moral qualities. Second, the way that it is "kindled and manifested" is quite strange: it is "'like a hidden force of nature', like stored-up electricity, discharging itself upon anyone that comes too near. It is 'incalculable' and 'arbitrary'."[14] The strange story of the ark of the Covenant in second Samuel is illustrative: when Uzzah reaches out his hand to steady the ark, he is immediately struck dead.[15] That the *tremendum* is experienced as such a force of nature is further evidence of the insufficiency of the analogy with the idea of "wrath," which has as its basis the idea of personal purposiveness.

Associated with the experience of awefulness is the experience of the *tremendum* as an overpowering might. Its concomitant is the feeling of the self as impotent, as a mere nullity, as something that is not entirely real. Abraham, for instance, refers to himself as "but dust and ashes" in the presence of the Lord (Gen 18:27). Only the numen is felt to be absolutely real. This apprehension of the numen has both ontological and valuational components; the numen is not only that which is absolutely real, it is also felt as that which has absolute worth. This experience is at the heart of mysticism, which witnesses that the I is not essentially real, and which rejects the delusion of selfhood as manifested in the ego. Lastly, partially implied by the experience of the *tremendum* as an overpowering might, but containing other elements as well, is the experience of the energy and urgency of the numen. This is the experience of the living God, of "a force that

---

12 Otto, *The Idea of the Holy*, 13.
13 Otto, 18.
14 Otto, 18.
15 2 Samuel 6:6. Another example is the story of the bubonic plague that the ark brings with it when it was captured by the Philistines in 1 Samuel chapters 5 and 6.

knows not stint nor stay, which is urgent, active, compelling and alive."[16] This energy is captured in the New Testament sayings "It is a fearful thing to fall into the hands of the living God" (Hebrews 10:31) and "indeed our God is a consuming fire" (Hebrews 12:29). The energy of the numen is absolutely unendurable; even Moses cannot see the glory of God, but only God's back, for "no one shall see me (God) and live" (Exod 33:21). In love mysticism it is experienced as the fire of divine love that the mystic can hardly endure.

The horrifying images in chapter eleven of the *Bhagavad-Gita* are especially apt in capturing the awefulness, overpoweringness, and energy of the numen. When Aryuna desires to behold God himself in his own form, his petition is granted and he sees Vishnu "touching the heavens, glittering, many-hued, with yawning mouths;" people "hasting enter into thy mouths grim with fangs and terrible; some, caught between the teeth, appear with crushed heads." And finally the grisly image spreads to includes whole worlds: "Thou devourest and lickest up all the worlds around with flaming mouths; filling the whole universe with radiance, grim glow Thy splendours, O Vishnu!" The image conveys the absolute power of the divine over all finite being. This power is, however, like a force of nature; it is an all-consuming energy, its horrifying indifference to human purposes demonstrated by the fact that it consumes whole worlds containing both good and bad alike.[17] After Aryuna has witnessed this, he asks to understand what he has seen, but the petition is not granted. What he has seen must remain incomprehensible to him. This brings us the next characteristic of the holy: its mysterious character.

The numinous is apprehended as *mysterium:* it is something that "strikes us dumb," and that brings with it "amazement absolute."[18] It is "wholly other" (*ganz Anderes*) since it is immediately grasped as something that is of a completely different nature than anything that can be known by the "natural" individual. The *mysterium* is "that which is quite beyond the sphere of the usual, the intelligible, and the familiar, which therefore falls quite outside the limits of the 'canny' and is contrasted with it, filling the mind with blank wonder

---

16 Otto, *The Idea of the Holy*, 24.
17 Lest anyone be tempted to think that this frightful image of the divine is merely indigenous to Indian religion, compare with the following statement from Luther: "Yea, He is more terrible and frightful than the Devil. For He dealeth with us and bringeth us to ruin with power, siteth and hammereth us and payeth no heed to us. ... In His majesty He is a consuming fire. ... For therefrom can no man refrain: if he thinketh on God aright, his heart in his body is struck with terror. ... Yea, as soon as he heareth God named, he is filled with trepidation and fear." Cited *Idea*, 99.
18 Otto, *The Idea of the Holy*, 26.

and astonishment."[19] As such, the numinous completely transcends the categories of the mundane. Concepts that are applied to things in this world are only analogically applicable to it, for it is of a radically different order than the world or anything in it. While we can have a positive experience of it through feeling, it eludes all apprehension through concepts.[20] Here lies the genesis of negative or apophatic theology that stresses the fact that all our concepts are inadequate to it. The concepts we use to refer to it, such as *mysterium*, are mere ideograms "for the unique content of feeling." In order to understand these ideograms the person "must already have had the experience himself."[21] What the numinous is "cannot, strictly speaking, be taught, it can only be evoked, awakened in the mind; as everything that comes 'of the spirit' must be awakened."[22] All of this carries with it the implication that the category of the numinous is *sui generis*, that is, it cannot be reduced to other categories such as that of psychology or the social sciences that strive to understand the human being in merely naturalistic terms.

Despite its daunting character, the numen is also experienced as *fascinating*. It is an object of search, desire, and longing. Augustine's famous words well express this fascination: "You have made us for yourself, and our hearts are restless until they rest in Thee." As such, the numinous ultimately must be sought out, for only it will quench the deepest desires of the soul. Otto notes that

> above and beyond our rational being lies hidden the ultimate and highest part of our nature, which can find no satisfaction in the mere allaying of the needs of our sensuous, psychical, or intellectual impulses and cravings. The mystics call it the basis or ground of the soul.[23]

The numen is ultimately experienced as the source of unspeakable bliss, a bliss that is of completely different order from natural happiness. Otto speaks of the "*wonderfulness* and rapture that lies in the mysterious beatific experience of the deity,"[24] an experience which is beyond comparison with any earthly joys. This el-

---

[19] Otto, 26.
[20] Otto notes, "The divine transcends not only time and place, not only measure and number, but all categories of the reason as well. It leaves subsisting only that transcendent basic relationship which is not amenable to any category" (*Religious Essays*, 87).
[21] Rudolf Otto, *Religious Essays: A Supplement to "The Idea of the Holy"* (London: Oxford University Press, 1937), 39.
[22] Otto, *The Idea of the Holy*, 7.
[23] Otto, 36.
[24] Otto, 32.

ement of wonderfulness is vaguely apprehended at the very beginning of the religious quest, and is at the heart of the fascinating element of the numen.

3 The Religious *A Priori* and the Ground of the Soul

But how does Otto envision that an *a priori* feeling for the numen (the non-rational aspect of the holy) is possible?[25] It is through sensation that individual objects are given to us or intuited, but sensation is an empirical faculty, not an *a priori* one. In the first *Critique* Kant argued that space and time are *a priori* forms of intuition, but it is hard to imagine that the *a priori* intimation of the feeling elements of the holy are analogous to those forms. The other two *a priori* elements discussed by Kant in the first *Critique* are the concepts of the understanding and the ideas of reason, neither of them suitable candidates for Otto's *a priori* feeling elements through which the numen is apprehended. Yet Otto stresses that without the *a priori*, the Word cannot be apprehended, received, or understood, and he invokes Kant's claim that while "all knowledge begins with experience, it by no means follows that all knowledge arises out of experience."[26] In a very significant passage he notes, "Kant's rational ideas of absoluteness, completion, necessity and substantiality, and no less those of the good as an objective value" refer back to "an original and underivable capacity of the mind implanted in the 'pure reason' independently of all perception." And he continues:

> in the case of the non-rational elements of our category of the Holy we are referred to something deeper still than the 'pure reason', at least as this is usually understood, namely, to

---

25 While critics of Otto have argued that his thought is inconsistent in that he moves from philosophy in his *Philosophy of Religion* to phenomenology in *Idea of the Holy*, this section demonstrates the consistency in Otto's thought in relation to the two books. This consistency is further evidenced if the Romantic reception of Kant's thought if fully understood, which brings together two elements, namely the emphasis on the feeling of Being and the impossibility of knowledge of the objects of Kant's regulative ideas of reason. The Romantic reception of Kant's thought, especially as found in Schleiermacher, had a huge influence on Otto. For a discussion of some of these criticisms, see Minney 519 ff. For another defense of the consistency of Otto's thought, see Philip C. Almond, *Rudolf Otto: An Introduction to his Philosophical Theology*, Chapel Hill: University of North Carolina Press, 1984. For a discussion of the Romantic reception of Kant's thought, especially as it came to bear on the understanding of religion, see my forthcoming "Romanticism and Religion," in *The Palgrave Handbook of Early German Romantic Philosophy*, ed. Elizabeth Millán.
26 Otto, *The Idea of the Holy*, 112–113.

that which mysticism has rightly named the *fundus animae*, the 'bottom' or 'ground of the soul' (*Seelengrund*). The ideas of the numinous and the feelings that corresponds to them are, quite as much as rational ideas and feelings, absolutely 'pure,' and the criteria which Kant suggests for the 'pure' concept and 'pure' feeling of respect are most precisely applicable to them.[27]

How are we to understand this element that is "still deeper" than pure reason? Is Otto still working within the parameters of Kant's philosophy?

Yes, he is. There are two important places where we need to look in Kant's philosophy. Both of these places were significant for the Romantic reception of Kant's work and its opposition to Fichte, especially in relation to how Kant's thought was applied to religion. The first place is Kant's remark at the end of his introduction of the first *Critique* where he notes that the two stems of human cognition, namely sensibility and understanding "may perhaps arise from a common but to us unknown root."[28] This unknown root is original consciousness, that is, consciousness prior to its reflection in the "I think." If there is any place to look for an idea corresponding to Otto's *fundus animae* in Kant, it would be here. The reception of Kant's work between 1785 and 1799 was marked by the attempt to understand the relation of this original consciousness to totality. For Fichte and those who followed him, an absolute philosophy of first principles was possible through a reflection on the activity of the I, that is, on the conditions of the possibility of the achievement of the identity of consciousness through the process of reflection: "the I posits itself as an I." Because the not-I is necessary for the positing of the I, it too was considered an achievement of consciousness. The Romantics countered this philosophy of first principles through their claim that original consciousness is factical and is given to us in feeling, namely the feeling of Being. While the totality of all existence is intuited in this original consciousness,[29] it cannot be penetrated by understanding and rea-

---

27 Otto, 112.
28 Immanuel Kant, *Critique of Pure Reason*, trans. and ed. by Paul Guyer and Allen W. Wood (Cambridge: Cambridge University Press, 1997) p. 246. B132. All references to Kant's *Critique of Pure Reason* are to the standard A and B pagination of the first and second editions, respectively. These are indicated by A/B in the body of the article, in this case A15/B29.
29 The point is made by Friedrich Schleiermacher, among others, in his *On Religion*, where he claims that "religion is sensibility and taste for the infinite" (23); he argues that intuition of the infinite is given in that "first mysterious moment" before "intuition and feeling have separated," that is, the infinite is given before the process of reflection. At this moment the soul "lies at the bosom of the infinite world." This moment is "the natal hour of everything given in religion" (32). Friedrich Schleiermacher, *On Religion: Speeches to its Cultured Despisers*, translated and edited by Richard Crouter, Cambridge: Cambridge University Press, 1988, 1996. There is no

son. There is, then, no philosophy of first principles, no absolute philosophy. The ground of existence surpasses consciousness and its conditions. We are confronted with the sheer facticity of our existence and are an enigma to ourselves. Instead of an absolute philosophy penetrating the very ground of being, what we have is epistemological modesty and a coherence theory of truth. What we can know is limited to what is given, and in reflection, that is, in self-consciousness. But the material given to reflection is but a fragment of the totality of original consciousness and its awareness, and can never come close to capturing it.

The second place to look for Kantian influences in Otto is Kant's third *Critique*. Kant's successors sought totality in original consciousness, in the moment prior to reflection through which the I distinguished itself from the not-I. The Romantics argued that this totality was given in original consciousness as a purely factual one that remained unknown and unknowable. Kant believed we have *ideas* of such totalities – ideas of God, the soul, and the world as a whole – but these are merely regulative. They can be thought, but we can neither prove the existence of their objects, nor can their objects be given to us in intuition. Nevertheless, these totalities are represented to us in what he calls *aesthetic ideas* – saturated intuitions symbolizing them. What we have in Otto's idea of the Holy is precisely such an aesthetic idea, one that opens up consciousness in such a way that it is brought back to that moment of original consciousness in which the soul stands in direct relation to existence and its ground.

In the third *Critique* Kant refers to the "ground of the unity of the supersensible that grounds nature with that which the concept of freedom contains practically."[30] Discussing his "critique of the faculties of cognition with regard to what they can accomplish *a priori*," he remarks on his division between understanding and reason, the former having to do with what can be known of nature *a priori*, and the latter having to do with the legislation of pure practical reason. But to this he adds an "intermediary between the understanding and reason," namely, the power of judgment, which contains "in itself *a priori*...a proper principle for seeking laws, although merely a subjective one" (*CJ* 5:177). These three,

---

doubt Otto was significantly influenced by Schleiermacher; in 1899 he produced a centenary edition of Schleiermacher's 1799 version of the *Speeches*, and discusses Schleiermacher in *Idea* (10) although he takes issue with Schleiermacher's understanding of the feeling of absolute dependence, stressing the phenomenological precedence of the intuition an "overpowering might" over the feeling of dependence.

30 Immanuel Kant, *Critique of the Power of Judgment*, trans. Paul Guyer and Eric Matthews (Cambridge: Cambridge University Press, 2000), 63. All future references to the third *Critique* are to this translation and will be indicated by the Academy Edition pagination, in this case *CJ* 5:176.

understanding, judgment, and reason are related to three faculties of the soul: "the faculty of cognition, the feeling of pleasure and displeasure, and the faculty of desire" (*CJ* 5:177). The third *Critique* is concerned with how an *a priori* feeling can be accounted for, or more precisely, how a judgment based on feeling can have universal validity. For example, aesthetic judgments have what Kant calls subjective universality. Here we have a judgment based on feeling, which is, as such, peculiar to the subject, but which nonetheless is valid for everyone. Kant answers that such judgments are possible in virtue of the harmonious exercise of the cognitive powers of the subject as it judges. This harmonious exercise pleases, and pleases universally. What then, is the power of judgment, and how does it shed light on Otto's category of the Holy, both in its rational and non-rational aspects?

The power of judgment is "the faculty for thinking the particular as contained under the universal" (*CJ* 5:179). There are two kinds of judgments possible: determining and reflective. When the universal is given, and the particular is simply subsumed under it, judgment is *determinative*. However, when only the particular is given, and the universal must be searched after, judgment is *reflective*. Now what is significant about reflective judgment is that it is concerned with a singular intuition, and how it is that this intuition is to be grasped in such a way that it can be taken *as an individual* that falls under a concept. Longuenesse rightly points out that there is an aspect of reflection even in the application of the categories, "for it presupposes a progress from sensible representation to discursive thought: the formation of concepts through comparison/reflection/abstraction, which is just what reflective judgment is: finding the universal for the particular." However, the third *Critique* is concerned with *merely* reflective judgment, and what happens in such a case is that "the effort of the activity of judgment to form concepts fails."[31] In reflective judgment we are first and foremost concerned with given intuitions. In the case of merely reflective judgment, an intuition is so saturated and rich that it is impossible to find a single rule of synthesis adequate to it, and as such the individual cannot be grasped in such a way that it can be subsumed under a given concept. This happens in the case of judgments concerning the beautiful and the sublime, as well as in the case of teleological judgments. In these cases, the particular is so saturated and has such an overplus of meaning that it breaks all bounds of inner-worldly significance and intimates the rational ideas of God, soul, and the world.

---

[31] Beatrice Longuenesse, *Kant and the Capacity to Judge*, translated by Charles T. Wolfe (Princeton: Princeton University Press, 1998), 164.

Kant defines spirit as "the animating principle of the mind" which works through the purposive setting of the "mental powers into motion, i.e., into a play that is self-maintaining" (*CJ*, 5:314). This setting of the mental powers into motion occurs as the mind tries to find a rule of synthesis for the saturated individual that we find in the aesthetic idea. Importantly, Kant relates the aesthetic idea to the ideas of reason. He notes that the animating principle of the mind

> is nothing other than the faculty for the presentation of *aesthetic ideas*; by an aesthetic idea, however, I mean that representation of the imagination that occasions much thinking though without it being possible for any determinate thought, i.e., *concept*, to be adequate to it, which, consequently, no language fully attains or can make intelligible. – One readily sees that it is the counterpart (pendant) of an *idea of reason*, which is, conversely, a concept to which no *intuition* (representation of the imagination) can be adequate. ...they [aesthetic ideas] at least strive towards something lying beyond the bounds of experience, and thus seek to approximate a presentation of concepts of reason (intellectual ideas), which gives them the appearance of an objective reality; on the other hand, and indeed principally, because no concept can be fully adequate to them, as inner intuitions.[32]

In what way is the aesthetic idea a counterpart of the idea of reason? In the first *Critique* Kant had argued that, unlike the concepts of the understanding, the ideas of reason cannot, in principle, have any objective validity. While the concepts of the understanding have corresponding schemata that direct and limit their application, these are lacked by the ideas of reason. Furthermore, because ideas of reason are ideas of unconditioned totalities, no intuition can be adequate to them. As Kant notes, "If they contain the unconditioned, then they deal with something under which all experience belongs, but that is never itself an object of experience; something to which reason leads through its inferences, and by which reason estimates and measures the degree of its empirical use, but that never constitutes a member of the empirical synthesis" (*CPR*, A 311/ B 368). On the other hand, all objects of possible experience are members of the empirical synthesis, and are, as such conditioned. The ideas of reason are greatly significant in two regards: first, they have a regulative function, in that lead us to unify principles ("the unity of principles is a demand of reason" [*CPR*, B 362]), and they have supreme importance in the practical sphere, since among them are found the ideas of freedom, the moral law, and a maximum of virtue. Moreover, it is through practical reason and our *interest* in the meaning of our existence from a first person point of view that ideas of unconditioned totalities such as God, the soul, and the world gain significance: these condition the core of our existence and the arena in which it must play itself out.

---

32 Kant, *CJ*, 5: 314.

While an idea of reason is one to which no intuition can be adequate, and is as such "indemonstrable," the aesthetic idea is a representation of an individual so rich in significance that no concept is adequate to it. It is what Kant calls an "inexponible representation" (*CJ* 5:342). Through its saturation and innumerable connections with the entire field of experience it intimates the supersensible objects to which the ideas of reason refer. Kant notes that the aesthetic idea "serves [the] idea of reason instead of logical presentation, although really only to animate the mind by opening up for it the prospect of an immeasurable field of related representations" (*CJ* 5:315). The aesthetic idea "cracks open" the understanding, which continually strives to grasp the intuition, but fails to find a concept adequate to it, as the realm of the understanding is limited to the conditioned appearances. The saturation of the aesthetic idea and its innumerable connections thereby become symbols of the comprehensive ideas of reason.

Since the aesthetic idea is the counterpart of an idea of reason, it is more closely associated with Kant's sublime than with the beautiful; earlier in the third *Critique*, Kant remarks: "the beautiful seems to be taken as the presentation of an indeterminate concept of the understanding, but the sublime as that of a similar concept of reason" (*CJ* 5:244). He lists the "wide ocean, enraged by storms, whose visage is horrible" (*CJ* 5:245) as provoking the sublime. In the dynamically sublime nature is presented as an overwhelming might that annihilates our own; as such, it invokes fear; so Kant, "nature can count as a power, thus as dynamically sublime, only insofar as it is considered an object of fear" (*CJ* 5:260). The sublime, however, is not constituted by this fear alone, but by the thought that the whole might of nature is inferior to the "moral law within." For Kant, the moral individual and her connection to the supersensible is superior to all possible terrors of the natural world.

It is, however, clearly the understanding of the aesthetic idea as *inexponible* that was to have such importance for both the Romantics and for Otto. Both in *Philosophy of Religion* and in his *Idea of the Holy*, Otto underscores Kant's understanding of spirit and its relation to both aesthetic and rational ideas as Kant's most important contributions. In *Philosophy of Religion* he mentions Herder as having fully grasped the importance of Kant's aesthetic ideas, noting that "in the whole of poetry Herder saw a creation that urges upwards from the secret and mysterious depths of the soul, a creation of the unconscious, the unwilled, and the uninvented; an inspiration that springs from the profound regions of the spirit, under divine influence...."[33] And in *Idea* the faculty of divination through which the Holy is intuited is related to Kant's aesthetic judgments, in particular

---

33 Otto, *Philosophy of Religion*, 184.

to that which is "not-unfolded" or inexponible: he notes: "in contrast to logical judgment, it [the aesthetic judgment] is not worked out in accordance with a clear intellectual scheme, but in conformity with obscure, dim principles...";[34] he further mentions Goethe's "daemonic" which "goes beyond all 'conceiving', surpasses 'understanding' and 'reason', and consequently is 'inapprehensible' and cannot properly be put into a statement"[35] in which all elements associated with the numen recur. Otto repeatedly affirms that *both* rational and non-rational elements of the numen are *a priori* elements, claiming that "in its content even the first stirring of 'daemonic dread' is a purely *a priori* element. In this respect it may be compared from first to last with the aesthetic judgment and the category of the beautiful."[36] It is clear, then that Otto conceived of the numinous in terms of Kant's aesthetic ideas as well as his understanding of the sublime.

The experience of the numinous is an experience of a *particular* that both terrifies and fascinates, and which, however, also represents unconditioned totalities. For example, insofar as it is experienced as an overwhelming might, the numen symbolizes the very ground of all power. The numen has an "overplus of meaning" and thereby functions in the same way as an aesthetic idea. Because it is given in an intuition in which distinct elements are united, *synthetic* judgments can be made of it. This brings us to one of the more obscure elements of Otto's presentation of the Holy, the necessary synthesis between its rational and non-rational aspects. The rational aspect is not contained in the irrational aspect; these are two distinct predicates, and one cannot be derived from the other.[37] They are, however, united in the object, and necessarily so; hence Otto claims "the same *a priori* character...belongs...to the connexion of the rational and non-rational elements in religion, their inward and necessary union."[38] He notes that the irrational element of the holy is "schematized" by its rational element and "is filled out and charged with rational elements." Now the schema, according to Kant, is a rule of synthesis, generated by the imagination, through which an image adequate to a concept is generated. In the case of aesthetic ideas, of course, these rules of synthesis are never adequate to the intuition, and conceptualization fails. The aesthetic representation is "inexponible." Otto, too, notes that even as this necessary schematization occurs, the non-rational aspect of the holy is never fully taken up into its rational aspects; there is an overplus that still eludes rationalization and is "even intensi-

---

34 Otto, *The Idea of the Holy*, 146.
35 Otto, 150.
36 Otto, 134.
37 Otto, 136.
38 Otto, 136.

fied" as the revelation proceeds.[39] Yet insofar as an aesthetic representation suggests the rational ideas, it must ultimately be taken up or synthesized in such a way that it is understood in accordance with moral and religious ideas having to do with the ultimate significance of human life.

How then, does the aesthetic idea illuminate the *a priori* structures of consciousness that make it possible for revelation to have significance for us? In the aesthetic idea we have a symbol of the mystery that is given in original consciousness. This symbol awakens the mind and brings it back to that first original moment prior to reflection. The Holy, much like the aesthetic idea, can only be adequately interpreted from the first person point of view. Both the aesthetic idea and the representation of the Holy have subjective universality. It is because each of us is a finite creature who acts, who must understand both self and world, and who must reflect on his or her own significance in relation to the indemonstrable totalities with which religion is concerned that the Holy is of utmost significance. Its non-rational elements concern our finitude and powerlessness in the face of an ultimate reality against which we must measure the significance of our lives;[40] its rational elements concern those moral concepts through which we must measure what we have done and should do, and which necessarily schematize and fill out the non-rational elements of the Holy. In the Holy, much like in the aesthetic idea, I am presented with a particular object of experience that works on the spirit in such a way that it is confronted with ultimate totalities, with the enormous power of the ground of being, both terrifying and fascinating, but which nevertheless is necessarily schematized by rational moral ideas. Otto notes that "once enunciated and understood, the ideas of the unity and goodness of the divine nature often take a surprisingly short time to become firmly fixed in the hearer's mind"[41] Rational ideas are always already present in our reason and need only be awakened.

Following Kant, Otto stresses that we cannot ignore the moral or rational element of the Holy. In *Religion*, Kant stressed that "on the basis of revelation alone," without the moral concepts of pure practical reason, "there can be no religion, and all reverence for God would be *idolatry.*"[42] Hence we cannot simply remain with the idea of God as "wholly other," which Otto coordinates with the idea that the intuition of the numinous is "inexponible." The intuition of the

---

[39] Otto, 135.
[40] On the development of this idea by the Romantics, see my "Romanticism and Religion," forthcoming.
[41] Otto, 139.
[42] *Religion and Rational Theology,* edited by Allen W. Wood and George di Giovanni (Cambridge: Cambridge University press, 1996), 6:169.

Holy must necessarily be schematized by moral concepts. As Otto notes, were we to fail to do so, God would remain *ex lex,* outside the law, and we could only relate to God in terms of power.[43] As Kant had argued in his *Religion within the Boundaries of Mere Reason*, we would then be left with a religion of mere servility, one bereft of the moral ideas that alone confer on the human being genuine worth:

> Although it certainly sounds questionable, it is in no way reprehensible to say that every human being *makes a God* for himself, indeed, he must make one according to moral concepts (attended by the infinitely great properties that belong to the faculty of exhibiting an object in the world commensurate to these concepts) in order to honor in him *the one who made him.* For in whatever manner a being has been made known to him by somebody else, and described as God, indeed, even if such a being might appear to him in person (if this is possible), a human being must yet confront this representation with his ideal first, in order to judge whether he is authorized to hold and revere this being as Divinity. Hence, on the basis of revelation alone, without that concept being *previously* laid down in its purity at its foundation as touchstone, there can be no religion, and all reverence for God would be idolatry.[44]

In the numinous, the individual is confronted with her finitude and conditioned character in a radical way. Otto repeatedly draws attention to the understanding of the self as "but dust and ashes" in the face of an overpowering might that is symbolized in ideograms whose significance is ultimately recognized by the soul at its ground. But how must the individual respond to this overwhelming might? To simply respond to it in such a way that *all* that an individual recognizes is an overpowering might ultimately leads to fear and the strategy of self-preservation. Here there are no higher values, and no way that the self can really move beyond itself to recognize the value of others for their own sake from within itself. Otto is of a mind with Kant on this: reason generates its own ideas of totality that must ultimately be synthesized with the totalities intuited at the ground of the soul. Hence the ideogram points upwards and downwards, downwards to the ground of the soul and the totalities intuited through original consciousness, and upwards to the ideas of reason in which totalities are thought but not intuited. In the ideogram and through the imagination's attempt to grasp it, the two, namely reason and intuition, are brought together. This synthesis is not one that can be proven, but is one that is achieved through the moral individual that makes a moral decision: *faith* that at the heart of existence there lies a moral order.

---

[43] Otto, *The Idea of the Holy*, 101.
[44] *Religion*, 6:169; cf., 6:189.

Christine Svinth-Værge Põder
Luther's Lectures on Romans in the Work of Karl Holl, Rudolf Hermann, and Karl Barth

1 Two Types of Theological Renewal in the Early Twenties and their Luther Reception

The two dominant theological movements of the interwar Germany, dialectical theology and the Lutherrenaissance may both be dated to the close of 1921, where, almost simultaneously, two groundbreaking books appeared in the bookstores.[1] One was the explosive second edition of Barth's commentary on Romans, *Der Römerbrief*[2], the entire revision and re-conceptualization of his first commentary on Romans from 1919 that reacted on the shock from the breakout of the First World War and the support to the war-policy by the 93 German intellectuals.[3]

The other book, also reacting to the First World War though from a different angle, is Karl Holl's *Luther*.[4] Holl, the professor for church history in Berlin, signaled and inspired a new start with Luther's theology – the German Lutherrenaissance – after the turbulent years of the ending war and the painful peace. In a situation of general public resentment, Holl in his interpretation of Luther's lectures on the Romans[5] emphasized that God intentionally "leads the human

---

[1] Cf. Johannes Wallmann, "Karl Holl und seine Schule," *ZThK Beiheft* 4 (1978): 1–33, 1, and Cornelis van der Kooi and Katja Tolstaja: "Vorwort," in Karl Barth, *Der Römerbrief (zweite Fassung) 1922* (Zürich: Theologischer Verlag, 2010), ix.
[2] Quotes from Karl Barth's *Römerbrief* from 1922 will refer to the page number of the authoritative second print from 1923 and in brackets to the new critical edition of the 1922 edition from 2010. I add references to the English edition (translation by Edwyn Hoskyns) from 1968 (here referred to as "Hoskyns' edition"). I have chosen, however, to provide English translation of the quotes myself, as I find that Hoskyns' version does not always very well capture and render the dynamic and explosive style of Barth's writing.
[3] Karl Barth, *Evangelische Theologie im 19. Jahrhundert*, ThSt 49 (Zürich: Evangelischer Verlag, 1957), 6.
[4] Karl Holl, *Luther, Gesammelte Aufsätze zur Kirchengeschichte*, vol. I, 1921 (Tübingen: Mohr (Siebeck), ⁶1932).
[5] Holl, *Luther*, 111–154.

being into darkness"[6] in order to lead it to salvation. A salvation, however, not conceived of as bliss but as moral fulfilment.

Thus, Holl took leave of the religious and ethical eudemonism of the previous century and focused instead on unity of wills between God and the human, who experiences the judgement of God in the conscience.

About the same time as these publications in the winter of 1921/22, Rudolf Hermann, who was professor in Breslau, began to lecture on Luther's theology. In the years to come, he too interpreted Luther's early works,[7] an effort resulting in a series of (partly posthumously published) articles on the significance of prayer to the understanding of justification in the theology of Luther. This is a theme that continues in his monograph from 1929, *Luthers These: Gerecht und Sünder Zugleich* (in English: Luther's Thesis: At the same time Righteous and a Sinner). Like Karl Holl, he emphasizes the significance of consenting to God's judgement as a central aspect of justification. Both are particularly interested in the early Luther and his lectures on the Romans that only just became public around the turn of the century.

How did the theology of the early Luther come to have such an attraction on the theologians of the early 20th century? An answer to this question would help to clarify common traits and shared concerns in the Lutherrenaissance and the Dialectical Theology, although Karl Barth and the leading figures of the Lutherrenaissance historically would see themselves as antagonists. Therefore, it is interesting to compare Barth, Holl and Hermann regarding their reception of Luther's Romans lectures and to question them on who their – early – Luther is and thus illuminating differences and similarities between these contemporaries in an epoch that had only just rediscovered the early Luther. That is, the Luther who, lecturing on the Romans in 1515–16, reflected on the disruptive and negative rhetoric of the letter: "The Spirit uses these negative expressions which are sweeter than the affirmative ones to describe the eternal nature of the things about which he is speaking. Because for death to be killed means that death will not return … a concept, which cannot be expressed through an affirmative assertion. For a person can think of life without eternity."[8] To Luther, negations

---

6 Holl, 136.

7 Cf. Rudolf Hermann, *Studien zur Theologie Luthers und des Luthertums, Gesammelte und nachgelassene Werke*, vol. II (Göttingen: Vandenhoeck & Ruprecht, 1981), 18–19.

8 Quotations from Luther in the body of the text are in English translation, which is either my own or with reference to *Luther's Works* (*LW*), vol 25, ed. Hilton C. Oswald (Saint Louis: Concordia Publishing House, 1972). The original Latin quote is provided in the footnote.

WA 56, 323,19–24: Istis autem Negatiuis orationibus, que sunt multo quam affirmatiue dulciores, vtitur spiritus ad expressionem eternitatum eorum, de quibus loquitur. Quia Mortem oc-

are the language of the Spirit (that is, of the Scripture). Similarly and almost programmatically, the opening lines: "The chief purpose of this letter is to break down, to pluck up, and to destroy all wisdom and righteousness of the flesh."⁹

Karl Barth, like Luther, had his theological breakthrough reading the Epistle to the Romans. He must have experienced the text in a comparable way. Thus in the second edition of his Romans commentary he questions all positive religious language and emphasizes judgement as the way humans meet the word of God. His commentary seems itself to convey this judgement upon its own readers. It is tempting to apply Holl's phrase and to say that Barth "leads his reader into the darkness" – almost literally with the disturbing opening chapter (after the introduction) "The Night." Thus, Barth is not, like Hermann and Holl, interpreting Luther in a direct sense but rather indirectly quoting him to express theological concerns. However, the three of them are all engaged in a disruptive effort over against the liberal theology and share an affinity to the reformers, perceiving their own time of crisis as a parallel to the time and controversies of reformation. Their epoch experienced a reappraisal of the doctrine of justification and, correspondingly, of the theological weight of negativity (emphasizing the judgment of God over humans) which resulted in new theological paradigms. They have had a vast impact on the protestant theology of the 20th century that is not over yet. Evaluating today this impact and this heritage means also evaluating the varying negativist approaches in terms of their theological significance and their actuality.

As a focal point of comparison, I suggest the idea of the believers' self-negation consenting to God's judgement, which implies being aware of oneself as a sinner. We will need to ask how this idea, this consent, is understood, in which concrete forms it occurs and what kind of rhetoric is used to express this idea of self-negation, in order to trace both obvious and more subtle similarities and differences between the three interpreters.

I will begin tracing Barth's use of, and his similarities to Luther's early theology. Though Barth is not primarily presenting an interpretation of Luther but rather of the Pauline letter to the Romans, he is strongly drawing upon Luther's theology. Subsequently, I will proceed to present Karl Holl's and then Rudolf Hermann's explicit interpretations of Luther's Lecture on Romans. Finally, in the comparison, I will point out both differences and common concerns among them.

---

cidi est mortem non reverti [...]. Que expressio per affirmatiua non potest fieri. Nam Vita potest intelligi sine eternitate.

9 *WA* 56, 157, 2–3: Summarium huius Epistolę Est destruere et euellere et disperdere omnem sapientiam et Iustitiam carnis.

2 Barth's Romans Commentary and its Affinity with Luther

In his later work, Barth has expressed an ambivalence against Luther – and in particular against the early Luther. If we turn to Barth's *own* early work, to his *Epistle to the Romans*, things look differently. In a letter to Eduard Thurneysen just after his second Romans commentary had been published, he quotes Luther's Lecture's on Romans, asking:

> ... don't you think, too, Eduard, *that* is somehow our place: There, in the shadow before the Reformation, when there was yet no "assurance of salvation" no "evangelical freedom" etc., when Luther still made statements like "God is righteous, because he so willed and it pleased him from eternity, and for his will there is no law and obligation at all."[10] Or: "we can never know whether we are justified or whether we believe"[11] Or "God, who is the negative essence and goodness and wisdom and righteousness, who cannot be possessed or touched except by the negation of all of our affirmatives."[12] However, if you like the monk Luther better that the reformer Luther, this you cannot even tell to your shirt, let alone this generation of theologians.[13]

The quotes express a striking preference for the early Luther in the lecture on Romans. A couple of years earlier, Barth mentioned to Thurneysen, that the second Romans represent a turn from Osiander to Luther, which he now experienced like a "catastrophe."[14] One might hear this rather as a metaphor for the turn to thinking in negations, and at any rate, we do not find Luther in the preface to the second edition, where Barth lists his new sources of inspiration, Plato, Dostoyevsky, etc.[15] However, the statement corresponds with the fact that the references to Luther are more numerous in the second Romans than in the first (ca 50 against ca 30, respectively). Here particularly the early quotes from the Romans lecture

---

10 *LW* 25, 82 (glossa 12). Cf. *WA* 56, 91, 18.
11 *LW* 25, 239. Cf. *WA* 56, 252, 20–21.
12 *LW* 25, 383. Cf. *WA* 56, 392, 33–393,3.
13 Karl Barth, letter on January 22, 1922, in *Karl Barth – Eduard Thurneysen. Briefwechsel, vol. II, 1921–1930* Gesamtausgabe, V. Briefe (Zürich: Theologischer Verlag, 1974), 30.
14 Karl Barth, letter on December 3, 1920, in *Karl Barth und Eduard Thurneysen: Ein Briefwechsel aus der Frühzeit der dialektischen Theologie* (Hamburg: Siebenstern-Taschenbuch-Verlag, 1966), 57.
15 Cf. also Henning Theisen's contribution to this volume, where he investigates comprehensively, how Barth receives Luther, and how, for the Romans commentary, he mainly makes use of the Eberle Luther edition, which seems to be one reason for not mentioning Luther in the prefaces.

match the spirit of Barth's own Romans commentary very well. It is somewhat disappointing that they are hardly as numerous as could be supposed from the letter to Thurneysen. There are only four quotes from Luther's Lecture on Romans. The majority of the references are to sermons by Luther. But Edgar Thaidigsmann has made an interesting observation: he notices that Barth, when quoting from the later texts by Luther in his second Romans, interprets and even changes the quotes "in the sense of the negative early theology of Luther. The *promissio* of the gospel according to Luthers mature theology is now only present in the negative-paradox shape of judgement. God's "Yes" in the *promissio* of the gospel is neither accessible nor perceptible for humans in this world as finite and creaturely beings."[16]

2.1 Faith as the Void

According to Barth's implicit interpretation of Luther, faith must be expressed negatively as the consent to God's judgement. In Barth's words, faith is to respect the qualitative difference – or even distance – between God and humans, affirming "the divine No! in Christ,"[17] wanting to be only a void[18]. Right at the beginning of the disquieting chapter on Romans 1, 18–32, he refers to Luther: "Who believes, loves with Job the God, who, only, is to be feared in his unapproachable height, loves with Luther the *deus absconditus*. To *him*, the righteousness of God unveils itself."[19]

Immediately after this consent follows a quote (somewhat freely rendered) from Luther's lecture on Romans, which suggests that the term "void" might actually be inspired by Luther: "Only the captive is freed; only the poor becomes rich; only the weak strong; only the humble is exalted; only the void is filled; only what is nothing becomes something."[20]

---

16 Edgar Thaidigsmann, *Identitätsverlangen und Widerspruch: Kreuzestheologie bei Luther, Hegel und Barth* (München: Chr. Kaiser Verlag, 1983), 145. In the following, I shall mention an example from the book where this (in my view) is the case.
17 Karl Barth, *Der Römerbrief 1922*, 14 (63). Cf. Karl Barth: *The Epistle to the Romans*, trans. Edwyn Hoskyns (Oxford: Oxford University Press, 1933, 1968), 39. Hereafter referred to as Hoskyns' edition.
18 Cf. Barth, *Der Römerbrief 1922*, 17 (66).
19 Barth, 18 (67). Cf. Hoskyns' edition, 42.
20 Barth, 18 (67). Cf. WA 56, 218, 17–21: "Vbi 'non est opus medico nisi male habentibus', Non queritur ouis nisi quę periit, Non liberatur nisi captiuus, Non locupletatur nisi pauper, non Roboratur nisi infirmus, non exaltatur nisi humiliatus, Non impletur nisi quod vacuum est, Non construitur nisi quod inconstructum est."

Luther, followed the tradition of the German mystics, connects the thought of a transition from negative to positive to the philosophical thought, that a new form presupposes the annihilation of the old one, also familiar to Tauler.[21] In this passage, he enhances that thought negatively using the conditional form: "Only..." We will have to mention that Luther employs a corresponding figure in another mode, namely as praise: "Oh how willingly we are empty that you may fill us...."[22]

Accordingly, Barth – though he would not add the "in nobis" of Luther – can speak of the wish or the willingness to be void but also warns against "*Selbstaufhebung*," self-abolition, as a human achievement.[23] In addition, negation itself is negated. While Luther – here closer to the mystics – can express the desire for God in the self-negating praise, Barth can only denote this self-negation, speaking of the power or force of God as the crisis of all known powers.[24] For this end, he can make use of Luther's language from the Romans lectures with its double negations: "the death of death and the sin of sin, the poison of poison, and the captivity of captivity".[25] Sin is to avoid this negation, this crisis of God, again with Luther's Romans lectures: "Whoever is unwilling to suffer tribulation should never think that he is a Christian."[26]

2.2 God as the Crisis

Luther in the Romans lecture is not yet, as in his later writings, explicit about the word of God as *promissio* or as consolation, where the spoken word communicates real divine presence to the believer. Rather, presence or realization of the

---

[21] Cf. the German translator of Luther's Romans lecture, Eduard Ellwein's notes of explanation in Martin Luther, *Vorlesung über den Römerbrief 1515/1516* (München: Chr. Kaiser Verlag, 1965), 487.
[22] WA 56, 219, 5–7: "*Ideo satur veritate et sapientia sua non est capax veritatis et sapientie Dei, Quę non nisi in vacuum et inane recipi potest. Ergo dicamus Deo: O quam libenter sumus vacui, ut tu plenus sis in nobis!*"
Cf. *LW* 25, 204: "Therefore he who is sated with his own truth and wisdom is incapable of receiving the truth and wisdom of God, which can be received only in an empty and destitute heart. Hence, let us say to God: 'O how willingly we are empty that Thou mayest dwell in us!'"
[23] Karl Barth, *Der Römerbrief 1922*, 17 (66), cf. also 32 (86), 37 (93), 84 (153). Cf. Hoskyns'edition, 42, 57, 62, 109.
[24] Barth, 11 (59). Cf. Hoskyns'edition, 36.
[25] Barth, 174 (268), cf. Hoskyns'edition, 194. Cf. also WA 56, 323, 1f.: "*Ideo Deus contulit mortem mortis et peccatum peccati, venenum veneni, captiuitatem captiuitatis.*"
[26] Karl Barth, *Der Römerbrief 1922*, 132 (213), cf. Hoskyns'edition, 155. Cf. WA 56, 302, 10–11.

relation between God and humans is conveyed sub contrario, when the humbled sinner consents to the judgement of God, thus gospel and law are at this time not as distinct as later. As I mentioned above, to Thaidigsmann Barth interprets later words by Luther on consolation and grace according to the early sub contrario scheme. Consolation must then be understood as the crisis of human consolations, that is, judgement.[27] Sin is in the first place not very distinct from the limitations and finality of creature. This could lead to the misunderstanding that here, Barth confuses sin and finality. Rather, sin is the way creatures relate to their finality. Creation, then, is also a matter of crisis, so that sin, further (and in view of grace which is judgement) means not consenting to the judgement of God. Grace, accordingly, is God's questioning the human: "'Grace is against sin and devours it' (Luther), namely the sin of disbelief, which erupts in the sin of anthropomorphism, culminating in religion. Grace attacks the sin in its roots. It questions us, as the humans that we are." [28]

The notion of religion as sin in the second Romans culminates in the crisis of the church, as the church would have no other justification than in living through judgement[29]. Barth quotes (in latin) from Luther's Romans lecture: "*Sed vere verbum Dei, si venit, venit contra sensum et votum nostrum. Non sinit stare sensum nostrum, etiam in iis, que sunt sanctissima, Sed destruit ac eradicat ac dissipat omnia*" ("If the Word of God comes, it comes contrary to our thinking and our will. It does not allow our thinking to remain, even in those matters which are most sacred, but it destroys and eradicates and scatters everything").[30]

What does this mean for the activity that Barth is performing writing his commentary – that is, for his idea of theology? Like faith consenting to judgement, theology consents to the crisis of all human imaginations and notions – observing the qualitative difference between God and human. Doing this, the theologian – or the preacher – must be, at the very most, afflicted by the message he or she delivers.[31] So one might ask, does the theologian then have a vicarious role? That is, does the theologian in doing theology or the pastor in

---

27 Cf. Karl Barth, *Der Römerbrief 1922*, 286–287 (414–416); WA 41, 303,3–11; 35–38; 306, 16–17. Cf. Hoskyns'edition, 302–304. Cf. also Karl Barth, *Der Römerbrief 1922*, 310–311 (446f.); WA 48,203,1–7. Cf. Hoskyns'edition, 326. Cf. also Edgar Thaidigsmann, *Identitätsverlangen und Widerspruch*, 158–159.
28 Barth, *Der Römerbrief 1922*, 170 (262–263); WA 22,94,11–12. Cf. Hoskyns'edition, 190–191.
29 Barth, 354 (502), cf. Hoskyns'edition, 370.
30 Barth, 355 (503), cf. Hoskyns'edition, 371, cf. WA 56, 423, 19–21. English translation by me, cf. German translation by Eduard Ellwein in Martin Luther, *Vorlesung über den Römerbrief* (München: Ch. Kaiser, 1965), 341.
31 Karl Barth, *Der Römerbrief 1922*, 355 (503), cf. Hoskyns'edition, 371.

preaching enact the necessary self-negation, consenting to divine judgement, in a way, that is not possible for everyone to do? And does Barth elaborate further on this? We shall keep this problem in mind and return to question Barth on this after the following account on Holl and Hermann's interpretation of Luther's lecture on Romans.

3 Karl Holl on Justification in Luther's Lecture on Romans

Karl Holl, born 1866, was professor for Church history at the University of Berlin since 1906. He was a student of Jülicher and von Harnack, with patristics as his special field of research. His academic road to professorship in Berlin was paved with personal and professional crises, a fact, that is mirrored in his increasingly religious anti-eudaimonism, seeing the religious existence dialectically coming into being through struggle and hard crises.[32] In 1910, he begins the work with Luther's theology that would result, finally in his collected volume on Luther in 1921. Thus, like Karl Barth's Romans, Holl's "Luther" was a revision of earlier works. Yet, unlike Barth, claiming to have left no stone unturned in his second edition, Holl is remarkably discreet about his works of revision with its additional stress on negativity in relation to the original texts of an entire decade, beginning with the article from 1910. It had the title: "The doctrine of justification in Luther's lectures on Romans particularly regarding the question of assurance of salvation."[33] I will give a short account of the 1910-article and afterwards, of the 1921 revision.

3.1 1910: Justification and Assurance of Salvation

In his interpretation of Luther's lectures on Romans, Holl did in part engage in a discussion with Johannes Ficker, who edited the lectures in 1908. In his preface to the edition, Ficker considered the lectures to be a document of the transition from pre-reformation to reformation theology, as they seemed to be ambiguous

---

[32] Karl Holl, *Gesammelte Aufsätze zur Kirchengeschichte*, vol. 3 (Darmstadt: Wissenschaftliche Buchgesellschaft 1965), 560.
[33] Karl Holl, "Die Rechtfertigungslehre in Luthers Vorlesung über den Römerbrief mit besonderer Rücksicht auf die Frage der Heilsgewißheit," *ZThK 20* (1910), 245–291.

about the assurance of salvation.[34] Holl argued that Luther did not deny assurance of salvation but only of election. Another challenge in the lectures was that there would seem to be still a notion of merit as, on the one hand, Luther speaks of justification of sinners but, on the other hand, of the justification of the already just.

We need to be aware, here, that Holl has a double concern: to argue that the lecture expresses a full-fledged reformation theology, and, to make compatible this dialectical notion of assurance with his own anti-eudaimonism. Therefore, he chooses a procedure of separately accounting for the divine and the human perspective of justification, grounding its certainty exclusively in the divine self-assurance and sole agency. He argues thus for a proleptic concept of justification: God, whose intention is to make the sinful human being righteous, justifies it in anticipating its future righteousness, of which he is certain.

Therefore, to Holl, the human being actually made righteous, must substantiate God's imputing righteousness to the human being. At the same time, in consequence with his religious and ethical anti-eudaimonism, Holl excludes every notion of merit.

Hence, Holl develops a highly dialectical and even antinomy-tense notion of assurance of salvation. From the human perspective, assurance is only possible in an ongoing existential tension between faith and repentance, between hope and anxiety. Indeed, the anxious human can win assurance from the promise of God even in its imperative character (Luther at this point does not yet distinguish sharply between gospel and law): the constancy and persistence of the demanding God then becomes dialectically the most reliable promise. The one who clings to this promissional imperative is actually saved, so Holl confidently states.

However, Holl even overrules this certainty in face of the mystery of predestination, though not everyone can face this final and decisive uncertainty. Facing the possibility that one might be condemned to perdition can lead to an even deeper assurance – the assurance not of justification, but of predestination, through the experience of the mystical *resignatio ad infernum*. Taking perdition freely upon oneself – if this should be the will of God – is the ultimate experience of unity with the will of God, even overcoming perdition, as there can be no God-forsakenness in the ultimate consent to the judging will of God. The fig-

---

34 Cf.. Holl, "Die Rechtfertigungslehre," 251. Cf also Johannes Ficker, "Die Auslegung," in Johannes Ficker, ed., *Luthers Vorlesung über den Römerbrief 1515/1516* (Leipzig: Dieterich'sche Verlagsbuchhandlung, ⁴1930), LXXVII.

ure of *resignatio ad infernum* is to Holl thus the way Luther makes tangible the severity of the doctrine of justification.

3.2 1921: Justification as Self-Surrender

In the course of the First World War, Holl increasingly turns to Luther as a way of theologically coping with the historical events. He writes a number of works on Luther's theology including the well-known speech for the reformation jubilee in 1917, "What did Luther understand by religion." However, otherwise than is the case with Barth, it is not the outbreak of the war that has an impact on his theology, but it is the November revolution, the defeat and the peace treaties. Holl perceives these events as the judgement of God over a Germany where the society has degenerated concerning ethics and sense of community.[35] This is part of the background for his revision of his works on Luther for the publication of the first volume of *Gesammelte Aufsätze zur Kirchengeschichte*, which in a very programmatic way begins indeed with the jubilee speech, now three times longer that in 1917 but still beginning with the words "Hochansehnliche ...." The powerful opening lines correspond with the new stance throughout the book, where Luther seems to be, to Holl, a symbol of ethical restoration of the nation.

This shimmers through the final lines of the article on justification in Luther's lecture on Romans:

> The lecture on Romans shows Luther yet in his fullest might; its doctrine of justification breathes all the heroism that Luther maintained as far as he stood on his own, and the concern for others, for the average people, did not yet hinder him from demanding the utmost.[36]

The 1921 version of the work on the Romans lectures is marked by an enhanced anti-eudaimonism concerning, in particular, the concepts of salvation and assurance. The idea of *resignatio ad infernum* – taking on oneself perdition for the sake of God's judgement – is no longer just a question of rhetorically intensify-

---

[35] Cf. Heinrich Assel, *Der andere Aufbruch: Die Lutherrenaissance – Ursprünge, Aporien und Wege: Karl Holl, Emanuel Hirsch, Rudolf Hermann (1910–1935)* (Göttingen: Vandenhoeck & Ruprecht, 1994), 118–124. The interpretation of these events as judgement, Holl expresses in a sermon in 1918, which Andrea Hoffmann has contextualized within the genre of war sermons in a paper given at the 13th International Congress for Luther Research, Wittenberg 2017. Cf. also Karl Holl, 'Kaufet die Zeit aus; denn es ist böse Zeit!', Predigt am 1. Dezember 1918 im akadem. Gottesdienst über Ephes. 5, 15–17, (Berlin: Verlag von Martin Warneck, 1918), 5.
[36] Karl Holl, *Luther*, 153–154.

ing justification. Rather, it is the fundamental logic of justification, that believers must ultimately abolish hope of salvation so as not to compromise with selfish motives the pureness of the surrender to God. Further, this notion of self-negation is combined with an emphasis on particular individuals (in this case Luther) standing in a unique immediacy to the acting God.

Practical-ethical concerns play an important role in this conception, as Holl was distressed over the condition of community in Germany. Thus, he understood the readiness to self-sacrifice in an active and even political way, as "strong Christians" acting as instruments of God, and not just as an affect. Assel has analyzed traits of this political theology and of how Holl's student, Emanuel Hirsch, further elaborates it.[37] Two difficulties also pointed out by Assel are the following: One is the soteriological or pneumatological differentiation between strong Christians and weak Christians, which Holl does not keep clear of psychology, attributing soteriological significance to affects.[38] The other is how the notion of the non-communicable *resignatio ad infernum*, as it seems, overrules the verbal-oral communication. Assel has thus observed the inclination towards hermeneutics of signification in Holl.[39] Both difficulties are present as tendencies in 1910 and are enhanced in the 1921 version.

4 Rudolf Hermann

4.1 Justification and Doxology

Rudolf Hermann, like Holl, was part of the Lutherrenaissance, though he did not belong to the Holl School. Hermann was a student of Carl Stange in Göttingen and was influenced by the theology of Martin Kähler. In the first half of the 1920's he taught in Breslau and around this time he studied Luther's theology while also working critically on Schleiermacher. Particularly, he engaged in interpreting Luther's lectures on Romans, an effort resulting in a number of articles, some of which were published posthumously.

Like Holl, Hermann had a high opinion of religious experience as a point of reference to theology, but unlike Holl, he would be far more specific about the role of religious language. There can be no speechless unity of wills between

---

[37] Heinrich Assel, "Politische Theologie im Protestantismus 1914–1945," in *Politische Theologie: Formen und Funktionen im 20. Jahrhundert*, ed. Jürgen Brokoff and Jürgen Fohrmann (Paderborn: Ferdinand Schöningh, 2003), 67–80.
[38] Heinrich Assel, *Der andere Aufbruch*, 78.
[39] Assel, 146.

God and humans. Rather, *something* happens in religious language that cannot happen otherwise. Particularly, in the mid-twenties, Hermann focuses on prayer as the subjective correlate of justification: we cannot understand justification – which is a relational event – Hermann claims, isolated from the prayer for the forgiveness of sins. Hermann observes that Luther, at an early stage (Psalm lectures 1513–16), develops his concept of justification with references to biblical texts that have the form of a dialogue with God, for example: "'Against you, you only, have I sinned …, so that you may be justified in your words and blameless in your judgment'[Ps 51]. By this Psalm word Luther develops his fundamental thought on justification, both in his first Psalms lectures and in his Romans commentary."[40]

Both Holl and Hermann identify human acknowledgement of God with the consent to the judgement of God (thus sharing the new negativistic paradigm of Lutheran theology): one who acknowledges God as just *is* justified. Whereas Holl, however, perceives this consent in the silent act of *resignatio ad infernum*, Hermann finds this consent only in the language of prayer and praise of repentance, declaring, "This acknowledgement must be an act that is very rich in relations."[41] It is his point, that only in this form – in the dialogue – can the repentance be real, and happy (!), repentance, and not just self-accusation.[42]

Happy repentance is (with a term coined by Old Testament Form criticism[43]) a doxology of judgement, a concept describing the praise of God in face of sin and judgement, which matches the phrase from Luther quoted above: "Oh how willingly we are empty …."[44] We should notice here, that Hermann quotes from the same passage in the lectures on Romans as Barth did, of being empty in order to be filled by God, but he chooses Luther's second mode of the phrase. Not, like Barth, "…only the void is filled, etc…," but: "Let us say to God: Oh how willingly we are empty that you may fill us,"[45] illustrating thus the dialogical nature of

---

[40] Rudolf Hermann, *Gesammelte und nachgelassene Werke*, vol. II (Göttingen: Vandenhoeck & Ruprecht 1981), 45. (Hereafter, *GnW*)

[41] Rudolf Hermann, *Gesammelte Studien zur Theologie Luthers und der Reformation* (Göttingen: Vandenhoeck & Ruprecht, 1960), 13. (Hereafter, *GSt*)

[42] Cf. Hermann, *GSt*, 30. This is also significant in the posthumously published article by Hermann from the same time, "Rechtfertigung und Gebet," in *Gesammelte und nachgelassene Werke, vol. II* (Göttingen: Vandenhoeck & Ruprecht, 1981), 55–87.

[43] Cf. Gerhard Von Rad, *Gesammelte Studien zum alten Testament II* (München: Kaiser, 1973), 245–54.

[44] *WA*, 56, 219, 5–7, cf. footnote 22 above.

[45] *WA*, 56, 219, 6–10. Not "*Non impletur nisi quod vacuum est…*" etc. but, "*Ergo dicamus Deo: O quam libenter sumus vacui, ut tu plenus sis in nobis!*"

the recognition of sins.⁴⁶ Acknowledging God as just thus implies the self-awareness of being a sinner, that is, of being in need of God. In other words, praying for forgiveness, which transforms the knowledge of sins, is the subjective correlate of justification.⁴⁷ With Luther: "Thus, who recognizes this, who groans to God and humbled prays, may be lifted up and healed by this will. But he, who does not recognize it, does not pray, and who does not pray does not receive, and thus he is not justified because he is ignorant of his own sin."⁴⁸

The concept "Doxology of judgement" is thus central, signifying here this dialectic language event of prayer and acknowledgement and justification, which is Hermann's answer to Holl's *resignatio ad infernum*.

4.2 Assertions as Events

The significance of prayer in Hermann's thought concerns justification, but it also concerns the active nature of new life. Prayer is the way of correlation between faith and works. Luther in the Romans lectures⁴⁹ claims that good works prepare for justification, which one might take as a pre-reformation concept of meritorious works. However, Hermann interprets this view in the sense that works have the character of prayer and repentance in the believers, who perceive themselves as sinners. Similarly, speech has a passive character, even to the person speaking – it is an event. This dynamic and dialectical connection of act, speech and experience links to Hermann's attempt at a *theology of time*, as pointed out by Assel. The progress of the believer is not a silent increasing of the new life, but it is the continuous recurrence of baptism, affirming the dependence upon Christ with the Pauline assertion "to me to live is Christ"⁵⁰ meaning negatively, "without Christ we are nothing,"⁵¹ thus stating in a non-paradoxical way the simultaneous being sinner and just.

---

46 However, Barth is in his later writings more explicit on this, seeing prayer (along with Anselm of Canterbury) as fundamentally similar or even identical to the theological "Denkbewegung". This view would seem to be at the most implicit in the methodological approach of his Romans commentary. Cf. also Christine Pöder, *Doxological Hiddenness. The Fundamental Theological Significance of Prayer in Karl Barth's Work* (Berlin: De Gruyter, 2009).
47 Rudolf Hermann, *GSt*, 27.
48 WA, 56, 254, translation from *LW*, 25, 240. Cf. Rudolf Hermann, *GSt*, 27.
49 WA, 56, 254, 23–24.
50 Rudolf Hermann, *Luthers These, Gerecht und Sünder zugleich* (Darmstadt: Wissenschaftliche Buchgesellschaft, (1930) ²1960), 184; Philippians 1:21 (Hermann is conscious, that he is using the phrasing with a different accent from the Pauline).
51 Hermann, *Luthers These*, 184, cf also 182. My italics.

Thus, Hermann can speak, like Holl, of a progress in the Christian life, though not in terms of a sole agency of God working through humans as his instruments, but in terms of dialogue and relation. There can be no pre-linguistic level of understanding or receiving grace and judgement from God. The assertions are themselves events of reception and transition from sinner to just in a reciprocal act, as described in the following expression that we repeatedly come across in Hermann's work: "Such revelation [of the justice of God] can only be understood in confession. And this confessing is confession towards God, prayer, imputation of justice to the sinner."[52]

Here, *speaking* – in terms of confession and prayer – is at the same time understanding, experiencing being spoken to.

5 Comparison

5.1 Speech and Experience

In Hermann's Luther-interpretation, speech plays a crucial role – it is not possible to understand what *justification* is, isolated from speech. In *Holl's* interpretation, by comparison, the spoken *promissio*, which is simultaneously demand and promise, is an important, though also an underexposed part of his argument. Although he attempts to see human fears, hopes, consolation, certainties etc. as reactions to *hearing* God's word, on the other hand he overrules these attempts through a tendency to see the intuitive and immediate effects of God in the conscience as more crucial than the oral speech. Exemplarily, this is the case by the silent act of *resignatio ad infernum*. It is essentially non-communicable. What really matters is the unity of wills in the conscience that happens before and inaccessibly from any account of it. Oswald Bayer in his book, *Promissio*, has argued that the early Luther's thought in the Romans lectures is still characterized by hermeneutics of signification in an Augustinian way, seeing the res as beyond and previous to communication about it, whereas in his later theology, the res itself is present in the word. While this assumed hermeneutic of signification might accordingly be detectible, also in the Luther interpretation by Holl (who is not explicit about this approach) Hermann would probably disagree that it is central to the lectures on Romans. If it were, this would ascribe to the verbal communication event a lower and deficient status, as it would not be an adequate vehicle of the event that it communicates (in Luther's phrasing,

---

[52] Hermann, 299.

thoughts are much more trustful witnesses than the words[53]). Holl, though he is aware of the significance of the spoken *promissio*, ultimately finds the decisive event, the *resignatio ad infernum* and its ensuing certitude, happening in a pre-lingual way. To Hermann this is different: as the event of justification is relational, it does not happen apart from or prior to the communication about it.

5.2 Ideas of Negation and Self-Negation

This has consequences for the concept of negativity. The question we have to pose over against the idea of self-negation in the consent to the judgement of God in justification is how the transition to the positive, which is presupposed, happens: that is, from whence does the assurance of justification or of a relation with God come? Holl would answer that we will need the perfect and ultimate self-negation – the *resignatio ad infernum*. However, this criterion of utter selflessness means that a relation exists only in the form of instrumentally acting out of God's will.

Herman does not mention the *resignatio ad infernum*, but he is aware of the dangers of non-communicative self-negation, which he describes as "conscience-ascetical self-dumping."[54] It is thus consistent that Hermann also has no concept that equals Holl's distinction between strong Christians and ordinary/weak Christians. Holl's strong Christians are of course not "strong" in any plain or undialectical sense of the word, but nevertheless the concept draws a divide between the those who can experience self-negation in the sense of consenting to God's judgement and those who are not capable of this. Herman contrarily can locate the negation in elementary religious language forms like prayer and praise.

5.3 Karl Barth – Language and Negativity: The Difference Between Holl and Hermann as Mirror for the Theology of Barth

Turning now to Barth, we have to keep in mind that his aim is not to interpret Luther, like Holl and Hermann, but that he, by using Luther as he does, interprets him according to his own aim to show how the word of God disrupts

---

53 Vgl. *WA*, 56, 204, 4–5.
54 Rudolf Hermann, *GSt*, 43. Deutsch: "*gewissensaschetische Selbstwegwerfung*".

human religious speech. As quoted above, he emphatically asserts the disruptive character of the letter to the Romans: "If the Word of God comes, it comes contrary to our thinking and our will. It does not allow our thinking to remain, even in those matters which are most sacred, but it destroys and eradicates and scatters everything."[55] While not overlooking the various dissimilarities between the three of them, I would suggest that the difference between Holl and Hermann might function as a mirror for the theological development of Barth. Considering his critique of religious speech, it is not surprising that he at this point seems ambivalent over prayer as stated above comparing Barth and Hermann on the "*O quam libenter sumus vacui.*"[56] However, what Barth actually is doing is referring theologically – and religiously – to God by disrupting and negating the ability of religious language to refer to God.

So language does (of course) have the character of an event in Barth's commentary. In his famous phrase, "As theologians we must speak of God. However, we are human beings and as such, we cannot speak of God. We must know both – our obligation and our inability – and in so doing give God the glory,"[57] he suggests a correlation between doxology and negativity, similar to the doxology of judgment in Hermann. The point is that theology praises God in negating the human possibilities to refer to God. Thus, theology – the act of theological thinking, the "Denkbewegung"[58] – *is itself an event of justification.* This, I suggest, Barth implies in the commentary on Romans. Only later does he become more explicit about theological assertions as a way of enacting this negation, and much later, he connects this understanding of doing theology with prayer.

Considering Barth's Romans commentary in this light (and keeping Holl in mind) leads to the question: if the claim that the word of God disrupts the human speech of God signals a justification event, meaning that the criterion

---

55 Karl Barth, *Der Römerbrief 1922*, 355 (503), cf. Hoskyns' edition, 371. Cf. WA, 56, 423, 19–22. Cf. latin quote above.
56 Cf. Karl Barth, *Der Römerbrief 1922*, 300–301, (432–34), 482 (615). Cf. Hoskyns' edition, 316–317, 458.
57 Cf. "*Das Wort Gottes als Aufgabe der Theologie,*" 1922 in *Vorträge und kleinere Arbeiten 1922– 1925 (GA III.19)*, 151: "As theologians, we ought to speak of God. But we are humans and as such cannot speak of God. We ought to do both, to know the 'ought' and the 'not able to,' and precisely in this way give God the glory." Translation by Amy Marga in Karl Barth, *The Word of God and Theology* (London, New York: Bloomsbury T&T Clark, 2011), 177.
58 Cf. Karl Barth, *Fides quaerens intellectum*, 1931, GA II, 13 (Zürich: Theologischer Verlag, 1981). Cf. also Bent Flemming Nielsen, *Die Rationalität der Offenbarungstheologie: Die Struktur des Theologieverständnisses von Karl Barth* (Aarhus: University Press, 1988), 62, emphasizing the (passive) event character of acting.

for theology is consenting to this judgement of God over human speech, then *what does this mean to those uttering this claim?* Barth doesn't speak explicitly of a *resignatio ad infernum*, but his reflections on Romans 9:1–5 (the passage, where Paul wishes to be cursed for the sake of his people, and which Luther interprets as *resignatio ad infernum*) are relevant for this thought. Here the preacher or the prophet who must communicate to the church the distressing message of the crisis, is the one to be the most afflicted by it. This *solidarity* is *resignatio ad infernum*, and the closest Barth gets to saying this is in the following:

> Every moment, as he raises his voice to remind himself and thus the church of eternity, he would rather be with the church (and thus also e.g. with theology) in Hell, than with the pietists of higher or lower order, of elder or more modern orientation in a Heaven – that doesn't exist.[59]

This is what theology should be, according to Barth. He conceives of the theological thinking and speaking in the sense of a methodological *resignatio ad infernum*, meaning that the theologian or preacher consents entirely to the judgement of God over human, religious speech and thought. As it is the case in Holl's Luther interpretation, this vicarious self-negation is essentially an event of justification, but unlike Holl, it is not happening in experience but in a theological crisis: *faith culminates in theology,* we might say. However, in the course of Barth's theological development, he attempts at connecting this concept with more elementary language forms, praise, confession, witness, prayer. In this regard he moves closer to the language theology of Rudolf Hermann, though he is actually following the course demarcated by the commentary on Romans only with different emphases. Reading his later work through the prism of Luther reception, we would thus need to consider, if Luther's doctrine of justification, which Barth criticizes so sharply in CD IV/1 actually remains an underlying structure of thought in Barth's – very different – theological approach.

---

[59] Karl Barth, *Der Römerbrief 1922*, 321 (461). Cf. Hoskyns' edition, 337.

Part II: **Parallel Movements**

Henning Theißen
Barth's Explicit Reception of Luther
An Auxiliary Tool for the Study of Karl Barth

1 Preliminary Remarks

Let me start my reflections* with a few remarks on why systematic theology should engage with questions of reception at all. Of course, if we are to understand what a given author says, it is essential that we study the sources they have received. But fulfilling this demand of historical interpretation or exegesis still will tell us next to nothing about *why* they chose to draw on this or that particular source. This question can only be answered if we presuppose that there is some sort of common problem to unite both the author and their sources even if to identify that common problem in advance runs the risk of setting aside the methodology of historical interpretation for a while. Christine Svinth Værge-Põder has argued convincingly that it was the epistemological phenomenon of negativity that linked Barth, Hermann, and Holl to each other.[1] I must confess that in the case of Barth's reception of Luther I have been unable to identify such a common problem beforehand since it cannot be Barth's historical curiosity of studying what Luther thought about this or that particular theological issue. I will only identify the common problem which drove Barth more or less unconsciously towards Luther in the final section of my paper.

I will start with some methodological reflections, followed by an outline of my study design and the results which I am going to discuss in the end. The composition of my contribution thus resembles the way in which empirical studies normally proceed, and even if the following is still a piece of hermeneutical, not empirical research in the strict sense of the term, I understand it to do no more than offer an auxiliary, but useful tool for further investigation.

---

* Funded by the Deutsche Forschungsgemeinschaft (DFG; German Research Foundation) – project number 261105911.
[1] Cf. Christine Svinth Værge-Põder, "Luther's lectures on Romans in the works of Karl Holl, Rudolf Hermann, and Karl Barth," in this volume.

2 Methodological Reflections

Modern theology, so E. Troeltsch taught us,[2] is based on three principles it has in common with historical research no matter whether the object studied is profane or not. These principles include analogy and correlation which allow for comparing any historical source – most commonly a text – to other sources. The third and in some sense overarching principle is criticism since it is by criticism that scholars become ready to question a given source they work with and treat it as a document among others open to historical comparison in the aforementioned manner. It is well known that critical theology in the sense of Troeltsch has celebrated its greatest successes since the second half of the 19th century which is when the critical Weimar edition of Luther's works (*Weimarer Ausgabe, WA*) began to be published. However, still almost a century later E. Jüngel stated that he "could not quite see the point behind the enormous amount of scholarly expertise on Luther if it did not make an attempt at [...] exegetical commentaries on his main writings."[3] In Germany, a series of such historical commentaries started no earlier than 2007, when R. Rieger of Tübingen published a commentary on Luther's *Treatise on Liberty*.[4] As for Barth, there is no historical critical edition of his writings until the present day, so the question what texts by Luther Barth did actually read and receive needs deepened study to which I want to contribute in this essay.

If we turn to this question, it is important to note that it asks for Barth's *explicit* reception of Luther. This needs explanation. Even if the *Gesamtausgabe (GA)* of the edited author's works is not a historical critical edition in the sense of giving comprehensive evidence of all reachable sources and printings of the texts edited, its editors have spent a great deal of work on identifying the sources particularly where quotations from other authors are concerned. The problem with

---

[2] Cf. Ernst Troeltsch, "Über historische und dogmatische Methode in der Theologie," in, *Gesammelte Schriften*, vol. 2 (Tübingen: J.C.B. Mohr, 1913), 729–53, particularly 731.

[3] Cf. Eberhard Jüngel, "Zur Freiheit eines Christenmenschen. Eine Erinnerung an Luthers Schrift [1978]," in *Indikative der Gnade – Imperative der Freiheit. Theologische Erörterungen* 4 (Tübingen: Mohr Siebeck, 2000), 84–160, here 115 fn. 89 (translation by H.T.). G. Ebeling's commentary on Luther's *Disputatio de homine*, whose first volume (*Lutherstudien*, vol. II/1 [Tübingen: Mohr Siebeck, 1977]) postponed the exegesis of Luther's own text until the second (1982) and third volumes (1989), is probably not the target of Jüngel's criticism, since he welcomes it in a footnote passage added while the first publication of his essay (1978) was already in print (Jüngel, "Freiheit," 96 fn. 24).

[4] Cf. Reinhold Rieger, *Von der Freiheit eines Christenmenschen = De libertate christiana*, Kommentare zu Schriften Luthers 1 (Tübingen: Mohr Siebeck 2007).

this sort of text editing is that the editors may have extended this kind of referencing the edited author's texts beyond the source material as such, thereby adding their own interpretation to the presentation of the texts. This problem applies to the editing of other important theologians' works form the 20th century, too. E. g., the contextualizing remarks which the leading German Bonhoeffer edition (*Dietrich Bonhoeffer Werke, DBW*) offers for many text passages strikingly often refer to his contribution to the anti-Nazi resistance even where the source material does not necessarily encourage this. It is also this kind of problem one is faced with when studying Barth's reception of Luther. There are hosts of Luther footnotes in the Barth *GA* including detailed references from the *WA*, but in a number of cases these were added by the editors and are only implicit in Barth's texts. They serve mainly to give these texts a more detailed and colorful overall impression. This would certainly be a nice thing for a textbook, but can be twilight in an edition since it suggests a closer and more thorough relationship between Barth and Luther than the texts themselves might support.

There is another reason why I will in this contribution content myself with Barth's *explicit* reception of Luther, and this becomes obvious if we take a look at the earlier research on our topic. There are particularly two essays which require attention, one by the distinguished Luther scholar G. Ebeling (1985) and the other by one of the world's leading Barth researchers, G. Hunsinger (1998).[5] Both do not only differ in their confessional backgrounds, but also methodologically. Ebeling, who began his academic career as a church historian, follows Barth's major writings chronologically identifying certain periods of intensified study of Luther, which then receive closer doctrinal investigation. Hunsinger, on the other hand, places some methodological reflections at the beginning of his essay which state that any theological idea in Barth's texts which stems originally from Luther ought to be considered a piece of influence by the Wittenberg reformer himself even if there is no evidence that Barth actually drew it from Luther rather than one of his pupils or the relatively anonymous complex of "Lutheran church and theology".[6]

What unites Ebeling and Hunsinger despite their many differences is that for them the question of Barth's reception of Luther is a *doctrinal* question. And as

---

5 Cf. Gerhard Ebeling, "Karl Barths Ringen mit Luther," in *Lutherstudien*, vol. 3 (Tübingen: J.C.B. Mohr [Paul Siebeck], 1985), 428–573, and George Hunsinger, "What Karl Barth Learned from Martin Luther," in *Disruptive Grace: Studies in the Theology of Karl Barth* (Grand Rapids MI: W.B. Eerdmans, 2000), 279–304.

6 Cf. Hunsinger, "What Karl Barth Learned," 282. Hunsinger adds that this criterion applies in particular to such instances where Luther's teaching on a given topic differs substantially from Calvin's and thus from Barth's own Reformed tradition.

Troeltsch taught us is always the case with doctrinal theology, once you reach out your hand towards it, it will seize you entirely.[7] Likewise, Ebeling and Hunsinger do not content themselves with questions of reception, but offer reflections on the whole of Barth's theology against which Ebeling takes a Lutheran stance[8] whereas Hunsinger emphasizes that there is hardly any topic in Barth's theology that could not in one sense or another be derived from Luther.[9] This hardly comes as a surprise since Hunsinger's definition of what reception of Luther means in Barth suggests that every text dealing with Protestant theology must receive Luther at least to some extent in the background. If the following reflections are confined to *explicit* receptions they do so in order to achieve results on some level other than doctrinal.

By "explicit reception" I mean *quotes with references* as this is the only way to be sure that Barth did actually work with the texts he refers to. This implies that if the following reflections are to be successful in any sense of the term, they must provide us with information on *what particular writings* by Luther Barth did work with. The focus will not be on doctrinal topics or keywords.

One could object that there might also be a sensible reception of Luther's writings in Barth's works merely on the basis of keywords or scientific terms; in fact it is characteristic of scientific discourse that it tends to discuss things on a more abstract level where terms and concepts play a more important role than single quotes or wordings. Although this is true in general, it cannot direct our research in this study because if we allowed reception on a mere keyword level into our reflections, we could not avoid the following problem: How can one be sure that Barth learned those concepts and keywords from the source texts and not somewhere else?

This, by the way, is a problem which even affects quotes with references. As the editing of Barth's first version of his commentary on *Romans* in the *GA* has shown, he drew many of his Luther references at that time from a book by a certain Ch. Eberle entitled *Luthers Episteln-Auslegung* (1866).[10] However, I think that

---

[7] Cf. Troeltsch, "Methode," 734: "Wer ihr den kleinen Finger gegeben hat, der muß ihr auch die ganze Hand geben."
[8] Cf. in particular Ebeling, "Barths Ringen," 537–39, where Ebeling observes a "fundamental difference" ("Grunddifferenz") between Barth and Luther.
[9] Cf. Hunsinger, "What Karl Barth Learned," 304, where Hunsinger, who is not unaware of "real disagreements" (303) between the two, refers to Barth's "substantive christocentrism, the theology of the cross, the primacy of God's Word, the doctrine of simul iustus et peccator, and the use of the Chalcedonian pattern" as Luther's legacy in Barth's thought.
[10] Cf. Karl Barth, *Der Römerbrief [Erste Fassung] 1919* = idem, *Gesamtausgabe. II. Abteilung: Akademische Werke*, vol. 16, ed. Hermann Schmidt (Zürich: TVZ, 1985), XXIV.

in order to classify a given quote as an explicit reception of some source text there is no need for that source text to be taken from a particular edition rather than a quote in secondary literature. The explicit reference as such will do to make sure that the quoted source text has really been received. Whether it is best scientific practice not to disclose the literature from which the source reference is taken is a different problem.

3 Study Design

In what follows I will argue that only cases of explicit reception of identifiable texts ought to be included in a study of Barth's reception of Luther. On this methodological premise the practical question arises how to spot the relevant passages of Barth's work. I would therefore like to add a few remarks on the study design behind this small essay.

Neither Ebeling nor Hunsinger had the opportunity of using the electronic devices which theology has at its disposal today. I have used the advanced search tools of the *Digital Karl Barth Library (DKBL)* published by Alexander Street Press. This database displays digitalized versions of the *GA* (except for its most recent volumes), Barth's main work that will not enter the *GA*, the *Kirchliche Dogmatik (KD)* or *Church Dogmatics (CD)*, and a number of additional Barth texts that have not yet been edited in the *GA*, but will be in the future. Even if *DKBL* is incomprehensive and regularly misrepresents some German characters, it is still a very valuable and powerful tool to conduct a study of the type that is required in order to answer the question of Barth's explicit reception of Luther.

Some have discarded the use of digital search tools such as *DKBL* as brute and unintelligent data mining, but I think that if it is used in a smart manner, it will lead us further than earlier generations could get. I have used *DKBL* to set up a table that contains all of Barth's quotes from Luther I could identify. Of course this presupposes that there are indeed references in the *GA* for Barth's reception of Luther which the search engine can match.

This poses an additional problem in terms of study design since there may be quotes without references in the sense of some bibliographically detailed evidence in such cases where very popular writings like, e.g., Luther's Catechisms are quoted. This, in fact, is a point which already Ebeling has raised. He states in a certain passage of his essay that the mature Barth seems to have appreciated

Luther for his elementary wording ("elementare[.] Formulierungen")[11] that is so typical for his catechisms and his Bible translations. No doubt such popular quotes (as one might call them) ought to be considered explicit receptions even if they might in some instance or another be close to mere "keyword dropping." But as a student of mine has checked for the volumes of the *KD* where Luther is received the most, such popular quotes are quite rare.[12] Thus I think we can safely say that by far the majority of Barth's Luther quotes are accompanied by references. Whatever Barth's use of Luther's texts may have been like, he seems to have used them with scrutiny. There is a nice letter by Barth to Lollo von Kirschbaum (April 2nd, 1931) which supports this view. Barth wrote it when working on the first volume of the *KD*.

> Dearest Lollo!
> Well, I have now left you alone for an indecently long time, and there is no comfort in the fact that there are many others whose urgent calls are also waiting in vain for an answer from me. At least I can now send you the first [part] together with this small letter. I have continuously worked on it and do hope now that it was worthwhile and will be so for my listeners and readers. Well, the thought really scares me that I am now more or less obliged to proceed exactly in this manner and on such a broad background. Our dogmatics is thus certainly going to be a beautiful book, don't you agree? But what an amount of work is that going to be for me – and for you! Here are some technical details for copying: 1 Would you not like to acquire some better paper for the main copy? 2 Wouldn't it be good to have a ribbon half black and half red for the footnotes? Such do exist and our little typewriter is prepared for them (see the switch on the right!). 3 Would you and could you locate all the quotes from the W.A.? In the case of the epistle to the Galatians you should try to find out in the E.A. to what biblical passage Luther's words belong. Use the Latin text for this which you will find in the New Testament on my desk or in your own Vulgata copy. In the W.A. the biblical passages are at the top of the pages. It will be more difficult to find the passages from De servo arbitrio. But you are so clever that you will certainly succeed. Please verify also the text provided by me and add the first line numbers from W.A. together with the page numbers. [...][13]

This letter reveals several things about Barth's reception of Luther. Though some have suspected that von Kirschbaum's contribution to the *Church Dogmatics* was much greater than her function as private secretary suggests,[14] I think

---

11 Ebeling, "Barths Ringen," 533.
12 I am indebted to Verena Pütz for her support at this point.
13 Karl Barth – Charlotte von Kirschbaum, *Briefwechsel* = Karl Barth, *Gesamtausgabe. V. Abteilung: Briefe*, vol 45, ed. Rolf-Joachim Erler (Zürich: TVZ, 2008), 174 (letter no. 82; English translation by H.T., disregarding the italics in the German original).
14 For a brief discussion of this issue cf. Hinrich Stoevesandt, "Charlotte von Kirschbaum," in *Barth Handbuch*, ed. Michael Beintker (Tübingen: Mohr Siebeck, 2016), 54–58, hier 56–57.

Barth is somewhat flattering her here when he refers to "our" joint dogmatics. I suppose that the Luther references were generally implemented into the text body by Barth himself and not some assistant or student of his even if there is evidence from Barth's correspondence with von Kirschbaum that it was she who had gathered suitable quotes from Luther's sermons since 1929.[15]

What seems more important in terms of our study design is that Barth obviously used the Erlangen edition (*Erlanger Ausgabe = EA*) of Luther's works until the 1930s, which is some forty years after the first volumes of the *WA*. Of course this was inevitable in the case of texts that were still unpublished in the *WA*. The rather rare instances where Barth stuck to the *EA* even when the respective texts had already been published in the *WA*, too, might suggest that these quotes indicate Barth's use of older secondary literature like the aforementioned Eberle who had no better source than the *EA*, but the total number of these instances is too low to make an argument. What Barth's letter seems to suggest is that he did not switch to the leading scientific edition until preparing his main work, the *KD*.

Based on the assumption that Barth quoted Luther (whether directly or according to secondary literature) using both the *EA* and the *WA*, the most important step of our study is to spot all occurences of *EA* and *WA* in *DKBL*. This search largely confirms Ebeling's findings that Barth's engagement with Luther generally declined during his academic career. There are obvious peaks in his first Göttingen year when his lecture on Zwingli inspires him to a study in Luther's theology of the eucharist that almost bursts with source references.[16] Another important example is the first volume of Barth's *Church Dogmatics* which is loaded with Luther references.[17] The decline, Ebeling notices,[18] coincides with Barth's move to Switzerland and the publication of *Evangelium und Gesetz* (1935) – a text critical of Lutheran theology. As E. Busch says in his biography, Barth's interest in Luther was raised again in 1953 when *KD* IV/1 was published[19]

---

15 Cf. Christiane Tietz, Karl Barth. Ein Leben im Widerspruch, München: C.H. Beck: 2018, 198: The quotes were supposed to enter into the reworked edition of the CD, which never appeared, but they may have become part of the 'Zeddelkasten' which Barth used later on to compose the excursus passages of the KD.
16 Cf. Karl Barth, "Ansatz und Absicht in Luthers Abendmahlslehre [1923]," in *Gesamtausgabe. III. Abteilung: Vorträge und kleinere Arbeiten*, vol. 19: 1922–1925, ed. Holger Finze (Zürich: TVZ: 1990), 248–306.
17 Cf. Karl Barth, *Die Kirchliche Dogmatik. I: Die Lehre vom Wort Gottes*, vol. 1: Prolegomena zur Kirchlichen Dogmatik (München: Chr. Kaiser, 1932).
18 Cf. Ebeling, "Barths Ringen," 441 and 460.
19 Eberhard Busch, *Karl Barths Lebenslauf: Nach seinen Briefen und autobiographischen Texten* (München: Chr. Kaiser, 1975), 409 with reference to Barth's academic teaching on Luther in the summer of 1953.

– the volume containing the doctrine of justification which according to Ebeling simply demanded engagement with Luther.[20] By that time Barth or rather his publisher, the *Evangelischer [later: Theologischer] Verlag Zürich*, had modernized the spelling of the *WA*. Before the Second World War this abbreviation (and *EA* alike) was printed with a blank between the two capitals and a dot after each of them; after 1945 both the blank and dots were omitted. A lot of *WA* occurences (with blank) in *DKBL* do not refer to Luther quotes, but to Barth's correspondence with W. A. Visser 't Hooft or his numerous mentions of W. A. Mozart, whose initials also meet the search criteria.

As this example shows, using the *DKBL* search engine runs the risk of producing false results, but it also gives us more detailed information about the particular writings Barth received from Luther. In this respect Ebeling propounded in a rather generalized manner that Barth drew more on the "churchy" side of the Wittenberg reformer and his "hymns, catechisms, and bible translations" than his academic writings, which Ebeling considered in accordance with Barth's own move from dialectical theology to the *Church Dogmatics*.[21] An important piece of evidence for this hypothesis is that in working on his commentary on *Romans*, Barth did not show much interest in Luther's early lecture on Romans (1515/16) which had only been discovered in 1908 and edited for the first time two years later by J. Ficker (the *WA* edition appeared no earlier than 1938). This lecture, as is well known, gave rise to the Luther Renaissance in K. Holl, R. Hermann and others, which is nowadays considered "another departure" (H. Assel) in 20th century theology besides the Dialectical Theology which largely built on Barth's second version of his commentary on *Romans*. What would have become of this chapter of the history of theology if in reworking *Romans* Barth had dedicated himself more to the study of the lecture that stimulated Holl's and Hermann's works? There are about thirty references to Luther in the first *Romans*, but the majority of them follow the aforementioned study by Eberle which was published in 1866 well before the discovery of Luther's lecture. There are only four passages[22] where the *GA* editors were able to spot Barth's use of Luther's early lecture on Romans. In the second edition of Barth's *Romans*, by which the contours of his dialectical theology had become clearer, the total number of references to Luther has increased to almost sixty, among which the Romans lecture remains rather insignificant.[23]

---

20 Cf. Ebeling, "Barths Ringen," 492.
21 Cf. Ebeling, "Barths Ringen," 533 (translation by H.T.).
22 Cf. Barth, *GA* II, vol. 16, 154; 213; 284; 395.
23 In fact, two of the four passages mentioned in the previous footnote also appear in Karl Barth, *Der Römerbrief (Zweite Fassung) 1922* = *Gesamtausgabe. II. Abteilung: Akademische*

More important than the number of occurences, though, is the variety of Luther texts quoted by Barth. I spent a seven-hour train journey with K. Aland's *Hilfsbuch zum Lutherstudium* on my knees in order to reidentify the single writings. And the result of this I think gives a good overall image of Barth's reception of Luther.

4 Results

There are hundreds of references to Luther throughout Barth's writings, but, considering his literary productivity, certainly not to an extent that one would have to consider Barth an extensive and lifelong thorough reader of Luther's texts. However, there are the aforementioned exceptions to this rule of thumb. At certain stages of his theological career Barth dramatically intensified his engagement with Luther's texts. The following three stages which deserve particular interest have already been identified by Ebeling.

The first stage is one of Barth's first lectures as a professor at the university of Göttingen where he read on *The theology of Zwingli* in the winter term of 1922/23. The *GA* edition of this lecture contains an astonishing 400 *WA* references in the paragraph on Zwingli and Luther alone.[24] Most of them were added by the editors, since Barth here quoted Luther according to the *EA* giving only the volume and page numbers, which would make it difficult to spot these in *DKBL* if there were no redactional remarks. Barth's essay on Luther's doctrine of the eucharist, published in 1923 in *Zwischen den Zeiten*, is the quintessential result of this lecture[25] and contains another 250 Luther references from the same writings: almost all of Luther's writings on the topic from the late 1510s (e. g., *Sermon dem hochwürdigen Sakrament des heiligen wahren Leichnams Christi und von den Bruderschaften*) and 1520s (e. g., *De captivitate babylonica ecclesiae praeludium*) up to *Vom Abendmahl Christi. Bekenntnis* (1528). Never before or after this have Luther's works had a similar impact on any single text by Barth. However, even if it is undeniable that for some reason Barth must have felt driven to engage deeply with the reformer's texts, the overall significance of this enormous bulk of quotes

---

Werke, vol. 47, ed. Cornelis van der Kooi/Katja Tolstaja (Zürich: TVZ, 2010), 213, 268. Two other passages from that lecture have been newly introduced into Barth's second *Romans*: ibid., 67, 503.

24 Cf. Karl Barth, *Die Theologie Zwinglis 1922/23. Vorlesung Göttingen Wintersemester 1922/23* = id., *Gesamtausgabe. II. Abteilung: Akademische Werke*, vol. 40, ed. Matthias Freudenberg (Zürich: TVZ, 2004), particularly § 4, 251–498.

25 Ebeling, "Barths Ringen," 444 calls it the "eigentliche Frucht" of the lecture.

is not quite as high as the statistical figures might suggest. One reason for this is that Barth quotes so thoroughly from Luther's writings in this essay he is rather meditating Luther as a whole than discussing the details of his position. If H. Assel is right in suggesting that there is a distinct thesis on the representation of the cross concealed in this kind of arguing with Luther,[26] it still seems to use Luther's sacramental thought as a dialectical counterpart needed to affirm Barth's own position, as Ebeling has argued.[27] Ebeling's argument is in perfect harmony with what Barth says in an unpublished draft for the preface to his first *Romans* about the function of quotations in the book: they were integrated into the book in order to support and underline what the text of the book says itself.[28]

The second period of Luther influence on Barth's thought is in the composition of the opening volume of the *Church Dogmatics* (I/1–2) from which period of time the letter quoted above originates. This is particularly interesting in comparison to the imperfect *Christian Dogmatics* which Barth reworks here. Beginning with his famous paragraph on the threefold shape of the word of God (§ 4 *KD* I/1), Barth multiplies the Luther references of the corresponding *Christian Dogmatics* passages by five, thus foreshadowing the excursus passages of the *Church Dogmatics* volumes to come. The exact reason why Barth obviously sought to defend his argument against objections from theologies drawing on Luther's texts still needs research, but one should realize that just like under his first Luther impact Barth receives a particular group of the Reformer's writings here. This time, however, it is not a doctrinal topic like the eucharist, but obviously Luther's engagement with the Bible that attracted Barth's interest. The vast majority of Luther quotes in *KD I* is from Luther's different collections of model sermons (*Postillen*)[29] or other printed sermons while his exegetical writings take the second rank: his lecture on Galatians (1535)[30] in particular and, though much less used, the second lecture on the Psalms (1519–21).[31] Even if

---

[26] Cf. Heinrich Assel, "Barth und Luther zur Repräsentation des Kreuzes Jesu," in *Zeitschrift für dialektische Theologie* 22 (2006/special issue): 40–46.
[27] Cf. Ebeling, "Barths Ringen," 444–45.
[28] Cf. Barth, *GA* II, vol. 16, 590: Quotations serve as "eine bes. treffende, kräftige und gleichsam prophetische Formulierung des Textgehaltes."
[29] Cf. Martin Luther, *Werke. Kritische Gesamtausgabe. I. Abteilung: Schriften*, vol. 7, 466–537; 10/ I,1–2; 17/II, 21–22; 52 (Weimar: Böhlau, 1897/1910/25/27/28/29/15).
[30] Cf. Luther, *WA* 40/I–III (1911/14/30).
[31] Cf. Martin Luther, *Operationes in psalmos 1519–1521*, part 2, *Archiv zur Weimarer Ausgabe* 2, ed. Gerhard Hammer/Manfred Biersack under the auspices of Heiko A. Oberman (Weimar: Böhlau, 1981).

the majority of the former is probably[32] borrowed from Eberle's book (like in *Romans*), it is clear that in *KD I* Barth has taken considerable efforts to integrate Luther's work both on the academic chair and in the pulpit into his own argument.

The third period after a long decline in Luther engagement is in vol. IV/1 of the *Church Dogmatics*. Ebeling argued that this newly arising interest in Luther had doctrinal reasons since it was the doctrine of justification Barth had to deal with in KD IV/1 – and how could one do so without referring to Luther?[33] However sensible this may seem on doctrinal terms, the evidence of Luther's writings Barth quotes in *KD* IV/1 tells a different story. Again it is Luther the bible theologian who appears in these quotations taken mainly from the sermon collections (*Postillen*) and the exegetical lectures.

5 Discussion

The overall image we get from these results is that the seemingly plausible idea of Luther's gradually declining significance for Barth once his doctrinal development had settled in the *Church Dogmatics* needs correction. I think the problem with hypotheses of the kind Ebeling suggests is to presuppose that the question of Barth's reception of Luther was primarily a doctrinal one. Quite to the contrary it seems that the textual evidence plays a crucial part. Considering the concrete texts by Luther which Barth quotes it is obvious that doctrinal texts are only of minor significance to him. Of course we do encounter quotes that reference doctrinal texts like *De servo arbitrio* or *De libertate christiana*, e.g. in several paragraphs of the *Christian Dogmatics*,[34] but their total number is rather low. It is likewise noteworthy that Barth hardly draws on those texts which Lutheran theologians usually consider characteristic of the reformer's social ethics like *Von weltlicher Obrigkeit*. An exception to this rule seems to be the early lecture on

---

32 This seems likely not just because many of the references stem from lesser known sermons like the ones used by Eberle, but also because Barth's letter to von Kirschbaum (quoted earlier in this essay) seems to suggest that the manuscript von Kirschbaum was supposed to work with did not yet contain the proper references from the scientific editions of the *EA* and the *WA*.
33 Cf. Ebeling, "Barths Ringen," 492.
34 Cf. Karl Barth, *Die christliche Dogmatik im Entwurf. Erster Band: Die Lehre vom Worte Gottes. Prolegomena zur christlichen Dogmatik 1927* = id., *Gesamtausgabe. II. Abteilung: Akademische Werke*, vol. 14, ed. Gerhard Sauter (Zürich: TVZ, 1982), §§ 16; 20–21.

Ethics II (1928/29) where Barth dwells a bit over Luther's concept of the law.[35] But these passages are certainly not enough to support the overall impression that the reception of Luther's texts was in itself a doctrinal question.

The only stage in Barth's theological career to support a doctrinal approach to our question seems to be his *Zwingli* lecture and resulting essay on Luther's doctrine of the eucharist in 1922/23. I suppose the reason why this is so is that this was one of Barth's first academic lectures he had to deliver without ever having earned the normally required academic degrees – which is to say that Barth here had to make his way into academic practice. It is well known that in this situation he took shelter from the history of theology: the medieval scholastics, later on the Reformed and Lutheran orthodoxies – why not Luther himself? If the massive Luther impact from 1922/23 was rather a transient period of trying to find his own style as an academic teacher, this would perfectly account for the fact that the impact was scarcely sustainable. Barth did try once to do what was expected of him at Göttingen, namely deliver academic lectures as a doctrinal theologian – but he must have found out quickly that he was not going to be a doctrinal theologian in the sense academic conventions of that time did doctrinal theology! It would be an interesting question to ask what the style of the *Church Dogmatics* is that finally represented the results of this transient stage of self-finding in Barth's theological career – but it is certainly not building doctrinal theology, rather it is something prior to that which we might call the architecture of theology. I would like to add a few more remarks about this suggestion.

To speak of theological architecture (not in the Kantian sense of the term) evokes the idea of some sort of mental building which theologians may enter to walk through its rooms. It also suggests that theology was done best behind closed doors or at least in a clear distinction of what is inside of theology and what is outside of it. Classic or neo-orthodox aesthetics of perfection come to mind if one develops theology in this line of thought. However, all these ideas would be misleading if they were to conduct our study of Barth's theology. From the fragmentary shape of his famous dialectical 1922 lectures to the *KD* which remained just as imperfect as its predecessor from Münster, Barth was hardly ever inclined to that sort of architecture. On the other hand it is true that in the *KD* the argument is all in the structure and composition – the architecture – of the book. E.g., it would be pointless to practice close reading of *KD*

---

[35] Cf. Karl Barth, *Ethik II 1928/29. Vorlesung Münster Wintersemester 1928/29, wiederholt in Bonn, Wintersemester 1930/31* = id., *Gesamtausgabe. II: Akademische Werke*, vol. 10, ed. Dietrich Braun (Zürich: TVZ, 1978), particularly § 11, 9–167. Again it is Luther's exegetical lectures (on Genesis, Isaiah, and both psalm lectures) Barth draws on.

texts since the significance of a given passage depends so much on its particular position in the overall architectural framework that two identical formulations may have opposite argumentative value in different places of the book. The relevance of these architectural features is most obvious, as E. Jüngel has shown, in Barth's doctrine of reconciliation,[36] but it also applies to many other chapters of his dogmatics, since the ingredients of which that architecture of reconciliation is made combine the doctrines of Christ and that of predestination with the doctrine of the Trinity as the probably most comprehensive doctrinal unit. Even if this architecture is rather easy to reconstruct, the whole point about it is that it is *not* a combination of doctrinal elements resulting in doctrinal integrity. As numerous scholarly contributions have shown, this Trinitarian and/or Christological architecture is something which theologians are supposed to *narrate in the church*. This is why I prefer to speak of an architecture of Barth's dogmatics rather than an "ontology" albeit "narrative ontology" (K.J. Bender).[37] It was H.W. Frei who thus emphasized the correlation between theology, church, and narrative,[38] and this is in my opinion one of the most important parts of the legacy of Barth's theology. As the late D. Ritschl has elaborated in his "story" concept,[39] it turns the architecture of theology into a lively reality rather than a mentally constructed building called "ontology."[40]

The problem which I think Barth research should discuss today is what sort of narration suits theology best. In some way, it is a question of the rhetorics of theology. Different suggestions have been made as to what rhetorics to adopt into theology, and I am doubtful if we are to expect one single and definitive answer to the question; it is perfectly possible that theology should have a flexible rhetorics according to the contexts in which theologians find themselves. This has led some to the idea that despite the enormous bulk of dogmatic work he

---

[36] Cf. Eberhard Jüngel, "Barth, Karl," in *Theologische Realenzyklopädie,* vol. 5 (Berlin: de Gruyter, 1980), 251–68, here 265.
[37] Cf. Kimlyn J. Bender, *Karl Barth's Christological Ecclesiology,* Barth Studies Series (Aldershot: Ashgate, 2005), 119 et passim.
[38] Cf. Hans W. Frei, "Theology and the Interpretation of Narrative. Some Hermeneutical Considerations," in *Theology and Narrative: Selected Essays,* ed. George Hunsinger and William C. Placher (New York NY: Oxford University Press, 1993), 94–116.
[39] Cf. Dietrich Ritschl/Hugh O. Jones, *"Story" als Rohmaterial der Theologie, Theologische Existenz heute,* new series 192 (München: Kaiser, 1976).
[40] The significance of ontology for Barth's theology has been discussed in German theology particularly since the book by Wilfried Härle, *Sein und Gnade: Die Ontologie in Karl Barths Kirchlicher Dogmatik, Theologische Bibliothek Töpelmann* 27 (Berlin: de Gruyter, 1975).

does Barth was something like a godfather of postmodern theology.[41] But here we encounter a severe problem since the Trinitarian architecture at least of his *KD* clearly "eats up the background," as D.F. Ford said,[42] and this would mean that it tells the sort of great or meta narrative postmodernity is supposed to have overcome.

My suggestion is that the sort of rhetoric we encounter in Barth, particularly his *KD*, is an indirect rhetoric: a rhetoric of witness with Christ as primary witness and the church as the cloud of witnesses gathered around him so that each and every believer bearing witness to Christ directly echoes his primordial witness. It is through the mediation of witness that God reveals Godself to the world. I should like to emphasize that the witness type of rhetoric is the inspiration I draw from Barth in respect to the question of how to narrate the architecture of theology; it is probably not compulsory. But whatever sort of rhetoric theology is to adopt, the one presupposition in the background will always be that there is something to narrate throughout theology in its entirety. Of course this also applies to the work of Barth if Barth is to inspire this or that particular theological narrative. What this something was in Barth's theological career, I will now try to make a few remarks about turning back to the different stages of his reception of Luther.

There was a second Luther impact on Barth after his first Göttingen lecture, and it stands at another important turning-point of Barth's career when he reworked the unfinished *Christian Dogmatics* into the first volume of the *Church Dogmatics*. It would seem that to establish an entire dogmatic system Barth needed to trespass the boundaries of a professor of Reformed theology he used to be when working at the universities of Göttingen and Münster. But as our survey of the actually received and quoted Luther texts suggests, Barth's concern in the opening volume of the *Church Dogmatics* was a different one. It was centered around his famous doctrine of the threefold shape of the word of God – a piece of doctrinal theology at first sight, but to solve a highly practical question that had haunted Barth ever since his Safenwil days: It was the dilemma of the proclamation of the word of God trapped between the expectations of the Bible on the one hand and of the congregation on the other, as Barth portrayed it in his famous lectures delivered in 1922 (e.g., *Not und Verheißung der christlichen*

---

41 Cf., e.g., Stephen H. Webb, *Re-figuring Theology. The Rhetoric of Karl Barth*, SUNY Series in Rhetoric and Theology (Albany NY: State University of New York Press 1991); Graham Ward, *Barth, Derrida, and the language of theology* (Cambridge: Cambridge University Press, 2004).
42 David F. Ford, *Barth and God's Story. Biblical Narrative and the Theological Method of Karl Barth in the "Church Dogmatics,"* Studien zur interkulturellen Geschichte des Christentums 27 (Frankfurt: P. Lang, ²1985), 92 (borrowing the wording from J.P. Stern).

Verkündigung)⁴³ when the experience of Safenwil was still very fresh. It is easy to trace the ways this dilemma makes through all of Barth's work in the *Göttingen Dogmatics* and his accompanying essays from these years.⁴⁴ And it was not until the *Church Dogmatics* that Barth found the Christological and Trinitarian solution to this dilemma which the doctrine of the threefold shape of the word of God expounds (§ 4 *KD*).

It is my suggestion that Barth's reception of Luther in the time of *KD I* was determined by the two factors that made up the Safenwil dilemma: Luther the exegete of the bible and Luther the man in the pulpit. This suggestion fits perfectly well in the body of referenced writings we encountered in *KD* I, *Ethics* II and Barth's first and second *Romans* alike, particularly the exegetical lectures on Galatians (Genesis and Isaiah, too, though much less) and of course the great bulk of quotes from Luther's model sermons. What seems to favor this suggestion additionally is that the Safenwil dilemma is nothing else than the heart of Barth's dialectical theology – which amounts to saying that the dialectics the pastor of Safenwil had experienced did not cease when Barth entered into an academic career. Ever since B. McCormack's study on Barth's theological development⁴⁵ it has been widely accepted that these dialectics was the most sustainable factor in Barth's theology – so sustainable, I should like to add, that it also accounts for the third and last impact Luther had on Barth when in 1953 he intensified his engagement with the Wittenberg reformer once more, and once again centered on Luther's bible theology and his preaching.

What seems to follow from all these observations is that Barth's reception of Luther is not an item of doctrinal theology. Rather, it is first of all biographically contextualized in Barth's theological career. Another point worthy of notice is that there is an important theological issue behind it, but this again does not really belong to doctrinal theology but to the ecclesial fundamentals and practical corollaries of any constructive Christian theology: the Bible and the task of preaching it.

---

43 Cf. Barth, *Vorträge und kleinere Arbeiten 1922–1925*, 65–97.
44 For a closer investigation of this, cf. Henning Theißen, *Die berufene Zeugin des Kreuzes Christi. Studien zur Grundlegung der evangelischen Theorie der Kirche*, Arbeiten zur systematischen Theologie 5 (Leipzig: Evangelische Verlagsanstalt, 2013), 373–85.
45 Cf. Bruce L. McCormack, *Karl Barth's Critically Realistic Dialectical Theology. Its Genesis and Development 1909–1936* (Oxford: Clarendon Press, 1997).

Claire E. Sufrin
Martin Buber between Revelation and Scripture

To understand the work of German Jewish philosopher Martin Buber (1878–1965), we must begin a bit earlier with the *Wissenschaft des Judentums* movement, which was started in 1819. The founders of this movement strove to understand Judaism as a historical phenomenon, that is, as a religion and culture that had evolved over time. Though the society collapsed just a few years later, its impact is immense. One of the *Wissenschaft des Judentums* founders, Leopold Zunz writes of his research that

> Only by considering the literature of a nation as a gateway to a comprehensive knowledge of the course of its culture throughout the ages, by noting how at every moment the essence of the given and the supplementary, i.e., the inner and the external, array themselves; how fate, climate, customs, religion and chance seize one another in friendly or hostile spirit; how, finally, the present is the necessary result of all that preceded it – only thus will one tread with true reverence.[1]

In claiming that Jewish practice and ideas at any given moment reflect the intellectual currents of the time, Zunz proposed to take a radically different attitude toward the history of Judaism. as he intended that study of the past would reveal Judaism's course of evolution so that it might change in the present. Zunz's call for "true reverence," however, signals that he saw his approach as being more respectful of the rabbinic tradition than that of Jews who might abandon it as hopelessly irrelevant as they grew distant from traditional Jewish practice or that of Jewish traditionalists who were unable to recognize the tradition's dynamism.

The *Wissenschaft des Judentums* movement was short-lived but deeply influential. Zunz and others understood that a Judaism that had evolved over time should surely continue to evolve. The ideas proposed by the Society for the Culture and Science of the Jews supplied an intellectual foundation for the liberalization of Judaism. For illustration of this point, we can turn to the work of Abraham Geiger (1810–1874), who was both a historian and a rabbi. While Geiger's scholarship focused on early Christianity, his theological writings offer an impor-

---

[1] Leopold Zunz, "On Rabbinic Literature," in *The Jew in the Modern World: A Documentary History*, ed. Paul R. Mendes-Flohr and Jehuda Reinharz, 2nd ed (New York: Oxford University Press, 1995), 223.

tant picture of the relationship between the historicization of Judaism and its liberalization in the nineteenth century.² In an 1838 sermon, Geiger admonished his audience to

> be very mindful of the pure and genuine grain of wheat in your faith, of the pure fear of God, so that you will work in behalf of the welfare of mankind. The outer shell, the ritual forms, are but bearers of the spirit in which that spirit becomes visible and by which it may mature; but do not forget that they are of no further use to piety once they no longer bear that spirit within them. Times and circumstances change, and necessitate many modifications and new institutions which, in keeping with contemporary circumstances, are needed to keep our religion alive.³

Using a stalk of wheat as a metaphor, Geiger portrayed Jewish ritual as existing solely to nurture and protect the precious core of Judaism as the outer husk protects the grain of wheat. At a certain point in the grain's development, the husk is no longer necessary and even blocks access to the nourishing potential of the grain. Geiger argued that ritual similarly threatens to outlast its purpose; the impulse to reform Jewish practice is an attempt to discard the dry husk that blocks the true teaching articulated in the Bible and nurtured through generations of Jewish history. Thus, he wrote, "do not complain when it seems to you that things are changing. The truth is that nothing has really changed. All that changes is the outer shell, only some outward forms undergo modification; the essence of things remains intact."⁴

This liberalization of Judaism – influenced ideologically by the *Wissenschaft des Judentums* and spurred on as well by a desire to demonstrate to their Christian neighbors that Judaism was an inherently rational faith and thus that the Jews were worthy of civic emancipation – began to take institutional form with a series of rabbinic conferences in the 1840s and then the establishment of the *Hochschule für die Wissenschaft des Judentums* in 1872 as a liberal rabbinical seminary that would promote the scientific study of Judaism. But the liberalization of Judaism ironically gave rise to what today we call modern or neo-Orthodoxy: a defense of the rabbinic tradition developed and preserved in the Talmud but with a limited number of concessions to the modern world. Samson Raphael Hirsch, one of the ideological leaders of this movement, was the first to call for a formal separation between liberal and Orthodox Jews in the city of Berlin.

---

2 Susannah Heschel, *Abraham Geiger and the Jewish Jesus* (University of Chicago Press, 1998).
3 Abraham Geiger, *Abraham Geiger and Liberal Judaism: The Challenge of the Nineteenth Century*, ed. Max Wiener (Cincinnati: Hebrew Union College Press, 1981), 247–48.
4 Geiger, 248.

It is against this Jewish background that we must begin to understand Buber. Born in Vienna in 1878, Buber grew up with his grandparents in Polish Galicia, in a household devoted to the *Wissenschaft des Judentums*. (His grandfather, Solomon Buber, was a prominent *Wissenschaft des Judentums* scholar and edited a critical edition of *Midrash Rabbah* that remains the standard today, more than a century later.) Unlike in Germany and places further west, in Eastern Europe, Jews were not split between liberal and Orthodox forms of Judaism but rather between a pietistic movement known as Hasidism and a second movement defined by its opposition to Hasidism and known for its devotion to textual study and strict adherence to the letter of the law. The area where Buber grew up included many Hasidic communities and what made his upbringing truly unusual was that he and his grandfather were also participant-observers in the traditional Jewish life of the Galician Hasidim that surrounded them. The spirited prayers and imaginative storytelling of these pietistic communities and courts influenced Buber's thinking throughout his life.[5]

In this article, I offer an overview of Buber's work through an examination of some of his writings about the Hebrew Bible. Neither strictly liberal nor orthodox in his orientation toward Judaism, Buber's engagement with the Bible was driven by his desire to understand and articulate the relationship between the past of the biblical Israelites and the present of modern Jews. In particular, what Buber pursued in his many writings about the Hebrew Bible was, first, a better understanding of how the historical relationship between the biblical Israelites and God might inform the spirituality or religiosity of the modern Jew, and, second, how the modern Jew might access that understanding and then act on it to enrich her own existence. In short, history and hermeneutics were for Buber interwoven as he hoped that together they might motivate a renewal of Jewish spirituality in the modern world.

In the years from 1909 through 1945, Buber understood revelation both as an abstract concept and as an event described in the biblical text. Here I show how his basic definition of revelation as divine presence and not divine speech grew more complex over this time as he became a more and more careful reader of the Hebrew Bible. The paper is divided into three sections, each one devoted to a particular period of Buber's writings. The first section addresses the 1910s and early 1920s, years that include Buber's *Early Addresses on Judaism*, his "Religion as Presence" lectures, and *I and Thou*. The second section examines Buber's thinking about revelation in the context of his translation of the He-

---

[5] For more on the circumstances of Buber's life, see Paul Mendes-Flohr, Martin Buber: *A Life of Faith and Dissent* (New Haven: Yale University Press, 2019).

brew Bible into German with his friend and colleague Franz Rosenzweig in the late 1920s. Finally, the third section considers the books of biblical commentaries Buber wrote in the 1930s and 1940s. As we move through these writings, I focus in particular on Buber's discussions of two biblical scenes of human-divine encounter that might be seen as prototypical moments of revelation: Moses meeting God at the burning bush in Exodus 3 and the Israelites encountering God at Mount Sinai in Exodus 19. Each of these scenes challenges the modern reader seeking to understand how it is that God might speak to human beings.

1 Religion, Revelation and the Bible in Buber's Writings of the 1910s and Early 1920s

In his *Early Addresses on Judaism* of the 1910s, Buber defines Judaism as a struggle to overcome the difference between religiosity and religion.[6] By religiosity, he means the actual and immediate experience of connection with God or even the pursuit of that experience, while by religion he means stable forms of religious expression such as literature, ritual or law. These forms are necessary, but there is always a danger that they will replace the original religiosity that gave rise to them. In line with liberal critics of traditional Judaism, this is exactly Buber's diagnosis of the neo-Orthodoxy advocated by followers of Samson Raphael Hirsch. But Buber is also critical of liberal Judaism, accusing its defenders of stifling the dynamism of Jewish teaching by limiting it to ethical monotheism, little more than a dogmatic insistence on God's oneness and an emphasis on the importance of love of one's neighbor and other moral commandments.[7]

---

6 On the terms religion and religiosity, see Paul Mendes-Flohr, *From Mysticism to Dialogue: Martin Buber's Transformation of German Social Thought* (Detroit: Wayne State University Press, 1989).

7 In a sentence suggestive of the work of Hermann Cohen, Buber writes that with the liberal version of Judaism, "Judaism appears to be a curious awkward detour to some modern philosophical theorems – as, for instance, the idea of God as a postulate of critical reason, or the categorical imperative.... The originators of such theories overlook the fact that religious truth is not a conceptual abstraction but has existential relevance; that is, that words can only point the way, and that religious truth can be made adequately manifest only in the individual's or the community's life." Martin Buber, "Herut: On Youth and Religion," in *On Judaism* (New York: Schocken, 1996), 161; "Cheruth: Eine Rede Über Jugend Und Religion," in *Reden Über Das Judentum* (Frankfurt am Main: Literarische Anstalt Rütten und Loening, 1923), 217. For Cohen's understanding of Judaism, see Hermann Cohen, *Religion of Reason out of the Sources of Judaism*, trans. Simon Kaplan (New York: Frederick Ungar, 1972); *Die Religion der Vernunft aus den Quellen des Judentums* (Leipzig: GFock, 1919).

Buber's first three addresses are the likely target of Franz Rosenzweig's "Atheistic Theology," written in 1914. (The two will become close friends and colleagues but at this point they barely know one another.) In his essay, Rosenzweig compares modern Jewish thought to the Life of Jesus movement that had swept through liberal Christianity in the 19th century. He argues that a parallel "Jewish People's Theology" began with the view of the scholars of the *Wissenschaft des Judentums* who, in their efforts to portray Judaism as a rational religion, emphasized the experience and the creativity of the Jewish people as the forces that had shaped Judaism and not the activity of God in human history. They saw myth as the process by which human beings created the divine. But in doing so, Rosenzweig argues, these thinkers deny the reality of revelation: "The distinctness of God and man, this frightful scandal for all new and old paganism, seems to be removed; the offensive thought of revelation, this plunging of a higher content into an unworthy vessel, is brought to silence."[8] In contrast, Rosenzweig insists that revelation consists of the exposure of something true about human experience by a divine force beyond the realm of human beings. It has happened and will happen again; the reality of revelation as a historical event cannot be denied, and revelation will re-assert itself against all attempts to explain it away in rational terms. To those who would attempt a rational understanding of revelation, Rosenzweig warns: "Let his theology be as scientific as it wants to be and can be: it cannot circumvent the notion of revelation."[9]

The last of Buber's *Early Addresses on Judaism*, the 1919 "Herut," already reveals the influence of Rosenzweig's "Atheistic Theology." In this essay, Buber focuses on youth, which he defines as the time of life in which one is open to the call of the "Unconditioned," God. If the call of God is the defining moment of youth, responding to the call is the defining challenge of youth, and Buber describes resources available to the young Jew seeking to respond with authenticity and creativity. In the Hebrew Bible, a youth finds that "mankind's wordless dialogue with God is condensed for him into the language of the soul, which he is not merely able to understand, but to which he himself can add new expressions, as yet unspoken. Without this language, he could do no more than stammer and falter."[10] The biblical text portrays human beings responding to God's call. In studying the biblical text, a young person does not find a script for re-

---

8 Franz Rosenzweig, "Atheistic Theology," in *Philosophical and Theological Writings*, ed. Paul W. Franks and Michael L. Morgan (Indianapolis: Hackett, 2000), 19; "Atheistische Theologie," in *Zweistromland*, ed. Reinhold Mayer and Annemarie Mayer (Derdrecht: Martinus Nighoff, 1984), 693.
9 Rosenzweig, "Atheistic Theology," 24; "Atheistische Theologie," 697.
10 Buber, "Herut," 155; "Cheruth," 209.

sponding to God but a set of images and words that might inspire her own response, in her own language and her own context: a response to divine presence that is creative, and just barely derivative.

"Herut" marks an important transition in Buber's thinking about religion.[11] His emphasis has moved from the tension between living religiosity and stale religious forms that dominated his thinking a decade earlier to God as an immediate presence. The pursuit of the Absolute that defined religiosity fades, and the religious challenge is the recognition of the divine and response to it. Revelation is a reality insofar as every human being – at some point or another in her life – has the opportunity to respond to God as an immediate presence in this way. Furthermore, in "Herut" Buber recognizes a connection between the record of past revelations found in the Hebrew Bible and the present-day divine callings that characterize youth. The biblical text preserves the responses made by earlier generations to God's calling. The text does not preserve the calls themselves, a distinction that will grow sharper as Buber's thinking about the Bible matures over the next two decades.

The transition in Buber's thinking about religion that we observe in "Herut" develops more fully in the "Religion as Presence" lectures he delivers at Frankfurt's Freies Jüdisches Lehrhaus in early 1922. The presence of religion to which Buber refers is the presence of God, universally available at any moment and in any place, but only to those human beings who turn toward it. As he tells his audience in the first lecture,

> presence is a concept of the soul; every presence is a moment of the human soul that is followed by another moment. An absolute present that did not become past would have to be one that did not merely exist in man as a moment of his soul, but one in which man stood, something in which man lived, yet which he could fulfill only in his inner being, by the dedication of his entire inner being.[12]

In the seventh lecture, he acknowledges that this absolute presence is God: "religion… is presence, is a present that by its nature does not and cannot become

---

[11] Hugo Bergman reads "Herut" as an anticipation of *I and Thou*. In light of Rivka Horwitz's work on the "Religion as Presence" lectures, I think this is an overreading. See Hugo Bergman, "Martin Buber and Mysticism," in *The Philosophy of Martin Buber*, ed. Paul A. Schilpp and Maurice Friedman (La Salle, IL: Open Court, 1967).

[12] Rivka Horwitz, *Buber's Way to "I and Thou": The Development of Martin Buber's Thought and His "Religion as Presence" Lectures* (Philadelphia: Jewish Publication Society, 1988), 20. The original German text for these lectures may be found in an earlier edition of the book: Rivka Horwitz, *Buber's Way to I and Thou: An Historical Analysis and the First Publication of Martin Buber's Lectures "Religion als Gegenwart"* (Heidelberg: Lambert Schneider, 1976).

past. And when we comprehend this correctly, when we feel that here is something that is no longer time-bound... when we feel this we also feel that this present of which we speak is the presence of God."[13] Religion is thus not an attitude but an experience. It relies upon openness, emotion, and intuition.

In the final lecture, Buber recognizes the confrontation between the divine and the human as revelation. It is

> something that happens everywhere and all the time, that can happen to every human being, every human being who opens himself up completely, being completely collected and unified in himself. The basic meaning, therefore, of this revelation and of all revelation is a sending forth of the human being.... This calling, this sending forth to the test, to the deed, to humanity, into the world, into the We, to the place of actualization – that is the strength, that is what revelation gives.[14]

Revelation as confrontation is a transformative event in the life of the individual, an assurance of divine presence that sets one on a path toward meaningful relationships among human beings who themselves can now be present within a community.

As Rivka Horwitz has demonstrated, large parts of the "Religion as Presence" lectures can be read as a rough draft for *I and Thou* (1923), Buber's most well-known work and the centerpiece of his dialogical philosophy. With this in mind, I turn now to *I and Thou* for a brief consideration of Buber's presentation of revelation as a form of dialogue.

The central argument of *I and Thou* is that human beings interact with others in the world within either instrumental I-It relationships or dialogical I-Thou encounters. While an I-It orientation is often necessary to support life and society, taking on an I-Thou orientation enriches human engagement with the world and lifts it above a purely animal existence. A second piece of this argument is that these two orientations toward the world are "word-pairs": dialogue for example is an I-Thou encounter, not a Thou encounter. The idea of word-pairs captures Buber's claim that the "I" is always constituted in relationship to an Other, whether that Other is used as an It or encountered as a Thou. My I is never alone but exists, from moment to moment, in orientation toward an It or toward a Thou. For Buber, there can be no solitary individual, for our way in the world will always be shaped by the presence of others and our interactions with them.

In the book's third and final section, Buber describes God as the Eternal Thou and revelation as a particular sort of I-Thou dialogue. As in the "Religion

---

13 Horwitz, *Buber's Way*, 106–7.
14 Horwitz, 121.

as Presence" lectures, the defining feature of revelation in *I and Thou* is the presence of God, here called the Eternal Thou. Buber insists that revelation has no content; God does not speak to human beings in human language. Revelation is instead divine presence:

> I do not believe in God's naming himself or in God's defining himself before man. The word of revelation is: I am there as whoever I am there. That which reveals is that which reveals. That which has being is there, nothing more. The eternal source of strength flows, the eternal touch is waiting, the eternal voice sounds, nothing more.[15]

Though Buber does not formally acknowledge it, this passage from *I and Thou* builds on Exodus 3:14 and the Hebrew phrase *ehyeh asher ehyeh*, "I will be who I will be" or "I am that I am" that appears therein.[16] These words are spoken by God in response to Moses' concern that the enslaved Israelites will ask the name of the deity who has all of a sudden arrived to redeem them. Here, in his unmarked reference to Exodus 3:14, Buber begins with "*Ich bin da als ich bin da*," which is a reasonable, more-or-less literal translation of the Hebrew. He then parses the phrase to define divine existence ("*Ich bin*," I am) as divine presence ("*da*," here). Divine language enacts that which it describes, and God's saying "*ehyeh asher ehyeh*" is God's presence.[17]

Buber's rendering of "*ehyeh asher ehyeh*" within his discussion of revelation in *I and Thou* allows him to imply subtly that his understanding of revelation has a biblical basis. But divine speech – substantive words issued by God or through a divine messenger in human language to human beings in their own particular situations – is an essential part of the biblical narrative and would seem to contradict Buber's insistence that God does not speak actual words to human beings. Within *I and Thou*, Buber does not address how revelation might have come to be recorded as the divine speech found in the Hebrew Bible. Ironically, Buber's reference to *ehyeh asher ehyeh*, though it is itself a citation of divine speech as recorded in the Hebrew Bible, serves to limit divine speech and deny it everywhere else it appears within the biblical text. Furthermore, by not acknowledging that he is drawing from the Hebrew Bible, Buber

---

15 Martin Buber, *I and Thou*, trans. Walter Kaufmann (New York: Scribner, 1970), 160; *Ich und Du*, 8th ed. (Heidelberg: Lambert Schneider, 1974), 132.
16 Robert Alter, *The Five Books of Moses: A Translation with Commentary* (New York: W.W. Norton, 2004), 321n14.
17 For a different perspective on Exodus 3:14 in German Jewish thought, see Francesca Albertini, "Èhyeh Asher Èhyeh: Ex 3, 14 According to the Interpretations of Moses Mendelssohn, Franz Rosenzweig, and Martin Buber," in *Jewish Studies at the Turn of the Twentieth Century*, ed. Judit Targarona Borrás and Angel Sáenz-Badillos (Boston: Brill, 1999), 19–26.

makes a claim about God that can be understood in terms that are less particularly Jewish than might be the case if he had acknowledged it.

In both *I and Thou* and the "Religion as Presence" lectures, what is revealed in revelation is that there is a revealer, i.e. that God is present. In the lectures, Buber uses distinctly sensual imagery to capture this sensing of divine presence:

> The voice, the eternal voice, becomes word through contact with the human being, with the surface of the human being that it touches, so to speak, with the skin, the ear, the living person that it touches. Through contact with the human being the voice becomes the Word; it becomes God's word. But only in the human being does the voice become a word of God, a word that speaks of God.[18]

Voice is the primary metaphor for revelation, while touch serves as a metaphor for the process that transforms the divine voice into Word. Stressing the multiplicity of religions that have existed over time, Buber writes of the "forms of God" created by human beings emerging from confrontation with God. Multiple forms of God reflect different encounters and motivate different religions; so long as human beings remain open, any religion might guide them anew into the encounter with God that is revelation.

The relationship between revelation and sacred text becomes pressing for Buber as he and Rosenzweig begin translating the Hebrew Bible into German in 1925. Over the next four years, until Rosenzweig's death in 1929, they make their way from Genesis through Psalms. (Buber later finishes the translation on his own in Jerusalem.) The translation work pushes Buber to read the text more carefully, with attention both to its language and grammar and to its theological message, and this change is reflected in his writings about the Bible from this time.

2 The Buber-Rosenzweig Translation (1925–1929)

Buber and Rosenzweig's translation of the Hebrew Bible relies upon a unique method of translation they devise based on literary principles they called cola and Leitworte, leading-words, both of which they consider to be essential features of the Hebrew text. A cola is a "breath unit," or the number of syllables that can be spoken aloud within the span of a breath. A Leitwort is "a word or word root that is meaningfully repeated within a text or sequence of texts

---

18 Horwitz, *Buber's Way*, 150.

or complex of texts; those who attend to these repetitions will find a meaning of the text revealed or clarified, or at any rate made more emphatic."[19] Together all the text's many Leitworte produce what Buber calls "the circulatory system of a great text."[20] Buber and Rosenzweig attempt to reproduce this feature of the biblical text by treating German as though it were Hebrew, namely, by identifying word-roots shared between related verbs and nouns. Each time a particular Hebrew word appears, Buber and Rosenzweig render it with the same German word. They insist as well that Hebrew words linked by a shared word-root be translated with German words that are similarly linked. At times, this works well; at other times, this principle of translation stretches the limits of the German language, forcing the creation of neologisms and even obscuring the meaning of the text. The words of the biblical text, of course, appear within particular verses and contexts that help to determine their meaning. While one appearance of a word might be well translated by a particular German word, it is not necessarily the case that the same German word will capture the word's contextual meaning elsewhere in the text. The translation that results from Buber and Rosenzweig's strict reproduction of the text's Leitworte is distinctly different from the standard German translation completed by Luther in the early 16th century. It was also distinctly different from translations by other German Jews in the modern period including Moses Mendelssohn and Leopold Zunz.[21]

"*Ich werde dasein, als der ich dasein werde.*" This is how Buber and Rosenzweig translate Exodus 3:14. It is Rosenzweig, not Buber, who writes about the particular choices they make in translating this verse, but his explanation is in line with Buber's thinking as we have seen it so far: "In the narrative context, then, the only justifiable translation is one that makes prominent not God's being eternal but his being present, his being present for and with you now

---

19 Martin Buber, "Leitwort Style in Pentateuch Narrative," in *Scripture and Translation*, trans. Lawrence Rosenwald and Everett Fox (Bloomington: Indiana University Press, 1994), 114; "Leitwortstil in der Erzählung des Pentateuchs," in *Die Schrift und ihre Verdeutschung* (Berlin: Schocken, 1936), 211.
20 Martin Buber, "Leitwort and Discourse Type: An Example," in *Scripture and Translation* (Bloomington: Indiana University Press, 1994), 150; "Das Leitwort Und Der Formtypus Der Rede," in *Die Schrift und ihre Verdeutschung* (Berlin: Schocken, 1936), 275.
21 On the phenomenon of Jews translating the Hebrew Bible into German, see Maren Ruth Niehoff, "The Buber-Rosenzweig Translation of the Bible within Jewish-German Tradition," *Journal of Jewish Studies* 44, no. 2 (1993): 258–79; W. Gunther Plaut, *German-Jewish Bible Translations: Linguistic Theology as a Political Phenomenon* (New York: Leo Baeck Institute, 1992); Naomi Seidman, *Faithful Renderings: Jewish-Christian Difference and the Politics of Translation* (Chicago: University of Chicago Press, 2006), 153–98; Abigaill Gillman, *A History of German Jewish Bible Translation* (Chicago: University of Chicago Press, 2018).

and in time to come."²² In Rosenzweig's defense of this translation, grammatical evidence ultimately serves a theological argument in line with Buber's account of revelation in both the "Religion as Presence" lectures and *I and Thou*, namely, that God is defined by presence. Rosenzweig presents divine presence not in contrast to divine speech, as Buber does, but in contrast to a more commonsense understanding of the verse as an indication of God's eternal nature.

Buber addresses biblical revelation in his 1926 essay "People Today and the Jewish Bible."²³ This essay expands beyond a discussion of the technicalities of the B-R translation into an account of the connection between revelation as an event and the record of God's words in the biblical text. This account also goes far beyond what we saw in Buber's earlier works and thus merits our careful attention here. In "People Today," Buber defines the central theme of the biblical text as "the encounter of a group of people with the Nameless Being whom they, hearing his speech and speaking to him in turn, ventured to name; their encounter with him in history, in the course of earthly events."²⁴ He presents the revelation at Sinai from Exodus 19 as an illustration of revelation. This episode raises several specific questions and issues. First and foremost, the Sinaitic revelation is a collective revelation: God appears before the Israelites to enter a covenant with them as a nation. How is this like or unlike Buber's description of revelation within the terms of I-Thou dialogue? Second, when the Israelites are overwhelmed by the divine presence, they send Moses as their emissary to receive the rest of God's message. What Moses delivers to them is commandments, which he presents as God's expectations of what the Israelites will do to uphold their side of the covenant. Because it is presented by Moses as part of the revelation, this extensive content poses a second major challenge to Buber's account of revelation as being specifically without content. Finally, in addition to this verbal content, the biblical account of the scene at Sinai includes extensive sensory imagery such as thunder, trumpets, fire, and smoke. This imagery – and the fear it engenders in the Israelites – poses a third challenge to Buber's definition of

---

22 Franz Rosenzweig, "'The Eternal': Mendelssohn and the Name of God," in *Scripture and Translation* (Bloomington: Indiana University Press, 1994), 105; "'Der Ewige,'" in *Die Schrift und ihre Verdeutschung* (Berlin: Schocken, 1936), 194.
23 The original title, "Der Mensch von Heute und die Jüdische Bibel," might also be translated as "The Man of Today and the Jewish Bible." But the German "mensch" is more gender neutral than "man" suggests, and I follow Everett Fox and Lawrence Rosenwald in referring to the essay as "People Today and the Jewish Bible." See Martin Buber, "People Today and the Jewish Bible," in *Scripture and Translation* (Bloomington: Indiana University Press, 1994), 4n1.
24 Buber, 4; "Der Mensch von Heute und die Jüdische Bibel," in *Die Schrift und ihre Verdeutschung* (Berlin: Schocken, 1936), 13.

revelation. Can revelation be accompanied by signs such as these? If so, are they necessary? If not, why does the text include them?

In "People Today," Buber describes the biblical account of revelation at Sinai as

> the verbal trace of a natural event, i.e., an event having occurred in the common sensory world of humankind and having fitted into its patterns, which the assemblage that experienced it experienced as God's revelation to it and so preserved it in the inspired and in no way arbitrary formative memory of generations.[25]

This description is multi-layered, describing both the text of Exodus – the "verbal trace" – and the event itself. In regard to the latter, Buber makes several points: first and foremost, whatever the revelation at Sinai was, it was not supernatural but happened within the ordinary world in which we continue to live. Second, the people present experienced this natural event as revelation. Because they experienced it in this way, they took extra efforts to record an account of it. The text that we have represents that attempt; it is inherently inadequate and, particularly as the authors suggest it was supernatural when it cannot have been, it should not be read as a literal or complete account. Nevertheless, despite its inadequacy, the Torah's account of Sinai offers a model of revelation as an intense event that demands response. It changed the lives of those who were there, and it plays an important role in the Jewish people's collective self-understanding.

In "People Today," Buber engages briefly with some of the commandments that appear within the biblical text as God's articulation of the covenant. But it is the building of the Ohel Mo'ed – the Tent of Meeting – that is commanded in Exodus 25 and then actualized in Exodus 36 that Buber presents as an illustration of the sort of action demanded by divine presence: "history at least is a dialogue. People learn to build [the Tent]; but their hands are not guided."[26] Buber develops this point through comparison of God's creation of the world in Genesis and the Israelites' construction of the Ohel Mo'ed in Exodus. In particular, and in line with the theory of Leitworte, Buber highlights repetition of the verb 'asah throughout the two passages and the verbs yaḥal and ra'ah at the conclusion of both the divine creation and the human construction. These Leitworte call the reader to examine these passages together; in the examination, the differences between them that emerge reveal a deeper meaning.

---

25 Buber, "People Today," 10; "Der Mensch von Heute," 25.
26 Buber, "People Today," 19; "Der Mensch von Heute," 42.

More specifically, Buber argues that the Leitworte shared between these two passages alert us to the differences between creation and revelation as two distinct epochs within the biblical conception of history. In creation, God's words are answered by the "dumb genesis of things"[27]; that is, God speaks and the things he names are created and appear. In the epoch of revelation – the epoch of human history – it is human beings, not things, that must respond, and they must do so with intention and purpose. In the case of the *Ohel Mo'ed* specifically, God's revelation calls for the tent and human beings respond by collecting the necessary materials, taking up their tools and creating the tent themselves. Buber argues that the *Ohel Mo'ed* illustrates more broadly that human response is a necessary element of revelation. This is in line with his discussion of revelation in *I and Thou* and his other earlier works, but at the same time the *Ohel Mo'ed* is by far the most specific and concrete example of response to revelation to be found in Buber's writings about the Bible up to this point.

As his discussion of the *Ohel Mo'ed* illustrates, Buber's translation work makes explicit the tension between his definition of revelation as divine presence and the claims of the biblical text to be a record of divine speech. But Buber does not retreat from his insistence that revelation in biblical times was no different from the revelations possible in other times and other places. He continues to argue that revelation and decisive response are possible and real for any human being at any time.

3 Commentaries

Buber's biblical commentaries provide a final case for our examination of his understanding of revelation. In *Kingship of God* (1933), *Prophetic Faith* (1942), and *Moses* (1945), Buber approaches the text with a methodology he calls Tradition Criticism. Though he does not directly reference German biblical scholar Hermann Gunkel, who developed the more standard version of Tradition Criticism, Buber's method overlaps with Gunkel's in important ways. In particular, Buber and Gunkel both assume that the text's stories and ideas record an earlier, oral tradition, and Buber reads the text as a collection of these oral traditions that was later written down rather than as a collection of disparate written sources redacted into a single whole. Beyond this, Buber relies upon the concept of

---

[27] Buber, "People Today," 19; "Der Mensch von Heute," 42.

Leitworte he developed while translating as a key for unlocking deeper meanings embedded in the written text.[28]

In line with his description of the text in "People Today," in his commentaries Buber reads the Bible as a record of encounters between the Israelites and God. He argues further that the written accounts of these events simultaneously represent stages in the development of a distinctive Israelite theology. Determining stages in the development of the human-divine relationship through particular historical events becomes the reader's primary challenge.

The central argument of *Kingship of God* is theo-political,[29] namely, that the Israelites understood God as king and that the Hebrew Bible preserves both the development of this theology and the efforts of the Israelites to realize it within the structure of their society. In seeking support for his argument from the Pentateuch in particular, Buber focuses on the name of God and illustrations of God's omnipresence, understanding both as departures from pagan beliefs that gods are located in specific places and can be summoned by name. *Ehyeh asher ehyeh*, Exodus 3:14, again serves as a locus point for Buber's discussion of divine presence and divine-human interaction in *Kingship of God*:

> The first *ehye* simply gives the assurance: I shall be there (ever and ever with My host, with My people, with you) – and thus you do not need to conjure me. And the following *asher ehye*, according to all parallels, can only mean: as I Who will always be there, as I ever and ever will be there, that is, as I ever and ever will want to appear.... In short: you do not need to conjure Me, but you cannot conjure Me either.[30]

Yet again, Buber uses the theophany at the burning bush to define revelation as divine presence rather than divine speech. His specification that divine presence need not be and cannot be summoned is intended to separate the one God of the Israelites from the multiple gods of the pagan traditions the Israelites were rejecting. These gods could indeed be conjured or summoned to respond to specific human needs. The God of the Israelites *is* presence and is thus *always present*. This is in line with Buber's account of revelation in *I and Thou* and also reflects Rosenzweig's grammatical argument in the context of the B-R translation.

---

28 For further consideration of Buber's hermeneutic method in his commentaries, see Claire Sufrin, "History, Myth, and Divine Dialogue in Martin Buber's Biblical Commentaries," *Jewish Quarterly Review* 103, no. 1 (2013): 74–100.

29 On Buber and theo-politics, see Samuel H. Brody, *Martin Buber's Theo-Politics* (Bloomington: Indiana University Press, 2018).

30 Martin Buber, *Kingship of God*, 3rd ed. (Amherst: Humanity Books, 1990), 106; *Königtum Gottes* (Berlin: Schocken, 1932), 84.

Buber's account of revelation as presence is of course complicated by the Bible's claim to be a record of the word of God. In *Moses*, the last of his commentaries, Buber traces the central events of the exodus from Egypt. In this account, Buber's discussion of *ehyeh asher ehyeh* is far more detailed than any of his earlier discussions of Exodus 3:14, as he takes care to understand the verse within the larger chapter in which it appears. He begins with Exodus 3:6, where God identifies himself as the "God of the Fathers" who was known to Abraham, Isaac and Jacob. Buber argues that connections between God, the ancestors, and the Israelites enslaved in Egypt is further underscored by the Leitworte *'ami* (my people) and *Mitsrayim* (Egypt). Using these Leitworte, Buber argues that God's connection to the ancestors is stronger than God's connection to the enslaved Israelites themselves, for the latter connection will only truly be established at Mount Sinai:

> With this repeated 'my people' [*'ami*] at the commencement and close of the passage, YHVH recognizes Israel in a fashion more powerful and unequivocal than would have been possible by any other verbal means. To be sure, he has not yet designated himself their God. He will become the God of Israel as a people solely through the revelation to the people; now he wishes to be known only as the God of their forefathers, to whom he had once promised the land whither he would lead Israel.[31]

Buber's emphasis on the connection between the God of the Fathers and the God speaking at the burning bush seems intended to build on his earlier arguments that *ehyeh asher ehyeh* represents a refutation of pagan traditions that associated gods with particular places. But more significantly for our inquiry, in this discussion Buber seems to suggest that God revealed a specific content to Moses, namely, the connection between this revealing God, the Israelites, and the Israelite forefathers.

As Buber's analysis of the burning bush encounter continues, he describes Moses and God's conversation as "the great [dialogue] in which the God commands and the man resists."[32] He then describes several moments in which God "states" something or makes a particular promise. But ultimately it is not clear whether Buber believes that God spoke specific words aloud for Moses to hear or if the words that the text ascribes to God were Moses' interpretation of his experience of revelation, as they would have to be within the model of rev-

---

31 Martin Buber, *Moses: The Revelation and the Covenant* (New York: Harper Torchbooks, 1957), 45–46; *Mosheh* (Jerusalem: Schocken, 1999), 68.
32 Buber, *Moses*, 46; *Mosheh*, 69.

elation as divine presence that runs through so much of his work. In his concluding statement on *ehyeh asher ehyeh*, Buber writes that the account

> does not belong to literature but to the sphere attained by the founders of religion. If it is theology, it is that archaic theology which, in the form of a historical narrative, stands at the threshold of every genuine historical religion. No matter who related that speech or when, he derived it from a tradition which, in the last resort, cannot go back to anybody other than the founder.[33]

Even if it was not Moses himself who recorded the words we have, by the nature of what they describe, we can be certain that they point to an actual event in his life and thus in history. At the same time, Moses is responsible for the content of the revelation. That is to say, even while we can be certain that something happened at the burning bush, we must give credit to Moses for his response, namely, the covenant he brings to the Israelites and its many theological implications. But the line between the revelation of divine presence and the human response is notably blurred in Buber's discussion of the event. Without the background of Buber's earlier discussions of revelation, it is possible, even likely, that the separation between the two would barely be noticed at all.

In discussing Moses in his commentaries, Buber occasionally even repeats the biblical language of "God said" to explain how the divine presence moved Moses to draw the tribes of Israel together through a covenant. I would suggest his slippage into this language reveals the power of speech as a model for interaction, an essential point of Buber's *I and Thou* and his emphasis there on the word-pairs that define human existence in the world from moment to moment. And, ultimately, whatever words Moses used to describe his encounter with God at the burning bush and whatever words the Israelites used to describe what happened at Sinai, that they chose to create a record serves to teach us too of divine presence and the possibility of encountering and responding to it.

---

33 Buber, *Moses*, 55; *Mosheh*, 78.

Volker Leppin
Luther and Mysticism
The Case of the Seebergs and Vogelsang

Whoever is interested in the question of Luther and mysticism is confronted with the distressing fact that this interest was shared by the Deutsche Christen; to see Luther as a mystic seems to have made him more agreeable for Nationalist Ideology. This also had consequences for Post World War research. Mainly in German Luther research, the question of a mystical Luther was politically infected and set aside. Only international researchers, such as Heiko Augustinus Oberman and his student Steven Ozment, brought it back onto the agenda of research, but it took a long while until an unburdened discussion about this topic was possible. Against this background, the following deliberations try to look for the forming of the question in the time of the Weimar republic to see the deeper roots of it, beginning before the Third Reich itself.

1 Luther and Mysticism: The Shaping of a Question in the 19th Century

To understand the debates on mysticism and Protestantism one has to take into account that the reception of Meister Eckhart in the 19th century, for a long while, had taken place in the context of the Hegel school: Eckhart, here, seems to prelude German idealism, and with this, protestant convictions. Ferdinand Christian Baur, for example contrasted the vital concept of God in mysticism to a hollow concept of God in scholasticism.[1] A more comprehensive image was depicted by Wilhelm Preger who wrote a history of mysticism: he also saw mysticism as a way to understand God more concretely than scholasticism did by the concept of the Holy Spirit,[2] which Preger interpreted as an "idea" in the sense of German idealism.[3] To show the protestant framework, Preger drew as a consequence that

---

[1] Ferdinand Christian Baur, *Die christliche Lehre von der Dreieinigkeit und Menschwerdung Gottes in ihrer geschichtlichen Entwicklung*, vol. 2, (Tübingen: Osiander, 1842), 885.
[2] Wilhelm Preger, *Geschichte der deutschen Mystik im Mittelalter: Nach den Quellen untersucht und dargestellt*, Geschichte der deutschen Mystik bis zum Tode Meister Eckhart's (Leipzig: Doerffling und Franke, 1874), 371.
[3] Preger, *Geschichte der deutschen Mystik*, 389.

mysticism stood in sharp contrast to "Roman hierarchy,"[4] and to do even more, he pointed out that Eckhart did not see any merit in good works,[5] so putting him in the line of protestant doctrine of justification: "So geht ein Geist evangelischer Freiheit durch Eckhart's Sittenlehre."[6]

As the Hegelian school saw in this way a strong connection between Protestantism and mysticism, not surprisingly Ritschl's critique against Baur and his school also affected the understanding of mysticism, even more inspired by his rejection of pietism: In the first volume of his *Geschichte des Pietismus*, published just six years after the first part of Preger's *Geschichte der Mystik* had appeared, Ritschl stated: mysticism is "...nur die prononcirte Stufe der katholischen Frömmigkeit."[7] The conclusion was: as far as pietism was mystical, it was catholic all the same. While Baur and Preger had seen mysticism as a kind of Protestantism before the Reformation, now, the line was drawn sharply between both, and this sharp line would remain in the following years. It seems as if Ritschl was directly attacking Preger's concept when he criticized the idea of mystical freedom as being evangelical:

> Die Freiheit ist nach Luther die geistige Beherrschung der Welt, welche aus der Versöhnung mit Gott oder der Rechtfertigung durch Christus dem Gläubigen zusteht, als eine Bestimmung, die er nur durch seine Zuversicht auf Gott auszuüben braucht. Die Freiheit des Mystikers ist die Abgezogenheit von der Welt, welche seiner Vereinigung mit Gott entspricht; denn Gott ist eigentlich nur die Verneinung der Welt.[8]

In contrast to all rhetorical as well as substantial critique the dialectical theology posted against Ritschl and his school, the negative assessment of mysticism was set forward, not with the identification of Catholicism and mysticism but rather, blaming Schleiermacher to be the founder of modern mysticism, as Emil Brunner did in his *Die Mystik und das Wort*.[9] Brunner could presuppose full convenience with Barth in this point. Critically, the Leipzig theologian Albrecht Oepke sum-

---

4 Preger, 449.
5 Preger, 451.
6 Preger, 452.
7 Albrecht Ritschl, *Geschichte des Pietismus*, Der Pietismus in der reformierten Kirche, vol. 1 (Bonn: Marcus, 1880; Berlin: de Gruyter, 1966), 28. For Ritschl's critique against mysticism see Wiberg Pedersen, "Mysticism in the Lutherrenaissance," 89.
8 Ritschl, *Geschichte des Pietismus*, Der Pietismus in der reformierten Kirche, vol. 2, 11.
9 Emil Brunner, *Die Mystik und das Wort*, Der Gegensatz zwischen moderner Religionsauffassung und christlichem Glauben dargestellt an der Theologie Schleiermachers (Tübingen: Mohr, 1924), cf. the revised edition, 1928.

marized in 1928: "Im Kampf gegen die Mystik sieht er [Barth] einen, vielleicht den wesentlichen Teil seiner Lebensaufgabe."[10]

Nevertheless, as it is well known, from here a dispute within the dialectical theologians arose, when Brunner in *Natur und Gnade*[11] tried to communicate with Barth about a necessary anthropological point of contact with God. In his: *Nein!*[12] Barth said what he had to say – and what is said in the title: Brunner himself, now, was seen as a mystic. So, the negative view on mysticism still was maintained, but the exponents of this kind of theology and piety changed.

In the following years, Barth in his *Kirchliche Dogmatik* developed this criticism: In 1938 he identified mysticism as the sister of atheism.[13] And in the second volume of the *Kirchliche Dogmatik*, he blamed the mystics for adoring a God without patience.[14] This meant: the mystical God was not able to be patient with a human being far from him, he wanted to identify God and human beings. With this, mysticism was not able to be accepted in the frame of a Biblical theology. One might think that with this Barth not only set forward the Ritschlian position, but that he more and more saw difficulties in the position of the Deutsche Christen and their appraisal of mysticism.

2 Luther and Tauler: The Discovery of Alphons Victor Müller

Obviously, against the Ritschl school and besides the dialectical theology, the Luther Renaissance worked out a different view on mysticism and Reformation which became quite important for the developments to be told here.[15] In the shadow of both movements, the Luther Renaissance as well as the dialectical

---

10 Albrecht Oepke, *Karl Barth und die Mystik* (Leipzig: Doerffling & Franke, 1928), 7. Actually, the aim of Oepke was to show, that nevertheless Barth's theology represented a special kind of mysticism (see ibid., 81).
11 Emil Brunner, *Natur und Gnade: Zum Gespräch mit Karl Barth* (Tübingen: Mohr, 1934).
12 Karl Barth, *Nein! Antwort an Emil Brunner*, Theologische Existenz Heute 14 (Munich: Kaiser, 1934).
13 Barth, "Die Lehre vom Wort Gottes," *Die Kirchliche Dogmatik*, vol. 1 (Zollikon: Verl. d. Evang. Buchh., 1938), 348 (§ 17).
14 Barth, *Die Kirchliche Dogmatik*, vol. 2, 460 (§ 30).
15 For my own view, please see Leppin, "Mystik und Neuzeit: Die Lutherinterpretationen der Holl-Schule in den theologischen Debatten der Weimarer Republik," in *Martin Luther. Monument, Ketzer, Mensch. Lutherbilder, Lutherprojektionen und ein ökumenischer Luther*, Leppin and Holzem, eds. (Freiburg: Herder, 2017), 269–291.

theology, a tiny study appeared which preluded insights into the close relationship of Luther and the late medieval mystic: *Luther und Tauler*, published by Alphons Victor Müller in 1918.[16] The author was an outsider in many respects: a former Catholic and Dominican who had converted in 1897, but still mainly lived as a journalist in Rome,[17] he fought against Heinrich Suso Denifle's Luther image alongside other protestants,[18] but he did it not by praising Luther's irreducible ingenuity, but by showing his roots in late medieval Dominican mysticism. He referred to Luther's annotations to the Tauler print of 1508, rediscovered in 1889 or 1890[19] and he stressed Luther's letter to Spalatin from December 14th 1516, in which Luther praised the doctrine of John Tauler.[20] Müller went through a lot of theological topics to show the close references between Luther and Tauler, but his main point was to show that Tauler had taught a pure Augustinism, and that he had done this in a practical way by means of sermons.[21] With the first idea, he directly referred to Preger,[22] showing that he tried to build a bridge over Ritschl and his successors to the 19th century appraisal of "mysticism". Müller blamed all theologians who divided Luther from Tauler of making Luther a "Neuerer" instead of an "Erneuerer", a newmaker instead of a renewer[23] – and, as Müller pointed out, this played into the hands of Denfile and Grisar who were be able to blame Luther for misinterpreting Tauler.[24]

With this position, Müller made himself counterpart to all Luther interpretations of his time, Catholic as well as Lutheran ones – and his small booklet published in 1918 soon was outflanked by Karl Holl's *Luther* from the year before. His special approach had not the power and even more not the fitting form to get a major impact. But it might present the deepest and most correct insights into the relationship between Luther and mysticism in his day.

---

16 Alphons Victor Müller, *Luther und Tauler auf ihren theologischen Zusammenhang neu untersucht* (Bern: Wyss, 1918).
17 See Christian Trapp, "Müller, Alphons Victor," in *Biographisch-bibliographisches Kirchenlexikon*, vol. 24, Friedrich Wilhelm Bautz and Traugott Bautz, eds. (Nordhausen: Bautz, 2005), 1113 – 1115.
18 Alphons Victor Müller, *Luthers theologische Quellen: Seine Verteidigung gegen Denifle und Grisar* (Gießen: Töpelmann, 1912).
19 Müller, *Luther und Tauler*, 15.
20 WA, B 1, 79; 30, 58 – 63; Müller, *Luther und Tauler*, 23.
21 Müller, *Luther und Tauler*, 24.
22 Müller, *Luther und Tauler*, 24.
23 Müller, *Luther und Tauler*, 28.
24 Müller, *Luther und Tauler*, 29.

3 Luther in His Medieval Setting: Reinhold Seeberg

The one who put Luther into his medieval setting anew was Reinhold Seeberg – not surprisingly in a theological context that was directed against Ritschl and Harnack and not yet against the dialectial theology. In his essay *Die religiösen Grundgedanken des jungen Luther und ihr Verhältnis zu dem Ockhamismus und der deutschen Mystik* from 1931, he directly attacked Albrecht Ritschl for denying any essential and lasting relationship of Luther to mysticism.[25] To him, Luther was influenced by Ockhamism as well as by mysticism.[26] The way to show this was more a typological than a philological one.[27] Seeberg did not look so much for direct reception of mystics by Luther, but for similar concepts which he could set into an overall view of history of mind. So, in his concept of mysticism, Tauler, whom Luther actually had read, played a minor role compared to Meister Eckhart.

However, more important than mysticism to Seeberg was Ockhamism here. He could argue that Luther's concept of the authority of scripture[28] as well as his concept of God[29] was based in late medieval scholasticism. Nevertheless, there were also some influences by mysticism: Seeberg pointed out that Luther's theology of the cross might be based in the central role of the cross in mysticism,[30] and even Luther's concept of faith should be inspired by mysticism,[31] while not fully dependent on it.

What makes Seeberg's approach interesting, now, for the understanding of the theology and *"Zeitgeist"* of the Weimar republic, is his combination of scholarly work and ideological framework. In contrast to most of his colleagues who saw in Heinrich Suso Denifle not more than the polemicist against Luther, Seeberg knew that Denifle had made known the Latin work of Eckhart to the scholarly world. This can be seen in his *Dogmengeschichte*. In 1930, the fourth edition

---

25 Reinhold Seeberg, *Die religiösen Grundgedanken des jungen Luther und ihr Verhältnis zu dem Ockhamismus und der deutschen Mystik*, Greifswalder Studien zur Lutherforschung und zur neuzeitlichen Geistesgeschichte 6 (Berlin: de Gruyter, 1931), 3.
26 Seeberg, *Grundgedanken*, 13.
27 Cf. Else Marie Wiberg Pedersen, "Mysticism in the Lutherrenaissance," in *Lutherrenaissance: Past and Present*, Christine Helmer and Bo Kristian Holm, eds., FKDG 106 (Göttingen: Vandenhoeck & Ruprecht, 2015), 95.
28 Seeberg, *Grundgedanken*, 15.
29 Seeberg, *Grundgedanken*, 16.
30 Seeberg, *Grundgedanken*, 21.
31 Seeberg, *Grundgedanken*, 30.

of the third volume, dedicated to the Middle Ages had been published. And here we find a description of mysticism, mainly focused on Eckhart. In it, Seeberg combined the German texts of Meister Eckhart with the Latin ones, not only those published by Denifle, but also the Paris Questions, just recently (1927) brought to light by Martin Grabmann.[32] This shows that Seeberg was absolutely outstanding compared to his protestant colleagues in receiving current medieval research which was still mainly Catholic.[33]

But this astonishing scholarly achievement is just one side of Seeberg's approach. The other can be seen in his nationalist concept of history of mind. Here, mysticism played a major role: In his essay mentioned above, Seeberg quoted Luther's statement in the preface to the edition of the complete *Theologia deutsch* in 1518, that "die Deutschen Theologen an zweyffel die beßten Theologen seyn."[34] This was not just an allusion, but a prelude to the consequence Seeberg drew at the end of the essay: however Luther might be influenced by scholasticism and mysticism, Seeberg stated here, he was a groundbreaking thinker whose achievement was to transform the theology of Paul into "die deutsche Denk- und Empfindungsweise."[35] Again, this was not just a secondary thought, but in his Dogmengeschichte Seeberg gave Luther a place in the history of Christendom as the one who had founded a new epoch of Christendom, forming Christianity in German mind. With this, as Seeberg had pointed out as early as the 1917 edition of volume 4 of his *Dogmengeschichte*, the Reformation might be a successor of Greek and Latin Christianity, but also a new step in their history.[36] This shows that the national framework for Luther interpretation was far

---

32 Martin Grabmann, *Neuaufgefundene Pariser Quaestionen Meister Eckhardts und ihre Stellung in seinem geistigen Entwicklungsgange: Untersuchungen und Texte*, Abhandlungen der Bayerischen Akademie der Wissenschaften – Philosophisch-philologische und historische Klasse 32/7, vol. 3 (Munich: Verlag der bayerischen Akademie der Wissenschaft, 1927), 679. These parts are fully revised and impressively extended compared to the 1913 edition (see Seeberg, *Lehrbuch der Dogmengeschichte*, Die Dogmenbildung des Mittelalters, vol. 3 (Leipzig: Deichert, ⁴1930 [= Darmstadt: Wiss. Buchges., 1959]), 597–599.
33 Actually, he was not the only one to notice the new discoveries, see Emanuel Hirsch's review to Grabmann's book in *ThLZ* 53 (1928): 41–44. Interestingly enough, Hirsch here states a "tiefe Nähe zum deutschen Idealismus," in Eckhart's Latin work (ibid., 44).
34 WA 1, 379, 11p; cf. Seeberg, *Grundgedanken*, 12.
35 Seeberg, *Grundgedanken*, 34.
36 Seeberg, *Lehrbuch der Dogmengeschichte*, vol. 4, bk. 1, 7, Die Entstehung des protestantischen Lehrbegriffs (Leipzig: Deichert, ²/³1917), 7. The same can be seen in the new 1933 context of the fourth edition (Leipzig: Deichert, ⁴1933 [= Darmstadt: Wiss. Buchges., 1974], 7).

older than the National Socialist ideology.³⁷ Reinhold Seeberg in terms of politics had always been a follower of the German national party.³⁸ So here, he combined his political option with his analysis of streams of the history of mind, showing that the combination of mysticism and national concepts was not just the result of National Socialist ideology, but somehow a presupposition of it.

4 Differences and Mystical Underlaying: Erich Seeberg

The combination of the issue "Luther and mysticism" with National Socialist ideology began with Reinhold Seeberg's son Erich Seeberg. One of his early works had dealt with mysticism in a quite critical way. In 1921, in an essay about *Zur Frage der Mystik*, Erich Seeberg analyzed mystical theologians form the 17ᵗʰ century. His result was to point out that mysticism was not a fundamental religious category – and he might have had Rudolf Otto's recently published book "*Das Heilige*" in mind, criticizing this conviction.³⁹ To him, mysticism was a universal anthropological endeavor to find unity, comparable to sexual appetite.⁴⁰ With this, mysticism was not fully set apart from religion, but its basis to Seeberg was different.

Later on, he had to find a more sophisticated way to deal with mysticism, when he wrote his comprehensive work on *Luthers Theologie* explicitly beholden to his father's work, but shaped to find his own paths.⁴¹ Published in 1929, the first volume was concentrated on the *Gottesanschauung*, the view of God. Seeberg here, tried to impose a peculiar methodological approach. He wanted to argue with "*Totalitäten*"⁴² which means, comparing Luther with others, he did

---

37 Nevertheless, Reinhold Seeberg in the Third Reich adapted national Socialist ideology into his thoughts; see Stefan Dietzel, *Reinhold Seeberg als Ethiker des Sozialprotestantismus: Die "Christliche Ethik" im Kontext ihrer Zeit* (Göttingen: Univ.-Verl., 2013), 203–257.
38 For his political position see Brakelmann, *Protestantische Kriegstheologie*; for the relationship between national political position and his idea of Christendom and nationalism see Michael Basse, *Die dogmengeschichtlichen Konzeptionen Adolf von Harnacks und Reinhold Seebergs*, FKDG 82 (Göttingen: Vandenhoeck und Ruprecht, 2001), 269.
39 Erich Seeberg, *Zur Frage der Mystik: Ein theologischer Vortrag* (Leipzig/Erlangen: Deichert, 1921), 42p; cf. Rudolf Otto, *Das Heilige: Über das Irrationale in der Idee des Göttlichen und sein Verhältnis zum Rationalen* (Breslau: Trewendt und Granier, 1917).
40 Seeberg, *Frage der Mystik*, 42.
41 Erich Seeberg, *Luthers Theologie: Motive und Ideen*, Die Gottesanschauung vol. 1 (Göttingen: Vandenhoeck und Ruprecht, 1929), 5*.
42 Seeberg, *Luthers Theologie: Motive und Ideen*, 5*.

not want to argue philologically in detail, but he wanted to compare systems of ideas. So, when he looked on Luther's relationship to Tauler, he compared system with system, *Gottesanschauung* with *Gottesanschauung*.

Tauler as seen by Seeberg, is completely based on the tradition of patristic dogma: the ground of the soul is a Trinitarian one, and the guide to it is no one else than Jesus Christ.[43] To get a clear picture of John Tauler, Seeberg stresses on the one hand that his ideas did not derive from philosophical questions, but from theological and ethical ones.[44] In this sense, Tauler is a pure theologian – but as a mystic nevertheless, he is quite different to Luther,[45] even if he comes close to him. The difference lay in both the understanding of God himself and the anthropology. Regarding the latter, Seeberg states that Tauler, however he might stress sin, even the original sin, can understand the encounter between God and the human being as an encounter between somehow equal entities.[46] It is precisely the Trinitarian ground in the inmost part of the human soul that establishes a divine basis in the human being. In his very core, the human being is godly. Seeberg sees here a logical problem of all mysticism. However the mystics enforce human beings to see themselves as pure nothing, there is a punctual rest of divine being in the ground of this nothing. Which means: "Die Mystik denkt von der Kreatur und nicht von der Sünde aus."[47] This causes, according to Seeberg, a fundamental difference to Luther's totus-anthropology: human beings are totally flesh, even including their mental parts, if they are not reigned over by God, while, the other way round, God's reign makes them totally spiritual.[48] So, what Seeberg sees as the main difference between Tauler and Luther, is the idea that there could be any creaturely basis within human beings making the human being adaptive for God.

The second problem, as said above, concerns the question of God himself. According to Seeberg, Tauler adopts a somehow neoplatonic model of God, who is not the hidden one who acts sub contrario as in Luther,[49] but he is the absolutely unknown, beyond all revelation[50] and without any properties.[51]

---

[43] Seeberg, *Luthers Theologie: Motive und Ideen*, 31.
[44] Seeberg, *Luthers Theologie: Motive und Ideen*, 41.
[45] Seeberg, *Luthers Theologie: Motive und Ideen*, 41.
[46] Seeberg, *Luthers Theologie: Motive und Ideen*, 48.
[47] Seeberg, *Luthers Theologie: Motive und Ideen*, 48.
[48] Seeberg, *Luthers Theologie: Motive und Ideen*, 48.
[49] Seeberg, *Luthers Theologie: Motive und Ideen*, 60; cf. Wiberg Pedersen, "Mysticism," 97.
[50] Seeberg, *Luthers Theologie: Motive und Ideen*, 61.
[51] Seeberg, *Luthers Theologie: Motive und Ideen*, 61.

So, the position Seeberg held in 1929 was highly sophisticated, but clear at the end: as close as Tauler came to Luther in some areas of thinking, he was far different from him in other, more important respects. Compared to this, his arguments were quite unclear once he reached the second volume of his theology which was published during the Third Reich, in 1937. Seeberg, now, was a famous member of the Deutsche Christen, and he did not hide this. In his preface, he mocked the Vandenhoeck publishers, "dem meine kirchenpolitische Stellung nicht gefiel" and who had given the advice to publish it with Kohlhammer's.[52] Indeed, now his position was quite clear to all – not only directly in questions of church politics, but also in terms of ideological influence of scholarship. He had entered the presidency of the commission for the edition of the works of Meister Eckhart – and had highly benefitted from the expulsion of Raymond Klibansky from the Third Reich. Klibansky had started an Eckhart edition under the auspices of the Heidelberg academy of sciences which now was replaced by the Seeberg enterprise.[53] And the new Eckhart edition now had no other publishers than Kohlhammer's!

The political context becomes even more obvious if one takes into account that Alfred Rosenberg, the National Socialist chief ideologist, in his *Mythus des 20. Jahrhunderts* had sketched the idea of a peculiar German religion based on his specific understanding of Meister Eckhart. There is no space here to outline Rosenberg's concept, so, a few words must be enough. Rosenberg took Eckhart as a thinker of the noble soul and its divinity. This concept, to Rosenberg means that the soul comes to a status where it does not need any grace anymore.[54] The theology of grace, to Rosenberg is a Pauline, not a Christian one,[55] and this means, it is Jewish influenced.[56] So, Rosenberg finds a "völkisches Bekenntnis"

---

52 Seeberg, *Luthers Theologie*, Christus, Wirklichkeit und Urbild, vol. 2 (Stuttgart: Kohlhammer, 1937 [= Darmstadt: Wiss. Buchges., 1969]), VIII. One might wonder, why in the German Republic in the late Sixties a book was reprinted unchanged with a sentence like this.

53 Ingeborg Degenhardt, *Studien zum Wandel des Eckhartbildes*, Studien zur Problemgeschichte der antiken und mittelalterlichen Philosophie 3 (Leiden: Brill, 1967), 295–297; Thomas Kaufmann, "'Anpassung' als historiographisches Konzept und als theologiepolitisches Programm: Der Kirchenhistoriker Erich Seeberg in der Zeit der Weimarer Republik und des 'Dritten Reiches,'" in *Evangelische Kirchenhistoriker im "Dritten Reich,"* Degenhardt and Oelke, eds., (Gütersloh: Kaiser, Gütersloher Verlagshaus, 2002), 123–272.

"'Anpassung'," 123–272, 193–196; cf. ibid., "Der Berliner Kirchenhistoriker," 216–243.

54 Alfred Rosenberg, *Der Mythus des 20. Jahrhunderts: Eine Wertung der seelisch-geistigen Gestaltenkämpfe unserer Zeit*, 91.–94. edition (Munich: Hoheneichen-Verlag, 1936), 237.

55 Rosenberg, *Mythus*, 235.

56 Rosenberg, *Mythus*, 235.

in Eckhart[57] and sees the founder of a new religion in him[58] who frees Christianity from the protestant sin to maintain the Old Testament.[59] The work is already done to show that Rosenberg's Eckhart has little or nothing to do with the historical one.[60] One of the reasons for this was that Rosenberg's image of Eckhart was just based on the distorted Eckhart translation of Hermann Büttner from the 19th century.[61] Now, Seeberg and the main editor, Josef Quint, went on to improve this edition with a new standard leading to the Eckhart edition which, nowadays, is still in progress. So, Seeberg could claim to act as a scholar on the one hand, as he did in his preface to the second volume of Luther's theology,[62] and on the other hand, he could assist the upcoming political adaption of Meister Eckhart, combined with Martin Luther.

Against this background one might understand why his statements about mysticism became quite less sophisticated and at the same time less distinct than in the first volume. One might even guess that the long lasting production of the second volume, with first preparatory work as early as in 1933, might be mirrored in different appraisals of mysticism in the work as published four years later. Here, Seeberg even came near to contrary assessments of mysticism. On the one hand, Seeberg stresses the differences that divide Luther from mysticism, pointing out, that we don't find a concept of imitation of Christ in the mystical shape of being dumped into Christ's passion itself.[63] Astonishing enough, in his chronological approach, Seeberg stated this difference as early as in the first chapter, devoted to the young Luther, before following him in the steps of Augustine and Paul. Even more, Seeberg seems to revoke this in the context of Luther's Augustinism. Here, he finds "den Gedanken der Nachfolge oder – besser – der mystischen Nachbildung Christi in unserer Seele."[64] However, in Seeberg's view, in the course of Luther's development the mystical parts become stronger, not weaker. Sure, he still holds the difference in the concept of God, stressing that the mystical concept of an unknown God is different to Luther's understanding of the hidden God,[65] but we might see in the second volume a far more positive view of Luther's relation-

---

57 Rosenberg, *Mythus*, 235.
58 Rosenberg, *Mythus*, 239.
59 Rosenberg, *Mythus*, 218.
60 Degenhardt, *Studien*, 261–74.
61 Degenhardt, *Studien*, 275.
62 Seeberg, *Luthers Theologie*, vol. 2, VII.
63 Seeberg, *Luthers Theologie*, vol. 2, 47.
64 Seeberg, *Luthers Theologie*, vol. 2, 91.
65 Seeberg, *Luthers Theologie*, vol. 2, 63.

ship to mysticism than before. Obviously, the ideological context in the National Socialist reign had influenced this view.

5 Erich Vogelsang: A Case of "*Anpassung*"

For generations, the most influential thinker on Luther and mysticism was Erich Vogelsang. His essay on Luther and mysticism[66] shaped the framework for scholarly research about this issue until the beginning of our millennium[67] – despite the fact that it was published during the Third Reich in 1937 and that its author used to be a member of the SA. Even more, one might argue that Vogelsang developed his positive evaluation of the relation between what he called "*Deutsche Mystik*" and Martin Luther, in answer to and in agreement with National socialist ideology.

Actually, at the beginning of his career, the question of Luther and mysticism was present in his work, but mainly he stressed the difference between both. In his dissertation on Christology in Luther's first lecture on the Psalms, Vogelsang remarks that Luther quoted authors like John Gerson or Bernard of Clairvaux[68] – but, as Vogelsang pointed out in this book published in 1929, Luther differed from them stressing faith as a core category of connection between the believer and God.[69] This position was not changed in Vogelsang's *Habilitationsschrift* about the "*angefochtene Christus*", which at least partly was published three years later.[70] Obviously, the term "*Anfechtung*", temptation, led to reflections about mysticism. So, he integrated a short excursus about the question of mystical background of Luther's theology, concentrated on Tauler and *Theologia deutsch*. Actually, at this moment, Vogelsang had no specific interest nor a specific concept of mysticism: in another excursus on scholasticism, he refer-

---

66 Erich Vogelsang, "Luther und die Mystik," *Luther-Jahrbuch* 19 (1937), 32–54.
67 See Karl-Heinz zur Mühlen, "Mystische Erfahrung und Wort Gottes bei Martin Luther," in *Mystik: Religion der Zukunft – Zukunft der Religion?*, Johannes Schilling, edition (Leipzig: Evangelische Verlagsanstalt, 2003), 45–66.
68 Erich Vogelsang, *Die Anfänge von Luthers Christologie nach der ersten Psalmenvorlesung insbesondere in ihren exegetischen und systematischen Zusammenhängen mit Augustin und der Scholastik dargestellt*, AKG 15 (Berlin/Leipzig: de Gruyter, 1929), 66.
69 Vogelsang, *Anfänge*, 74–76.
70 Erich Vogelsang, *Der angefochtene Christus bei Luther*, AKG 21 (Berlin/Leipzig: de Gruyter, 1932). Ohst, "Lutherdeutungen," 19–50, 46, shows the aim of this book to present a Christology that is fully able to take in account the humankind of Jesus Christ. (Martin Ohst, "Die Lutherdeutungen Karl Holls und seiner Schüler Emanuel Hirsch und Erich Vogelsang vor dem Hintergrund der Lutherdeutung Albrecht Ritschls," in *Lutherforschung im 20. Jahrhundert: Rückblick – Bilanz – Ausblick*, Rainer Vinke, edition [Mainz: Zabern, 2004], 19–50).

red to a passage in Luther's table talks: "Solus Gerson scripsit de tentatione spiritus, alii omnes tantum corporales senserunt, Ieronimus, Augustinus, Ambrosius, Bernhardus, Scotus, Thomas, Richardus, Occa; nullus illorum sensit, solus Gerson de pusillanimitate spiritus scripsit. (…) Sed scholastici doctores nunquam pervenerunt ad catechismi cognitionem."[71]

Strange enough, among all those scholastics, Luther himself mentions Bernard of Clairvaux – whom in other passages he used to estimate very much. However, Vogelsang just implicitly corrected this confusion, speaking of "Scholastik wie (…) Augustin und Bernhard," differing the latter from the group of scholastics. But he did not insist on this distinction.

Interestingly enough, in Vogelsang, we find a reception of Alphons Viktor Müller,[72] whose concentration on John Tauler was fitting to Vogelsang's aim. For his concept, he did not need Bernard or even Gerson: the excursus on mysticism mentioned above just spoke about Tauler and *Theologia deutsch* – and clearly denied any connection in terms of dependency. Vogelsangs's arguments here were two:

- First, he argued, based on his dissertation, that the beginning of seemingly mystical thoughts – especially concerning the special understanding of hell and purgatory – could be found as early as in Luther's first lecture on the Psalms.[73] This argument in itself shows that Vogelsang reduced mysticism to the so called German, or as one nowadays would better say: Rhenish mysticism. He himself had shown in his dissertation that Luther knew Bernard and Gerson in 1513, who could have been possible mystic authorities.
- Second, and this seems more convincing, Vogelsang argued with a passage in Luther's *Resolutiones*, where Luther spoke about the fear in the soul as the purgatory itself. Here, in explanation of thesis 15, Luther first gave a number of quotations of Psalms, and then spoke about John Tauler's German sermons as a witness of this.[74] For Vogelsang, this is an expression of intellectual development, because in the next passage, Luther speaks about himself and his Reformation breakthrough.[75] Nevertheless, the argument must not be seen as cogent, as one might understand the succession of arguments not as a chronological report, but as a list following the weight of argu-

---

71 WA, TR 2, 64, 22–29: no. 1351); cf. Vogelsang, *Der angefochtene Christus*, 12.
72 Vogelsang, *Der angefochtene Christus*, 40n39.
73 Vogelsang, *Der angefochtene Christus*, 41.
74 Vogelsang, *Der angefochtene Christus*, 41.
75 Vogelsang, *Der angefochtene Christus*, 41n42, referring to WA 1, 557, 33–35. Vogelsang here speaks about "das bekannte große Selbstzeugnis," obviously referring to and criticizing Stracke, *Luthers Großes Selbstzeugnis*, which had been published just six years ago.

ments, particularly since the recollection of psalms is just the fourth point in Luther's list, which starts with a referral to the consensus of *"omnes."*[76]

However one might evaluate Vogelsang's arguments, both of them show that he looks to make Luther independent of mysticism – Tauler and *Theologia deutsch* just gave a confirmation of ideas he had developed earlier by the Bible itself.

Nevertheless, Vogelsang admitted a certain connaturality ("gewisse Verwandtschaft")[77] between mysticism and Luther, which cannot be understood in terms of dependence, but in terms of resemblance. According to Vogelsang, this can be found in the idea of a non local concept of hell, but it is associated with a clear difference given first in the central role Luther gave to the Word of God in his theology,[78] and second, in anthropology.[79] While the mystics believed in a residue of the divine in human beings, called the *funkelîn*, Luther emphasized the difference between the human and the divine.[80]

As early as 1932, one sees Erich Vogelsang as a scholar who puts philological and theological reflections like these into a setting of the contemporary *"Zeitgeist"*. Even if he in his preface claimed to argue purely historically,[81] in his wording can be seen the horizon of the twenties. When he defined temptation as "ein Lebensbegriff, kein Lehrbegriff,"[82] he alluded to the *"Lebensreformbewegung"* as an important part of the mentality in the Weimar Republic, preferring affective concepts of life against rationality in its intellectual, cultural and economic dimensions, and he gave an elitist shape to this when he picked up the widespread distinction of "individual human being" and "the mass" and spoke about the *"Mensch der Masse"* who would never be able to understand the deepness of being.[83] With the term of being, *"Dasein"*, another kind of terminology is reached. Vogelsang also played with Heideggerian vocabulary, not only when he spoke about being and being like this ("Dasein und Sosein"),[84] but even more, when he defined life as a "life to death," a "Leben zum Tode."[85] It seems, as if Vogel-

---

76 WA 1,556,8.
77 Vogelsang, *Der angefochtene Christus*, 41.
78 Vogelsang, *Der angefochtene Christus*, 42.
79 See Steven Edgar Ozment, *Homo spiritualis: A comparative study of the anthropology of Johannes Tauler, Jean Gerson and Martin Luther in the Context of their theological thought*, Studies in Medieval and Reformation Thought 6 (Leiden: Brill, 1969).
80 Vogelsang, *Der angefochtene Christus*, 42.
81 Vogelsang, *Der angefochtene Christus*, 4.
82 Vogelsang, *Der angefochtene Christus*, 4.
83 Vogelsang, *Der angefochtene Christus*, 7.
84 Vogelsang, *Der angefochtene Christus*, 18.
85 Vogelsang, *Der angefochtene Christus*, 18.

sang's claim not to reshape Luther's thinking by modern philosophical concepts was not conducive for all of his reflections.

These observations might be a hint to a basic line of Vogelsang's work. While arguing historically, his construction of Luther's theology was highly adaptive to the Zeitgeist – and this showed problematic effects in the time of the Third Reich. Still in 1934, Vogelsang saw a huge difference between mysticism and Christendom.[86] But at the same time, he started re-thinking the phenomenon of mysticism, and quite openly, he referred to Alfred Rosenberg, mentioned above, as his inspiration in reflecting on the question of mysticism anew. In a footnote he wrote:

> Ich kann hier weder auf Rosenbergs Eckhart-Deutung noch auf das weitschichtige Problem der 'Deutschen Mystik' eingehen. Die Frage nach dem deutschen Charakter bekommt m. E. erst dann ihr Gewicht, wenn man nicht nur wie Denifle Eckharts Abhängigkeit von der Scholastik kennt (ohne sie zu übertreiben), sondern auch Dionysios Areopagita, Avicenna und Augustin einbezieht und nun versucht herauszustellen, was die deutsche Mystik von der indischen, christlichen, spätjüdischen, areopagitischen usw. unterscheidet.[87]

In contrast to the defiance of finer differences in the understanding of mysticism as seen above, here Vogelsang argued with a special typology of mysticism that basically was an ethnic or national one. This was the starting point for his interpretation of Luther and mysticism as explained in the 1937 essay in the *Luther Jahrbuch*. Here, the typological approach was used to argue for a positive relationship between Luther and mysticism, which obviously expresses a quite different view compared to *Der angefochtene Christus*, not just concerning the overall question of Luther and mysticism, but also his relationship to peculiar mystics or other theologians.

Vogelsang now distinguishes Aeropagite, Roman and German mysticism and declares: "zu der areopagitischen fand er [i. e. Luther; V.L.] ein schroffes Nein, zu der romanischen stets ein Ja und Nein, zu der Deutschen ein fast reines Ja."[88] This seems to be astonishing. While the excursus about mysticism in *Der angefochtene Christus* had the aim mainly to show differences between Luther and the Rhenish or German mysticism, now, for Vogelsang, there was an almost pure affirmation of them in Luther. And while in *Der angefochtene Christus* the excursus on Luther and scholasticism had distinguished between Gerson on

---

86 Erich Vogelsang, *Umbruch des deutschen Glaubens: Von Ragnarök zu Christus* (Tübingen: Mohr, 1934), 13.
87 Vogelsang, *Umbruch*, 71n76.
88 Vogelsang, "Luther und die Mystik," 33. The difference between "Romanic" and "German" mysticism is made by the same points, Vogelsang pointed out in his book on *Anfechtung*: Bernard just knew the carnal temptation, not the spiritual one (ibid., 40).

the one side, and the Scholastics together with Augustine and Bernard on the other side, now Vogelsang dissimulated this insight. Among the mystics Luther knew, he mentions Gerson,[89] but when he shaped his typology, he skipped this name. Obviously, Gerson could not be part of the German mysticism, but among the Roman mystics Vogelsang only mentioned Bernard, Bonaventure and Hugh of Saint Victor.[90] There was no longer a place for Gerson, as he did not fit into the idea of a Luther based in German mystical traditions.

One cannot avoid the consequence: it is Vogelsang's reading of Rosenberg that made him aware of differences within mysticism and made him able to develop a more complex idea of it. This, without a doubt, is a scholarly process, but at the same time it is also a process of "*Anpassung*," adaptation to National Socialist ideology, as at the end, Vogelsang has the result that Luther is part of the "*Deutsche Mystik*" which was favored by Rosenberg as a basis of National Socialist ideology. So, in this way, Luther was made acceptable in the context under the regime of the Third Reich.

At the same time, Vogelsang made boundaries clear to other theological options. Already in the 1937 essay, one might see in the formulation of "Ja" and "Nein" an allusion to Barth's famous essay against Brunner, called *Nein*.[91] While Reinhold Seeberg had held his positive image of mysticism against Ritschl, now the dialectical Theology came into the focus, obviously for reasons of church politics. This confrontation became more explicit one year later in an essay on *unio mystica* in Luther in the *Archiv für Reformationsgeschichte*. Here, he made clear, that Karl Barth was his target:[92]

> Daß Karl Barth mit der Erneuerung der melanchthonischen rein forensischen Rechtfertigung und der ganz unreformatorischen eschatologischen Auffassung der Heiligung der abgesagte Feind jeglicher unio mystica ist, verwundert nicht.[93]

---

89 Vogelsang, "Luther und Mystik," 32.
90 Vogelsang, "Luther und Mystik," 33. Obviously, Vogelsang knew about this lack of argumentation. So he gave just a short footnote to his report on romanic mysticism: "Über Gersons Sonderstellung vgl. E. Vogelsang, Der angefochtene Christus bei Luther (1932), S. 15 Anm. 56; W. Dreß, Die Theologie Gersons (1931) S. 141 ff., 166 ff." (Vogelsang, "Luther und Mystik," 40n2): Following this footnote one could find his differing reconstruction, mainly based on Gerson, but he did not allow Gerson to destroy his ethnical construction made in 1937.
91 Barth, *Nein*.
92 Erich Vogelsang, "Die unio mystica bei Luther," Archiv für Reformationsgeschichte 35 (1938), 65.
93 Vogelsang, "Die unio mystica," 65.

Vogelsang blamed Karl Barth for introducing Melanchthonian thinking into Protestantism, and at the same time, he praised Brunner for coming back to insights about Luther's mysticism.[94] This meant, alternately: coming back to Luther against Melanchthon and Barth's Calvinism would mean to come back to mystical roots.

Actually, implicitly with this, Vogelsang revoked, or at least reshaped, his own earlier convictions about a sharp distinction between Luther and mysticism. Clearly, for Barth, it was the anthropology that made human beings unable to unite with God. The anthropology of sin distinguished the Reformation from mysticism – and this, exactly had been the position of Vogelsang in his *Der angefochtene Christus*. It was Vogelsang, who had changed his mind on this point, and as we have seen, he did this following Rosenberg and dissimulating earlier scholarly insights. So, both, intellectual as well as ideological development had deepened the gap between Vogelsang and dialectical theology by means of mysticism.

6 Conclusion

The fact that an understanding of Luther against mystical background was favored by the Deutsche Christen remains challenging. The development of research, as shown above, might give an understanding of the dense interaction between scholarly work and ideological adaptation. This is seen even in the generation of Reinhold Seeberg, who obviously had developed his ideas before National Socialism arose.

The following generation dealt with Nationalist Socialist ideas, and both thinkers examined above did this with obvious sympathies for the National Socialist ideology. So, in both, we can observe a complicated mixture of scholarly interest and political. Vogelsang, even more than Seeberg, developed his ideas further, mainly under the influence of Rosenberg. Nevertheless, both wanted to maintain their scholarly respectability. This made their ideas compatible even for research after the Second World War. Seeberg's works were reprinted in the early German Federal Republic, and Vogelsangs's essay on Luther and mysticism was still received as an authority in recent years. It is a duty today to discern between research and ideology in their work.

---

94 Vogelsang, "Die unio mystica," 65.

David W. Congdon
Desperatio Fiducialis
Barth and Bultmann on the Anthropological Significance of Revelation

1 Barth, Bultmann, and the Early Luther

Scholars frequently analyze the divergence between Karl Barth and Rudolf Bultmann in terms of their theological traditions – Reformed and Lutheran, respectively – and for good reason, since Barth himself frames their differences in these terms. In his 1952 "attempt to understand him," Barth considers whether Bultmann is best understood as an apologist, historian, or philosopher before finally proposing that "the nearest solution will be that Bultmann is simply a Lutheran – *sui generis*, of course!" Barth sees Bultmann's ethics as cohering well with the Lutheran doctrine of the two kingdoms and warns that "those who throw stones at Bultmann should be careful lest they accidentally hit Luther, who is also hovering somewhere in the background."[1] Eberhard Jüngel furthers this line of thinking when he connects Bultmann's concept of paradoxical identity with the Lutheran *est* and argues that "what finally separates Barth from Bultmann is the same reservation which Barth also has towards Luther's teaching on the Lord's Supper."[2] Christophe Chalamet pushes this further still by arguing that each develops a confessionally different approach to dialectical theology: Bultmann with a Lutheran Law-Gospel dialectic and Barth with a Reformed Gospel-Law dialectic.[3] The distinction between Barth and Bultmann along confessional lines has much to commend itself as an explanation of their later disagreements, but it has the disadvantage of oversimplifying Lutheran thought

---

1 Karl Barth, *Rudolf Bultmann: Ein Versuch, ihn zu verstehen* (Zollikon-Zürich: Evangelischer Verlag, 1952), 46–48; ET: Karl Barth, "Rudolf Bultmann – An Attempt to Understand Him," in *Kerygma and Myth: A Theological Debate*, vol. 2, ed. Hans-Werner Bartsch (London: S.P.C.K., 1962), 121–23. Barth indicates that this is his guiding thesis toward the start of his essay, where he says "perhaps we should call him in all essentials a Lutheran, though, of course, a Lutheran *sui generis*, and on a higher plane!" (Barth, *Rudolf Bultmann*, 10; ET, 90).
2 Eberhard Jüngel, *God's Being Is in Becoming: The Trinitarian Being of God in the Theology of Karl Barth. A Paraphrase*, trans. John Webster (Edinburgh: T&T Clark, 2001), 74.
3 See Christophe Chalamet, *Dialectical Theologians: Wilhelm Herrmann, Karl Barth and Rudolf Bultmann* (Zürich: TVZ, 2005), 195–97.

and thereby missing the Lutheran aspects of Barth's own theology, particularly in his early dialectical years. Chalamet, for instance, suggests that "since the events of 1914, perhaps without fully realizing it, Barth had already 'become who he was', namely a Reformed theologian,"⁴ and as true as this may be in certain respects we should not overlook the fact that in 1921 Barth told Martin Rade that "I have recently been moving rapidly towards Lutheranism in more than one aspect."⁵

There is another way of understanding Barth and Bultmann, namely, as representing two different trajectories *internal* to Lutheran theology. One way to illustrate this is by looking at the way each develops a different insight from the writings of the early Luther. Bultmann rarely cited Luther directly, but one of the few passages he quoted repeatedly is a line from Luther's *scholia* in his 1515–1516 *Lectures on Romans*: "And so God, in going out of himself, brings it about that we go into ourselves, and through knowledge of him he brings us to knowledge of ourselves" (*Et ita Deus per suum exire nos facit ad nos ipsos introire et per sui cognitionem infert nobis et nostri cognitionem*).⁶ These lectures, published in 1908 and edited by Johannes Ficker, formed a key basis for the Luther Renaissance that emerged during the Weimar period in response to the quadricentennial of the Reformation. While it is hard to say when Bultmann actually read the *scholia*, he first quotes this line in his 1927 essay on "The Concept of Revelation in the New Testament," and in the citation he includes a reference to Barth's 1927 *Die christliche Dogmatik im Entwurf* to complement Luther.⁷ In

---

4 Chalamet, 96.
5 Karl Barth to Martin Rade, 31 January 1921, in Karl Barth and Martin Rade, *Karl Barth – Martin Rade: Ein Briefwechsel*, ed. Christoph Schwöbel (Gütersloh: Gütersloher Verlagshaus, 1981), 154.
6 WA, 56:229.20–22, *scholion* on Rom 3:5. Bultmann was possibly referring to the first interpretation of this text in the Luther Renaissance by Rudolf Hermann in "Das Verhältnis von Rechtfertigung und Gebet nach Luthers Auslegung von Röm. 3 in der Römerbriefvorlesung [1926]" in *Gesammelte Studien zur Theologie Luthers und der Reformation* (Göttingen: Vandenhoeck & Ruprecht, 1960), 11–43.
7 Rudolf Bultmann, *Der Begriff der Offenbarung im Neuen Testament* (Tübingen: Mohr, 1929), 38, 48n11. Reprinted in Rudolf Bultmann, "Der Begriff der Offenbarung im Neuen Testament [1929]," in *Glauben und Verstehen: Gesammelte Aufsätze*, 4 vols. (Tübingen: Mohr, 1933–1965), 3:1–34, at 29; hereafter *Glauben und Verstehen* (*GuV*). Future references to Bultmann's essay will be to the *GuV* version. See Karl Barth, *Die christliche Dogmatik im Entwurf*, ed. Gerhard Sauter, Gesamtausgabe 2.14 (Zürich: Theologischer Verlag, 1982), 516. Bultmann originally wrote the lecture in 1927 in preparation to present at the spring holiday course held by the Marburg theological faculty each year in coordination with the Hessian pastorate, which was to occur that year on April 19–21. He apparently expected it to be a comedic event, since he told both Heidegger and Gogarten that it would likely be a "satyr play." He tells Gogarten that, because he will be presenting first, "I will throw some sticks between the legs of the following speakers." See Rudolf Bultmann

1935 he quotes the phrase "through knowledge of him he brings us to knowledge of ourselves" in a letter to Barth himself, but by this time he recognizes it no longer represents Barth's own theology. Bultmann in fact acknowledges that Barth will likely "smell heresy" in his *Glauben und Verstehen*.[8] He uses Luther's statement two further times: in his 1940 essay on "The Question of Natural Revelation" (which Bultmann originally published in 1941 with the programmatic lecture on demythologizing, "New Testament and Mythology") and in the 1952 response to his critics, "On the Problem of Demythologizing."[9]

Barth, by contrast, latches on to a different statement from Luther. On 8 April 1516, at the same time he was giving his *Lectures on Romans*, Luther wrote a letter to Georg Spenlein, an Augustinian friar at the Memmingen monastery. While the letter is most famous for Luther's line that "Christ dwells only in sinners," Barth picked up on a statement a few lines later in which Luther concludes: "Therefore you will only find peace in him [i.e., Christ] through a confident despair in yourself and your works" (*Igitur non nisi in illo, per fiducialem desperationem tui et operum tuorum, pacem invenies*).[10] The phrase "confident despair" (*desperatio fiducialis*) – translated into German as "getroste Verzweiflung" – appears roughly twenty times in Barth's writings between 1920 and 1953.[11] Barth

---

to Friedrich Gogarten, 3 April 1927, in Rudolf Bultmann and Friedrich Gogarten, *Briefwechsel 1921–1967*, ed. Hermann Götz Göckeritz (Tübingen: Mohr Siebeck, 2002), 105; Rudolf Bultmann to Martin Heidegger, 3 April 1927, in Rudolf Bultmann and Martin Heidegger, *Briefwechsel 1925–1975*, ed. Andreas Grossmann and Christof Landmesser (Tübingen: Mohr Siebeck, 2009), 28. Unfortunately, it was cancelled at the last minute because there were only ten registrants (Bultmann to Heidegger, 18 April 1927, in ibid., 31). Bultmann instead gave the lecture at the following year's holiday course on 12 April 1928 (Bultmann to Heidegger, 11 April 1928, in ibid., 60). He gave the lecture again on October 9 at the holiday course in Malente, held on 9–12 October 1928 (Bultmann to Heidegger, 29 October 1928, in ibid., 73n7).

8 Rudolf Bultmann to Karl Barth, 10 December 1935, in Karl Barth and Rudolf Bultmann, *Briefwechsel 1911–1966*, ed. Bernd Jaspert, 2nd ed., Gesamtausgabe 5.1 (Zürich: TVZ, 1994), 161.

9 See Rudolf Bultmann, "Die Frage der natürlichen Offenbarung," in *GuV*, 2:79–104, at 99; cf. Rudolf Bultmann, *Offenbarung und Heilsgeschehen* (Munich: A. Lempp, 1941). See Rudolf Bultmann, "Zum Problem der Entmythologisierung," in *Kerygma und Mythos, Band II: Diskussion und Stimmen zum Problem der Entmythologisierung*, ed. Hans-Werner Bartsch (Hamburg-Volksdorf: H. Reich, 1952), 179–208, at 200.

10 Martin Luther, *Briefwechsel*, 18 vols., Martin Luthers Werke, Kritische Gesamtausgabe (Weimar: H. Böhlaus Nachfolger, 1930–1985), 1:36.33–34. Cf. Martin Luther, *Dr. Martin Luther's Briefwechsel*, ed. Ernst Ludwig Enders, 18 vols., Martin Luther's sämmtliche Werke in beiden Originalsprachen (Frankfurt am Main: Schriften-Niederlage des Evangel. Vereins, 1884–1923), 1:29.46–48.

11 Barth uses the translation of Martin Rade and others in Martin Luther, *Luthers Werke für das christliche Haus*, ed. Georg Buchwald, et al., 8 vols. (Braunschweig: C. A. Schwetschke, 1889–1892), 8:313–14. Interestingly, in his 1749 edition of Luther's letters, Johann Georg Walch (mis)translates "per fiducialem desperationem" as "durch völlige Verzweiflung," replacing "confi-

first used the phrase as the title of a sermon on 20 June 1920, while he was in the midst of refining his new theology and about to revise his Romans commentary.[12] Barth's sermon on Reformation Sunday that year (November 7) was an extended reflection on the letter and quoted at length from it. In the sermon he says that the Reformation is an attempt to answer the question, "How does one start to become a Christian?," or more generally, "How does one become a true, living human being?"[13] Both Paul and Luther, he says, answer this question by first acknowledging who we are, namely, "a lost and damned sinner, incapable of good, handed over to death and worthy of death."[14] For this reason our only hope is "*Christ, the crucified one*," who "*dwelled among sinners* in the deepest affliction" and thereby shows us that we are "*saved* by God, *held* by God, *belong* to God." It is in this context that Barth refers to the "confident despair" that points us away from ourselves to Christ, in whom we hear God's yes to us.[15] If there is any consistent theme throughout the entirety of Barth's dialectical theology, it is this pointing away from ourselves to God's action in Christ. Luther's "getroste Verzweiflung" appears subsequently in numerous writings: a letter to Eduard Thurneysen on 27 July 1921; the second edition of *Der Römerbrief*; his dispute with Paul Althaus in 1922 over Christian social ethics; his 1922 essay on "The Problem of Ethics in the Present Situation"; the 1927 *Die christliche Dogmatik im Entwurf*; the Münster *Ethik* of 1928–1929; and finally *Die kirchliche Dogmatik* I/2 and IV/1.[16]

---

dent despair" with "complete despair." See Martin Luther, *Dr. Martin Luthers Sämmtliche Schriften (1740–1753)*, ed. Johann Georg Walch, 23 vols. (St. Louis: Concordia Publishing House, 1880–1910), 21.1:21.
12 See Karl Barth, *Predigten 1920*, ed. Hermann Schmidt, Gesamtausgabe 1.42 (Zürich: TVZ, 2005), 224–35.
13 Barth, 369.
14 Barth, 371.
15 Barth, 373–74. Emphasis in original unless otherwise noted.
16 See Karl Barth to Eduard Thurneysen, 27 July 1921, in Karl Barth and Eduard Thurneysen, *Briefwechsel, Band I: 1913–1921*, ed. Eduard Thurneysen, Gesamtausgabe 5.3 (Zürich: TVZ, 1973), 506; Karl Barth, *Der Römerbrief (Zweite Fassung) 1922*, ed. Cornelis van der Kooi and Katja Tolstaja, Gesamtausgabe 2.47 (Zürich: TVZ, 2010), 61; Karl Barth, "Grundfragen der christlichen Sozialethik: Auseinandersetzung mit Paul Althaus (1922)," in *Vorträge und kleinere Arbeiten 1922–1925*, ed. Holger Finze (Zürich: TVZ, 1990), 39–57, at 47–48; Karl Barth, "Das Problem der Ethik in der Gegenwart (1922)," in *Vorträge und kleinere Arbeiten 1922–1925*, ed. Holger Finze (Zürich: TVZ, 1990), 98–143, at 140; Barth, *Die christliche Dogmatik im Entwurf*, 87; Karl Barth, *Ethik II: Vorlesung Münster, Wintersemester 1928/1929, wiederholt in Bonn, Wintersemester 1930/31*, ed. Dietrich Braun, Gesamtausgabe 2.10 (Zürich: TVZ, 1978), 19, 260; Karl Barth, *Die kirchliche Dogmatik*, 4 vols. (Zollikon-Zürich: Evangelischer Verlag A.G., 1932–1970), I/2:409; IV/1:692–93, 700, 707, 710.

Barth and Bultmann's respective uses of the early Luther highlight, more clearly than almost anything else, that their diverging approaches to dialectical theology stem from the same root and cannot be pitted against each other as easily as many scholars would like. The divide between the "Reformed Barth" and the "Lutheran Bultmann" is attractive as a theory of everything, but it ultimately fails to illuminate the underlying logic animating their theologies, neither of which comfortably fits its given category. A more productive approach is to see Barth and Bultmann developing two aspects or possibilities internal to the same Lutheran family tree. Both theologians structure their dialectical theologies around a broadly Lutheran doctrine of justification as the event of divine grace, but Bultmann highlights the question of epistemology (how do we come to know God in this event?) while Barth highlights the question of soteriology (how are we reconciled to God in this event?). This difference in perspective leads Bultmann to identify theology paradoxically with anthropology, but it leads Barth to subordinate, or even sublate, anthropology within theology.

We will explore the difference between Barth and Bultmann by looking at their respective doctrines of revelation in the year 1927, comparing Bultmann's lecture on "The Concept of Revelation in the New Testament" with Barth's *Christliche Dogmatik* – to which Bultmann positively refers. Both works refer to the early Luther in ways that foreshadow the insurmountable differences that would become manifest in later years.

2 *Ad Nos Ipsos Introire:* Bultmann's Doctrine of Existential Revelation

Bultmann's first use of Luther's line from the *Lectures on Romans* occurs in his 1927 lecture, "The Concept of Revelation in the New Testament," the nearest thing to a systematic account of his theology that Bultmann had produced to that point. The document warrants a close reading for two reasons: (a) it clarifies the basic compatibility of Bultmann's dialectical theology with Barth's regarding the character of revelation as an *event*; and (2) it highlights the aspect of Bultmann's project that most concerned Barth, namely, the *preunderstanding* of revelation. The latter issue eventually led Barth to dissociate himself from the other dialectical theologians, even though Bultmann's position was still in flux and more nuanced than Barth recognized.

2.1 Revelation as Existential and Eschatological Event

Ernst Baasland has correctly observed that "throughout all of his work Bultmann wanted to establish the essence of religion or of faith. This issue – whether explicitly or implicitly – is the point of continuity in his development."[17] In his early years Bultmann defined this essence in terms of religious experience along the lines of his teacher, Wilhelm Herrmann. Following his turn to dialectical theology in the 1920s – catalyzed by his encounter with Friedrich Gogarten's 1920 Eisenach lecture, "The Crisis of Culture," and the second edition of Karl Barth's *Römerbrief* in 1922 – Bultmann rejected the experiential, religious essence of liberal theology but did not have a clearly defined positive norm with which to replace it. The error of liberalism, as Bultmann understood it, was attempting to discover the essence of Christianity by means of the general, scientific methods of historical research, seen most notably in the nineteenth-century quests for the historical Jesus, which Bultmann refers to as "Christ according to the flesh."[18] The object of theology that results from using these methods is something given within the world and is thus incompatible with the eschatological transcendence of God, as theorized by dialectical theology.[19] The focus of Bultmann's earliest dialectical writings is therefore on opposing talk of God, or anything else, as a given object – *eine Gegebenheit*. His guiding thesis is "the constantly repeated statement of Barth and Gogarten: There is no direct knowledge of God; God is not a given object."[20] This negative epistemological criterion becomes the basis for Bultmann's early theological program.

---

[17] Ernst Baasland, *Theologie und Methode: Eine historiographische Analyse der Frühschriften Rudolf Bultmanns* (Wuppertal: Brockhaus, 1992), 19. Original emphasis removed.
[18] Rudolf Bultmann, "Zur Frage der Christologie," in *GuV*, 1:85–113, at 101.
[19] Bultmann summarized the position of early dialectical theology well in his 1926 statement: "For God is the 'wholly other' – not, however, in the sense of R. Otto, which is based on mysticism, but in the sense of early Christian *eschatology* (expectation of the end)." Rudolf Bultmann, "Die evangelisch-theologische Wissenschaft in der Gegenwart [1926]," in *Theologie als Kritik: Ausgewählte Rezensionen und Forschungsberichte*, ed. Matthias Dreher and Klaus W. Müller (Tübingen: Mohr Siebeck, 2002), 156–66, at 161. Bultmann makes this statement in the context of presenting Barth and Gogarten's dialectical theology as "a kind of revolution in theology" that speaks of "the faith of the Christian as faith in God's revelation, and not as a phenomenon of the history of religion, a function of the human spirit, a human spiritual attitude," and in this sense the movement of dialectical theology returns to "Luther and Calvin as the theologians who grasped the genuine theme of theology" (ibid., 160–61).
[20] Rudolf Bultmann, "Die liberale Theologie und die jüngste theologische Bewegung [1924]," in *GuV*, 1:1–25, at 6. He associates direct knowledge of God with liberal theology's "pantheism of history," which claims to access religious truth about God through the use of historical research" (ibid., 5–6).

Under the guidance of Barth and Gogarten, Bultmann differentiates in 1925 between two different modes of God-talk: a speaking *about* God (*Reden über Gott*) and a speaking *of* God (*Reden von Gott*).[21] To speak *about* God is to treat God as a *Gegebenheit*, as an object that is directly accessible to any person. Bultmann associates this with orthodox theologies that view God as something "fixed in knowledge" as well as with liberal theologies of experience that view God as directly accessible in historical research, spiritual states, creative life forces, or the irrational.[22] To speak *of* God, by contrast, is to view God as wholly other and thus not as a given entity that one can supposedly demonstrate through rational proofs or historical research. For Bultmann this means that "if one wishes to speak of God, one must evidently *speak of oneself.*"[23] The opposite of a theology of divine givenness is an existential theology of God's action upon the individual. He argues that "God is the reality that determines our existence," by which he means God is the one who justifies the sinner, but he does not yet have the language to crystallize this into a new essence of Christianity that could serve as a norm for dialectical theology.[24] Bultmann thus understands *how* one must speak of God, but at this stage he does not yet have a clearly defined account of *why* one must speak of God in this way. In order to establish this he needs an account of *what* God does – and by implication, who God is – to determine what counts as responsible God-talk.

Bultmann's 1927 essay on the concept of revelation is his first sustained effort to supply the positive norm for his new theological orientation. He begins by acknowledging that his inquiry is "guided by a certain understanding of the concept of revelation," which he later calls a "preunderstanding of revelation."[25] We presuppose a general view of revelation as the disclosure of what was hidden, but there are two kinds of disclosure. According to the first type, revelation is the communication of information "by which what was previously unfamiliar becomes familiar and thus known." Revelation in this sense is knowledge that can be taught and passed to others; it is something mediated. According to the second type, revelation is an occurrence or event "that places me in a

---

[21] Rudolf Bultmann, "Welchen Sinn hat es, von Gott zu reden? [1925]," in *GuV*, 1:26–37, at 26.
[22] Bultmann, "Die liberale Theologie und die jüngste theologische Bewegung," 18. Bultmann says in 1926 that the historicist theologians believed that, in their understanding of history, "the revelation of God was directly visible." See Rudolf Bultmann, "Geschichtliche und übergeschichtliche Religion im Christentum? [1926]," in *GuV*, 1:65–84, at 67.
[23] Bultmann, "Welchen Sinn hat es, von Gott zu reden?," 28.
[24] Bultmann, 29.
[25] Bultmann, "Der Begriff der Offenbarung im Neuen Testament," 1, 4. Original emphasis removed.

new situation with respect to myself."[26] Revelation in this sense is an existential reality that can be a kind of knowing but may not always become explicit. Both forms of revelation address some human limitation, whether this is a lack of information requiring new knowledge or an existential limitation requiring an occurrence. Either way revelation is something highly personal in nature, like love and friendship, so that "to know about revelation is to know about our authenticity."[27] It is not like "visit[ing] an exhibition of old locomotives" or asking about "the boundaries of Persia and Afghanistan."[28] Bultmann has thus replaced the abstract distinction between "speaking about" and "speaking of" with the concrete distinction between two kinds of revelation: "revelation as communication" and "revelation as event." The contrast is an either/or: "one understanding or the other must be false, must be a misunderstanding."[29] It is this existential need to clarify which understanding of revelation is the correct one that motivates his study of revelation in the New Testament.

In order to answer his guiding question Bultmann investigates *what* is actually revealed according to the New Testament witness and reaches the conclusion that revelation is, first and foremost, an *existential* reality. Drawing on a vast array of texts, he argues that, negatively, the decisive human limitation is death (Rom 7:14; 1 Cor 15:26), and, positively, revelation addresses this limitation by giving life – eternal life. Revelation is a saving event that leads to new life and gives a person victory over death, not a communication of information. The problem that death poses is not merely rational in nature, as if the revelation of the "*idea* of life" could be sufficient to address our existential predicament. On the contrary, revelation can only bring about authenticity if it actually "destroys death" itself. "Revelation can only be the gift of life that overcomes death," and therefore "revelation is an *occurrence* that abolishes death, not a doctrine that says it does not exist."[30] The obvious objection to this, of course, is that death still occurs. One could argue then that revelation is at present a possibility that only becomes an actuality in the future, either at the end of one's life or at the end of history. But this would be merely the "prolongation" of our present life, "the fulfillment of our natural longing" to hold on to our lives, and not something genuinely new.[31] Moreover, Bultmann finds in the New Testament a clear witness to the *present* reality of revelation and new life, since ultimately

---

26 Bultmann, 1–2.
27 Bultmann, 6.
28 Bultmann, 3, 6.
29 Bultmann, 4.
30 Bultmann, 15.
31 Bultmann, 16.

"revelation consists in nothing other than the fact of Jesus Christ."[32] Christ has already come and his presence is the reality of revelation itself, and yet this reality is not self-evident or generally discernible. Revelation has indeed occurred, but its occurrence "is not visible, demonstrable, or provable in the categories and with the means of perception native to 'everyday' existence."[33] Or as Bultmann puts it, revelation "is perceptible neither with the eyes nor with the conscious mind or with feeling."[34] The fact of Christ is not an objective reality for all but rather a "veiled revelation" that is "hidden for [the world]," since the world wants a publicly visible demonstration of revelation and so "cannot see the risen one."[35] The objectivity (the what) of revelation thus demands a specific subjectivity (the how) – namely, faith.

Revelation in the New Testament is not merely a what but also a how: the revelation of life in Jesus Christ coincides simultaneously with the revelation of faith and the word of the gospel. The New Testament concept of revelation is, in a sense, a double revelation. Bultmann finds support for this especially in 2 Corinthians 2:14–6:10, where the apostle Paul can speak of the "word" or "ministry" of reconciliation having the power of salvation and life (2 Cor 5:18–19). Moreover, this revelation of life only produces life "wherever it finds *faith*," so that one can also say "faith is revealed" (e.g., Gal 3:23, Heb 9:8, John 16:33).[36] The New Testament concept of revelation requires that we keep both aspects of revelation clearly in view. The dual character of revelation rules out any attempt to go behind the Christ encountered in word and faith to find the "historical Jesus" or a cosmic process that is fixed in a particular time and place.[37] The what of revelation – Christ and life – means that "revelation is not enlightenment or a communication of knowledge, but rather an occurrence"; the how of revelation – word and faith – means that "the occurrence of revelation is not a cosmic process that takes place outside of us," in which case the word would be a merely informational report and thus "nothing other than a myth."[38] Revelation is not hidden from us metaphysically, as in myth, but eschatologically, as in the reality of God. The

---

[32] Bultmann, 18. Original emphasis removed.
[33] J. Louis Martyn, *Galatians: A New Translation with Introduction and Commentary* (New York: Doubleday, 1997), 104.
[34] Bultmann, "Der Begriff der Offenbarung im Neuen Testament," 16.
[35] Bultmann, 18–19. Original emphasis removed. The fact of Christ as revelation is "not an innerworldly fact . . . but rather an 'eschatological' fact, i.e., one in which the world comes to an end" (ibid., 22).
[36] Bultmann, 21.
[37] Bultmann, 23.
[38] Bultmann, 21.

event of revelation confirms its eschatological, even apocalyptic, character in the way it "*breaks in from the outside*" and is thus "not demonstrable within this life."[39] The eschatological hiddenness of revelation requires and includes faith. Faith is the necessary subjective corollary of the objective event of new life. Without the objective event – the fact of Christ – revelation would be the projection of our natural longings and not something eschatologically new. Without the subjective corollary of faith, the occurrence of revelation would be a given object in the world and not something that existentially concerns the human person facing death. The two aspects of revelation occur together and require each other: "revelation is not visible outside of faith; ... therefore faith itself belongs to revelation."[40] Or as he puts it in his theological lectures from 1933, "*Revelation and faith* are together the object of theology."[41]

While Bultmann does not use these terms, we can say that Christ and the word are respectively the *empirical forms* of revelation's what and how, while life and faith are respectively the *existential effects* of revelation's what and how.

	The What	The How
Empirical Form	Christ	word
Existential Effect	life	faith

Schematizing Bultmann's interpretation of revelation this way does not mean we can cleanly separate these concepts. Indeed, the point of this analysis is that each term necessarily implies all of the others. Christ is a historical fact, but this fact is only revelation insofar as it gives life; and one only receives eternal life insofar as revelation evokes faith, which takes place in response to the word of proclamation; and this word only grants faith insofar as Christ is present in it, and so on. Bultmann thus treats Christ, life, word, and faith as virtual synonyms, since each is an aspect or mode of the singular event of revelation.[42]

---

39 Bultmann, 15.
40 Bultmann, 23.
41 Rudolf Bultmann, *Theologische Enzyklopädie*, ed. Eberhard Jüngel and Klaus W. Müller (Tübingen: Mohr, 1984), 159.
42 "Thus it becomes completely clear that *revelation, the action of God*, is *an occurrence*, not a supernatural communication of knowledge. Further, it is clear that revelation reveals *life*; it liberates the human person from the provisional and the past and gives them the future. Even so it is clear that *Christ* is revelation and that revelation is *the word*; for the two are one and the same. ... And once again, the word is what it is, namely revelation, not because of its timeless meaning but rather as an address that is brought to us by ordinary people. And thus, like the word, *faith*

The dual or dialectical character of revelation as simultaneously objective and subjective leads Bultmann to Luther. If both the empirical forms and existential effects are ontologically located in the singular event of revelation itself, then not only are the forms-as-revelation hidden from the eyes of the world, but the effects-as-revelation do not subsist in themselves outside of the event. Life and faith do not become properties of the person who encounters revelation. For this reason "the understanding of the Reformers is correct: righteousness is 'imputed' to us as *iustitia aliena*." Bultmann clarifies that this does not mean "justified sinners are 'seen only as if' they were righteous. No! They *are* righteous."[43] But this righteousness or life, like the revelatory significance of Christ, is actual only in the event itself, and thus only for faith. Revelation, like justification, is present and real (the what), but hidden and eschatological (the how). The hiddenness of revelation means that revelation is always existential, and the only way to speak of God's revelation is, as Bultmann said two years earlier, by speaking of ourselves in our encounter with God. Bultmann finds support for this in Luther's understanding of the knowledge of God as a going-into-ourselves:

> *What therefore is revealed?* Nothing at all, insofar as the question concerning revelation asks for doctrines – doctrines that no person could have arrived at – or for mysteries that, when they are communicated, are known once and for all. But everything, insofar as *persons have their eyes opened about themselves and they can understand themselves anew.* It is as Luther says: "And so God, in going out of himself, brings it about that we go into ourselves, and through knowledge of him he brings us to knowledge of ourselves."[44]

In the footnote following the reference to Luther, Bultmann then quotes from Barth's *Christliche Dogmatik*: "Hearing God's word does not mean wandering in the metaphysical clouds, but rather finally – finally – coming to oneself, learning to see oneself, becoming revealed as one is."[45] Revelation is a new reality, but its newness is only available to me as the one who hears and responds to God's justifying word.

Bultmann's doctrine of revelation is an ever new occurrence that, paradoxically, does not reveal anything new. It is an alien revelation in the sense that it comes from outside of us as an act of God, but its permanent alienness means that it never becomes some *thing* outside of us that we can grasp or possess.

---

too is revelation, because it is only faith in this occurrence and otherwise it is nothing" (Bultmann, "Der Begriff der Offenbarung im Neuen Testament," 30–31).
43 Bultmann, 31.
44 Bultmann, 29.
45 See Barth, *Die christliche Dogmatik im Entwurf*, 516.

The existential event of revelation always remains event and so always draws us into ourselves, opening our eyes to the truth of our own existence. For Bultmann, this paradox points us to Christ as the eschatological fact of revelation, but without careful articulation, it can also point us away from Christ to natural revelation.

2.2 The Question of Natural Revelation

Bultmann's lecture on the concept of revelation marks a transitional moment in his theological development. Following Baasland we can identify this as the start of his existentialist phase, in which he began to construct his theology in active dialogue with existentialist philosophy.[46] We see this most clearly in the new conceptuality he employs. When originally composed this lecture was the first time Bultmann had used the concept of "preunderstanding," a term that would play a significant role in his later hermeneutics.[47] He spends the first half of the lecture developing the general meaning of revelation on the basis of both preunderstanding and church history before turning to his exegesis of the New Testament. While he gives the theological rationale for existential theology in the second half of the lecture, he begins by giving a philosophical and historical rationale. This methodological decision results in an unresolved internal tension.

Much of this is perhaps attributable to his optimism in the late 1920s about the possibilities of fruitful theological engagement with Martin Heidegger. In Tübingen on 9 March 1927, a month before Bultmann was originally scheduled to deliver his lecture, Heidegger presented his lecture on "Phenomenology and Theology," a document developed in close conversation with Bultmann on the relationship between theology and philosophy. Heidegger gave this lecture again in Marburg on 14 February 1928.[48] Two weeks later, on 25 February, and six weeks before Bultmann was finally able to deliver his lecture on the concept

---

[46] Baasland, *Theologie und Methode*, 76.
[47] Because the revelation lecture was delayed until April 1928, Bultmann first used the concept publicly in his lecture in Eisenach on 19 October 1927, "The Significance of 'Dialectical Theology' for New Testament for the Scientific Study of the New Testament," published in early 1928. And his very first use of the term, at least based on the available sources, is in the same letter to Gogarten on 3 April 1927, in which he mentions the upcoming lecture on the concept of revelation (indeed, only a few sentences earlier). See Bultmann and Gogarten, *Briefwechsel 1921–1967*, 105.
[48] Konrad Hammann, *Rudolf Bultmann: A Biography*, trans. Philip E. Devenish (Salem, OR: Polebridge Press, 2013), 209.

of revelation at Marburg, Heidegger received a call to the University of Freiburg. This prompted Bultmann, on the eve of giving his talk at the holiday course, to consider sending "both lectures to a publisher as a unified publication. That seems to me to be a beautiful public conclusion to our shared time at Marburg."[49]

While Heidegger turned down this offer, the suggestion in itself indicates a proximity between Bultmann and Heidegger during this period, which manifests itself in Bultmann's ambivalence regarding the newness of revelation. On the one hand, he claims that revelation is an event that "places me in a new situation," whose content is a new creation that places a person "in this new mode of being, in this new history."[50] On the other hand, he suggests several times that revelation does not bring about anything new at all. Revelation, he argues, is a return to the old, original revelation of creation and law. Justification reproduces the "original relation of creation" and makes "the old revelation visible again."[51] Bultmann immediately follows his reference to Luther on knowledge of God occurring as knowledge of ourselves by saying that the light that shines in Jesus is the same light that was already shining in creation. We do not understand anything in the "revelation of redemption" that we should not have already understood from the "revelation in creation and the law."[52] He even says that "the revelation in Christ is not the first," that people could have known God earlier because the light of revelation was already available in the knowledge of our creatureliness. It follows that, though it has been misunderstood and lost in practice, "there is thus a '*natural revelation.*'"[53] Bultmann makes no effort to reconcile the various claims in this essay. The lecture is a rigorous inquiry in every other respect, but there is an awkward ambivalence when it comes to the question of the exclusive identification of revelation with Christ – an ambivalence that no doubt would have raised suspicions for Barth. Is revelation nothing other than the fact of Jesus Christ, or is there revelation outside of Christ in creation? Bultmann does not resolve the question in this essay, per-

---

49 Bultmann to Heidegger, 11 April 1928, in Bultmann and Heidegger, *Briefwechsel 1925–1975*, 60. When Heidegger declined – declining both the joint publication and Bultmann's offer to be a coeditor of the journal *Theologische Rundschau*, on the grounds that discussing the relation between philosophy and theology was a "practical" matter that would cause him trouble within the philosophical guild – Bultmann published his essay on its own in 1929. Heidegger's lecture remained unpublished until 1969.
50 Bultmann, "Der Begriff der Offenbarung im Neuen Testament," 2, 27.
51 Bultmann, 26. Original emphasis removed.
52 Bultmann, 29.
53 Bultmann, 26.

haps because he was torn between his allegiance to the material norms of dialectical theology and his interest in the conceptual insights afforded by Heidegger's philosophy.

In 1929 Gerhardt Kuhlmann addressed a series of critical questions to Bultmann focusing especially on his apparent reduction of revelation to the profane self-understanding of natural existence as theorized by philosophy.[54] Bultmann attempted to clarify his position the following year by replacing the distinction between old revelation and new revelation with the Heideggerian distinction, presented most clearly in "Phenomenology and Theology," between the ontological and the ontic – that is, respectively, the general structures of existence and the particular existential reality of the individual. Revelation does not change the former (what we might call "creation"), but it does change the latter. Bultmann's point is that revelation does not make the recipient of new life a visibly different creature: "What takes place in the Christian occurrence that is realized in faith, in 'rebirth,' is not a magical transformation of the human person that removes the believer from Dasein. ... If prefaithful existence is existentially-ontically overcome in faith, that does not mean that the existentialist-ontological conditions of existing are destroyed."[55] Revelation, he argues, provides the "definitive clarification" of one's existence, analogous to the way falling in love definitively clarifies one's prior concept of love. But Bultmann's clarification at this stage only goes so far. On the one hand, he emphasizes that "through the *event* of revelation the *events* of one's life become new – 'new' in a sense that is valid absolutely only for those with faith and is visible only to faith, that indeed *becomes* visible only in each now and becomes visible always *anew*."[56] But no sooner does he say this than he adds that faith's self-understanding presupposes the *lumen naturale*, reveals natural existence as being "always already graced," and rediscovers "natural Dasein as *creation*."[57]

---

[54] Gerhardt Kuhlmann, "Zum theologischen Problem der Existenz: Fragen an Rudolf Bultmann," *Zeitschrift für Theologie und Kirche* N.F. 10 (1929): 28–57, esp. 51–57.
[55] Rudolf Bultmann, "Die Geschichtlichkeit des Daseins und der Glaube: Antwort an Gerhardt Kuhlmann [1930]," in *Neues Testament und christliche Existenz: Theologische Aufsätze*, ed. Andreas Lindemann (Tübingen: Mohr Siebeck, 2002), 59–83, at 65–66. Bultmann here uses Heidegger almost verbatim. Compare "*Im Glauben ist zwar existenziell-ontisch die vorchristliche Existenz überwunden*" (Heidegger) with "*Ist im Glauben die vorgläubige Existenz existentiell-ontisch überwunden*" (Bultmann). See Martin Heidegger, "Phänomenologie und Theologie," in *Wegmarken*, 2nd ed., ed. Friedrich-Wilhelm von Herrmann, Gesamtausgabe 1.9 (Frankfurt am Main: Klostermann, 1978), 63.
[56] Bultmann, "Die Geschichtlichkeit des Daseins und der Glaube," 71.
[57] Bultmann, 72.

No wonder then that in January 1930, when Bultmann showed Barth this new essay, Barth immediately wrote Eduard Thurneysen to say that what he heard "before and afterwards in private conversation with Bultmann, I did not like." He added:

> My dear Eduard, a very bad business is developing along the entire line, in which I do not wish to have a part under any circumstances. Is it not the case that gradually all the people who seemed to stand alongside us want something that we ... precisely did not want and which stands in the closest connection with, if it is not identical to, what we were inherently opposed to: to put on the table a justification, not of the actuality of course, but the possibility of faith and of revelation? ... Thus: Bultmann with his theology of believing Dasein, which derives its legitimacy from a corresponding existentialist philosophy. Thus – certainly not least of all – the solemn Friedrich [Gogarten] with his framing doctrine of historicity and his already openly admitted proximity to Schleiermacher's "anthropology."[58]

Barth recognized that the dispute came down to the anthropological significance of revelation. Given the convoluted nature of Bultmann's argumentation, it is little wonder that Barth only heard the statements suggesting anthropology as the presupposed basis for revelation and missed the other statements indicating that revelation includes, sublates, redefines, and clarifies anthropology. During these pivotal years Bultmann was still in the process of figuring out his new theological program – and, unfortunately, at the same time Barth was in the process of rethinking his own theology. In the years immediately following, Bultmann would move away from Heidegger and write strongly against the notions of "natural revelation" and "revelation in creation" in direct opposition to the orders-of-creation theology of the German Christian Faith Movement.[59] But by that point the damage to his relationship with Barth had already been done.

---

58 Karl Barth to Eduard Thurneysen, 26 January 1930, in Karl Barth and Eduard Thurneysen, *Briefwechsel, Band II: 1921–1930*, ed. Eduard Thurneysen, Gesamtausgabe 5.4 (Zürich: TVZ, 1974), 700.
59 See Rudolf Bultmann, "Das Problem der 'natürlichen Theologie' [1933]," in *GuV*, 1:294–312; Rudolf Bultmann, "Die Bedeutung des Alten Testaments für den christlichen Glauben [1933]," in *GuV*, 1:313–336; Rudolf Bultmann, "Die Aufgabe der Theologie in der gegenwärtigen Situation," *Theologische Blätter* 12, no. 6 (1933): 161–66; Rudolf Bultmann, "Der Arier-Paragraph im Raume der Kirche," *Theologische Blätter* 12, no. 12 (1933): 359–70; Bultmann, "Die Frage der natürlichen Offenbarung," in *GuV*, 2:79–104.

3 *Desperatio Fiducialis:* Barth's Doctrine of Historical Revelation

In the brief space remaining we turn now to Barth's doctrine of revelation from the same period, found especially in *Die christliche Dogmatik im Entwurf* of 1927, comprising his lectures in dogmatics from the winter semester of 1926–1927. Barth had recently had a dispute with Bultmann over hermeneutics and the theological exegesis (*Sachkritik*) of the Bible,[60] but they were still by and large allies in the nascent movement of dialectical theology. For this reason – unlike the later *Kirchliche Dogmatik*, written after the dialectical honeymoon had effectively ended – the *Christliche Dogmatik* reveals the early fractures in their common theological vision over the very essence of Christian theology.[61]

Like Bultmann's lecture on the concept of revelation, Barth's *Christliche Dogmatik* occupies a transitional moment in his theological development, and this is nowhere more evident than in his doctrine of revelation as "primal history" (*Urgeschichte*).[62] The concept of *Urgeschichte* first appeared in Barth's work in early 1920, following the Christmas gift in 1919 from his brother Heinrich of Franz Overbeck's *Christentum und Kultur*.[63] While the concept occurred a handful of times in his revision of *Der Römerbrief* – where it served as a synonym for Kierkegaard's "paradox" and Johann Christoph Blumhardt's "victor" as a way of un-

---

[60] In 1922, after Bultmann reviewed Barth's *Römerbrief*, the two of them disputed over *Sachexegese* and *Sachkritik*, leading ultimately to Bultmann's 1925 essay on theological exegesis. This was followed by Bultmann's review, published in early 1926, of Barth's *Die Auferstehung der Toten*. See Rudolf Bultmann, "Karl Barths 'Römerbrief' in zweiter Auflage [1922]," in *Anfänge der dialektischen Theologie*, 2 vols., ed. Jürgen Moltmann (Munich: C. Kaiser, 1962–1963), 1:119–42; Rudolf Bultmann, "Das Problem einer theologischen Exegese des Neuen Testaments [1925]," in *Neues Testament und christliche Existenz*, 13–38; Rudolf Bultmann, "Karl Barth, 'Die Auferstehung der Toten' [1926]," in *GuV*, 1:38–64.
[61] In my previous work I called the period 1929–1939 the stage of "dogmatic dissonance" in Barth's theology, because of a misalignment of subject and object in his thought. I would now extend this to 1927, given the confusion manifest in the *Christliche Dogmatik*. See David W. Congdon, *The Mission of Demythologizing: Rudolf Bultmann's Dialectical Theology* (Minneapolis: Fortress, 2015), 129.
[62] Barth, *Die christliche Dogmatik im Entwurf*, 310: "*Offenbarung ist Urgeschichte.*"
[63] Franz Overbeck, *Christentum und Kultur: Gedanken und Anmerkungen zur modernen Theologie*, ed. Carl Albrecht Bernoulli (Basel: Benno Schwabe, 1919). See Karl Barth, "Unerledigte Anfragen an die heutige Theologie [1920]," in *Vorträge und kleinere Arbeiten 1914–1921*, ed. Hans-Anton Drewes (Zürich: TVZ, 2012), 622–61.

derstanding Jesus as the Christ[64] – the term played almost no role in subsequent writings, only appearing once in the entirety of the Göttingen Dogmatics.[65] That is to say, it played no role until the "false start" of the *Christliche Dogmatik*, where the idea of *Urgeschichte* appears over sixty times and serves as the dominant category by which Barth interprets the meaning of revelation. Moreover, the term takes on a new meaning: whereas in *Der Römerbrief* he uses the concept of primal history to refer to an event that is protologically and eschatologically "timeless," in 1927 he uses the term to refer to "a historical event, an event that is itself in time" but also "not bound to the irreversible sequence of temporal history."[66] As deployed by Barth, the master category of *Urgeschichte* functions to secure both the existential and the eschatological dimensions of revelation analyzed by Bultmann, while avoiding the potential for natural theology. On the one hand, *Urgeschichte* roots revelation in history. Barth rejects the notion that God's "eternal history" in the trinity is revelation in itself; revelation is instead "more than eternity." God's history only becomes revelation when God enters time and "encounters us."[67] On the other hand, we encounter not just anyone in revelation but rather *God*, and for this reason history in general is not revelation but only history as it is taken up by God in the event of incarnation. History is a predicate of revelation, rather than the reverse. For this reason, revelation is also "more than history."[68] The *Ur-* thus represents this *more than* character of revelation, irreducible to either eternity or history, either the present or the past – and so "wholly undiscoverable in history" but available instead where eternity and history definitively intersect, namely in the "prophetic, adventual history" of Jesus Christ.[69] Like Bultmann, Barth posits a correlation, not between the

---

64 See Barth, *Der Römerbrief (Zweite Fassung)*, 50–51. For more on this, see Bruce L. McCormack, *Karl Barth's Critically Realistic Dialectical Theology: Its Genesis and Development, 1909–1936* (New York: Oxford University Press, 1995), 226–35.

65 Karl Barth, *Unterricht in der christlichen Religion, Teil 1: Prolegomena 1924*, ed. Hannelotte Reiffen, Gesamtausgabe 2.17 (Zürich: TVZ, 1985), 182. Barth here says that revelation is historical in the sense of being "*prä*historisch, *ur*geschichtlich," so that faith is the only means of accessing it.

66 See Barth, *Der Römerbrief (Zweite Fassung)*, 51, 344; Barth, *Die christliche Dogmatik im Entwurf*, 310, 320. This is something of a paradox: despite working with a vertical, punctiliar concept of revelation in the *Römerbrief*, Barth's understanding of primal history refers protologically to the origin of history and eschatologically to the end of history. By contrast, in *Christliche Dogmatik*, which has a more temporal concept of revelation, *Urgeschichte* refers to a vertical relationship between observable history below and eternal history above.

67 Barth, *Die christliche Dogmatik im Entwurf*, 311.

68 Barth, 312.

69 Barth, 314, 320.

what and the how but between two whats: the eternal and the historical. While this does not generate an existential theology for Barth, it does lead him to the same conclusion regarding the hiddenness of revelation – on which point, again like Bultmann, Barth also quotes from the *scholia* of Luther's 1515–1516 *Lectures on Romans*, though in this case from the commentary on Romans 3:11: "The word was made flesh and wisdom incarnate *and thus it is hidden* and graspable only by the proper understanding, just as Christ is knowable only by revelation."[70]

The concept of *Urgeschichte* does heavy lifting for Barth – perhaps more than it is capable of bearing. He admits he uses the term as "a dogmatic concept" in clear distinction from the way Overbeck himself defines it.[71] The word is something of a cipher that becomes the master solution to every theological problem. Barth wants to ground revelation more thoroughly in history than he did in either *Der Römerbrief* or *Unterricht in der christlichen Religion*. But Barth also wants to maintain the eschatological character of revelation as an act of God that remains nonobjectifiable. The term accomplishes both goals. *Urgeschichte* locates revelation in a divine event that encounters us existentially but takes place outside of us in history, though not a history that we can analyze and domesticate. But therein lies the problem: Barth's concept of revelation at this stage is entirely formal and has no real grounding in history at all or even any real content. Barth's exposition lacks the exegetical richness of Bultmann's lecture. If pressed to identify the what of revelation, Barth's answer in the *Christliche Dogmatik* is simply "God." This allows him to vacillate between existential and nonexistential claims. On the one hand he can say that the human recipient of revelation is "coposited" in the event of the word of God, and thus "the word of God is a concept that is only ever accessible to an existential thinking."[72] Later Barth claims "the correlate of truth, of revelation, of the word of God, is the human person. ... The *individual!* That is the correlate of truth, not humanity, not even the mass of Christians, ... but rather *this* person, the I."[73] This is the section in which Barth writes the line about "coming to oneself" that Bultmann quotes. He also here defines interpretation of scripture as "thinking-after, thinking-with, thinking-for-oneself" (*Nachdenken, Mitdenken, Selberdenken*), a terminological triad first mentioned in the Göttingen Dogmatics.[74] On the other hand, Barth declares – implicitly against the idea of preunderstanding – that

---

70 Barth, 314.
71 Barth, 313.
72 Barth, 148.
73 Barth, 517–18. Cf. ibid., 310: "The reality of revelation consists in the fact that our I is addressed by God in the form of a human You."
74 Barth, 513. See Barth, *Unterricht in der christlichen Religion, Teil 1*, 311.

"we have no access to God's revelation on our own, no possibility of comprehending it," and against the fatal mistake of "theological modernity," there is "no human organ for revelation."[75] We cannot attribute the preacher's knowledge of God "to an original or acquired suitability of the human subject for this knowledge (neither to a religious organ or *a priori* nor to a religious experience!)," but rather this knowledge has to be understood as a modification of the preacher's "unsuitability, as 'docta *ignorantia*' [*learned ignorance*], as an obedient and promising (and insofar as it grasps its object, because it is grasped by it) *not-knowing*."[76] Whereas Bultmann speaks of a "not-knowing knowledge" (*nichtwissende Wissen*) as our preunderstanding *before* encountering revelation,[77] Barth speaks of a kind of "not-knowing" knowledge *after* the encounter with revelation, as the existence of the human person in faith. With respect then to the preacher's action of speaking of God, Barth says, invoking the key phrase from Luther, "we can speak of a *desperatio fiducialis*, of a 'confident despair,'" a human despair in the self that only finds confidence in the fact that the *ius divinum* covers like a garment "an ultimately insufficient and deeply illegitimate *ius humanum*."[78] God's claim on the preacher is alone what makes God-talk possible, and this claim does not give security to the preacher; it is not something to which the preacher can lay claim but instead a divine act to which the preacher merely submits. For this reason "there can be no talk of anthropologizing" this divine equipping, either by trying to prove the truth of religion on human grounds or by trying to expose the error of religion along the lines of Feuerbach. God's commission alone makes possible talk of God.[79]

A year later, from November to December 1927, Barth gave a series of lectures on "God's Revelation according to the Teaching of the Christian Church."[80] While this material largely repeats what was said in the *Christliche Dogmatik*, there are certain notable changes. For instance, Barth here abandons the concept of *Urgeschichte* and speaks instead of *Geschichte*. The concept of "self-revelation," used only a handful of times in both Göttingen's *Unterricht* and the *Christliche Dogmatik*, appears over twenty times in these lectures, though in keeping with the dogmatic experimentation of this period Barth uses the concept primarily in a *pejo-*

---

75 Barth, *Die christliche Dogmatik im Entwurf*, 382.
76 Barth, 86.
77 Bultmann, "Der Begriff der Offenbarung im Neuen Testament," 4, 6.
78 Barth, *Die christliche Dogmatik im Entwurf*, 87.
79 Barth, 87.
80 For the latter see Karl Barth, "Gottes Offenbarung nach der Lehre der christlichen Kirche [1927]," in *Vorträge und kleinere Arbeiten 1925–1930*, ed. Hermann Schmidt (Zürich: TVZ, 1994), 215–95.

rative sense to refer to "the self-revelation of *human beings*."⁸¹ Theology is only possible, he says, if revelation is neither human self-revelation nor the revelation of God to Godself, neither purely subjective nor purely objective. Bultmann makes a similar critique of both liberalism and orthodoxy in his lectures in theology from the same period,⁸² but whereas his solution is an existential theology rooted in an event that includes human faith in the divine act of revelation, Barth has yet to find a solution that satisfies him. One can almost see him trying out ideas in real time in these lectures. He speaks of revelation as "a concrete event in our life," in which "we are placed in our own existence before God's revelation."⁸³ But instead of developing the material content ("the what") of this event, he takes refuge within the formal language of an encounter ("the how"), in which God objectively confronts us as a "temporal You" and – because this revelation "occurs in the incognito" – subjectively enables us to see God through "the miracle of the Holy Spirit."⁸⁴ In an effort to oppose all anthropologizing, he rejects the possibility of understanding the subjective side of revelation as either history or religion, as he claims is the case in both the new Protestant theology and Roman Catholic theology. He wants to secure revelation in something outside of us immune to objectification without retreating into an abstract orthodoxy. But his solution does not move beyond a formal appeal to Jesus Christ and the Holy Spirit – until, that is, at the end of the fourth lecture, when Barth unknowingly anticipates the direction of his future theology by declaring without elaboration: "Divine revelation means divine *election*."⁸⁵

4 Conclusion: Beyond the Whale and the Elephant

In the hindsight of history the year 1927 appears like a fork in the road in the relationship between Barth and Bultmann, though in the moment it was more a calm between the storms of the early 1920s and the early 1930s. And yet, intellectually speaking, the two of them were in the midst of rethinking their theological programs and deciding which values were going to dominate their future work. Both were experimenting with what it means to do dialectical theology.

---

81 Barth, 218.
82 Bultmann, *Theologische Enzyklopädie*, 28–34.
83 Barth, "Gottes Offenbarung nach der Lehre der christlichen Kirche," 254, 274.
84 Barth, 251–52. Regarding the incognito, see ibid., 277.
85 Barth, 281.

On 19 October 1927, Bultmann gave his lecture on dialectical theology, arguing that it referred to a theology that speaks of God in relation to the historical existence of the human person, a method perfectly consistent with his new account of revelation as the essence of Christian faith.[86] Revelation is essentially dialectical for Bultmann since human faith is included in revelation. By contrast, in Barth's lectures on revelation a month later, he says that theology is only dialectical because we do not have access to God's self-knowledge and have not yet arrived at the "coming perfection" of seeing God face-to-face. Instead we are stuck doing theology in the "fragmentary nature of existence" (*Bruchstückwesen*).[87] Barth has abandoned his notion in *Römerbrief* of an "inner dialectic" in revelation, but he has neither embraced a nondialectical theology nor has he yet grasped the inner dialectic implicit in his christology, something that would not occur for over another decade.[88]

When the two theologians finally realized their respective programs, they represented the two pathways to knowledge of God available within the reformational vision of Luther: the one leading to an existential self-knowledge as the location of God's event of justifying grace and the other leading away from the dead, sinful self to the confidence and security of God's electing grace in Jesus Christ. Both are legitimate approaches *internal* to the same Protestant theological tradition. Seeing dialectical theology synoptically in light of both pathways, we can conclude that dialectical theology in general is a *desecuring*, a denial of the human attempt to secure our relation to God in ourselves. Barth desecures by removing security from the individual self and locating security in God. We must have a "confident despair": despair in ourselves but confidence in God's election. Barth's theology thus establishes a new security outside of ourselves. Bultmann, by contrast, establishes a *permanent* desecuring by constantly removing security and refusing to relocate security somewhere stable. Because the event of revelation includes the historical existence of the individual, security is found always only in the moment and thus has to be found ever anew. Bult-

---

86 Rudolf Bultmann, "Die Bedeutung der 'dialektischen Theologie' für die neutestamentliche Wissenschaft [1928]," in *GuV*, 1:114–33, esp. 115–20.
87 Barth, "Gottes Offenbarung nach der Lehre der christlichen Kirche," 293–94.
88 Regarding the "inner dialectic of the *Sache*," see Barth, *Der Römerbrief (Zweite Fassung)*, 16. I agree here with Jüngel that Barth abandons the "inner dialectic" in the mid-1920s, restricting the dialectic to the human side. See Eberhard Jüngel, "Von der Dialektik zur Analogie: Die Schule Kierkegaards und der Einspruch Petersons," in *Barth-Studien* (Zürich-Köln: Benziger Verlag, 1982), 127–79, at 143–44. This is further supported by the *Christliche Dogmatik*, where Barth says that "God … speaks an undialectical word. … *God's* theology, God's knowing and speaking, is in itself … undialectical theology" (Barth, *Die christliche Dogmatik im Entwurf*, 583).

mann's path tends toward an embrace of natural revelation, while Barth's path tends toward an abstract formalism and metaphysical orthodoxy. Neither error is necessary to their respective projects. Perhaps a revitalized dialectical theology will come through renewed attention to their shared reformational origin.

Part III: **Disruption**

Hent de Vries
Theologia paradoxa, theologia crucis
Heidegger's Luther

1 Introduction

There is no doubt that Heidegger was an avid reader of Luther, to begin with the latter's commentary on Paul's Letter to the Romans, which effectively enabled him to break away from "the system of Catholicism" in which he had been groomed for a possible special chair in Freiburg im Breisgau. It is in an invited contribution to Rudolf Bultmann's seminar, in February 1924, that we see Heidegger for the first time expound his thoughts on the concept of "sin" in Luther's theology in the context of Genesis 3:8–10 and in terms of a modality or affect (*affectus*) of human existence (of factical life experience or *Dasein*, as he will early on say), which is characterized by its formal and general feature, that is to say, its tendency to "fall," its *aversio Dei*, rather than by any ontic-empirical occurrence or mental event that would single it out in particular. In so doing, Heidegger thereby prepares a radical and relentless critique of the ecclesial and confessional, historical and liberal theology of his days, both in its Roman Catholic, Neoscholastic or Neo-Thomist and its Protestant, that is, Lutheran and Calvinist, variants. Natural theology or onto-theology and so-called *Kulturprotestantismus* suffer the same fate in his early and later "phenomenology of religion" for reasons that the present contribution will seek to spell out, with special emphasis on Heidegger's early and later reading of Luther.

In apparent proximity to the early dialectical and later hermeneutic theology, Heidegger first introduces and then refines central elements of his idea of "destruction [*Destruktion*]," the procedure to take a "step back" into the very origins of Western metaphysics, whose all too naïve understanding of the privilege of "presence," not to mention the "subject," would have made us forget the primary "question" of the very "meaning of Being." The latter is taken to convey that of Being "as such [*als solches, kath'auto*]" and of Being "*in toto* [*als Ganzes, kath'olou*]," thereby slipping all too easily into misunderstanding the latter two in terms of mere generality and of "the highest" (which is where metaphysics or, later, ontology touches upon theology or onto-theology). In taking to task this historical syndrome, Heidegger is influenced by the emerging reception, in his days, of Søren Kierkegaard's writings, just as he echoes a return to Augustine and, via him, Paul.¹ But the role played by Luther is equally, if not more, important in this very context.

In fact, both *affectus* and *destructio* (or, indirectly, *annihilatio*) are terms Heidegger borrows from Luther. Following a patient preparation in his lecture courses, correspondence, and manuscript drafts, the introduction to Heidegger's *Being and Time* (*Sein und Zeit*), published in 1927, opens with a scathing reminder of theology's original task, invoking Luther explicitly. We will come to this. And the later introduction to his 1929 inaugural lecture, "What Is Metaphysics? [Was ist Metaphysik?]," has a Lutheran ring as well as it cites I Corinthians 1:20, even though it inscribes its fundamental theological question – and admitted madness – in a much longer and decidedly Greek tradition of thought in whose light its scandal is all the more visible (and should have remained that way)²: "Will Christian theology one day resolve [*entschliesst*] to take seriously the word of the apostle and thus also the conception of philosophy as foolishness [*Torheit*]?"³

The present contribution retraces the essential steps leading up to this position and reassesses the crucial stakes of Heidegger's lifelong engagement with the early Luther, to begin with their different receptions of Aristotle's thought and with special emphasis on their respective concepts of the *theologia crucis* (to be distinguished from the triumphalist and presentist *theologia gloriam*, characterized by the early Heidegger in terms of the "system of Catholicism," the "system of dogmatics," or, indeed, of "Christendom" and "Christlichkeit," as Franz Overbeck conceived them).

As Hans-Georg Gadamer noted, in Heidegger's 1922 "theologische Jugendschrift," also known as the "Natorp-Bericht" and recently published under the title *Phänomenologische Interpretation zu Aristoteles* (*Anzeige der hermeneutischen Situation*) (Phenomenological Interpretations of Aristotle [Indication of the Hermeneutic Situation]), we see the author still very much in search of "an adequate in-

---

1 Cf. Hent de Vries, "The Kierkegaardian Moment: Dialectical Theology and Its Aftermath," *Modern Language Notes* 128.5:Dec 2013, 1083–1114; "Inverse versus Dialectical Theology: The Two Faces of Negativity and the Miracle of Faith," in *Paul and the Philosophers*, ed., Ward Blanton and Hent de Vries (New York: Fordham University Press, 2013), 466–511.
2 Cf. Hans-Christoph Askani and Christoph Chalamet, eds., *La sagesse et la folie de Dieu: Lectures exégétiques de théologique de 1 Corinthiens 1–2* (Geneva: Labor et Fides, 2017).
3 Martin Heidegger, "Einleitung," in idem, *Was ist Metaphysik?* (Frankfurt am Main: Vittorio Klostermann, 1969), 20.

terpretation and anthropological understanding of Christian consciousness."[4] What Heidegger aimed at, Gadamer continues, was to justify

> why one must once again resort to Aristotle if one wants to really understand the Christian history of the West in its productive possibilities and to clarify our own situation in our present. The aim was to give Aristotle's anthropology, notably as it can be found in his rhetoric and ethics, a voice out of the understanding of life in the present moment. One reads with respect the intimate knowledge of the history of dogma in the Middle Ages, which the young researcher Heidegger had, and how he in the footsteps of Luther, via Augustine and Neoplatonism, followed the path back to Paul and the gospel of John so as to elucidate his own questions in life in returning to Aristotle.[5]

Presumably, it was Heidegger's early motivation, in sync with some of the Protestant and notably dialectical theologians of his days, to highlight a quest for self-transparency and self-understanding against the backdrop, not of self-presence, but of "'reaching-out' with regard to something [*das 'Aus-sein' – auf Etwas*]."[6] In the range of ontological possibilities that Aristotle characterized on an spectrum stretching from *sophia* to *phronesis* or theoretical and practical wisdom, this would lead Heidegger eventually to an analysis of a certain *ethos* as opposed to its "habituation [*Gewohnheit*]," which he eventually associated with *Dasein*'s tendency toward so-called "fallenness," which is a falling away and flight from what he would come to describe in terms of proper existence.[7] And in fallenness, "occultation [*Verdunkelung*]" and "distortion [*Verstellung*]" take preeminence over the perspicuity of the "illumination [*Erhellung*]" of the self by the self.[8] It is against this thing-like quality of presentness qua present-at-handness, of the occurring and objects, that Heidegger launches a defying gesture, inspired in this by Luther's dismissal of the "theology of glory [*theologia gloriae*]."

It is, Gadamer continues, in the Aristotelian physics that Heidegger finds the "true middle" of his conception as the latter discipline's theme is "being qua movement" – more precisely, "that which is or exists in the how of its movement [*das Seiende im Wie seines Bewegtseins*]" – as distinguished from the immobility of Platonic-Pythagorian "ideality,"[9] which necessarily falls short of expressing the *flux* and *enactment* of our existence (and, Heidegger leaves no

---

4 Hans-Georg Gadamer, "Heideggers 'theologische' Jugendschrift," in Martin Heidegger, *Phänomenologische Interpretation zu Aristoteles (Anzeige der hermeneutischen Situation* (Frankfurt am Main: Vittorio Klostermann, 2013), 67–75, 67.
5 Gadamer, "Heideggers 'theologische' Jugendschrift," 70.
6 Gadamer, 73.
7 Gadamer, 74.
8 Gadamer, 74.
9 Gadamer, 74.

doubt, of *our Dasein* alone). On this reading, Aristotle is read against Aristotle or, at least, against the Aristotle of Neoscholasticism and Neothomism, including its Protestant analogues. Behind the appropriation of Aristotle in the early Heidegger there lies, Gadamer concludes, "the eschatological aspect of the Christian gospel and the unique temporal character of the moment [*Augenblick*]."[10]

These questions that guided Heidegger early on, I would suggest, have lost nothing of their relevance in the later work, nor for us, here and now. Their premises and implications are delineated nowhere more clearly than in the lecture "*Phänomenologie und Theologie* [Phenomenology and Theology]" likewise from 1927. The latter can be seen as an appendix to the *Being and Time* and has often rightly been treated as an integral part of its project and this not least because of its far more explicit discussion of the principle and procedure of "formal indication [*formale Anzeige*]," which organizes the *magnum opus* and which I have treated elsewhere in the context of Heidegger's destruction of onto-theology.[11] I will not return to this here. Of equal or even greater importance is the motif that Heidegger espouses in the contemporaneous lecture and throughout some of the lecture courses, namely that of the *theologia crucis*. It is on this particular motif and its underlying – I am tempted to say, near-Lutheran – motivation that the following pages will dwell.

2 Lutheran Sensibilities

Numerous scholars, most recently Judith Wolfe, in her lucid *Heidegger's Eschatology* and its compagnon volume *Heidegger and Theology*, have spoken of Heidegger's "Lutheran sensibilities."[12] Speaking in the first person, the early Heidegger claims:

---

10 Gadamer, 75.
11 Cf. Hent de Vries, *Philosophy and the Turn to Religion* (Baltimore and London: Johns Hopkins University Press, 1999, 2000), the chapters "Formal Indications" and "The Generous Repetition," 158–304.
12 Judith Wolfe, *Heidegger's Eschatology: Theological Horizons in Martin Heidegger's Early Work* (Oxford: Oxford University Press, 2013), 157; idem, *Heidegger and Theology* (London: Bloomsbury, 2014); Christian Sommer, *Heidegger, Aristote, Luther. Les sources aristotéliciennes et néotestamentaires d'Être et Temps* (Paris: PUF, 2005); Philippe Büttgen, *Luther et la philosophie* (Paris: Vrin/EHESS, 2011), 54–55, 62, 66, 80–85; Jean-Claude Gens, "Martin Luther ((1483–1546)," in Philippe Arjakovsky, François Fédier, and Hadrian France-Lanord, eds., *Le Dictionnaire Martin Heidegger* (Paris: Les Éditions du Cerf, 2013), 787–790.

The one who has accompanied me in my investigations was the young Luther and my model was Aristotle, who was despised by the first. Several impulses came from Kierkegaard and in my eyes, it is Husserl who implanted them.[13]

If we bracket the question of Kierkegaardian "impulses" as well as that of the Husserlian phenomenological gaze, then what is striking is Heidegger's invocation of the "young" Luther who "accompanied" him perhaps even more so than that philosophical "model," which for a long tradition ranging from the Middle Ages and Scholasticism up to Neo-Scholasticism and Neo-Thomismen, including Husserl's teacher Franz Brentano, would, indeed, be Aristotle. It seems implied here that the latter's conceptual framework as read through the Hussserlian gaze was best suited to highlight and profile as well as think through and realize the Lutheran impulse. But then, the grave reservations of Luther vis-à-vis the Aristotle are well-known, if often exaggerated, and Heidegger's own early efforts clearly consist in radically recasting some of Aristotle's major premises, preoccupations, and ulterior aims. It is, precisely, by offering a rigorously and original *phenomenological* interpretation of Aristotle's metaphysics and physics, by way of his ethics, that a significantly new and different type of inquiry will slowly emerge.

The two invocations and ongoing references are, in fact, far from easy to situate. For while Heidegger's discovery of Aristotle clearly precedes his reading of Luther, it should be explained why and how the latter is said to be the one who "accompanied" him in the investigations, which consist of lectures and seminars, articles and drafts, leading up to a provisional culmination, the publication of *Being and Time*. What would it mean for a theologian – and a resolute anti-philosopher, at that – to "accompany" the emergent philosophy and methodic phenomenology that, without this company, might not have forged its very own path, much less come into its own?

In a letter, dated January 19, 1919, to Father Engelbert Krebs, a Catholic priest and professor of theology who had officiated his wedding, Heidegger made it official that his recent reading, notably Luther's commentary on Paul's Letter to the Romans had suddenly placed his earlier studies and understanding of the Middle Ages in an altogether new light and had further given him a "radically new" grasp of "the development of Christian religiosity." But the letter also and, perhaps, first of all, speaks of a strictly and rigorous or serious *philosophical* conversion and, from here on, "calling," which are, surprisingly, phrased in unmistakingly Lutheran terms. In the letter, Heidegger insists on a necessary break with a

---

13 Martin Heidegger, *Ontologie. Hermeneutik der Faktizität* (Summer Semester 1923), ed. K. Bröcker-Oltmanns (Frankfurt am Main: Vittorio Klostermann, 1988, 2nd edn. 1995), 5.

"*system* of Catholicism" that has become "problematic and unacceptable" on the basis of "epistemological insights that extend to historical knowledge," even though these insights do not thereby affect "Christianity and metaphysics" as such, since these are now understood in a strikingly "new sense." At any rate, any such new appreciation, Heidegger leaves no doubt, leaves the value of the Christian "lifeworld" intact, just as its shuns all too facile polemics. Apostasy, reneging on the faith of the past generations, much less of the Fathers of the Church, would thus not be an option. As Heidegger says:

> Over the last two years I have set aside all scientific work of a specialized nature and have struggled instead for a basic clarification of my philosophical position. This has led me to results that I could not be free to hold and teach if I were tied to positions that come from outside of philosophy.
>
> Epistemological insights that extend to the theory of historical knowledge have made the *system* of Catholicism problematic and unacceptable to me – but not Christianity and metaphysics, which however [I now understand] in a new sense.
>
> I believe that I – perhaps more than those who work on the subject officially – have perceived the values that the Catholic Middle Ages holds within itself, values that we are still far from truly exploiting. My research into the phenomenology of religion, which will draw heavily on the Middle Ages, should prove beyond dispute that even though I have transformed my basic standpoint, I have refused to be dragged into abandoning my objective high opinion of and regard for the Catholic lifeworld or into mouthing the vacuous polemics of an embittered apostate.
>
> (...) It is hard to live as a philosopher – inner truthfulness toward oneself and toward those one is supposed to teach demands sacrifice, renunciation, and struggles that remain forever foreign to the academic "tradesman."
>
> I believe I have an inner call to philosophy and, by fulfilling it in research and teaching, a call to the eternal vocation of the inner man – *and for that alone* do I feel called to achieve what is in my powers and thus to justify, before God, my very existence [*Dasein*] and work.[14]

Heidegger would later claim that he had, in fact, never left the Church and it would become clear that he had originally hoped to obtain a chair in Catholic Philosophy in Freiburg. Indeed, he characterized his philosophical project as the dedicated effort of "making the intellectual riches stored up in Scholasticism available und usable for the spiritual battle of the future over the Christian-Catholic ideal of life."[15] Yet he was passed over for the chair and would soon intensify

---

14 In Theodore Kisiel and Thomas Sheehan, eds., *Becoming Heidegger: On the Trail of His Early Occasional Writings, 1919–1927* (Evanston: Northwestern University Press, 2007), 96; cf. also Sheehan, "Reading a Life: Heidegger and Hard Times," in Charles B. Guignon, ed., *Cambridge Companion to Heidegger* (Cambridge: Cambridge University Press, 1993), 71–72.
15 Cited after Sheehan, *Cambridge Companion to Heidegger*, 75.

his reading of Protestant theologians such as Friedrich Schleiermacher, Søren Kierkegaard, and notably Luther (begun between 1909 and 1911, when he started to study the latter's commentary on Paul's Letter to the Romans, but undertaken with far more fervor even some ten years later).[16] In the process, one commentator notes,

> Heidegger came to believe that Luther had correctly identified Scholasticism as an illegitimate fusion of Christianity and Greek metaphysics. Luther's purge of Christian theology from Aristotelian-Scholastic concepts became Heidegger's paradigm for the phenomenological destruction of the ontological tradition. Luther reduced theology to primordial Christian faith; Heidegger would reduce ontology to historical life.[17]

And, as yet another commentator observes, "when Heidegger returned to full-time teaching in 1919, he understood himself to be a Luther of Western metaphysics."[18]

3 "A Luther of Western Metaphysics"

Husserl had helped Heidegger obtain a grant that allowed him to purchase the complete version of the Erlangen edition of Luther's works. Hence, when Heidegger went from Catholic Freiburg im Breisgau to Protestant Marburg, he was already familiar with Luther's work as would soon become clear in his participation in Rudolf Bultmann's seminars, devoted to "Paul's Ethics." The collaboration with Bultmann for years to come would be intense, if not without reservations, mostly on Heidegger's part. Yet Heidegger's investment in the topic would not be a passing affair. The Marburg connection and conversations with Bultmann would find a much later echo, long after the war, during Heidegger's participation in Gerhard Ebeling's seminar. There he would, once again, pronounce himself on Luther.

This said, as several scholars have demonstrated, it is not only the reading of Luther's commentary on Paul's Letter to the Romans, but notably his *theologia paradoxa* and *theologia crucis* that formed stages on Heidegger's way towards

---

16 Cf. Otto Pöggeler, *Philosophische und hermeneutische Theologie: Heidegger, Bultmann und die Folgen* (Munich: Wilhelm Fink Verlag, 2009), 95–105.
17 S. J. McGrath, *The Early Heidegger and Medieval Philosophy: Phenomenology for the Godforsaken* (Washington: The Catholic University of America Press, 2006), 151 and 151 n. 1 and 151 n. 2.
18 John Van Buren, *The Young Heidegger: Rumour of the Hidden King* (Bloomington: Indiana University Press, 1994), 167.

a thinking that would eventually break with the "system of Catholicism" and much beyond. The reason is twofold.

First, Heidegger notes in his early lecture course on the *Phänomenologie des religiösen Lebens* (*The Phenomenology of Religious Life*) that,

> Protestant faith and Catholic faith are *fundamentally different*. Noetically and noematically separated experiences. In Luther an *original* form of religiosity – one that is also not found in the mystics – breaks out.
>
> The "holding-to-be-true" of Catholic faith is founded entirely otherwise than the *fiducia* of the reformers.
>
> Phenomena which first come to be understood within the doctrine of the constitution of the religious world in general.
>
> From there also the concept of "grace" differentiates itself, and with it, the entire "relationship" of grace and freedom, nature and grace, and the meaning of the phrase "gratia supponit naturum" [grace underlies nature]; the doctrine of "justification" and the conception of the sacrament.
>
> In turn the religious sense complexes are qualitatively entirely otherwise in primordial Christianity. The development of theology [takes place] out of its various motives and its relationship to faith.[19]

Second, Heidegger finds in Luther's destruction of Aristotelian-Scholastic metaphysics the pretext for discovering another, "primitive" Aristotle, which will allow him to leap backwards to yet another origin from which the whole edifice of Western thought can be put in a different light and recast, from the ground up. In fact, as also the early Luther had noted in 1517 in his controversy with Scholastic theology: "It is highly unlikely that the thought of Aristotle can be found among the Latins [i.e., the Church Fathers, preceding Scholasticism]." (WA 1, 226). And recent scholarship has brought out more fully why and in what sense Aristoteles' work contains potentialities that the subsequent philosophical and Christian appropriation of theology and the amalgam of onto-theology has glossed over, distorted, and made us forget.[20]

What underlies Heidegger's early work, then, is the influence and confluence of two sources, which could not be more different, the New Testament conception of *Urchristentum* and its factical life experience, as read with the help of Luther and subsequently with Bultmann, and the conception of the "primitive"

---

[19] Martin Heidegger, *Phänomenologie des religiösen Lebens*, Gesamtausgabe vol. 60 (Frankfurt am Main: Vittorio Klostermann, 1995), 310; *The Phenomenology of Religious Life*, trans. By Matthias Fritsch and Jennifer Anna Gosetti-Ferencei (Bloomington and Indianapolis: University of Indiana Press, 2004), 236.

[20] Gwenaëlle Aubry, *Dieu sans la puissance: dunamis et energeia chez Aristote et chez Plotin* (Paris: Vrin, 2006) and idem, *Génèse du dieu souverain* (Paris: Vrin, 2018).

as opposed to Scholastic Aristotle. This primordial Aristotle will turn out to be as distinct from Brentano's as it will be from Luther's and is distilled and culled, as Gadamer claims, from his model's *Metaphysics, Ethics,* and *Physics* alike. An old-new sense of *sophia* and *phronesis* goes hand in hand with an original understanding of *Dasein's* – modal – moods and movement at once.

Together with these observations, then, we can retain two crucial elements: the moment of annihilation or destruction, mentioned earlier, and the understanding of theology as a science of the calling of faith, of a faith, that is, which is centered on the "crucified God" and, indeed, must itself be seen – and see itself – as a form of self-effacement, of sorts.

Hence, the two themes are interrelated and, on closer scrutiny, the expression of one unique thought and its spiritual exercise: the thought namely that faith (*Glaube*) is given by, in and through, what is believed (*das Geglaubte*) and, thereby, "generated,"[21] as one commentator puts it, "*not out* of Dasein and *not through* it on its own account [*nicht aus* dem Dasein und *nicht durch* es aus freien Stücken]," but as a mode of existence that stands in inner relation to the "cruficied God," here and now, and *cannot do otherwise* (to echo and parody Luther famous, if apocryphal, dictum).

4 *Poenitentim agite, metanoeite, Tut Busse*

Not the least important aspect of the transition that the Protestant Reformation brought about is the shift from an understanding of man in broadly Aristotelian concepts that privileges man's essential *genus* and *differentia specifica* to that of a calling, *klesis, Berufung* or *Bestimmung*, a calling or vocation, privileging man's service and servitude, becoming *Knecht*. Luther's first and most public statement, the 1517 *Disputation for Clarifying the Power of Indulgences*, starts out with the assertion that what Christ in matter of literal fact asks of us is not what the established Roman Catholic Church has ended up teaching:

> Our Lord and Master Jesus Christ, in saying "Do penance . . . [*poenitentim agite, metanoeite, Tut Busse*, "Repent, for the kingdom of heaven is at hand," *Matthew* 4:17]" wanted the entire [sic, HdV] life of the faithful to be one of penitence. (Thesis 1).

It should be noted that the Latin Church Fathers translated the Greek term *metanoia* with *poenitentia*, that is, an act of penance. And the "phrase" in question – "repent, for the kingdom of heaven is at hand," Luther adds in the second the-

---

21 Konrad Hammann, *Rudolf Bultmann: Eine Biographie* (Tübingen: Mohr Siebeck, 2012), 200.

sis – "cannot be understood as referring to sacramental Penance, that is, confession and satisfaction as administered by the clergy." A letter to his spiritual mentor, von Staupitz, dated May 30, 1518, states this explicitly. Yet to repent, to do penance, to turn around and be reborn, the third thesis goes on to say, "does not mean solely inner penitence [which would be "contrition"] – indeed such inner penance is nothing unless it outwardly produces various mortifications of the flesh." Consequently [*itaque*], Luther ends this opening salvo in thesis 4, a logical conclusion imposes itself: "penalty [*poena*] remains as long as hatred of self (that is, true inner penitence) remains, namely: until our entrance into the kingdom of heaven)."

The motif of hatred of self, of the former and present self, is, of course, as old as Christianity itself, and, perhaps, best known from Blaise Pascal's famous dictum, in *Pensées*, that "*le moi est haïssable*." But, significantly, it also resonates with the downright dismissal of self-love and, perhaps, even self-care – or "care of the self" – that the tradition of ancient spiritual exercises and, indeed, of philosophy seen and practiced as a "way of life" inaugurated in the history of Western thought. As a matter of fact, Pierre Hadot, whose lifelong work demonstrated this insight in a variety of ancient, early modern, and modern contexts and, in so doing, helped us see how philosophy in its most telling countercurrents was neither a matter of theoretical contemplation or speculation nor of normative ethics and politics primarily, but instead took the form of a spiritual practice, was inspired from the outset by Heidegger's questioning. Indeed, Hadot is closer to Heidegger, in this respect, than he is to Michel Foucault's massive investigations into the so-called "care of the self." After all, as in Hadot's writings, *Selbstsorge* is not a locution one will find in Heidegger. Rather, in the earliest Heidegger there is an appeal to *Entselbstung*, which Wolfe, who translates this term as the "offering up of self," wrongly characterizes as the contrary of the later *Eigentlichkeit*, the term that translates as "authenticity" (and not so much "mineness,"[22] as she further suggests, as that term renders *Jemeinigkeit*, a concept that implies no self-centeredness, much less self-care, per se).

Luther, again in the *Heidelberg Disputation*, puts it neatly: "through the cross works are dethroned and [the old] Adam, who is especially edified by works, is crucified." In other words, it is the cross that crosses out works – and all that they stand for – and it is the old man, informed or, rather, formed by works who is crucified as a result. *Bildung*, as the later idiom, analyzed by Gadamer, will have it, concerns the shining forth an inner image, itself left by the Creator in the soul and heart of His creatures.

---

22 Judith Wolfe, *Heidegger's Eschatology*, 17.

It is clear that, for Heidegger, our ownmost mode of existence – which is a *modal* possibility, first and foremost – lies in its relationship to the cross, which is a concrete ontic, if not always explicitly ontological, character of *Dasein*'s historical being. But then, this historical aspect, indeed, this original historicity, is given in a fundamental experience, namely that of faith, alone. It discloses or, indeed, reveals and shows itself "in faith," that is, "for the one who finds or has faith."[23]

5 The Lutheran Schema

The Lutheran schema of spiritual exercise is that of Greek *metanoia*, Latin *conversio*, and German *Umstellung*, in English *reversal* or, rather, *inversion*. All these technical terms, it seems, are premised upon a process and task, which is that of a preparatory and preliminary *annihilatio*, a term and notion we find in Luther and two of his closest readers on whom I would here like to focus somewhat more directly, namely Heidegger, and somewhat more indirectly, namely Karl Barth.

The concept of annihilation testifies to the strange prevalence and privilege of Non-Being, whether it takes the form of a *lex redigit at nihilum*, of a law reducing man to a nullity before God, as Emil Brunner and others put it, or, with Heidegger, is found in the assumed nihilism of human finitude, given with the fundamental experiences of anxiety, boredom, transcendental homelessness, and our so-called being-towards-death or, finally, in the problem of ineradicable evil, discussed by Barth in the paragraph 50, in *Kirchliche Dogmatik* (Church Dogmatics), devoted to "Gott und das Nichtige [God and the Nothing]," and a notion, it has been claimed, Barth may have borrowed in part, if not from Heidegger's inaugural address, "Was ist Metaphysik?," then at least from the widespread circulation of the "Nothing" in the existential philosophical literature of the day. Conversely, other attributions have been made, perhaps all too quickly, as well. Erich Przywara, for example, in a 1928 essay, portrayed Heidegger's interpretation of being-towards-death as "a metaphysics of sin and salvation – concretely the religious metaphysics of Kierkegaard and Barth."[24] But the actual history and explanation of such apparent convergences and their correlative divergences is, it seems, far more complex.

---

23 Cf. Wolfe, 17.
24 Cited after Wolfe, 138 n. 3.

For Luther, Heidegger, and Barth this privilege of a certain *annihilatio* and the *nihil* is neither one of chronological nor of logical priority. Its prevalence is that of a horizon or rather dimension of critical thought and fundamental experience that accompanies us each step of our way. As such, it is *given with, ahead of,* and *surrounding* all we think, do, and judge or even refrain and withdraw from. Indeed, it is the originally given, the originary phenomenon, even though we cannot leave it at that and even though it is neither possible nor permitted to turn this "given" into a foundational "myth" that would ground and orient us epistemologically, normatively, and criteriologically.

The motif and motivation of *annihilatio* and the *nihil* it faces lies behind the so-called "*exitus* and *reditus* from and to 'factical life experience,'" to cite one commentator, Wolfe aptly notes. And it is this movement, including the "nothing" that surrounds it that theology and philosophy share in common, as the latter offers, in her view, "merely an ontologically more basic traversal of theology's *exitus* and *reditus* from and to faith,"[25] just as, we might add, theology almost inevitably adopts and reiterates some of philosophy's basic assumptions and arguments in the same vein.

The philosophical moment in early Luther and the theological moment in early Heidegger converge in destruction (in Latin: *destructio*, in German: *Destruktion*). They coincide in a mental, indeed, spiritual process of destruction or annihilation that forms the very basis for everything new, for a "re-formation" of thought and experience, ethics and politics. As one commentator, Benjamin Crowe, summarizes:

> *Destructio* is a name for a way of doing theology that attempts to block the influence of humanity's pervasive urge for self-glorification on the concrete experience of religious life... Heidegger transcribes this program into his own philosophical outlook by developing a practice of "*Destruktion*," which, like Luther's *destructio*, attempts to counter the tendencies toward complacency and conformity that encroach upon an individual's attempt to live an "authentic" life.[26]

It has been observed, most recently by Marius Timmann Mjaaland in his book *The Hidden God: Luther, Philosophy, and Political Theology,* that it is notably in the 1518 *Heidelberg Disputation* – often considered the classical text outlining the contours of the *theologia crucis* – that we find this influential philosophical topos, even concept, namely that of "destruction." In that text, he reminds us,

---

[25] Wolfe, 112.
[26] Benjamin D. Crowe, *Heidegger's Religious Origins: Destruction and Authenticity* (Bloomington and Indianapolis: University of Indiana Press, 2006), 38.

Luther "argues for a *destruction* of metaphysics – and a subversion of our moral intuitions concerning the difference between good and evil. These arguments are puzzling and they demonstrate some basic paradoxes that run counter to the presuppositions of hermeneutic theology and philosophy."[27] Following a New Testament motif, best known from Paul's words – in I Corinthians 1:19, "For it is written, 'I will destroy the wisdom of the wise, and the discernment of the discerning I will thwart'" – Luther could be said to offer

> an intriguing argument for the *destruction* of metaphysics, beginning with a destruction of Aristotelian anthropology in the "crucifixion" of the old Adam. More precisely, he argues that *crucifying and destroying man* is necessary in order to acquire truth and unveil illusions: Since human beings naturally tend to be self-possessed, self-assertive, and potentially destructive to others as well as to themselves, they simply *need* this destruction of their illusions.[28]

Mjaaland's observation is hardly new. Indeed, he departs from the suggestive question, discussed by numerous philosophers and most tellingly by Reiner Schürmann in his book *Broken Hegemonies* (*Des hégémonies brisées*), namely whether "the philosophy of the modern era," seen through a phenomenological lens, has it roots in Martin Luther's most daring thoughts.

While some had suggested that in addition to the critique of Aristotelian metaphysics, there can be found "a transcendental turn at the heart of Luther's approach," forcing us to reconsider a well-established modern philosophical genealogy, known since Hegel and Heidegger, according to which modernity begins with Descartes, Schürmann, by contrast, sees an even earlier relevant motif and motivation originating in Luther. It is the impetus of "passive transcendentalism" which, on his reading, inaugurates a very different, "recessed" and "obedient" aspect of modernity that is far more "tragically" and mostly "covertly" connected with modern reason's autonomy and self-assertion. This motif and motivation stands opposed to modern philosophy's representational, egological, and formal accounts of its own genesis and structure in that it inserts a distinctive event-character of "grace" into all that exist, all that befalls us and falls upon us. After all, Christian "freedom" is a freedom from all things, from all others, just as it is, *ipso facto* and not merely subsequently, *post factum*, a matter of being or becoming subservient to all.

---

[27] Marius Timman Mjaaland, *The Hidden God: Luther, Philosophy, and Political Theology* (Bloomington and Indianapolis: University of Indiana Press, 2016), 54.
[28] Mjaaland, *The Hidden God*, 1–2, the reference is to the *Heidelberg Disputation*, WA 1, 362.

This paradoxical theo-logic, I would like to add, was identified by an avid reader of especially the young Luther, namely the young Heidegger, at the time rumored to be the "hidden king" of early twentieth-century German philosophy. Indeed, it is in Heidegger's appropriation of central tenets of Luther's *theologia crucis*, perhaps more than anything else, in addition to the emphasis on *sola fide* and *sola scripture* motifs in so many words, that we find the prism or prisms through which the uniquely philosophical repercussions of the Protestant Reformation (at the time, some 400 year after its historical event) find themselves filtered and fractured in distinctly phenomenological and dialectical, existential and hermeneutical, and eventual more political theological – indeed, new theologico-political – patterns.

Yet compared to their idioms and methods Heidegger's insight into the formal or structural relationship between philosophy or, in his early terminology, phenomenology and ontology, the "science of Being," the *Urwissenschaft* that is "absolutely" different from all others, on the one hand, and theology, the "science of faith," of the Cross, on the other, is deeply paradoxical, not to say, aporetic. In the lecture "Phenomenology and Theology" which Heidegger delivered in a rough, schematic version in 1926 and then again in 1927 (again, the very year *Sein und Zeit* was published) and 1928, that puzzling, indeed, dazzling aspect of their relationship is further deepened by the fact that he does not think of two actual sciences but of two "possible sciences," whose "ideal type" and "construct" he lays out in basic countours: one ontological and one ontic for which the designation "science," in either case, is somewhat of a stretch or whose distinct scientific features have a *sui generis* character (philosophy or phenomenology and ontology being at the furthest, indeed, absolute remove from what historically and empirically defines ontic, say, positive sciences, while theology resembles the latter seemingly more, without being reducible to them either; closer to chemistry or mathematics than to philosophy, as Heidegger provocatively claims, theology nonetheless anticipates or should we say retains some of the elementary forms philosophy's method, at the very least. As a *Kreuzeswissenschaft*, to cite Edith Stein's, but not Heidegger's, terminology, although he might have agreed, its fundamental experience and operation is that of *Umstellung*, reversal or inversion, and not mere *Fortführung*, say, explication and elaboration, and in this shares the essential trait that demarcates philosophy from all positives sciences, which, as Heidegger later explicitly will say, do not properly "think." And what it, theology, thereby expresses and also produces is everything but the "knowledge of God," but, quite to the contrary, the painful realization of its, of our *Gottvergessenheit*.

And yet, a religious, theological, or Christian philosophy, blending theology and fundamental rather than merely regional science (and, perhaps, strictly speaking any science), would be best pictured as a *hölzernes Eisen*, a wooden iron, meaning a coincidence of opposites (a *coincidentia oppositorum*), borrowing Nicholas Cusanus' expression, as taken up by Pierre Hadot in his introduction to French translation of Ernst Bertram's *Nietzsche. Versuch einer Mythologie*[29] and used to capture the equally strenuous relationship between objective history, philology, and historiography, on the one hand, and existential appropriation and import, on the other; an eminently Heideggerian topos and tension and one explicitly addressed by Bultmann in roughly these terms as well.

The reference to an *hölzernes Eisen* Heidegger may have found, in philosophical context, in Arthur Schopenhauer and Friedrich Nietzsche. Heidegger uses the same oxymoron as a rhetorical tool to indicate that there is a ostensible self-contradiction residing in the fact that just as something wooden cannot be amalgamated with iron or a circle not squared, so, likewise, philosophy and theology do not match or add up.

Pairing contradictory or incongruent terms, the expression conveys a predicament of all predication, which is that to predicate something of something – and *a fortiori* to *philosophically* predicate something *theological* in theological and be it Biblical and dogmatic, practical or homiletic discourse – at the very least *risks* distorting what was claimed (intended or gestured). This, Heidegger would seem to intimate, is already clear from the "idea" and "possibility" for which these peculiar "sciences" stand, never mind how they turn out to relate to – and, indeed, invert – the places they pretend cover (and, in the process, tend to cover over, just as they end up "concealing" and "distorting" themselves as well).

It is this *contradictio in terminis* or *contradictio in adjecto* in which a kind of discourse (or, indeed, discourse *tout court*) adds itself on to the decision and choice – call it "faith," the "call" of faith – that presumably guides it (but that is as much guided by that same discourse, in turn). Indeed, it is this paradoxical or, more precisely, aporetic insight and experience that leads us to the heart of the *theologia crucis*, to the necessary "crossing out" or *kreuzweise Durchstreichung*" of which the later Heidegger (and, in his footsteps, others such as Jacques Derrida and Jean-Luc Marion) will make so much. But the premises of this motif and motivation lie, I claim, in the early engagement with Luther. For the relationship between philosophy or phenomenology and theology this means that both of these terms and disciplines coincide as opposites and,

---

29 Pierre Hadot, "Préface," in Ernst Bertram, *Nietzsche. Essai de mythologie*, trans. Roger Pitrou (Paris: Éditions du Félin, 2007), 5–44; "Introduction to Ernst Bertram, *Nietzsche: Attempt at a Mythology*," trans. Paul Bishop, in *The Agonist* III.1 (2010), 52–84.

I will add, also obey a strangely dialectical and political outlook. They do so contingently and, ultimately, arbitrarily, based on choice and decision, a call made in faith and through faith alone. And this, finally, affects philosophy no less than theology proper.

6 Phenomenology and Theology

As Jean Greisch has keenly observed in his massive commentary on *Being and Time*, "the lecture [on "Phenomenology and Theology"] can be read as the developed version of a thesis relative to the crisis of the foundations of theology that is formulated as early as par. 3 of *Sein und Zeit*."[30] Here, Heidegger references the *Grundlagenkrisis* that affects a host of so-called ontic sciences, theology among them, from within:

> *Theology* is seeking a more primordial interpretation of man's Being towards God, prescribed by the meaning of faith itself and remaining within it. It is slowly beginning to understand once more Luther's insight that the 'foundation' on which its system of dogma rests has not arisen from an inquiry in which faith is primary, and that conceptually this foundation not only is inadequate for the problematic of theology, but conceals and distorts it.[31]

In different contexts, Heidegger adds that "traditional systematics and dogmatics" and the "philosophical system" and "conceptuality" they are based on have "turned the question of man and especially the question of God as well as the relationship between man and God upside down [*auf den Kopf gestellt*]."[32] The theo-

---

[30] Jean Greisch, *Ontologie et temporalité: Esquisse d'une interprétation intégrale de* Sein und Zeit (Paris: PUF, 1994), 427.
[31] "Die *Theologie* sucht nach einer ursprünglicheren, aus dem Sinn des Glaubens selbst vorgezeichneten und innerhalb seiner verbleibenden Auslegung des Seins des Menschen zu Gott. Sie beginnt langsam die Einsicht *Luthers* wieder zu verstehen, dass ihre dogmatische Systematik auf einem 'Fundament' ruht, das nicht einem primär glaubenden Fragen entwachsen ist und dessen Begrifflichkeit für die theologische Problematik nicht nur nicht zureicht, sondern sie verdeckt und verzerrt." (Heidegger, *Sein und Zeit*, 10, cf. 9).
[32] Greisch, *Ontologie et temporalité*, 428, recalls a passage from the important lecture course, known as *Prolegomena zur Geschichte des Zeitbegriffs* (Gesamtausgabe 20, Summer semester 1925, ed. P. Jaeger [Frankfurt am Main: Vittorio Klostermann, 1979, 2nd edn. 1988, 3rd edn. 1994], 6), where Heidegger says the following: "*Die Theologie will aus einer Erneuerung des Glaubens, d. h. des Grundverhältnisses zur Wirklichkeit, die für sie thematisch ist, dazu vordringen, eine ursprüngliche Explikation des Seins des Menschen zu Gott zu gewinnen, d. h. vorzudringen zu einer Herauslösung der fundamentalen Frage nach dem Menschen aus der traditionellen Systematik der Dogmatik. Denn die Systematik ruht im Grunde auf einem philosophischem*

logical operation par excellence, then, would be the inversion of this inversion, the reversal of the *aversio Dei* that liberates man, who is *incurvatus in se*, as Luther says, in other words, in captivity of the "naturalist disposition" and "constative fallacy," as traditional and linguistic phenomenologists such as Husserl and J.L. Austin in the twentieth century will further add. It would do so through an act of "epoché" or, indeed, "*Konversion,*" as Husserl also says. Faith would be a radical reversal or "*Umstellung,*" as Heidegger insists.

And here is the catch. For while Heidegger insists on the absolute distinction between all ontic sciences, theology included, on the one hand, and philosophy proper, as an ontological science, on the other, at least the text of the lecture "Phenomenology and Theology" leaves no doubt that the philosophical calling and professional discipline, in its very exercise, operates under the exact same regime of reversal (terminologically and methodologically speaking). In this, Heidegger stood hardly alone, even though few would admit this apparent challenge of no less apparent distinctions with equal rigor.

We know that Karl Barth kept himself at a remove from the intricacies of the conversations, dialogues and debates, that Bultmann and Heidegger entertained for several years. He never quite agreed to meeting, much less to an open exchange or confrontation with Heidegger, of which Bultmann had held great hopes and which he continued to plan, if only in vain. In Wolfe's words:

> Unwilling to be pulled into a discussion he saw neither as his calling nor as his strength, he kept his distance from Heidegger from the beginning. In July 1927, Barth declined Bultmann's invitation to a weekend in Marburg to meet Heidegger and attend his lecture on "history and time" with mock self-irony: "As a lumbering Swiss, I am not so quick off the mark [alt. quick with concepts] that I could grasp fast enough what Heidegger, whom I don't even know, wants."[33]

It was Barth's brother, Heinrich, who would publish an extensive "*Auseinandersetzung*" with Heidegger on the problem of ontology and idealism, in *Zwischen den Zeiten*, in 1929, not Karl Barth himself. Barth, for his part, would continue to dismiss the "accommodation efforts" among the group of dialectical theologians (notably Emil Brunner, Paul Tillich, Rudolf Bultmann, and Friedrich Gogarten), stating in a letter to Thurneysen, dated March 13, 1925:

System und einer Begrifflichkeit die ihrem Sinne nach sowohl die Frage nach dem Menschen als auch die Frage nach Gott und erst recht die Frage des Verhältnisses des Menschen zu Gott auf den Kopf gestellt hat."

33 Wolfe, *Heidegger's Eschatology*, 107, cf. Barth, Bultmann, *Briefwechsel*, 36, cf. also 102–118, 122–127.

> The problem is not that one cannot honourably have some kind of philosophy in mind, much less that it musn't … be Heidegger's. It's that those people all want to run for shelter from philosophy; that, rather than from God, they want to start from some kind of "possibility"; [that they want to] avoid the scandal of theology by means of some kind of "pre-apprehension" or some trick to lead the pagans *ad absurdum* and look good. And then they boast to me about the clarity of their concepts, as if that were an art if one takes those concepts from anywhere except from within the matter itself.[34]

This lack of interest, however, is not the whole story and, this much is clear, it was not fully mutual. In fact, in his correspondence with Bultmann, Heidegger would eventually conclude that a theology that premises itself on – and seeks to express and serve – faith, that is, faith in the crucified God, alone best captures its spiritual vocation and academic profession with "Barth's indifference *against* philosophy [*Gleichgültigkeit* gegen *die Philosophie*], but with the understanding *of* it [*Verständnis* für sie],"[35] an understanding, Heidegger left no doubt, that his friend Bultmann had acquired more fully than any other advocate of so-called dialectical theology.

This indifference resonates, if one can say so, with Heidegger's own claim that, for a philosopher, silence with respect to all theology is, when all is said and done, *de rigueur*. Indeed, Heidegger's nod to Barth does not only shed light on a striking parallel, in this context at least, with Ludwig Wittgenstein's use of silence in his *Tractatus Logico-Philosophicus*, but also and more importantly on Heidegger's own understanding of an "a-theism" that is privative rather than negative (i.e., not based on a negation of theism or affirmation of atheist humanism at all).

Yet Heidegger's a-theism is not merely methodological either, entertained for descriptive and analytical, hermeneutic or otherwise explicative purposes alone. On the contrary, its format and formula – including its all too formulaic notions and idiom – is espoused and experimented in an almost spiritual, meditative as well as pragmatic guise, that is to say, exercised *ad maiorem gloriam Dei*, for the glory of God (or whatever it "is" that comes to take His place). Heidegger says so himself: "*Die Theologie ehren wir, indem wir von ihr schweigen.*"[36] Or, as he puts it elsewhere in a letter to Bultmann, it is "*reinlicher und ehrlicher, wenn die Philosophie zunächst einmal schweigt.*"[37] Or again, in yet another letter, he writes: "the more I think about these things … the more it seems to me that all explicit [sic] phil-

---

34 Wolfe, 141.
35 Rudolf Bultmann and Martin Heidegger, *Briefwechsel 1925–1975*, Andreas Grossmann and Christof Landmesser, eds. with an introduction by Eberhard Jüngel (Frankfurt am Main: Vittorio Klostermann/ Tübingen: Mohr Siebeck, 2009), 172, cf. Hammann, *Bultmann*, 203.
36 Cited after Rüdiger Safranski, *Ein Meister aus Deutschland. Heidegger und seine Zeit* (München: Hanser, 1994), 162.
37 Heidegger, Bultmann, *Briefwechsel*, 64.

osophical discussion ought to disappear from theology in favor of concentrated textual and historical work."³⁸ But then, it is precisely by committing oneself rigorously and resolutely to this philolological and historical aspect of things that, paradoxically, the other – proper theological and, dare I say, philosophical – other aspect (indeed, the other or inverse theology of Christianity's origins and eschatology) is either pressuposed or freed up, even obliquely involved, if only sideways.

Again, this would not be so different from Barth's longheld conviction, blocking any further interest on his part in Heidegger's philosophy or, for that matter, any other, namely that philosophy "has nothing to say to theology or in theology [*der Theologie und in der Theologie nichts zu sagen hatte*]"³⁹; a formulation that leaves fully open that only by crossing itself fully out philosophy acquires *for* and, perhaps, even *in* theology its possible relevance.

Yet, philosophy does and cannot target in and for theology any subject or object of faith *directly* or, let's say, *intentionally*. It can merely clear out the latter's ontic, non-theological remains, including and especially the correlative ontological misunderstandings that "conceal" and "distort" the very matter, the *Sache selbst*, the existence and "essence," of what is believed, of what it is to believe in the very act of faith and out of this faith alone. Moreover, while realizing, that is, inevitably imposing while also criticizing, the predicament of *its* predications, philosophy does not so much obey as it follows, mimics or reiterates, a distinctively theological and even religious topos. That is the cross, Heidegger shows, it will have to carry.

In his "What Did Luther Understand by Religion?" Karl Holl noted that "[b]ehind the annihilation, Luther sees a coming-to-be; behind the destruction a creation, the emergence of something eternal into the perishing of the finite."⁴⁰ Heidegger, it seems, sets out to radicalize precisely these assumptions. This is not to deny that Heidegger borrowed, adopted, and transformed motifs and motivations he found in the New Testament, in Augustine, the German mystics, Luther and Kierkegaard, well before Bultmann borrowed and adopted Heidegger's own, presumably "independently derived categories to illuminate the New Testament,"⁴¹ as Wolfe rightly observes. But Wolfe, in my view, gets things only partly right when she continues by saying that

---

38 Heidegger, Bultmann, 108, trans. in Wolfe, *Heidegger's Eschatology*, 113.
39 Cited after Hammann, *Bultmann*, 196.
40 Karl Holl, *What Did Luther Understand by Religion?*, ed., James Luther Adams and Walter F. Bense, trans. Fred W. Meuser and Walter R. Wietzke (Philadelphia: Fortress Press, 1977), 55.
41 Wolfe, *Heidegger's Eschatology*, 107.

> Heidegger derived his own categories partly [sic, HdV] from phenomenological reduction of New Testament experience ("reduction" not in the technicial sense in which Husserl used the term, but in that dictated by the *lex parsimoniae*). Although Heidegger later presents his work of the late 1910s and earl 1920s as one of uncovering essential structures which made the religious experiences of the early Christian community – as well a myriad other religious and non-religious experiences – possible... this is a *post hoc* interpretation from the perspective of an already developed distinction between ontic and ontological sciences. In its original stages, Heidegger's work on aboriginal Christian experience was the reason [sic, HdV], not merely the laboratory, of his characteristic development of the phenomenological method. Bultmann's reception of Heidegger requires re-evaluation in that light ...[42]

There are many things one can take issue with in this proposed reading (the exact difference between phenomenogical reduction and the heuristic device of Occam's razor, the *lex parsimonia*, being the first among them). But the one assumption that matters most here is the following. The relationship between philosophy (here: phenomenology, ontological science, or even "reason"), on the one hand, and theology (here: the Christian factical life experience), on the other, is not a question of either genesis and genealogy or structure and analogy. It is, rather, that the rigorous and resolute insistence on the fundamental premises and contours of either discipline and *disciplina* (a *disciplina arcani*, if ever there was one), paradoxically, that is, inexplicably, aporetically or mysteriously, *yields* or *gives us* the aspect, perspective and mode, even mood, of the other. Phenomenology and theology, then, while historically and categorically distinct, change places left and right, at their extremes, to the point of virtually collapsing into each other. Their relation-without-relation is that of a *coincidentia oppositorum* that eludes the conceptual and argumentative register and logic of each, while implying or involving both.

It is incorrect, then, to suggest, as Wolfe does, that "Heidegger's argument," in the lecture "Phenomenology and Theology" and elsewhere, is that "phenomenology is logically prior to theology because it lays bare the essential structures of which specifically Christian experiences and concepts are only particular *existentiell* outworkings."[43] Nor does it seem adequate to add, as Wolfe does here, that "Paul's First Letter to the Thessalonians does not instantiate but potentially subsumes Heidegger's interpretation" (here, that of the so-called "night").[44] Neither aspect comes first or last. That, in this lecture and throughout, is Heideg-

---

[42] Wolfe, 107.
[43] Wolfe, 114–115.
[44] Wolfe, 115.

ger's point. Wolfe seems to acknowledge as much with reference to the text, not of the lecture, but of *Being and Time:*

> Echoed by Heidegger's own contention that "philosophical questioning strictly 'knows' nothing of sin" [SZ par. 62, 306 n. 1], Barth's position was ironically closer to that of Heidegger than was that of Brunner [who had offered a 'quasi-Kantian' foundation (*Grundlegung*) of theology]. Indeed, Heidegger himself encouraged Barth's and Thurneysen's insistence on a thoroughly *theo*logical rather than philosophical grounding of theology: in 1923, he recalled Thurneysen to theology's task of calling to faith in faith.⁴⁵

This does not sound as if Heidegger attributed to theology, in its comparison, cooperation or confrontation, with philosophy, a "decidedly inferior role."⁴⁶ It merely states that only if both disciplines respect their respective angles, viewpoints and aims, they will be best positioned to fulfill their professional and vocational – indeed, existential – calling. Such "fundamental differences" could hardly be that of "anthropocentric" versus "theocentric approaches."⁴⁷ For arguably, Heidegger's concept and method of a fundamental ontology or existential analytic has nothing deeply human or humanistic per se (and only the much later 1947 "Brief über den Humanismus [Letter on Humanism]" will set this record straight, even if the magnum opus offers all the necessary demarcations from so-called philosophical anthropology one might wish for). And, by the same token, Heidegger's own early and, *a fortiori*, later concept of the *theos* in *theo*logy is not strictly theist or even "theo-centric" either. And, while Heidegger, not long after delivering his Marburg lecture wrote to Elisabeth Blochmann that his effort, primarily addressed at theologians, to sketch philosophy's usefulness for their own enterprise, had placed him "as a philosopher in a terribly skewed light ... and ma[de] the whole thing into an apology for Christian theology rather than ... confrontation" – an assessment Wolfe judges as "perhaps somewhat disingenuous" – there is no doubt that he intended to clearly demonstrate "'*how, given* that someone stands in the Christian, Protestant faith and busies himself with theology, he ought to take philosophy, assuming he wants it to be a help and not,*" as is really the case [Wolfe adds], "a fundamental agitation.'"⁴⁸ But then, "a fundamental agitation," on second glance, is precisely what both philosophy and theology, following Heidegger's very own definition of their very movement, their flux and tendency to lapse and collapse into each other, have also in common. It is for this reason that Heidegger rightly claimed that Luther

---

45 Wolfe, 110 and 110 n. 90.
46 Wolfe, 111.
47 Wolfe, 107.
48 Cited after Wolfe, 113, cf. 142.

had "accompanied" him at the very outset of his career, casting a long shadow that even the later and latest work does not fully outrun.

Bruce L. McCormack
The Man who became God or the God who became Man?

The Concept of Revelation in the Theologies of Karl Barth and Friedrich Gogarten

1 Introduction

Among the influences contributing to the emergence of the *Diastasentheologie* of Karl Barth's second commentary on Romans – and its corollary, the dialectic of veiling and unveiling in revelation – must surely be Luther. Though Kierkegaard's "infinite qualitative difference" has received the greatest attention (due to Barth's celebration of that phrase in the preface to the second edition[1]), Luther too had a role to play in shaping Barth's understanding of the act of revelation as occurring in "hiddenness." In a defining passage (where the *Sache* to which Paul bore witness is concerned), Barth says,

> If Christ is true God, He must be [so] in unrecognizability. Direct recognizability is characteristic of idols (Kierkegaard). The power of God for salvation is something so new, so unheard of and unexpected in this world, that it can only step forth, be perceived and received as its [the world's] contradiction. The message of salvation does not explain itself and recommend itself. It does not ask and negotiate. It does not threaten and it does not promise. It withdraws itself everywhere it is not heard for its own sake.

There is then immediately appended a passage from Luther's *Bondage of the Will.*

> Faith is directed to invisible things. In order, therefore, that there be occasion for faith, everything which is believed must be hidden. These things are, however, most deeply hidden when they are placed over against appearance, the senses and experience. If God therefore makes alive, He does it by killing. If He justifies, He does it by making us guilty. If He leads us into heaven, He does it by leading us into hell.[2]

---

[1] Karl Barth, *Der Römerbrief, 1922* (Zürich: TVZ, 1940), xiii.
[2] Barth, *Der Römerbrief*, 1922, 14; E.T. pp.38–39. Cf. Martin Luther, *LW* 33 (Philadelphia: Fortress Press, 1972), 62.

Clearly, what "kills" is, for Barth, the divine "hiddenness," the non-givenness of God in the givenness of God's Self-revelation. But it is also, at the same time, that which saves. For it is by not making God's Self directly available to the would-be human knower that God remains God in the revelation-relation, that God remains the God who cannot be commandeered for human agendas but is free to realize God's own gracious purposes. That this goes beyond what Luther wanted to say might well be the case; I leave that to the Luther specialists to decide. But Barth's use of Luther here surely belongs to the possibilities created by Luther's contention that God saves as the One hidden in human suffering.[3] And that tells us a good deal about the "Luther" Barth most deeply appreciated. This was the "Luther" he made rich use of in the elaboration of his understanding of revelation in terms of a dialectic of veiling and unveiling.

Barth would take up this theme once again in *Church Dogmatics* I/1 under the heading of "The Speech of God as Mystery," thereby testifying to a significant element of continuity is his theological development – and, at the same time, to the importance of "Luther" for his doctrine of the Word of God. The "form" of revelation, Barth there wrote, is profoundly "secular" in nature. "The veil is thick. We do not have the Word of God otherwise than in the mystery of its secularity."[4] This is true even in the case of Christ, the primary "form" of the Word.[5] There is no similarity of this "form" *as such* to the content of revelation.[6] The humanity of Christ belongs to this world, both as created and as fallen. If, in the act of divine Self-mediation through this human "form," a similarity of form is realized, that would mean the overcoming of the contradiction in which all that belongs to this world stands. In explaining this, Barth again has recourse to Luther – this time joining together the passage already cited from *The Bondage of the Will* with the theology of the cross set forth in the Heidelberg Disputation.[7]

I mention all of this for several reasons pertinent to the thesis I will defend in this paper. First, the possibility that Luther exercised some influence on

---

[3] See Martin Luther, "The Heidelberg Disputation, 1518" in *LW* 31, 52–53: "He deserves to be called a theologian, however, who comprehends the visible and manifest things of God through suffering and the cross. The 'back' and visible things of God are placed in opposition to the invisible, namely, his human nature, weakness, foolishness. The Apostle in 1 Cor.1 [:25] calls them the weakness and folly of God. Because men (sic) misused the knowledge of God through works, God wished to be recognized in suffering... Now it is not sufficient for anyone, and it does him no good to recognize God in his glory and majesty, unless he recognizes him in the humility and shame of the cross."
[4] Karl Barth, *Church Dogmatics* I/1 (Edinburgh: T & T Clark, 1975), 165.
[5] Barth, *CD* I/1, 165.
[6] Barth, 166.
[7] Barth, 167.

Barth's thinking in the second *Romans* helps to explain Barth's response to news of a possible call to an honorary professorship in Reformed theology in Göttingen which came to him in January 1921. In a letter to Martin Rade, Barth made it clear that everything in him spoke against accepting this call – not least because he had recently been moving "rapidly towards Lutheranism in more than one respect."[8] This self-assessment is all the more remarkable in that it comes only eight weeks after Barth had announced to Friedrich Gogarten that, in the root and branch revision of his commentary on *Romans* just then underway, "…the strong influence of Beck and Kutter must step back and Luther must leave the field."[9] Clearly, something had changed in the very short two months which separated these letters. One cannot help but wonder if it might have had something to do with Gogarten's reply. He had, he says, since visiting Barth in Safenwil in October,[10] been reading wonderful things in Luther; specifically, his theses for the Heidelberg Disputation"[11] – a way of suggesting, perhaps, "don't give up too quickly on Luther!"

Second, if it were Gogarten in particular who helped Barth gain access to a more "use-able" Luther, it might help to explain their early comraderie. It has long been a puzzle to many that Barth should have been drawn to Gogarten in the first place. And it helps little to reduce the explanation for their alliance to a slogan like "the enemies of my enemies are my friends." That such a slogan might explain why Barth would extend support and encouragement to Gogarten behind the scenes but it would not explain why he would take the very public step of founding and co-editing *Zwischen den Zeiten* with him – nor why he would remain on friendly terms with him as long as he did. A more positive explanation is needed. For there can be no question but that, even as Barth ex-

---

8 Karl Barth to Martin Rade, 31 January 1921 in *Karl Barth – Martin Rade: Ein Briefwechsel*, ed. Christoph Schwöbel (Gütershoh: Gütersloher Verlagshaus Gerd Mohn, 1981), 154.
9 Karl Barth to Friedrich Gogarten, 4 December 1920, *Friedrich Gogartens Briefwechsel mit Karl Barth, Eduard Thurneysen und Emil Brunner*, ed. Hermann Götz Göckeritz (Tübingen: Mohr Siebeck, 2009), 164–65.
10 It was after Gogarten's lengthy [a week? ten days?] visit with Barth in Safenwil in October that Barth announced to Thurneysen "And now a strange and frightening piece of news: after Gogarten left, the *Römerbrief* began to shed its skin, i.e. I saw clearly [*ich bekam die Erleuchtung*] that it may not simply be reprinted as it is now but must rather be reformed in head and members." Karl Barth to Eduard Thurneysen, 27 October 1920 in Eduard Thurneysen, ed., *Karl Barth and Eduard Thurneysen Briefwechsel, Band I, 1913–1921* (Zürich: TVZ, 1973), 435. The clear implication seems to be that it was his conversations with Gogarten that led quite directly to this decision. One would love to have some information on what was discussed between the two of them!
11 Friedrich Gogarten to Karl Barth, 14 December 1920 in ibid., 167.

pressed reservations with respect to Gogarten privately, he was able to convince himself that both were working – in their differing ways – on the same problem(s).[12] But, then, what was that problem or problems? And in what way(s) did their theologies constitute differing approaches to the same constellation of issues? That is the question which requires an answer.

Third, and most importantly for the purposes of this paper, I want to argue that both Barth and Gogarten were concerned to construct theological epistemologies which witnessed to a de-centering of the human subject and her re-centering in God. And both tried to achieve this in the concept of an *indirect* Self-revelation of God. To be sure, Barth was working on the objective side of the revelation-relation (in Christology); Gogarten on the subjective side (with a clear focus on faith). But both held – in theory, at least – that a distinction had to be maintained between God and any perceptible form of revelation precisely in the act of divine Self-revelation. That is the point of convergence which, for a time at least, bound the two together in a common enterprise – all other divergences notwithstanding. When, later, Barth became more confessionally-oriented, he began to worry that once Gogarten had acquired greater historical knowledge of the conflicts dividing the two great Protestant confessions, he would embrace confessional Lutheranism's sacramentology and its Christology[13] – which would set aside, in Barth's view, the just-identified convergence and bring an end to their co-operation. But at the point at which Barth voiced this fear, Gogarten responded, "I think we could do well not to reflect too early on possible differences between us which the future might one day bring."[14] The truth is that Gogarten had very little interest in confessional differences. It was Luther he had a stake in – and even Luther had to be handled critically in his view.[15]

---

12 On the eve of the publication of the first number of *Zwischen den Zeiten*, Barth wrote to Thurneysen of his thoughts on Gogarten, "Lukas Christ should have no concerns with regard to our relationship. I do not at all think that we are far from one another. On the contrary. ...I am more convinced than ever that we are chewing on the same bone..." See Karl Barth to Eduard Thurneysen, 19 December 1922 in *Barth – Thurneysen Briefwechsel II*, 125–26.
13 Karl Barth to Friedrich Gogarten, 31 October 1922 in *Friedrich Gogartens Briefwechsel mit Karl Barth, Idnuard Thurneysen und Emil Brunner*, 189–90.
14 Friedrich Gogarten to Karl Barth, 8 November 1922 in ibid., 191.
15 See Friedrich Gogarten, *Theologische Tradition und theologische Arbeit* (Leipzig: J. C. Hinrichs'sche Buchhandlung, 1927), 40: "...the change of direction towards Luther may not take place in such a way that one carries out a repristination of his theology, i.e. that one simply sets up and receives his doctrine once again. One would, in that case, have forgotten what the task of theology is." Cf. p. 39, where Gogarten makes it clear that it is the Luther Renaissance that he has in view here.

My focus, in what follows, will lie in those years in which the disagreements which would eventually bring about a break-down in the collaboration of Barth and Gogarten were first clarified – that is, in the years 1926 and 1927. At this point in time, however – and even after Gogarten violated Barth's oft-repeated preference that they keep their disagreements private by making them public starting in early 1929 – these material disagreements did not prevent either from thinking they still had a common concern. And so, Barth could still make a case to officials in Berlin that Gogarten should be his successor in Münster in December 1929.[16] But the truth is that the foundation was already laid for Gogarten's later political ethics in his major work of the 1920s, *Ich glaube an den dreieinigen Gott* ("I Believe in the Triune God") in 1926.[17] All that was required was a dramatic change in the political situation in Germany (which occurred in the national election held in September 1930). At that point, Gogarten's interests would turn in a new direction but he would everywhere be building on a foundation already laid. In any event, I will concentrate here on the foundations. I will begin with Gogarten – with his version of dialectical theology. I will then turn to Barth's *Die christliche Dogmatik im Entwurf* – scrutinized in the light of Gogarten's 1929 review of that book.

2 Gogarten's Subjective Anchoring of an Indirect Revelation

Gogarten's major work of the 1920s *Ich glaube an den dreieinigen Gott* was published in December 1926. But Barth's dear friend and confidant Eduard Thurneysen knew a fair bit about it already in late October because Gogarten had sent him the first half of it – and then explained it thoroughly in a conversation which took place in Thurneysen's home. An account of this conversation was given to Barth in a letter.

> When one listens to him – and I sat in these days and half the night if not at his feet, then very quietly before him – then one has the impression that the entire field of theology is constricted with Gogarten and one sees then cut out before oneself only a single (to be sure, central) problem. Or rather, one sees not this problem as such, one sees *him*, again and again him, the master, Gogarten, hacking, digging, shoveling in the area defined by

---

16 Karl Barth to Dr. Werner Richter, 3 December 1929 in *Friedrich Gogartens Briefwecksel mit Karl Barth...*, Appendix 2, 386–88.
17 Friedrich Gogarten, *Ich glaube an den dreieinigen Gott: Eine Untersuchung über Glaube und Geschichte* (Jena: Eugen Diederichs, 1926).

> this problem. ...You understand me: one asks oneself which really prevails over the other – Gogarten or his theme? And yet, the question is unjust, maliciously put; one really sees both, never the one without the other.[18]

Thurneysen is not wrong: Gogarten was a man with one doctrine – though he resisted thinking of his solution to the problem with which he concerned himself as a "doctrine" in the first instance. And he had a tendency to absolutize the significance of his solution and to tell himself that he alone had found the key that sets appropriate (but quite severe!) limits to what can and must be said in the realm of theology. And, as is clear from this report, Gogarten had a tendency in conversation to "hold court" in a way that allowed for little if any real engagement on the part of those present.

But, then, what is the single point? The problem which Gogarten is so utterly fixed upon? The problem, as Thurneysen understood it, lay in identifying "the essence of the living Word of God."[19] And the solution? "...[T]he incarnation, therefore, the kernal of Luther's theology, not the Trinity, not eschatology, but rather the doctrine of reconciliation and this understood as the becoming human of God. Where is God? In heaven? What does God in *heaven* have to do with me! In Christ, he is there for me. Therefore I am to seek him in his humanity..."[20] Thurneysen goes on to say that, for Gogarten, God's revelation of God's Self in the humanity of Christ authorizes seeking and finding God in the humanity of the other in relation to whom I stand in an I-thou relation. This is actually a very insightful "reading," though it has to be said that he was aided in providing it by hours of listening to its author.

Barth's response reflected a certain uncertainty:

> Just think: your lines on Gogarten have had the remarkable effect on me that I began immediately to make ready for publication...the paragraphs on *Feuerbach* from last summer ['s course on "The History of Protestant Theology since Schleiermacher"]... If the book is good, then Feuerbach may speak as testis veritatis *for it*; if it is not good, then he may speak as a specter against it.[21]

An interesting decision, to be sure – given the problems that emerge from close consideration of Gogarten's work.

---

18 Eduard Thurneysen to Karl Barth, 30 October 1926 in *Barth – Thurneysen Briefwechsel II*, 438. Thurneysen, it must be said, was much more patient and, indeed, generous in human relationships than was Barth – and I think we should take his description seriously.
19 Thurneysen, *Briefweschsel II*, 438.
20 Thurneysen, 439.
21 Karl Barth to Eduard Thurneysen, 8 November 1926 in ibid., p.442.

In what follows, I am not going to begin my analysis of Gogarten's dialectical theology with his *Ich glaube*... but with his inaugural lecture given in Jena just five months after the appearance of the book.²² My reason is simple. The inaugural lecture provides a rather clear summary of the leading ideas found in the book, a considerable advantage given that the book itself is often dark, raising many more questions than it is able to answer. I will begin with a bit of background – which will lead quite directly into Gogarten's inaugural address.

2.1 Overcoming the Idealist Subject

Between May 1921 and June 1922, Friedrich Gogarten engaged in an intensive letter exchange with Eberhard Grisebach, a philosopher who was just then developing the I-thou philosophy for which he was known. Through this exchange, Grisebach exercised a long-lasting influence on Gogarten's theology. The parallels between Grisebach's philosophy and Gogarten's theology are still clear four years later.

Grisebach had constructed his I-thou philosophy in reaction against the idealism of his teacher, Rudolf Eucken. For Grisebach, there could be no bridge leading from "subjective consciousness to reality, from thinking to being..."²³ Philosophy could no longer afford to concern itself with the "cloud cuckoo land of ideals" but should concentrate instead on "real goals on this earth."²⁴

> Only the encounter of the individual with the real world, above all with the "other" in whom he experiences its contradiction [of him], decides him for the present and real life. A revelation of the Absolute in finite concepts is impossible. And so, all that is left to philosophy is to trace the contradiction of the knowing "I" by a thou over which she exercises no control. This is the "real dialectic" which alone places one before reality.²⁵

---

22 Gogarten, *Theologische Tradition und theologische Arbeit*, In the "Vorwort" to this small monograph, Gogarten mistakenly dates his inaugural on May 15. This has been corrected by Göckeritz. See *Friedrich Gogartens Briefwechself mit Karl Barth*..., 255, n3.
23 Göckeritz, "Zwei Wege Zwischen den Zeiten: Zur Einführung," in *Friedrich Gogarten's Briefwechsel mit Karl Barth*..., 22.
24 The phrases here cited are found in Göckeritz' introduction to the Gogarten-Barth letters. He in turn is citing Eberhard Grisebach to Friedrich Gogarten, 27 October 1921 in Michael Freyer, ed., *Philosophie und Theologie in realer Dialektik* (Rheinstettin: Schindele-Verlag, 1979), 59.
25 Grisebach, 23.

Göckeritiz is right to conclude that Grisebach's I-thou philosophy would render impossible not only every metaphysical system but every theological "system" as well.[26]

Now even though Gogarten would never have an interest in theological system-building, he could not allow himself to be completely limited by Grisebach. No theological statements whatsoever were possible on the soil of Grisebach's philosophy. A material modification was needed. It took the following form. Gogarten too believed that it is through a decisive encounter with an "other" – with one who speaks to me a word which I cannot speak to myself – that the knowing subject that "I" am is judged, de-centered and re-centered. But his claim in the inaugural address is that the word in question is the word heard in the event of justification and that this hearing takes place "only" in the church.[27]

Gogarten's starting-point lay in bringing to light a hermeneutical problem common to all theologians, though scarcely realized or discussed. Most in his day would agree, he says, that theology requires a fundamental relationship to revelation in the Bible. But this is a largely formal claim and agreement with it breaks down the minute it is explained. On the one side are those who view the Bible as the witness of the writers to their own religious consciousness. On this showing, revelation takes place in that readers recognize in themselves the religious experience of the writers.[28] On the other side are those who would say that the Word of God which comes to us through the Bible calls our religious consciousness into question in a fundamental way.[29] The Word of God does not tell us what we already know about ourselves but what we do not know.

On the face of it, these two positions are antithetically related. But, says Gogarten, these two positions are closer to each other than most realize. For there is no guarantee that the Word of God we think to have been spoken to us is not still, at the end of the day, a "conception" which we have devised for ourselves in advance of real "hearing.".[30] And so, no "conception" of the Word which we might formulate can escape the suspicion that we are still speaking to ourselves. The sinfulness of every reader of the Bible is so great that no one can protect herself against the deeply ingrained tendency to paralyze the "allowing oneself to be spoken to" by a "speaking to oneself."[31]

---

[26] Grisebach, 22.
[27] Gogarten, *Theologische Tradition und theologische Arbeit*, 18.
[28] Gogarten, 4.
[29] Gogarten, 4
[30] Gogarten, 5.
[31] Gogarten, 4.

What then? Is there no way out of the dilemma created for the reader of the Bible by the his/her sinfulness? Gogarten thinks there is, obviously. And his strategy is twofold. First, he would like to close the door firmly on an option preferred by many in his day. He would like to demonstrate that modern idealism's attempt to find the "essence" of the human by means of a wholly rational inquiry into the "self" or "personality" can only end in a speaking of the human knower to him/herself – a situation which underscores the sinfulness of sin in that the would-be knower remains stuck in his/her preoccupation with self.[32] And where this human "essence" is then made the key to understanding the Bible, there the message of the Bible cannot be brought to expression. All of that is on the one side. But Gogarten wants to defend an alternative solution which has yet to find the kind of support he would like to attract with his lecture.

We begin to catch sight of Gogarten's proposed solution when he says that "allowing oneself to be spoken to" is not an occurrence which takes place in the realm of ideas, within the consciousness of the knowing "I." Rather it is an event which takes place in the real world as a speaking by one and a hearing by another. "It is an occurrence between two subjects, not an occurrence in *one* subject."[33] More concretely, however, it is (as already intimated) an occurrence that takes place in that the Word which justifies is heard in the church. What takes place in this event is that the Word that is Jesus Christ is proclaimed by a preacher – and heard by another human being. And to the degree that the word proclaimed is made effective by God, it brings about a shift in the hearer from speaking to herself to allowing herself to be addressed. Put another way, the response is made to be one of "obedient faith." It is in this way that Gogarten seeks to de-center the actual, the real human subject (and with that, the ideal epistemological subject) and to re-center that subject in God. Does he succeed? Or perhaps better; *how far* is he successful?

Again, Gogarten knows full well that even a true "hearer" of the word of justification spoken in the church remains a sinner. The "obedient faith" of the hearer is but partial. It is inadequate in that it does not fulfill the law (by which Gogarten means: the divine command to love the Lord for his own sake and the neighbor for her own sake). And for that reason, the "obedient faith" of the justified can never provide an adequate basis for her justification.[34] The "ground" of her justification will always – at every point in the Christian life – have to be sought elsewhere. Gogarten's analysis up to this point directs us to

---

[32] Gogarten, 29–37.
[33] Gogarten, 9.
[34] Gogarten, 12–14.

Christ – a move which holds forth the promise of a completion of his de-centering of the subject (in both the real and the ideal senses).

For Gogarten, Jesus Christ alone perfectly fulfilled the law. He alone loved God "for his own sake" and the sinner "for her own sake" without any admixture of self-interest.[35] In Jesus alone was there no self-speaking which might qualify his "hearing" of God – which is what made him to be the speech of God. And so, it is the man Jesus who is the "Du" who meets us in proclamation – breaking open the reasoning "I" turned in on itself and resting quite serenely (up to that point) in its own consciousness of itself as a self. It is thus the "obedient faith of Jesus which justifies – not our "hearing" as such.

I will break off from my commentary here to offer three comments with respect to Gogarten's description of the event of justification and the Christology it presupposes. First, the description of the event of justification which he sets forth is one that has some precedent in the Lutheran tradition. Certainly, he is on solid footing in treating justification as a kind of "effective word." That is not a phrase he uses but it is fittingly applied to him. At the same time, however, and this is the second point, Gogarten's Christological reflections have brought about a shift in the traditionally Lutheran law-gospel distinction in the direction of giving gospel a certain priority. It is Jesus' perfect fulfilment of the law which is the gospel whose proclamation effects obedience (however qualified) in its "hearers." No mention is made here of Luther's religious experience; of the terror which Luther thought the Law to bring about and which he himself had experienced. What is important about Luther for Gogarten is not his experience of justification as the consolation of a terrified conscience. He is critical of the Luther Renaissance at this point.[36] What is important about Luther is that he made the "humanity of Christ" to be the "center point of the whole of his theology."[37] He did so because he found in Holy Scripture "the man Jesus as the Son of God and our only righteousness."[38] But that then leads to the third and (for our purposes) decisive point. There is no need, Gogarten thinks, to engage as Luther often did in reflection on the relation of divine and human "natures" in Christ. There is no need to remain faithful to Luther's doctrinal teachings at all. To enter Luther's "school" is not to strive for fidelity to his theology but to do what he did, viz. to be find in Scripture the Jesus whose faithful obedience to the divine command constitutes the speaking of God. What is important is Luther's focus on the humanity of Christ.

---

35 Gogarten, 14.
36 Gogarten, 39.
37 Gogarten, 49.
38 Gogarten, 49.

The weakness in Gogarten's analysis has begun to emerge. He would like to have developed an indirect concept of revelation which would de-center the self. But by refusing to demonstrate an indirect identity of the Word of God with the humanity of Christ on the objective end of the revelation relation (as Barth wished to do), Gogarten made the distinction between the human preacher as "thou" from the hearing "I" do all the heavy-lifting where is ultimate goal is concerned. And one has to ask whether that goal can be adequately served in this way – which is why I asked *how far* Gogarten is successful. It seems to me that there is a grave danger here – given Gogarten's rather direct identification of the Word with Jesus' humanity – that there is little or nothing to prevent the human Jesus as the Word from being collapsed into the human who proclaims the word (the latter being then understood as the concrete instantiation in the "here and now" of the faithful and obedient Jesus). Were this to occur, all that would remain is the relation of the "hearer" of the proclaimed word to the preacher as her "thou." And the reason this is dangerous is that an authority proper only to the Word of God might then devolve upon the preacher as the Du in the event of justification – a human being who is every bit as sinful as the would be "hearer" of the Word – a move fraught with political implications quite obviously. That is a danger which emerges with even greater clarity in Gogarten's in his major work, to which I now turn.

2.2 *Ich glaube an den dreieinigen Gott*

In his "Preface," Gogarten tells his readers: "So that this book will not be read with false expectations, it is perhaps necessary to say explicitly that it does not want to be anything like a dogmatics but rather only an investigation into faith and history." But, he says, the problem of faith and history can only be addressed theologically in a "trinitarian" fashion. That is because the "history" referred to where the problem is treated theologically is "the event of the revelation of God the Father and of the Son and of the Holy Spirit."[39] The body of the work falls, then, quite naturally into three parts consisting in two chapters each which treat successively of creation, redemption and sanctification – which are preceded by two introductory chapters whose function is to get clear just what the faith and history problem is.

---

39 Gogarten, *Ich glaube an den dreieinigen Gott*, front matter (no page number).

According to Gogarten, "history is not possible where there is only one person."[40] History is what takes place between two persons. Idealism always finds its starting-point in the isolated individual, in the "idea of the I."[41] Where this occurs, the temptation is irresistible to identify the human I with the divine I[42] – a projection of the human self into an eternal essence which is made to be the thought of God. But the problem posed by "history" cannot come into view in this way. It is evaded. And the "sphere of history" has been abandoned.[43]

It should be noted that in defining the problem of "history" in this way, a difference over against the inaugural address has announced itself. Here, the decisive "encounter" in which the I is confronted by its thou does not take place in the event of justification but in the relation to the "neighbor" – or as Gogarten also frequently says, "the other." For faith in the Christ who is "the fulfilled Word," whose words (unlike the words of the prophets) are *the* Word because Jesus is what He speaks,[44] is a faith which issues immediately in love for the neighbor. And it is just here that the concept of "orders of creation" rears its head – a controversial topic which would become greatly divisive in the 1930s.

According to Gogarten, faith in "God the Creator" is not a matter of speculation about the world's origins or the result of a quest for the world's "essence." Such faith takes its rise in that one acknowledges oneself to have been "placed" in a "situation" in which one hears "the Word of Jesus Christ."[45] Gogarten becomes a bit vague at this point, offering no criterion for recognizing this Word "in a situation." On the contrary, he tells us that the acknowledgment of the Word in a given situation will only express faith where it is an "interpretationless acknowledgment." In that a person has been set free in faith in Jesus Christ from the accusation of the law to have failed to fulfil its demand, he is free as well to hear the "claim" of the other and to acknowledge this claim in its "peculiarity." "Only in this way is he able to grasp the great spirit-bodily contexts and orders in which a human has her life...as the orders of God, as orders of creation."[46]

Now Gogarten is quick to say that these "orders" are "wholly other" than what is customarily thought of as natural orders or natural laws. Just as a person makes herself to be the lord of "history" insofar as she seeks to understand and

---

40 Gogarten, 35.
41 Gogarten, 36.
42 Gogarten, 36.
43 Gogarten, 37.
44 Gogarten, 146.
45 Gogarten, 205.
46 Gogarten, 206.

interpret the world by means of a unifying concept (i.e. the concept of a "universal history"), so too here: to seek to establish by reason certain "laws" which are said to govern the lived existence of an actual individual is to make oneself lord over "life and being."[47] It is to confuse "orders of creation" with historical laws of cultural development. "Here, the only thing that helps is faith in the Creator, only the concrete encounter with the other, only the interpretation-less and responsible hearing of his claim and...faith in Jesus Christ."[48]

The weakness referred to earlier has now become evident in the realm of the social and the political. Since Gogarten offers no criteria for recognizing the Word in the claim of my concrete other, all we are left with is "faith" that the two are one in a concrete situation. Gogarten does not help matters in speaking of acknowledgment of this claim as "interpretation-less." I am tempted to say: where one fails to distinguish and relate the divine Word and the humanity of Christ by means of an explanatory model that is coherent and self-consistent, there it becomes almost inevitable that one will also fail to distinguish when relating the Word of God in a concrete situation to the claim of the other. I say "almost" because there is no necessity here that Gogarten should have moved in the direction he finally did politically. Still, where this last named failure occurs – as it did in Gogarten – a foundation had been laid for his later doctrine of an authoritative state.[49] Four years earlier, Karl Barth told his friend that he did not see how Gogarten would be able to avoid the "conservative romanticism"[50] which the latter had identified (in an earlier essay) as a pressing threat. A prescient remark, to be sure!

2.3 Provisional Conclusions

Like Karl Barth, Friedrich Gogarten wanted to set forth an indirect concept of divine revelation. Since he concerned himself primarily with the subjective end of the revelation-revelation (and with the objective end only as the presupposition of the subjective but not as a topic of close inquiry), he was unable to prevent the sought for indirection from being supplanted by an identity of Word and human "other" in the concrete situation of revelation. Notwithstanding his

---

47 Gogarten, 207.
48 Gogarten, 207.
49 See Heinrich Assel, "Luther Renaissance and Dialectical Theology: A tour d'horizon 1906–1935," included in this volume.
50 Karl Barth to Friedrich Gogarten, 23 December 1922 in *Friedrich Gogarten's Briefwechsel mit Karl Barth...*, 196.

often quite insightful criticism of the tendency of idealism to identify the human "I" with the divine "I," Gogarten would wind up all too close to an identification of the human "thou" with the divine "I."

3 Karl Barth's Objective Anchoring of an Indirect Revelation

Gogarten wanted to do theology out of a center in an existential encounter. Of course, Barth did that too – in his own way. But Gogarten's existential encounter consisted in an "interpretation-less acknowledgment" of a Du which placed severe limits on what could be said in the realm of theology. Barth's existential center consisted in the Spirit's "hearing" in us the Word of God addressed to us in Christ alone and, therefore, in a "hearing" which could never be treated in isolation from but only on the basis of close consideration of the address itself. And for Barth that meant: reflecting on Christ – and on the "how" of the revelation that took place in him.

That such reflection would take the form of a *doctrine* of Christ was, in his view, inevitable. "I was and am," Barth wrote in the preface to his *Die christliche Dogmatik im Entwurf*, "an ordinary theologian who does not have the Word of God at his disposal but at best a 'doctrine of the Word of God'...."[51] Throughout his life, Barth would remain quite clear that a doctrine of Christ is not the living Christ.[52] But a doctrine of Christ must always be the end result of any attempt to think carefully about the event of revelation on its objective side – even if its status is never more than that of a witness to the living Christ.

3.1 Karl Barth's Dialectic of Veiling and Unveiling

The dialectic of veiling and unveiling which provided the formal structure of Barth's concept of revelation was a constant in all phases of his theological development after his "departure" from so-called "liberalism" – though it would, in fact, undergo some material modification. In the second *Romans* commentary, the speaking of the Unintuitable God takes place through an intuitable occur-

---

[51] Karl Barth, *Die christliche Dogmatik im Entwurf*, ed. Gerhard Sauter (Zürich: TVZ, 1982), 8.
[52] See Eberhard Busch, *Glaubensheiterkeit: Erfahrungen und Begegnungen* (Neukirchen-Vluyn: Neukirchener Verlag, 1986), 24.

rence in human history, viz. the death of Jesus.[53] It takes place, that is to say, in that the light of the resurrection shines into the darkness surrounding the death of Christ, revealing the meaning of that death – and God gives to a would-be recipient of revelation the "eyes" to see what is remains hidden to view in the impenetrable veil that is death. After Barth's turn to dogmatics, the objective pole of that dialectic would undergo considerable expansion and explanation. It would no longer be confined to a single event but would focus on the "person" of Christ, i.e. on the formula "two natures in one person" in its Reformed orthodox iteration (as found in Heinrich Heppe's manual of doctrine[54]). In accordance with seventeenth century Reformed teaching, Barth's emphasis fell on the distinction of the "natures" – and the rejection of the Lutheran *genus majestaticum*. "Two natures unimpaired in their original integrity subsequent to their union"[55] was the Reformed teaching and it was sufficient to provide Barth with the critical leverage needed to prevent a collapse of the Word of God into the Christ's humanity – and, with that, a collapse of the Word of God in the present moment of "hearing" into other figures and events (Barmen I). And so, Barth had at his disposal a doctrine of revelation that found its center in the notion of an indirect identity of God (the Word) with the medium of his Self-revelation. The goal shared with Gogarten had been met but met differently, in a way that created a conceptual tool useful in destabilizing any political program which might make claims to ultimacy, to the allegiance proper to God alone. And this was a decided advantage. But Barth's solution was not without a quite serious weakness.

The problem with an all-too uncritical employment of Chalcedonian categories is that this model left unresolved the relation of the human "nature" to the "person." And this was no accident. Because the "person" was directly equated in the Chalcedonian Definition with the Logos – who, as God, was understood by

---

[53] The use made by Barth of Kantian epistemology in the second *Romans* to explicate a theological state-of-affairs (the relation of the Resurrection as a "un-historical" event to the cross as an occurrence in history is something I have already traced quite thoroughly. See Bruce L. McCormack, *Karl Barth's Critically Realistic Dialectical Theology; Its Genesis and Development, 1909–1936* (Oxford: Clarendon Press, 1995), 129–30, 218–26, 245–62; and idem., "Revelation and History in Transfoundationlist Perspective: Karl Barth's Theological Epistemology in Conversation with a Schleiermacherian Tradition" in idem., *Orthodox and Modern: Studies in the Theology of Karl Barth* (Grand Rapids, MI: Baker Academic, 2008), pp. 21–39. See also Johann Friedrich Lohmann, *Karl Barth und der Neukantianismus: die Rezeption des Neukantianismus im 'Römerbrief' und ihre Bedeutung für die weitere Ausarbeitung der Theologie Karl Barths* (Berlin and New York: Walter de Gruyter, 1995).
[54] Heinrich Heppe, *Die Dogmaik der evangelisch-reformierten Kirche, dargestellt und aus den Quellen belegt* (Elberfeld: R. L. Friedrichs, 1861).
[55] Here paraphrasing John Calvin, *Institutes* II.xii.1.

the bishops to be simple and impassible – no real relation of anything created to Him was conceivable. If a real communication of the properties of the human "nature" to the Logos were to have occurred (the so-called *genus tapeinoticum*), the Logos would no longer have been either simple or impassible. So the only "relation" conceivable on the soil of Chalcedon was a "relation" of the Logos to the human nature (with all traffic moving from the divine to the human) – and to even call it a "relation" is stretching a point. For it was really not so much a "relation" that was in view so much as it was a quite direct exercise (internal to the God-human) of omnipotent divine causality. The Logos, it was believed, acted through and even upon his human "nature" in order to "divinize" it. I won't say anything more about this here. Suffice it to say that the Orthodox constructed their Christology under the guidance of a prior commitment to the concepts of simplicity and impassibility as applied to God. And that meant in practice that a controlling function had been granted to the speculative metaphysics of the ancient Greeks. When, later, the Lutheran and the Reformed theologians developed their own versions of the Chalcedonian model, the one thing that they shared in common was a commitment to the doctrine of divine simplicity and impassibility. Each in its way, upheld the concept of God devised by the ancients.

And so it came about that Barth's reception of the older Reformed Christology had the positive consequence of a clear distinction between divine and human in Christ. But, unfortunately, it also meant resting content (for the time being) with its other features which included, above all a drift towards a "two subjects" Christology which had its roots in the attempt to preserve the received notions of the simplicity and impassibility of the divine Word while saying at the same time an emphatic "no" to the Lutheran Christology. In allowing this Christology to guide his thinking, Barth had opened the door to speculative metaphysics – in spite of himself, it now has to be said.

3.2 Barth's Construction of a Doctrine of the "Essential" or Immanent Trinity

That Barth shared with Gogarten a desire to overcome a foundation of theology in speculative metaphysics becomes clear in his construction of a doctrine of the "essential" Trinity. His starting-point lies in the economy of God. More specifically, it lies in the three "moments" of the divine Self-revelation. How he achieves this would become be the focus of Gogarten's review.

For Barth, only God can reveal God. Revelation does not consist in a bestowal of information about God but in *Self-* revelation. This being the case, Jesus

Christ can only reveal God if he himself is God. That is the fundamental significance for Barth of the early Christian confession "Jesus is Lord" (Phil. 2:11). And so, the content of revelation is "*Gott allein, Gott ganz, Gott selber.*"[56] And if it is the God made human who is all of this, then God is this "in the midst of our contradiction" – i.e. in the midst of our alienation from God and therefore also from ourselves and our neighbours. But to be the "Lord" in the midst of our contradiction requires explanation – not least of how God can remain Lord while entering into that contradiction. The Trinity then becomes a provisional answer to that question – a first consideration to which Barth will then add reflections on the incarnation.

The first "moment" – that "God is the Lord" as the One who speaks in Christ – requires little explanation. The same is true of the third moment. The thought that "God is the Lord" over the reception of revelation by those elected to "hear it" is a commonplace in the Augustinian and Reformed traditions. It is the second "moment" that requires close scrutiny – all the more so since it provides the foundation for the move "from below" to "above." "God is the Lord" in the midst of our contradiction and can be this because, Barth says, "God is completely revelation."[57] He can even say that if God "does not reveal himself completely, he does not reveal himself at all."[58] This is not at all to say that the human recipient of revelation can ever acquire an exhaustive knowledge of what has been revealed. And it is certainly not to say that there is no place in Christian theology for the concept of divine "incomprehensibility" or a hiddenness of God. But Barth thinks he has Luther on his side when he says that the hiddenness of God is not to be thought of in quantitative terms, as though a portion of God is revealed and a greater portion unrevealed, as though God in and for God's Self is more than what is given to us in the economic Trinity. On the contrary: "The hidden God ('Deus absconditus') is also the revealed God ('Dues revelatus') just as certainly as the reverse is always also to be said."[59] But, then, if the reverse is also true, if the "revealed God" *is* the hidden God, then of course Barth is right to say that "God is completely revelation." There is nothing proper to God that is left behind in that God's reveals God's Self. And so: "God is complete in his revelation... He is not only in his Person the *Revealer*, but also the *act* of revelation. His work [in revelation] is identical with his Person. *Deus = Deus loquens.*"[60]

---

56 Barth, *Die christliche Dogmatik im Entwurf*, 165, 297.
57 Barth, 177.
58 Barth, 179–80.
59 Barth, 180.
60 Barth, 180.

Taking a step back for just a moment from Barth's argument, we may note that if God *is* indeed *the act* of revelation, then the act itself can only be "proper" to God. It can only be an act which belongs to God essentially. And that has rather significant ramifications. A simple and impassible God like that found in the tradition cannot "add" anything to the perfect being God already is "in and for himself." But a God who *is* the act of revelation can take to himself the full consequences of a being in *this* act while remaining completely identical with God's Self. Were it not so, God would not be "completely revelation." And if God can have God's being *in this act* without becoming anything other than what God is, then the relation that is established to the humanity of Christ (and to all other humans in him) is proper to God too. In any event, to say that God's work is identical with God's "Person," that "God" equals "God speaking," must surely entail the view that God is revelation "in himself," that there can be no "in and for himself" if that is taken to mean an isolated, unrevealed God. The "in and for himself" is already a "for us."

Now notice: the line of thought I have developed here was made possible by Barth's contention that God is completely revelation, that God is God's work of revelation. Barth himself was less explicit about all of this – in all likelihood because his interest lay elsewhere. What Barth was seeking to construct was a doctrine of the "essential" Trinity that did *not* have its foundation in speculative metaphysics. He achieved this end by insisting that God is identical with the act of revelation. And if that is so, then God is identical with God's Self in all three moments.

Barth's next move was a quasi-transcendental one; one which sought in the eternal relations of the members of the Godhead the ontological condition of the possibility of their economic relations. Basically, he was asking himself "what must God *be* if Jesus is Lord?" Again, given the limits of this essay, I will say no more about that here. It is sufficient to say that there is no "metaphysical" gap here between the economic Trinity and the immanent Trinity. The relation between the two is not one of analogy but of identity.

But, now, if all of this be true, then Gogarten would have had little cause for complaint. Yes, Barth would have made rich use of the ancient dogmas of Christology and Trinity but they would have been stripped of their speculative foundations in the process. I turn then to Gogarten's critique.

3.3 Karl Barth – A Disguised Idealist?[61]

At the heart of Gogarten's critique of Barth lay the claim that the "contradiction" of which Barth spoke was nothing more than "the dialectical idea of a contradiction which is grounded and sublated in its absolute unity."[62] In support of this claim, Gogarten points to the fact that Barth can speak of God from time to time in abstraction from the relation to the human which is realized in revelation. He can speak of a God "in isolation," in a sphere outside of history, the sphere which he sometimes refers to as *Urgeschichte* [or "primal history"].[63]

Two things are happening here. First, Gogarten is rejecting all talk of a realm above or behind history. "If revelation is history and we are humans who are addressed by it, ... then there is no such thing, there can be no such thing, as suprahistory. Of *Urgeschichte*, one would do better not to speak."[64] Gogarten does not envision the possibility that God might *be* in a supra-history what God *is* in God's address to human beings in time. He is clearly convinced that the only means by which supra-history could be accessed is by means of a speculative leap.[65] But he has not grasped Barth's transcendental move and so misunderstands his procedure. Second, Gogarten equates Barth's talk of *Urgeschichte* quite directly with the idealist supposition of an originating unity of subject and object – as though Barth were attempting to propose a theological solution to that particular philosophical problem. Barth's problem, as we have seen, is to establish the ontological conditions in God for His Self-revelation in time. The idealistic attempt to overcome Kant's epistemological dualism by means of an *Identitätsphilosophie* could have provided Barth with a secular parable of the theological state-of-affairs he was seeking to describe. But even if that had been the case – and it is not clear that it is – it would only have been a parable (and one that Barth failed to mention in this context). Having said that, however, there are times when Barth's use of the ancient dogmas led him to think along with the speculative metaphysical commitmets of their authors for long stretches – and even, it would seem, to adopt them.

---

61 Karl Barth to Eduard Thurneysen, 15 May, 1927, in *Barth – Thurneysen Briefwechsel II*, 500: "He takes me for a disguised humanist and idealist and I him for a stubborn mule with whom, basically, one can only speak by listening..."
62 Friedrich Gogarten, "Karl Barths Dogmatik," *Theologische Rundschau* N.F. 1 (1929): 60–80.
63 Gogarten, 64, 67–68.
64 Gogarten, 75.
65 It is for this reason that Gogarten says that it is impossible to think *von Gott aus*; every attempt to think God will necessarily take place *von sich aus*. See Gogarten, *Ich glaube an den dreieinigen Gott*, 11.

At this time, Barth still joined the ancients in rejecting all thought of a *genus tapeinoticum* – which meant that he too had yet to find a way to speak coherently of the ontological significance of the relation of Christ's human "nature" to his "person" (and, therefore, to speak of the importance of the assumed humanity for an understanding of Christ's "person"). But, then, that also meant equating the "person" of Christ with a Logos "in himself" – i.e. a Logos with no real relation to His human nature. That, as we have seen, was central to the Reformed orthodoxy Barth was using as a source for his reflections. This commitment became conspicuous at the point at which Barth sought to explain the triumph of Jesus Christ over our "contradiction." For Barth, Jesus Christ is Lord in the midst of our contradiction precisely by remaining "above" it *in his person*.[66] In other words, the Logos triumphs over the contradiction by remaining "above" it. The so-called human "nature" is *in* the midst of the contradiction but the person whose nature this is, is above it. This is a very traditional solution, one that owes a great debt historically to the concept of impassibility (*Unberührbarkeit*). But it is also one which imports into Barth's Christology a great deal of the ancient metaphysics – a form of speculation which Barth clearly wanted to overcome.

At the end of the day, Gogarten's critique is quite insightful. He is not wrong to find in Barth a speculative concept of God – sitting loosely alongside of his non-metaphysical procedure in forming a doctrine of the "essential" Trinity. Gogarten is only wrong about its source.

4 Conclusion

The appellation "dialectical theology" is apt for both Barth and Gogarten, albeit in differing ways. Gogarten's dialectic had to do with an I-thou encounter in which God was thought to be indirectly revealed. Barth's dialectic had to do pre-eminently with God's Self-revelation in and through the flesh of Christ, an

---

[66] Karl Barth, *"Unterricht in der christlichen Religion." Dritter Band: Die Lehre con der Versöhnung / Die Lehre von der Erlösung, 1925–1926*, ed. Hinrich Stoevesandt (Zürich: TVZ, 2003), 26 and especially 44: "The *Son of God*, the *Logos*, is the God-human. *He* is *above* the antithesis." In the Münster Dogmatics, this language is softened without being substantively altered. On the one hand, Barth could now say that "the faithfulness of Gdo triumphed in the midst of the as yet un-sublated but precisely thereby limited antithesis of God and the human." See Karl Barth, typescript of Münster Dogmatics, § 50, 160–61 (in Karl Barth-Archiv, Basel). And yet, he could also say that "The hypostatic union in the God-human stands above, not in, the dialectic of God and man." Ibid., 150.

event which joins together the "there and then" of Christ's lived existence and the "here and now" of the believer in a relation of contemporaneity. Barth's version had the considerable advantage over Gogarten's that it immunized him against any and every attempt to identify the divine command with any human articulation of it. But Gogarten had put his finger on a weakness that would have to be addressed sooner or later – if not by Barth himself then by his later interpreters.

Heinrich Assel
Trinity, Incarnation, Political Theology
Gogarten's Luther between Luther Renaissance and Rudolf Bultmann

1 Introduction: Not Understanding Gogarten – Constellations

As the New Year 1933 began, Barth saw himself confronted with the unbearable situation of misunderstanding: it would have been dangerous, if Barth had *not* publicly declared a break with the authors of *Zwischen den Zeiten*.[1] The immediate targets were Paul Althaus and Emil Brunner.[2] Barth broke with both immediately. It was only in the case of Gogarten that everybody shied away: Thurneysen, Kirschbaum, and even Barth. They thought that it was too difficult to prove the intolerable misunderstanding[3] and so they preferred to speak of an "irrational impression."[4]

When Gogarten traveled through Cologne in January 1933, Barth urgently requested a meeting with him. However, the request reached Gogarten too late. The train had left the station! What follows between Barth and Gogarten is triggered

---

[1] Charlotte von Kirschbaum to Eduard Thurneysen (3.1.1933), in: Barth and Thurneysen, *Briefwechsel Bd. 3: 1930–1935. Einschließlich des Briefwechsels zwischen Charlotte von Kirschbaum und Eduard Thurneysen*, GA V, ed. Caren Algner (Zurich: TVZ, 2000), 337. It was Ernst Fuchs who visited Barth on New Year's Day in the evening 1933 and urged him to break publicly with Gogarten as Fuchs denied Gogarten had any *theological* intention. After 1945, Fuchs was the most genial and prominent exponent of the Hermeneutical Theology, and was then the laudator on the occasion of Friedrich Gogarten's *Emeritierung* in Göttingen (25th of February 1955) and gave his remarkable speech "Begegnung mit dem Wort: Eine Rede für Friedrich Gogarten" (Bad Canstatt: R. Müllerschön, 1955), declaring Gogarten his teacher.
[2] The breakup with Paul Althaus on January 2nd, 1933 with a letter (partly printed in TEH 1 [1933]: 155–157); the breakup with Emil Brunner on January 10th, 1933 (Barth and Brunner, *Briefwechsel 1916–1966*, GA V, ed. Eberhard Busch [Zurich: TVZ, 2000], 213–217; draft from January 2nd, 1933, Barth and Thurneysen, *Briefwechsel 1930–1935*, 337 Anm. 1).
[3] Barth prompted in his *Sozietät* a critical analysis of Gogartens *Politische Ethik* cap. 1 by Georg Eichholz. Eichholz sent his manuscript to Barth on 30.11.1932, Barth and Thurneysen, *Briefwechsel* 3, 305 Anm. 8; 336 Anm. 1. A copy of the Eichholz-paper does not exist in the Barth Archive in Basel.
[4] Kirschbaum to Thurneysen (3.1.1933), in Barth and Thurneysen, *Briefwechsel* 3, 338.

by Gogarten joining the *German Christians* early in August 1933. He left them again on November 17th 1933.⁵ What followed was a fight for superiority in the public perception of the misunderstanding and the heritage of Dialectical Theology, starting with Barth's *"Abschied von Zwischen den Zeiten"*⁶ (fall 1933), culminating in a conflict on January 23rd 1934,⁷ and ending with Gogarten's *Gericht oder Skepsis* in 1937.⁸

This story has a pre-history. Rudolf Bultmann initiated an internal debate between Barth and Gogarten in Marburg in 1929, but the two protagonists evaded the debate. At the same time, their letters become increasingly stale.

But what exactly were the points of theological division?

Had Gogarten not offered in 1928 a profound 20-page critique of Barth's *Christliche Dogmatik im Entwurf?*⁹ Had he not discussed the function of prolegomena as a basic conceptual consideration in the foundations of a Trinitarian doctrine of the Divine Word? Finally, had he not focused on two problems: on the task of theological anthropology as an integral dimension of the event of the Word of God; and on the temptation of Christ as the starting-point of incarnational Christology, that is, the humanity of Jesus the God-man in light of a particular *theologia crucis?*

Anyone could have seen the outline of another Trinitarian Word-theology in the spirit of Luther in this review, quite different from Barth's. It was presented in

---

5 D. Timothy Goering, *Friedrich Gogarten (1887–1967): Religionsrebell im Jahrhundert der Weltkriege*, Ordnungsysteme 51 (Berlin/Boston: DeGruyter, 2017), 268–276.
6 Karl Barth, "Abschied," *ZZ* 11 (1933), 536–544. Documents of the last meeting of ZZ (without Gogarten) on 30.9.1933: Hermann G. Göckeritz, *Friedrich Gogartens Briefwechsel mit Karl Barth, Eduard Thurneysen und Rudolf Bultmann* (Tübingen: Mohr Siebeck 2009), 389–416. Michael Beintker, "Barths Abschied von 'Zwischen den Zeiten': Recherchen und Beobachtungen zum Ende einer Zeitschrift," *ZThK* 106 (2009): 201–222. What is not convincing is the recent interpretation in: Goering, *Gogarten*, 284 f. The perspective of Gogarten-research is represented in Göckeritz, *Gogartens Briefwechsel*, 61–145.
7 Goering, *Gogarten*, 288 f.290–293.
8 Gogarten's originally planned title was "Ethische Skepsis oder gehorsamer Glaube." Ernst Fuchs' private copy of the book documented an intensive reading of the whole book (dated June 1937), similarily Bultmann, who agreed with Gogarten theologically against Barth, but not politically and ecclesially (Rudolf Bultmann, Friedrich Gogarten, *Briefwechsel 1921–1967*, ed. Hermann G. Göckeritz [Tübingen: Mohr Siebeck, 2002], 211–213 [18.4.1937]).
9 Friedrich Gogarten, Rez. Karl Barth, *Die christliche Dogmatik im Entwurf*, Bd. 1, München 1927, ThR 1 (1928/29 [published November 1928]): 60–80; also in *Gehören und Verantworten: Ausgewählte Aufsätze*, Hermann G. Göckeritz and Marianne Bultmann, eds. (Tübingen: Mohr, 1988): 14–30.

more detail in Gogarten's book *I believe in the triune God* from 1926,[10] Gogarten's first "main oeuvre."[11] I will argue that this book is a key to understanding the misunderstanding between Barth and Gogarten.[12]

Still, one could point out that in July 1931 Barth responded to Gogarten's review of his *Christliche Dogmatik* with two preprints from *Church Dogmatics* I/1. In these, he offers a sharp discussion of Gogarten's views on anthropology and Christology.[13] Barth's critique of Gogarten always focuses on one *specific* train of thought: the claim that Gogarten's anthropology necessarily leads to natural theology and that this 'natural anthropology' would be foundational for Christian doctrine as a whole. Unfortunately, it was now Gogarten who did not respond for one and a half years, allegedly because he was "too lazy."[14]

However, Gogarten did address the issue of the *Humanity and Divinity of Jesus Christ* in early 1932 – as if it were a last attempt at mutual understanding. He did so, of course, in the spirit of Luther and the theology of the cross, with a nod to Chalcedon. He understands the inner triune being of God in light of the wonder (*mirum*) of God's revelation in the cross of Jesus, veiled in divine ambiguity and human temptation.[15]

---

10 Gogarten and Barth discussed the book in April 1927 in Dorndorf over two days. Afterwards, Barth coined a very sharp critique in a letter to Thurneysen (15.5.1927): Gogarten is unable to engage in fashioned "real doctrine" (in contrast to the *Christliche Dogmatik*), he is terribly arbitrary regarding standards of sound academic scholarship, Gogarten knows only "seinen Luther in Auswahl und seine Grisebachschen Stichwörter dazu." Barth, Thurneysen, *Briefwechsel Bd. 2: 1921–1930*, GA V, ed. Eduard Thurneysen (Zurich: TVZ, 1974), 500f.
11 Barth to Gogarten, 23.9.1927, Göckeritz, *Gogartens Briefwechsel*, 255. Gogarten sent his book to Barth at the end of 1926, Barth confirmed his reading on 16.3.1927 and announced a visit on 19./20.4.1927 with some discussion, Gogarten confirmed the date of the visit on the 21.3.1927.
12 My starting-point is the observation that Barth, unlike Bultmann, never reviewed Gogarten's first "main oeuvre." He discussed it only briefly in his *Christliche Dogmatik* in regard to the concept of the "orders of creation," echoing the oral debates between them in April 1927. The most contentious criticism is that of the term "order of creation" in Karl Barth, *Die Lehre vom Worte Gottes: Prolegomena zur christlichen Dogmatik: Die Christliche Dogmatik im Entwurf* Bd. 1 (Munich: Kaiser, 1927), 91–93, which is presumably an echo of the oral discussions. Barth offers the category of man as "individual" and "member of the church" (ibid., 92) against the supposedly collectivizing notion of a *volk*-ish creation order. He counters this with a criticism of the alleged "abstraction" (ibid., 91), a standard topos of Barth's criticism of Gogarten since 1927.
13 These preprints are Karl Barth, "Prolegomena zur kirchlichen Dogmatik," *KD* I,1 (Munich: Kaiser, 1932), 128–136.177–180. The prints were sent on the 28.7.1931.
14 There was no reply from Gogarten, although Thurneysen asked him at the beginning of November 1932 (see Barth, Thurneysen, *Briefwechsel* 3, 288.)
15 See Friedrich Gogarten, "Die Menschheit und Gottheit Jesu," *ZZ* 10 (1932): 3–21, and Martin Luther, "Dictata super Psalterium, 1513–1515 zu Ps 4:4f.": "[Dominus] Mirabilis enim in sancto suo est, quod eum in tribulationes tradit et sic coronat. ... Crux enim Christi ubique in Scripturis

Certainly, Barth was simply not finished with Gogarten's critique in 1933. And Gogarten was quite clearly not finished with Barth's critique of his understanding of revelation in terms of an ethics of creation, that is, as holy and political law. Nor with Barth's critique of his highly ambiguous concept of bondage (*Hörigkeit*) of the "I" to the "Thou" or "the Other".

Gogarten was also not finished with Barth's critique of the starting-point of a theology of the cross, that is, a Christ who takes upon himself the curse and the hell *that is "the Other"* (to quote J. P. Sartre).[16] A Christ, who becomes the hostage of *all others*, and precisely, thereby, is God's witness and image.

Barth's "almost physiological" aversion to Gogarten,[17] and the split between the two could not be amended after 1933.[18]

Hence, I go back to the years between 1926 and 1932 and ask:

- What is controversial about Gogarten's "accentuated Lutheranism" – as Barth called it? What questions remain unexplored due to the intolerable misunderstanding? This is the historical anamnesis.
- What doctrinal possibilities were lost in the misunderstanding? Was a third position omitted? *Neither Barth nor Gogarten*, as opposed to the slogan *Either*

---

occurit." (WA 3,62,36f.40). Emanuel Hirsch had already claimed in 1920 in *Initium theologiae Lutheri* (Lutherstudien II, [Gütersloh: Bertelsmann, 1954], 9–35) that Luther's interpretation of Ps 4:4f. was the key to his *theologia crucis*. His pupil E. Vogelsang elaborated upon this thesis up until 1932: Erich Vogelsang, "Die Anfänge von Luthers Christologie nach der ersten Psalmenvorlesung insbesondere in ihren exegetischen und systematischen Zusammenhängen mit Augustin und der Scholastik dargestellt," AKG 15 (Berlin: De Gruyter, 1929), 97–101; Erich Vogelsang, "Der angefochtene Christus bei Luther (1932)," AKG 21 (reprint Berlin/Boston: De Gruyter, 2012). In 1932, Gogarten attempted to establish a third position beyond a *theologia crucis sensu* Hirsch and a Chalcedonian, incarnational Christology *sensu* Barth. After 1945, Gogarten's mature Christology criticizes Luther's reception of Chalcedonian incarnational Christology. He eliminates the Chalcedonian Christology in favor of an existential-hermeneutical Urbild-Christology: Friedrich Gogarten, *Die Verkündigung Jesu Christi: Grundlagen und Aufgaben* (Heidelberg: Schneider, 1948), 322–402, 405–545; Friedrich Gogarten, *Jesus Christus Wende der Welt: Grundfragen zur Christologie* (Tübingen: Mohr, 1966), 4f.234–244.

16 J. P. Sartre, *No Exit (Huis Clos)*, 1944; GT, *Geschlossene Gesellschaft: Stück in einem Akt*, transl. T. König (Hamburg: Rowohlt, 1991), 59. About *L' Etre et le Néant* (1943) and *Huis Clos* (1944), see M. Theunissen, *Der Andere: Studien zur Sozialontologie der Gegenwart* (Berlin: De Gruyter, 1965), 187–240.

17 Barth to Thurneysen, 7.10.1932, Barth and Thurneysen, *Briefwechsel* 3, 293.

18 Neither do we need to comment on their fight for interpretive superiority. After 1934, the rules of argument and interpretation did not apply any longer. It was war, and now the only rule was the racist idea of universality as expansion, as Lévinas called it. Emmanuel Lévinas, "Einige Betrachtungen zur Philosophie des Hitlerismus," in *Die Unvorhersehbarkeiten der Geschichte* (Freiburg: Alber, 2006), 23–36, 32.

Barth or Gogarten? However, this is the constructive question: *Otherwise than Barth or Beyond Gogarten.*

In the following, I consider two texts of Gogarten in two constellations: Gogarten and the Luther-Renaissance (section 2); Gogarten and Rudolf Bultmann (section 3).

2 An "Accentuated Lutheran" Critique of Barth's *Christliche Dogmatik* (1928)? Gogarten and the Luther Renaissance

Barth's statement in favor of Gogarten as his successor in Münster (in November 1929) attests:[19] "Unlike Bultmann, I am not too happy about Gogarten's closeness to phenomenology. I also have my reservations about the accentuated Lutheranism represented by Gogarten. Hence, it is indeed not easy for me to propose him as my successor."[20]

Barth's evaluation echoes Gogarten's critical review of the first volume of the *Christliche Dogmatik*.[21] But what does Barth mean by Gogarten's "accentuated Lutheranism"? What does Barth mean, when he called Gogarten a "modern Lutheran"[22] Word-of-God-theologian in 1927?

My claim is that, apart from Gogarten, there already existed another Lutheran Word of God theology in 1929, exemplified in the writings of R. Hermann and

---

[19] An unofficial, unsent draft from November 1929 (Barth, Bultmann, *Briefwechsel* 1911–1966, GA V, ed. Bernd Jaspert [Zurich: TVZ, 21994], 232–236) that names the disagreements to Gogarten, while Bultmann's separate vote for Gogarten is indirectly quoted and commented upon (Bultmann's separate vote was available at the Prussian Ministry of Science). A passage from the draft stated in a milder form was in a letter sent to Ministerial Director Prof. Dr. Richter dated 3.12.1929, Göckeritz, *Gogartens Briefwechsel*, 386–388.
[20] Barth and Bultmann, *Briefwechsel*, 233; in his official letter Barth continues: "For my part, I am alarmed by the certain narrowness of his theological circle of interest, earlier by his attraction to Grisebach's and now Heidegger's philosophy, and the influence this has had on him, and finally to accentuated Lutheranism, as he puts it." (ibid., 387).
[21] The review appeared in November 1928 (cf. fn. 10). It was probably sent to Barth immediately, if Barth's first reply was on the 4.2.1929 (Göckeritz, *Gogartens Briefwechsel*, 265).
[22] In 1927, Barth prefers the 'Gnesio-Lutheraner Thüringens' den 'Modernen' von Gogarten über Hirsch bis Merz: Barth to Thurneysen 15.5.1927 (see fn. 11).

H. J. Iwand.²³ Neither Barth nor Gogarten were familiar with *this* Lutheran teaching.²⁴ Hence, it is difficult to assess adequately their controversy about the specific character of "modern-Lutheran" theology. Gogarten's critique of Barth focuses on two aspects and one conclusion:²⁵

Barth's great achievement in the prolegomena is the focus on God's subjectivity and Lordship in revelation. However, Barth's Trinitarian explication of God's Word and revelation renders unnecessary any "pre-understanding about the meaning and the possibility of dogmatics" (17). Important conceptual work is missing: for example, the consideration of basic or foundational concepts, like the difference between form and content or subject and object (16.28). To say this in Kantian terminology: Gogarten diagnoses an "amphiboly of the concepts of reflection," that is, a tricky confusion about standard leading distinctions such as *form/content* or *in itself/for us:*

- The distinction between form and content, e.g., the form of the Word of God is Gospel and Law, but the content is the Gospel alone;
- The distinction between in itself/for us, e.g., God's Word in itself and God's Word for itself and for us.

Kant, in his famous appendix to the transcendental analytic of "the Critique of Pure Reason,"²⁶ deals with the confusion about the empirical and the transcendental use of reason. He asks for the transcendental place, where concepts of reflection produce either knowledge or illusion, and he calls for a transcendental phenomenology. Gogarten argues that Barth refuses to engage this issue of a phenomenology. Therefore, Barth's solution to the problem of the objectivity (Gegenständlichkeit) *and* non-objectivity of the *event* of God's Word and the knowledge of God remains unsatisfying for Gogarten (17).

Gogarten thinks it is the task of *theological anthropology* to tackle the problems that Barth's prolegomena left unresolved:

---

23 Rudolf Hermann's main work, "Luthers These gerecht und Sünder zugleich," was published in 1930 (preprints in 1929); Iwand's Dissertation, "Rechtfertigungslehre und Christusglaube," was published in 1930.

24 Gogarten did not know Hermann in 1928 (cf. Bultmann and Gogarten, *Briefwechsel*, 135); Barth only regarded the Lutheran theology of R. Hermann and H.J. Iwand to be true from 1934 onwards in Barmen.

25 Page numbers in the text refer to Gogarten's review of the "Christliche Dogmatik" of 1928 (cf. fn. 10).

26 Immanuel Kant, *Kritik der reinen Vernunft*, Akademie-Ausgabe Bd. III (Berlin: de Gruyter, 1970), A 214–233, B 316–349.

> Only when this *petitio principii* [i.e., the reality of God's Word] states that the starting-point of the Gospel is at the same time the starting-point of human reality, disclosed by the Word of the Gospel, has one really held on to the event of God's revelation as the starting-point, and one has [...] consistently held on to the theme of theology (20).

Gogarten elaborates on this claim in his essay on *The Problem of Theological Anthropology* in 1929.[27] Yet, his critique of Barth does not become clearer but more unclear and unfocused. This is because the essay turns prolegomena into "eristics" (as it was called a few years later), that is, the questioning of human self-understanding and the analysis of historical world-views.

Gogarten is not able to relate the *legitimate central problem* of the anthropology of God's Word as revelation – a problem that Barth immediately acknowledges – to the *legitimate resulting problem* of describing and locating human self-knowledge that occurs in revelation in an ethics of creation. In Gogarten there is also no preconception of the "temporal stages" (Zeitekstasen) of creation and atonement in relation to the temporality of the self, of individuality and singularity, of the dialogical and personal human being in God's revelation.[28]

The more Barth thinks that Gogarten's engagement of the *central* problem turns into a general revelation in creation,[29] the less he reflects on the *resulting* problem.[30] This is despite the fact that his own *Christliche Dogmatik* had discussed it under the title of the *transition from the phenomenological to the existential consideration of the Word of God*.[31]

Let me now confront these two critics' reductions with a third option: the Word-of-God-Luther-Renaissance.[32]

---

27 Friedrich Gogarten, "Das Problem einer theologischen Anthropologie," *ZZ* 7 (1929): 493–511; also in Gogarten, *Gehören und Verantworten*, 31–45. Actually, Gogarten deals here with anthropology as an analysis of historical and contemporary world-views sensu Wilhelm Dilthey, with man as sinner and the history of world-views as a history of decay, with the Word of God as the law and judgement of the concrete person.
28 These questions are discussed in: Rudolf Hermann, *Luthers These* (s.fn 25) and Heinrich Assel, *Der andere Aufbruch: Die Lutherrenaissance – Ursprünge, Aporien und Wege, Karl Holl, Emanuel Hirsch, Rudolf Hermann (1910–1935)* (Göttingen: Vandenhoeck & Ruprecht, 1994), 391.3–95.416–426.
29 Barth, *KD* I,1, 134: "God being revealed in human creatureliness."
30 Cf. Barth, *KD* I,1, 128–136 (§ 5), esp., 135f.
31 Barth, *Christliche Dogmatik*, 69–109 (§§ 5–6), esp. 69–71.
32 I freely summarize this view under the title *Beyond Law and Gospel?*, following Hans Joachim Iwand's review of *Church Dogmatics* I/1 in 1935. See Hans Joachim Iwand, "Jenseits von Gesetz und Evangelium: Eine kritische Besprechung der Lehre von dem Worte Gottes in Karl Barths 'Prolegomena zur Kirchlichen Dogmatik I,1,'" *Theologische Blätter* 14 (1935): 65–80;

Faith understands God's promise in particular human and ecclesial speech acts (e.g., baptism, absolution, the Lord's Supper, proclamation) by distinguishing God's Word from these speech acts. Faith thus distinguishes between God's Word and human words. It does so because of God's own condescension into human words and not because of God's alleged transcendence ("God's being in Himself"). Faith is the recognition of God's christologically determined humanity and lowliness in the word of the promise. Faith justifies *God* in his promise, insofar as it recognizes the "for you" of the crucified Christ, which *precedes every human recognition and foundation* and validates the promise "for itself" and "in itself." This is the event of *Christ's New Testament* as *moriturus promissor* and *victurus testator*.[33]

Faith is also justified *by God*, because a person recognizes himself or *herself as both righteous and guilty at the same time*. In accordance with this correlation of judgment, all promises are valid "in" Christ. The distinction between law and promise explains to what extent faith has to understand the condescension of the promising and covenanting Christ as its own temporality. However, since faith remains, by itself, unfree to enter into God's presence, it is always inquiring about the hidden, electing, and rejecting God, *beyond and apart from the promise*. In light of the temptation towards a theology of glory, the law is the reminder of the constant need to return to the promise of the God revealed in Christ and hidden precisely *in* the Word, that is, *in* revelation.

The *simul iustus et peccator* is a doctrinal rule about the *real* person in the reality of God's Word. It is not based on experience but opens up the variety of experiences that characterize faith as Christian faith. The *simul iustus et peccator* is an axiom of revelation as promise and assertion.

This was a possible answer to the *problem* of anthropology in prolegomena.

Let us return to Gogarten's review! This Lutheran doctrine of revelation as the Word of God was reduced by Gogarten to the accusation that Barth allegedly ignores human sin in light of the reality of God's Word. But this is much too simple! Gogarten offers no argument to support this claim.[34]

---

also in idem (ed.), "Um den rechten Glauben: Gesammelte Aufsätze," *ThB* 9 (Munich: Kaiser, 1959): 87–109.

33 Martin Luther, "De captivitate Babylonica ecclesiae praeludium (1520)," WA 6, 513, 34– 514,10.

34 Gogarten's objection against Barth states that Barth doesn't presuppose a realistic (*wirkliche*) dialectic of the sinner's person, but only a dialectical *idea* of the sinner's self-contradiction – a contradiction which is already solved in an *a priori* unity of the ideal person (Gogarten, *Rezension*, 21). But Gogarten himself does not explain to what extent his rather superficial explanation

Nevertheless, Gogarten draws a final conclusion: "Since Barth's doctrine of the Trinity operates in light of this [...] theologically inadequate concept of the human being, who stands in opposition to God and to himself or herself, it, unfortunately, remains opaque."[35] The objection concerns Barth's doctrine of God's revelation as Creator and, especially, as Reconciler.

> If one looks closely at Barth's teaching on the incarnation, it becomes rather clear that the starting-point of his thought is not the revealed God but the unrevealed God, "the being of God in God's self." Hence, Barth engages in a procedure that he himself criticized, when he claimed that the old Lutheran theologians had taught that the divinity *in abstracto* assumed humanity.[36]

Gogarten's critique is reasonable, but it does not really apply to Barth's view in the *Christliche Dogmatik*. Gogarten reduces Barth's incarnational Christology to specific *thin* concepts. This will lead to an unresolved dispute between the two about the *in itself* of God's *eternal* freedom, the "eternal history" *in God's self*, and the *for us* of God's "original historical" *Oikonomia*.[37] If you read Barth's commentary on the Prologue to the Gospel of John (1925/1933),[38] you will see Barth's imaginary and subtle description of the Logos as Creator and as Incarnate. Whenever he remains close to the text of the Prologue, he does not entangle himself in cumbersome talk about God-in-Himself and God-for-us. Gogarten's objection[39] misses the richness of Barth's thinking.[40]

Let me offer a first summary:

(1) Gogarten's review offers two objections against Barth and, in doing so, appeals to Luther's theology of the Word. These objections are sparsely supported, and the references to Luther are too selective to be convincing. This is especially clear when we see what the Luther Renaissance of Her-

---

of *simul iustus et peccator* implies a "humanism of the real human being" or a "humanism of the other human being."

35 Gogarten, *Rezension*, 22.
36 Gogarten, *Rezension*, 23; Gogarten's Barth citation is not to be taken literally, though it is possibly meant as such, see Barth, *Christliche Dogmatik*, 215, 231. 255.
37 Vgl. Barth, *KD* I,1, 179.
38 Karl Barth, "Erklärung des Johannesevangeliums [Kapitel 1–8]: Vorlesung Münster im Wintersemester 1925/1926, wiederholt in Bonn Sommersemester 1933," *GA* II, ed. W Fürst (Zurich: TVZ, 1999).
39 Compare Gogarten, *Rezension*, 24–26 with Barth, *Christliche Dogmatik*, 215–218.
40 In return, Barth rearranges KD I, 1, 179f. to cite Luther quotes against Gogarten. The actual Christological debate between the two is thereby shifted by Luther to the theme of the inner and revealed Word.

mann and Iwand had already offered in terms of a theology of revelation and the Word.
(2) Gogarten mentions neither the distinction of the Gospel as promise and law nor *simul iustus et peccator* as a basic anthropological rule. He mentions the central problem of anthropology, but he hardly elaborates on it.
(3) The resulting problem of the location of God and self in revelation and in terms of an ethics of creation is discussed ambiguously. This is the source of future misunderstandings.
(4) Gogarten's critique from the perspective of incarnational Christology is interesting, but it is remarkably close to Erich Vogelsang. Barth's Christology is interpreted below its own standard.
(5) The fundamental relationship between the incarnation and the cross of Jesus Christ, as well as between the election of Jesus and the economic Trinity, is discussed but only in outline.

3 "I believe in the triune God" (1926): Gogarten and Bultmann's Word-of-God-Phenomenology

Gogarten's *I believe in the triune God*[41] is his first central work. To date, there are hardly any good analyses.[42] Apart from the differentiation of Dialectical Theology, the book is as central as Barth's *Christliche Dogmatik im Entwurf* (1927). Right in between these two books, Heidegger's *Sein und Zeit* (*Being and Time*) was published (in the spring of 1927).[43]

Barth never reviewed Gogarten's book but Rudolf Bultmann did. Bultmann wrote a unique, sophisticated, 27-page commentary, which comments on the book almost page by page and which shows Bultmann's hermeneutical mastery. One can almost see Bultmann reading Gogarten's book with Heidegger's *Sein und Zeit* lying close by. While reading both books, Bultmann writes his meta-text, commenting on Heidegger in light of Gogarten and on Gogarten in light of Heidegger.

Gogarten's first "main oeuvre" and Bultmann's Commentary (or meta-text) are spotlights on an explosive discussion between the spring of 1927 and the fall of 1928. They are the fluid magma of Dialectical Theology and phenomenol-

---

[41] For the Genesis of the book see Goering, *Gogarten*, 179f.
[42] Characteristically, the most recent monograph on Gogarten quotes isolated citations from the book (Goering, *Gogarten*, 141–149), but doesn't analyze its systematic argument and structure.
[43] Martin Heideger, *Sein und Zeit* (Tübingen: Niemeyer 1927). Page numbers refer to the first edition.

ogy. Bultmann's text was never published and only a single complete copy exists. Hence, my discussion of it here is a first.⁴⁴

Before I engage with it, let me offer two observations: First, it is exciting to see how Bultmann tries to understand Gogarten better than Gogarten understands himself. He does so by using Heidegger's analysis of temporality and historicity. Secondly, it is equally exciting to ask: Where does Gogarten's text *not* fit Bultmann's interpretation? Could his phenomenological interest have led him to Buber and Lévinas instead of Grisebach and Heidegger? Or is Gogarten's fatal position in his *Political Ethics* from 1932 already visible in 1926, since his dialogical thinking becomes dialog*istic* and ideological?⁴⁵

Now let us turn to Bultmann's 27-page commentary. My close reading of it has three parts.⁴⁶

3.1 Gogarten and Bultmann on *"Faith and History"*

Gogarten's *Introduction, "Faith and History"* (G. 1–39), discusses "recognition" as the basic phenomenon of the "duality of human reality" (G, 36 f.) and of "I" and "Thou." But its critique of Troeltsch's theory of historical development gets entangled in Troeltsch's own categories. Gogarten speaks about history and the historical only polemically and not critically.

Bultmann (B, 2–5) brings forth valid objections in light of his reading of *Being and Time:*
- Gogarten underestimates temporality and historicity as modes of existence in the world.
- He does not use the Kierkegaardian concept of the "moment" (*Augenblick*).

---

44 See the circumstances of the genesis (preparation for a discussion in *Bultmanns Marburger Sozietät* in the fall of 1928), the proof of the authorship, and the edition of Rudolf Bultmann's Commentary on Friedrich Gogarten's *Ich glaube an den dreieinige Gott*, in the Appendix of this book. Page numbers in the text refer to Gogarten's work *Ich glaube an den dreieinigen Gott* (= G) or to *Bultmanns Kommentar* (= B, page number of the original typescript, see Appendix).
45 The distinction of dialogical (critical) and dialogistic (ideological) thinking refers to Theunissen, *Der Andere*, 363 Anm. 18.
46 Gogarten's argumentation is not forceful but partly indecisive, partly expectant. Problems, concepts, and hypotheses, which should have been unpacked in the introduction, do not appear until later. Therefore, Bultmann makes the following perceptive remarks: "It would have to be shown," "the missing problem at the beginning now presents itself", "it would probably have changed the whole system," "the investigation gets lost." I do not comment upon these points of criticism in detail, but refer to them in the appendix.

- The concept of the historical event as *Vorhandenes* or as *momentous event* is blurred.
- The relation between existence as created being or being-thrown-into-the-world and existence as redeemed being is unclear. Sometimes the two are identical, sometimes not – and of course Bultmann argues for a distinction according to his own convictions.
- The prevalence of the possible over against the actual is underestimated.
- Gogarten does not discuss the openness (*Erschlossenheit*) of existence as momentness, futurity, and pastness (*Augenblicklichkeit, Zukünftigkeit, Gewesenheit*).[47]

Bultmann later (B, 11) summarizes his objections in the question: What is the motivation for the return of faith to the *historical Thou of Jesus* and his word? In this regard, Bultmann says that Gogarten's introduction lacks basic concepts.

3.2 Gogarten and Bultmann on *Faith in God the Creator*

Gogarten's exposition in *Part I: Faith in God the Creator* becomes more affirmative.[48]

The belief in God the Creator is located in the encounter with the concrete Thou as God's creature. Faith is seen primarily as relational and practical, and therefore it is belief *in* the Creator. "This adjustment of faith to the I-Thou-relationship means that their faith in God necessarily implies faith in the other person, in the Thou – [...] the neighbor as God's creature, and through whom God actually speaks with us, and to whom we are thus irrevocably bound." (G, 60) Indeed, a strange and far-reaching statement!

Faith in the Creator is a *deed:* it is a *pure action* towards the Thou, by an I that is released *as a created person* only through this action. Faith in the Creator is a *decision:* either for the I, as that which is at hand, or for the Thou, as that which is not-at-hand. Finally, the "concepts of faith and of decision" are "impossible to use for the interpretation or the explanation of an event" (G, 61). One can

---

47 The last two critical points are not directly articulated by Rudolf Bultmann, but by Ernst Fuchs in his private copy of Gogartens book – perhaps an echo of the discussion of Gogarten in *Bultmanns Sozietät* in the fall of 1928.
48 Especially the summary of chapter 3, *Der Glaube an Gott den Schöpfer* (G, 60–62).

only encounter the Thou without any interpretation or explanation! This claim is pure Grisebach[49] – much to Barth's annoyance!

What does Gogarten mean? The other, the Thou, cannot be interpreted in the light of my own world-projection, since it interrupts and transcends my world-projection. Bultmann asks: Does one not at the very least have to "encounter the Thou with understanding?!" (B, 22, cf. 7f.17) Yet, Bultmann's hermeneutical term *Verstehen* (B, 2.5.6.12.13.15.16) is precisely not the term Gogarten seeks. The encounter with the transcendent and unavailable Thou shall reveal the wordly transcendence of the creature in general. The awareness of the ethical obligation must not depend on any "gesture" of claiming to "comprehend" the Thou. Ethical perception must fully respect the alterity of the Thou.

It is here that Bultmann and Gogarten reach an impasse and Heidegger cannot help either.[50] Gogarten erroneously views the Thou-I-relationship as subject-object-relationship in reverse: "the Thou [is] the subject, the determining instance, while the I is the object, which is determined" (G, 145, see also 108.111.187).[51] When the I, in the encounter with the Thou, loses its intentionality, its understanding, and its world-projection, it becomes passive, bound (*hörig*), responsible, and it is determined as the object of the Thou.[52]

I want to state here a constructive thesis: Lévinas' question about sensitivity and the passive sense of the "diachronic" proximity of other and self lingers in Gogarten's text but it is never addressed. Gogarten seeks for a passive sense-manifestation in the non-synchronic proximity of self and other (as Lévinas calls it). But his Thou-I-relationship is *too* immediate and *too* authoritarian. Right at the end of his book, Gogarten speaks of the Thou-I-bondage as the fundamental "order of creation," as if the genie has suddenly been let out of the bottle.

Gogarten's emphasis on an unconditional bondage to the Thou and his idea of a non-explanatory encounter with the actual, bodily Thou – and soon with the ethnic Thou – is the door through which the authoritarian ideology of ethical

---

49 S. on the thesis of the meaninglessness (*Deutungslosigkeit*) of the Thou in the encounter, see Eberhard Grisebach, *Gegenwart: Eine kritische Ethik* (Halle: Niemeyer, 1928), 6.15.191. Interpretation and criticism: Theunissen, *Der Andere*, 362.
50 In regard to the problem of *existence-with* (*Mit-Dasein*), ignored by Heidegger in "Sein und Zeit," cf. Theunissen, *Der Andere*, 164–167.
51 Similar to Gogarten, *Glaube und Wirklichkeit* (Jena: Diederichs, 1928), 26.28. This (published separately in 1928) epilogue to Gogarten's edition of Luther's *De servo arbitrio* (Munich: Kaiser 1924, 344–371) is problematic in its own right.
52 To this figure by Grisebach, *Gegenwart*, 577; reception by Friedrich Gogarten, *Politische Ethik: Versuch einer Grundlegung* (Jena: Diederichs, 1932); prepared in Gogarten's *Glaube und Wirklichkeit*, 28.31.32. For criticism: Theunissen, *Der Andere*, 361–363.

bondage and political "responsibility" will come in – in the Politische Ethik of 1932.[53]

In 1927 and 1928, however, there is still time for theological discussion. Bultmann asks: How can the situational Creator-faith be the basis of the past dimension of the Creator-faith, that is, the idea of creation as origin and "in the beginning"? (B, 6b) And how can one conceive of God's action regarding promise and law in relation to Israel? (B, 9) What is the relationship between the actual present and the past as a story that is remembered or that initiates a decision (B, 9, see B, 11)?

Gogarten becomes assertive. He suggests that the coherence of creation remains impervious to human reason. It can only be believed by faith in the Creator of the beginning and the end (G, 63). Bultmann remarks: The distinction between the coherence and unity of *life* and the coherence and unity of the *world* is missing. Gogarten should read Heidegger on *eigentliches Ganzseinkönnen* as ontological notion from *Sorge* (SuZ 301–334) and on *Welt-Geschichte, Weltlichkeit von Welt als Geschichte* (SuZ, 389–392)[54] (B, 8).

Gogarten's writings after 1927 show the extent to which he is indebted to Heidegger. He famously demands a theological concept of the worldliness of the world, a legitimate secularity, and secularism as the decline of the secular. The demand is certainly inspired by Luther (around 1918). Now, however, it is specified with the help of Heidegger and Bultmann (1927). And in 1933 it is reformatted politically through Carl Schmitt.[55]

Chapter 4 is entitled *Creation and History* (G, 65–85). Here, Gogarten seems to develop his connotation of history and historical understanding (*geschichtliches Verstehen*). At least, this is what Bultmann thinks, who once more is clearer than Gogarten himself. Bultmann insists: "The motivation of the question of past history must become clear. The same is true for the relation of the past that becomes present through the Thou to the past that becomes present through remembrance; the former cannot be without the latter. […] The demand of the past Thou (if one really wants to say so) has to become clear on the basis of

---

53 Gogarten's *Politische Ethik* 1932 is interpreted in the author's first essay in this volume.
54 Bultmann's references to page numbers refer to the first edition of Heidegger's *Sein und Zeit* (see fn. 43).
55 Friedrich Gogarten, "Säkularisierte Theologie in der Staatslehre" (presented on January 18, 1933 at the University of Wroclaw), in *Gehören und Verantworten*, 126–141. On the acquaintance of Gogarten and Schmitt: Goering, *Gogarten*, 223–229. D. Braun, Carl Schmitt und Friedrich Gogarten. Reflections on 'actual Catholic aggravation' and its Protestant equivalent in the transition from the Weimar Republic to the Third Reich in *Berliner Theologische Zeitschrift* 11 (1994): 219–242.

the present Thou." (B, 11) And Bultmann suggests how to distinguish between them: historicity encompasses the existential analysis of historical understanding and tradition. Faith means existential understanding of the eschatological kerygma, in which the Gospel of Jesus Christ determines each one's existence in faith (B, 10 f.).

3.3 Gogarten and Bultmann on "Faith in God the Reconciler"

Part II of Gogarten's book on *"Faith in God the Reconciler"* begins with *Chapter 5 Law and Promise*. It is now that Gogarten finally responds to Bultmann, but the response does not match Bultmann's expectations. It also contradicts Barth's objection from 1932 that Gogarten, allegedly influenced by Bultmann, gives priority to God's general revealedness in creation over God's special revelation in Jesus Christ.[56]

Gogarten explains the historical existence under law and promise by referring to the validity of the *Old Testament and Israel's* "past history of salvation." "The past, to which the history of the Israelites certainly belongs, is, until today, present for us as the past, and it calls us to make a decision. Our question, therefore, is whether this history can be present for us as the past, precisely with this existential meaning." (G, 90) The "historical quality" of existence is measured against the history of Israel in the Word as law and promise, which is a *witness* and *as such* becomes a concretely present Thou-encounter (G, 98 f.). Here, Bultmann cannot agree with Gogarten.[57]

Witness as *Israel's historical witness and as "living tradition"* is the basis of the unity as well as the distinction between law and promise. It is also the basis of the unity of and difference between creation and reconciliation. For Gogarten, faith in the Creator and in Creation as an event of historical quality presupposes *special* revelation, namely, *Jesus Christ and the Old Testament history of promise*. This implies, in turn, that there is no creaturely revelation in one's own ethnic group or ethnic law (*nomos*) as a second source of revelation besides this special revelation!

One wants to exclaim: "Gogarten, why did you not hold on to *this* position! Why did you in 1934 ask the fatal question about the German ethnic law (*Volks-*

---

56 Barth, *KD* I,1, 132–134.
57 In 1927, Bultmann already interprets the understanding of past witnesses in a Heideggerian sense as the understanding of a "past possibility to exist" (*gewesene Möglichkeit zu existieren*) and the understanding of faith as the possibility of having a existential history (*echte Geschichte*) (B, 12 f.).

gesetz) as God's law?"[58] And note that it is *Bultmann* who demands from Gogarten an explicit concept of *God's general revelation:* "Bei konsequenter Durchführung der revelatio generalis und specialis würde sich alles klarer sagen lassen. " (B, 17).[59]

Gogarten further sharpens his alternative position: the creaturely revelation in the history of Israel, as "witness-history" and history of election (G, 117), has a twofold character and content, it is law and promise (G, 119). It also refers to Christ as "Thou," as witness and Word of God.

The decisive *Chapter 6, "The Gospel,"* opens with a methodical remark about the possible participation in Israel's history of witness (G, 127–129). This participation is possible only indirectly and dialectically, because God could fulfill the promise only in taking it away from Israel. That is, the end of Israel as the beginning of that which is promised, and the beginning of that which is promised as the end of Israel. This model is well known from the genesis of Barth's Israel-theology up until 1942.[60] Bultmann does not comment on it and, in general, he now agrees more and more with Gogarten (B, 19–22).

Jesus' proclamation is Word, and "it is constitutive for this Word that it is spoken to the Other [with a capital O]. Indeed, it only exists as Word spoken to the Other. From the beginning, it is relation, and this is, at the same time, both its content and form. This Word cannot be an expression of the individual life of its speaker, because it has no content that is not at the same time in relationship to the Other." (G, 134) What does Gogarten have in mind here?

Jesus' proclamation speaks indirectly to the Other, it is the witness of the Father towards His creature as Jesus speaks directly towards the historical other (Pharisees, disciples). In Jesus' "instrumental" words, he reveals himself as the "medial" Word. For Gogarten, this is the form of the twofold Gospel of Jesus. Its content is the Lordship of the wrathful or merciful God. "Since this Word, from the beginning, is a responsible Word, it puts me into this responsible relationship." (G, 142) It provokes the decision to faith or unbelief.

The OT prophets and Jesus *as* prophet speak out of this relationship to the people of the promise, as it is *demanded* by God. Jesus as *witness* speaks out

---

58 Friedrich Gogarten, *Ist Volksgesetz Gottesgesetz? Eine Auseinandersetzung mit meinen Kritikern* (Hamburg: Hanseatische Verlagsanstalt, 1934).
59 Bultmann's summary of cap. 5 and 6 critic. –Bultmann will in 1933 contradict Gogarten's doctrine of ethnic law (Volksgesetz): Bultmann to Gogarten, 26.6.1933 (Bultman and Gogarten, *Briefwechsel*, 209 f.); s. Gogarten's memorandum on this topic from June 1933 (Bultmann and Gogarten, *Briefwechsel*, 301).
60 Cf. Eberhard Busch, *Unter dem Bogen des einen Bundes: Karl Barth und die Juden 1933–1945* (Neukirchen-Vluyn: Neukirchener Verlag, 1996).

of the *fulfilled* relationship (G, 146 f.). The law stands between prophet and faith, and love stands between witness and faith. Jesus speaks in the power of fulfillment, in the power of his listening to the Creator, and his bondage to the claim of the Other (G, 149).[61]

The law of Jesus annuls the subject's claim to dominion. Jesus is the only witness, who is unreservedly and without interpretation bound to and responsible for the claim of the Thou, the Other. There is no understanding of the cross of Jesus without hearing the Word of Jesus that calls us to love (*"Thou shall"*). And there is no hearing of this Word without the recognition of the crucified who somehow is the "original substitute"[62]: the human-being-for-others, although Gogarten doesn't use this term yet.

The OT prophets and Jesus *as* prophet disclose human sin. Jesus *as* witness and *as* Word forgives sin. "Jesus Christ, who knows my sin, hears and fulfills my claim in a much deeper way than I could ever conceive. Since he knows human sin, he knows better than any human being that the deepest human desire is to be redeemed from this sin" (G, 155).

Gogarten does not construe Jesus' knowledge by means of a metaphysical theory, for example, as intuitive knowledge of the *Logos asarkos* and the discursive knowledge of the *Logos ensarkos*.[63] Jesus' knowledge is the knowledge of the incarnate Judge, who *abstains* from judging the hidden maxim of the will, radical human sin, and the human future (*futurabilia*), that is, what human beings show themselves to be when they are led into temptation. Jesus *only* judges human deeds by forgiving, because His divine knowledge is love. "In this is love perfected with us, that we may have confidence for the day of judgment, because *as he is, so are we in this world*" (1 John 4:17, RSV). This argument, which extends from Luther via Kant to Gogarten, is the key to understanding the incarnation for Gogarten. His later works on Christology[64] elaborate this outline.

---

[61] Denial of the claim of the other is "sin." That no man is without sin – because sin is non-love – is nevertheless not a general proposition, but an existential one. (G, 151) "Only the Word of love is a genuinely real and responsible Word. [...] If a person hears the Word of Jesus Christ as an answer to his own demand, he plunges into an abyss, in which, one way or another, he loses the life he previously led." (G, 153, my translation).
[62] Regarding the term original substitution: Bernhard Waldenfels, *Hyperphänomene: Modi hyperbolischer Erfahrung* (Berlin: Suhrkamp, 2012), 41.
[63] Marilyn McCord-Adams, *Christ and Horrors: The Coherence of Christology* (Cambridge: Cambridge University Press, 2006).
[64] Gogarten, *Jesus Christus, Wende der Welt*, 226–231.

4 Conclusion

Let me stop here and offer a second summary and conclusion.[65] What is Gogarten's "accentuated Lutheranism"? What kind of phenomenology do we find?

(1) Gogarten's text includes problematic dialogistic and not only dialogical concepts of bondage to, and responsibility for the Thou. They stem from Grisebach and already appear in Gogarten's first book on Luther from 1924. In 1932, in his *Political Ethics* they are openly ideological.

(2) Bultmann's commentary reinterprets Gogarten *hermeneutically*, in light of Heidegger.

(3) It is Bultmann and not Gogarten who raises the question of whether this analysis of existence implies the idea of "general revelation" – an idea explicitly rejected by Gogarten. Gogarten's phenomenological starting-point – the Thou and the Other, their transcendence and unavailability (*Unverfügbarkeit*) – is different from Bultmann's starting-point.

(4) Gogarten's distinction between law and promise is developed in terms of a theology of Word and witness as well as in terms of a theology of Israel and of Christology. In 1926, it is not (yet) political-ethical, let alone ethnocentric or racist!

(5) Still, the future problematic development of Gogarten's thinking is already visible: as soon as he elaborates on a doctrine of God's general revealedness as Creator in the form of an analysis of existence, his central concepts can become political-ethical.

(6) Gogarten's theology of the cross understands the human being Jesus as a "human-being-for-others," as substitute in the place of sin and the curse, as hostage, etc. Here, he takes up Luther's ideas, but he turns them into a *foundational social ontology* in a precarious combination of Grisebach, Heidegger and (allegedly) Martin Buber.

(7) At least Gogarten offers a Word-and-revelation-theology of concrete command and concrete bondage, in which he seeks to develop the "*encounter with reality*"[66] in a Trinitarian way as law and promise.

(8) Only the last pages evoke the concrete "orders of creation" (almost in the terms of a phenomenology of the body).

---

65 The *3. Teil Heiligung*, and here the *7. Kapitel Die Gemeinde der Heiligen* should not be described here. Bultmann's commentary mostly agrees with these parts.
66 Gogarten, *Glaube und Wirklichkeit*, 23.

(9) Gogarten's first central work, *I believe in the triune God*, regards faith as genuine historical existence, as creaturely Thou-bondage, and only in this light as doctrine of creation, redemption, sanctification.[67]

---

[67] Funded by Theoria, Kurt von Fritz-Wissenschaftsprogamm zur Förderung der Geistes- und Sozialwissenschaften Mecklenburg-Vorpommern. – Translated from German by Dr. Matthias Gockel.

Christian Neddens
Werner Elert and Hans Joachim Iwand – Political Theology and Theology of the Cross

1 Introduction

If we look at the Luther Renaissance (broader speaking), no bigger contrast can be imagined than between Werner Elert (1885–1954) and Hans Joachim Iwand (1899–1960). The differing directions theological innovation took in Lutheranism after World War I can be demonstrated clearly in these two positions.[1]

Both were part of the Luther Renaissance from the 1920s onwards, but not of the Holl school. Both developed their theology through intensive debate with Karl Barth. They were in full agreement with him in their criticism of 19th century theology. In the course of the 1920s, however, their disparity became marked. While Elert attempted polemically to sharpen his own profile as a confessional Lutheran alternative in the Erlangen tradition *against* Barth, Iwand sought theological renewal in critical constructive discussion *with* Barth.

Both Elert and Iwand referred to Luther, but the ways in which they did so varied greatly. While Elert adopted Luther's later theology as found in Theodosius Harnack, in deliberate contrast to the Holl school, Iwand was interested in the newly discovered *young* Luther, as was Holl.

2 Werner Elert: *Völkisch*-Political Theology of the Law[2]

2.1 Luther, Schleiermacher and the Depression after WW I

Werner Elert has occasionally been named a "Lutheranissimus", an advocate of true Lutheran confessionalism.[3] In point of fact his theology is a pronouncedly

---

[1] The German sources and literature will be translated by the author if cited in the body of the text.
[2] Concerning this term and the different forms of Political Theology see Heinrich Assel, Aporien und Charaktere evangelischer Theologie: Neue Arbeiten zur Geschichte der deutschsprachigen Systematischen Theologie im 20. Jahrhundert," *VuF* 45 (2000): 3–55, 32.

modern form of transformation, clothing *völkisch*-vitalistic ideas in a Lutheran confessional robe. After 1933 this played a considerable role in compromising Lutheran theology.

Werner Elert was born in 1885. He belonged to a Lutheran minority church in Prussia, a fact which moulded his character, as did the academic tradition of experiential theology in Erlangen. Initially he sought a grounding for the certainty of faith by studying religious philosophy and religious psychology. Adhering to the Erlangen tradition, he used experience to connect a subjective approach to religion with the assertion that the subject of faith possesses objective reality. He sought ways to make this seem plausible to a general audience.

In 1919, after a period as pastor and army chaplain, Elert became director of the Theological Seminary in Breslau of the Ev.-Luth. Church in Prussia, in 1923 professor in Erlangen. Towards the end of World War I Elert's interpretation of the cross began to merge in a characteristic manner with national thought – also seen in Paul Althaus and Wilhelm Stapel.[4] The force of the battle ground experience but even more the need to legitimate the millions who died in the lost war demanded a religious interpretation. With recourse to Rudolf Otto's *Das Heilige* (1917) and Oswald Spengler's *Untergang des Abendlandes* (1918) he decoded the depression so prevalent in protestant milieus as a reemergence of Luther's "experience of justification".[5] Appalled by the relentless violence of an unpredictable wrathful God, Christ's obedient suffering becomes the "symbol for the fundamental law of all earthly reality".[6] True to his profession despite failure, the perspective of a future (national) resurrection begins to appear.[7]

Lutheran theologumena are now integrated successively into this basic concept. Initially Luther was not so much the central figure as it was an inversion of

---

[3] Reinhard Hauber, Werner Elert, "Einführung in Leben und Werk eines 'Lutheranissimus,'" *NZSTh* 29 (1987): 113–146. See Berndt Hamm, "Werner Elert als Kriegstheologe: Zugleich ein Beitrag zur Diskussion 'Luthertum und Nationalsozialismus'," *KZG* 11 (1998): 206–254, 210.

[4] See Klaus Scholder, *Die Kirchen und das Dritte Reich, vol. 1: Vorgeschichte und Zeit der Illusionen 1918–1934* (München: Ulstein [1977] 2000), 148.

[5] A characteristic example is Werner Elert, "Predigt zum Bußtage (Hebr 3,7–11)," *Kirchenblatt der Evangelisch-Lutherischen Gemeinden in Preußen* 76 (1921): 609–616.

[6] Werner Elert, Review of *Tragik im Weltlauf*, by Joseph Bernhart, *ThBl* 38 (1917): 397. See Werner Elert, "Die Transzendenz Gottes," *NKZ* 34 (1923): 521–546, 529: "Von denen, die am unmittelbarsten die Tragik allzufrühen Sterbens auf dem Schlachtfelde miterlebten, ist vielmals bezeugt worden, ihnen seien an dieser Analogie die biblischen Gedanken des Opfertodes, der Stellvertretung für andere oder auch der Sühnung nunmehr als zutreffender Ausdruck für Gottes Handeln in der Menschheit gewiß geworden."

[7] See Werner Elert, "Die Übriggebliebenen," *Der Tag* (Ausgabe A, No. 290; 12/12/1917): 1–2.

Schleiermacher's *Gefühl schlechthinniger Abhängigkeit:*[8] the fundamental religious experience is fear, a feeling of being completely at the mercy of God's wrath.[9] It was not until the mid 1920s that Elert began to fall back on Luther's theology and to link the feeling of fear with the concept of the law.

Elert developed a theology for a church milieu which was, on the one hand, traditionally Lutheran, and on the other hand, open to modern *völkisch* thought. Lutheranism, the "autochthonous religion of the German nation,"[10] became the characteristic of a political religious identity against "enemies in the West, the South and lately even in the East"[11]. The objective was to develop a Lutheran *Reichskirche.*[12]

2.2 *Die Lehre des Luthertums im Abriss* (1924/26)

Elert's first compact dogmatic theology *Die Lehre des Luthertums im Abriss* (*An Outline of Christian Dogmatics*) is indeed innovative and a fascinatingly stringent example for the *Verweltanschaulichung* of an antithetic doctrine of reconciliation "centered on enmity between God and man."[13] In the second edition of 1926 Luther quotations were included to lend it authority, and to emphasise its dependence on tradition. Luther's doctrine of justification as a matrix for an existential

---

8 See Werner Elert, *Morphologie des Luthertums*, vol. 1: *Theologie und Weltanschauung des Luthertums hauptsächlich im 16. und 17. Jahrhunderts* (München: C.H.Beck, 1931), 149, and Friedrich Schleiermacher, *Der christliche Glaube* (Berlin: Walter de Gruyter, 1960⁷), § 4 und § 46,2.
9 See Werner Elert, "Die Forderung unseres Zeitalters an die Sprecher der Christenheit," *AELKZ* 55 (1922): 386–390; 402–404; 418–421; 434–436, 420: The sceptical contemporary should feel, "daß er mit seinem gesamten Dasein [...] in der Gewalt des transzendenten Gottes steht, dessen Motive und Absichten ihm zunächst völlig unberechenbar sind." The deepening of awe of God into an abysmal horror can also be found in Rudolf Otto, *Das Heilige. Über das Irrationale in der Idee des Göttlichen und sein Verhältnis zum Rationalen* (München: C.H.Beck [1917] 1979), 13–27.
10 Werner Elert, "Das Erstarrungsgesetz des Protestantismus," *NKZ* 36 (1925): 912.
11 Werner Elert, *Die Die Lehre des Luthertums im Abriß* (München: C.H.Beck 1926²), 158. See also Werner Elert, "Zu den Waffen," *AELKZ* 56 (1923), 525.
12 The idea of an independent Lutheran national church had already been raised in 1870 by Theodosius Harnack. See Werner Klän, "Von der Reichsgründung 1871 bis zu den Reformationsjubiläen 1883," in *Nation im Widerspruch. Aspekte und Perspektiven aus lutherischer Sicht heute*, ed. Helmut Edelmann and Niels Hasselmann im Auftrag der VELKD (Gütersloh: Gütersloher Verlagshaus, 1999), 147.
13 Elert, *Lehre des Luthertums*, 136. See Theodosius Harnack, *Luthers Theologie*, 2 vol. (München: C.H.Beck, [1862/1885] 1927). See the very positive appreciation in Werner Elert's Review of *Luthers Theologie (neue Auflage München 1927)*, by Theodosius Harnack, *ThBl* 49 (1928): 330–332.

political fateful enmity, according to Carl Schmitt's logic, was perhaps Elert's most innovative and successful idea. The political concepts of submission and self-assertion, enmity and freedom are projected onto the theological situation of judgement and mercy, guilt and reconciliation, so that a theology of the cross as the core of a world view makes both political and theological enmity reciprocally plausible. As the highest form of obedience, Christ's sacrifice on the cross becomes the principle for surrendering life for a higher cause, specifically the sacrifice of those who died in the war.

2.3 The *Morphologie des Luthertums* (1931/32)

Elert's principle work, the two volumes of the *Morphologie des Luthertums* (*The Structure of Lutheranism*), published in 1931/32, on which he had worked since he was called to the chair for church history and denominational studies in Erlangen in 1923, is "undeniably inventive"[14] and makes extensive 16th and 17th century source material available. By combining criticism of modernity, historical reconstruction and normative claims to validity, Elert drafted a model which surpasses modernity, contrasting on the one hand with liberal academic culture and on the other hand with rival confessional models.[15] Contemporary reviews show how clearly the integration of "völkisch thought" in a Lutheran system of belief was perceived.[16]

---

14 Thomas Kaufmann, "Werner Elert als Kirchenhistoriker," *ZThK* 93 (1996): 193–242, 215.
15 For the mentality-historical background compare Werner Elert, "Christus im Abend Europas," *CuW* 2 (1926): 361–376.
16 By way of example may be mentioned Walter Künneth, "Zur Morphologie des Luthertums," *Zeitwende* 7 (1931): 372–374; Emanuel Hirsch, Review of *Morphologie des Luthertums I*, by Werner Elert, *ZKG* 51 (1932), 343–345 and *Morphologie des Luthertums II*, by Elert, *ZKG* 52 (1933): 434–437. Karl Barth has subjected the morphological method (especially Elert's) to harsh critique in *Kirchliche Dogmatik* vol. I/2 (Zürich: Evangelischer Verlag Zollikon, 1938), 935f.: "Zur Hälfte einfach ästhetisch historisierend, zur anderen, schlimmeren Hälfte aber bestimmten säkularen, insbesondere nationalistischen Stimmungen und Strömungen folgend, lebte man sich hinein in einen Typus von angeblichem ‚Calvinismus' und ‚Luthertum', mit denen man im Stillen längst und dann bald auch ausdrücklich etwas meinte, an das Calvin und Luther und die alten Calvinisten und Lutheraner mit ihnen bestimmt nicht einmal im Traum (oder eben höchstens in gelegentlichen bösen Träumen!) gedacht haben können: nämlich an die in diesen kirchlichen Gestalten ihren Ausdruck gewinnenden ‚Typen' des westeuropäischen und des germanischen Menschen, die Typen je einer besonderen, durch Rasse, Volkstum, Sprache und Geschichte bestimmten Frömmigkeit, des ihr eigenen ethischen Pathos und des mit ihr verbundenen Weltverständnisses. Eben in diesen Typen meinte man jetzt, nachdem man den Ernst des einstigen Fragens nach der Schriftwahrheit verlernt hatte, mit scheinbar um so größerem Ernst das Prinzip

Elert sees the nucleus of Lutheran *Weltanschauung* in Luther's fundamental experience (*Urerlebnis*), which he does not so much extract from Luther himself as he constructs it from an expressionistically strengthened traumatisation of the war generation.[17] In a second step, this experience is proved to be surpassingly modern.

a) Against Ernst Troeltsch,[18] Elert characterises modern times as a depravation of the Lutheran *Urerlebnis*. Lutheran thought anticipated Kant's antinomy of causality and freedom in the antithesis of law and gospel, making true secularism possible. Kant's idea of ethical autonomy is seen as an attempt to flee from the *deus absconditus* "which dictates expectations to mankind, making him responsible, but at the same time so determined that he is fatefully prevented from fulfilling expectations."[19] Genuine secularity arises from *true* religious freedom which bows to God's will. Lutheran ethos recognizes the fateful connection of nation, race and leadership as God's will and attempts to realize its normative content.[20] In this way Luther's brotherly love of the neighbor becomes a *völkisch* communal ethos of reciprocal obligation.

---

der konfessionellen Trennung zu erblicken." Barth saw in the "nicht genug zu verdammenden *Morphologie*," "romantischen und letztlich tief heidnischen Ahnenkult."

17 Elert describes the *Urerlebnis* as "Grauen, das einer empfindet, wenn ihn in der Nacht plötzlich zwei dämonische Augen anstarren, die ihn zur Unbeweglichkeit lähmen und mit der Gewißheit erfüllen: es sind die Augen dessen, der dich in dieser Stunde töten wird." (Elert, *Morphologie vol. 1*, 18.) The motif was common not in Luther but in contemporary expressionistic art and literature. See Christian Neddens, *Politische Theologie und Theologie des Kreuzes: Werner Elert und Hans Joachim Iwand* (Göttingen: Vandenhoeck & Rupprecht 2010), 274–303. For Elert's Luther reception compare Friedrich Duensing, *Gesetz als Gericht: Eine lutherische Kategorie in der Theologie Werner Elerts und Friedrich Gogartens* (München: Kaiser Verlag, 1970); Notger Slenczka, *Selbstkonstitution und Gotteserfahrung: Werner Elerts Deutung der neuzeitlichen Subjektivität im Kontext der Erlanger Theologie*, Studien zur Erlanger Theologie II (Göttingen: Vandenhoeck & Rupprecht, 1998).

18 About Elert's Troeltsch-reception see Slenczka, *Selbstkonstitution*, 141–146; Kaufmann, *Elert als* Kirchenhistoriker, 214–217.

19 Elert, *Morphologie I*, 358 f. For Elert's comparison of Luther and Kant see Slenczka, *Selbstkonstitution*, 219–244.

20 The term *Schöpfungsordnung* is Elert's guiding principle, which suggests a self-evident, immediate harmony of the factual (*Schöpfung*) and the normative (*Ordnung*). Compare Hans Joachim Iwand, *Von Ordnung und Revolution, Nachgelassene Werke vol. 2: Vorträge und Aufsätze*, ed. Dieter Schellong and Karl Gerhard Steck (Gütersloh: Gütersloher Verlagshaus, 2000²), 153–192, 192: "In den Bekenntnisschriften der lutherischen Kirche ist die Theologie der Ordnungen noch nicht der weltanschauliche Rahmen, innerhalb dessen die Verkündigung des Evangeliums ergeht. Die philosophische Ausweitung der Anerkennung natürlicher Lebensordnungen, wie wir sie in den Bekenntnisschriften vertreten finden, bildet sich erst, als die Vertreter des

b) This overlapping of Lutheran doctrine and a postwar psychogram of society was characteristic for Elert's thinking and transformed all theological *loci*, for example the doctrine of God. In Elert's description of the *Urerlebnis* God rears his ugly head of radical malice, which never fades, not even in view of Christ's revelation. Luther was haunted by "the terrible notion of demonic possession by a God, who forces his creation into guilt by the power of his superior ability, from which he derives the right to torment them mercilessly."[21] In his Christology we see the same phenomenon: obedience in fateful ties becomes a characteristic of Christ's work. Not only political obedience in times of war, but also the risk that God may decree failure, is thereby ensured Christologically.[22]

2.4 "Genuine Lutheranism" as Alternative to Hirsch and as Antithesis to Barth

Elert positioned his anti-modernistic innovation as genuine Lutheranism in opposition to the Holl school (above all against Hirsch) and as an antithesis to Barth, thereby defining his position for the coming conflicts.[23]

a) In many ways Elert's interpretation of Luther was close to that of the Holl school.[24] Like Holl and Hirsch, he reconstructed justification as an underivable experience of religious conscience.[25] Like Holl, the believer is justified by the

---

Christentums sich genötigt sehen, der Revolution und der Aufklärung eine christliche Weltanschauung entgegenzusetzen."

21 Elert, *Morphologie I*, 116.
22 See Heinrich Assel, "Politische Theologie im Protestantismus 1914–1945," in *Politische Theologie. Formen und Funktionen im 20. Jahrhundert*, ed. Jürgen Fohrmann & Jürgen Borkhoff (Paderborn: Schöningh, 2003), 79 (here concerning Hirsch): "Diese Überversicherung des politischen Risikos zweier industrieller Massenkriege scheint mir die Pointe politischer Theologie im Protestantismus zwischen 1914 und 1945."
23 Compare Karlmann Beyschlag about Elert's *Lehre des Luthertums im Abriss* (Werner Elert in memoriam, *Homiletisch-Liturgisches Korrespondenzblatt, Neue Folge* 7 (1991/92): 15: Elert habe "mit diesem 'Abriss' erstmals der Barthschen Wort-Gottes-Diktatur eine lutherische Kontrafaktur [...] entgegenstellen wollen."
24 See Heinrich Assel, "The Luther Renaissance," *Oxford Encyclopedia of Martin Luther*, ed. Paul Hinlicky and Derek Nelson (New York: Oxford University Press, 2017) and Kaufmann, *Elert als Kirchenhistoriker*, 220–222.
25 See Heinrich Assel, *Der andere Aufbruch: Die Lutherrenaissance – Ursprünge, Aporien und Wege: Karl Holl, Emanuel Hirsch, Rudolf Hermann (1910–1935)* (Göttingen: Vandenhoeck & Ruprecht 1994), 469 and 475.

failure of his will and its reconstitution in obedience.[26] Again like Holl, a theory of community formation is decisive, which merged *völkisch*-vitalistic ideas with Christological and pneumatological motifs of *Stellvertretung* and *Geisteinheit*. But unlike Holl, Elert ignored the newly available, quasi 'pre-confessional' young Luther[27] and emphasized – unlike Hirsch – the correlation between Luther and Lutheranism as a coherent doctrinal consistency.[28] Despite their many similarities, Hirsch and Elert were strident rivals. None of his contemporaries saw through Elert's hybrid theology so clearly as did Hirsch, who followed each of Elert's publications closely: "In my opinion Elert allies very modern judgements and sentiments with strictly confessional supra-naturalism of the old school, soured by pietism."[29]

b) In the first years after the First World War, Elert considered himself, despite differences, on a line with Gogarten, Brunner and even Barth against the theology of the Ritschl school. Elert emphasized that God could not be comprehended and writes of the "feeling of transcendency which is alive in us today" as a feeling of something wholly other and "completely inconceivable."[30] After Barth's appointment to the new chair for reformed theology in Göttingen in 1921, followed subsequently by some sharp attacks on Luther's theology,[31] he became Elert's greatest adversary. Elert's enmity with Barth became a structuring principle of his theology from the beginning of the 1920s, culminating in 1934. Ostensibly, the issues of concern were "natural theology" and "law and the gospel", but the dispute about national obligation and political theology was the core of the matter. Elert saw this just as clearly as did Barth. And he accused Barth of engaging in political theology in the name of Christ's sovereign rule ("theocracy").[32]

---

26 See Karl Holl, *Die Rechtfertigungslehre in Luthers Vorlesung über den Römerbrief, Gesammelte Aufsätze zur Kirchengeschichte I* (Tübingen: J.C.B.Mohr 1921¹), 288.
27 See Werner Elert, "Luthergeist und lutherisches Bekenntnis," *Luthertum* 45 (1934): 293–307, 304.
28 See Emanuel Hirsch, Review of *Die Lehre des Luthertums im Abriss*, by Werner Elert, *ThLZ* 49 (1924): 549, and Elert's answer in: *Lehre des Luthertums*, 149–151.
29 Emanuel Hirsch, Review of *Der Kampf um das Christentum Werner*, by Werner Elert, *ThLZ* 47 (1922): 282.
30 Elert, *Transzendenz*, 521, 524, 526.
31 See Gerhard Ebeling, "Über die Reformation hinaus? – Zur Luther-Kritik Karl Barths," in *Luther und Barth*, ed. Joachim Heubach (Erlangen: Martin-Luther-Verlag, 1989), 85–126, 87f.
32 Werner Elert, *Karl Barths Index der verbotenen Bücher* (ThMil 2) (Leipzig: Deichertsche Verlagsbuchhandlung 1935), 6.

2.5 *Völkisch*-Political Theology of the Law and its Christological Core

After the National Socialists came to power, Elert – who was not a member of NSDAP – recommended his association of Lutheranism with nationalism and his political-theological "two-spheres-model" as a probate model for a Lutheran *Reichskirche* in the NS-state. The *"völkisch* revolution" was interpreted as a historical fruit of the Reformation.[33] Governmental autonomy (*Eigengesetzlichkeit*) received an immediate theological foundation as an order of creation (*Schöpfungsordnung*), thereby suspending not only Gods commandment but also conscience.[34] The church should now comply with their commitment to nation and race in their proclamation. What this meant is explained in the *Theologisches Gutachten* of 25 September 1933 written by Elert and Althaus "concerning the accreditation of Christians of Jewish origin for holding office within the German Protestant Church".[35] In February 1934 Elert demanded an oath of loyalty to the National Socialist *Führer* state and disciplinary measures for ministers who engaged in political opposition.[36]

Elert's political theological programme manifested itself in a series of publications. As a first class partner for the totalitarian state, he positioned his "genuine" German Lutheranism as an alternative to the "theocratic" ambitions of the Confessing Church and the heresy of the *Deutsche Christen*. Since the God given "orders," including those from the state, are designed "to regulate our whole natural existence unconditionally and without any provisional clauses"[37] (an allusion to the *clausula Petri*, Acts 5:29), preaching on the law cannot fall afoul of the *völkisch* state. The *Ansbach Ratschlag*, a confession drafted by

---

[33] See Werner Elert, "Luther und der revolutionäre Gedanke," *Der Reichsbote* 61 (1933), No. 267 (19/11/1933).
[34] Werner Elert, "Politische Aufgaben und Schranken des Pfarrers," *Korrespondenzblatt für die ev.-luth. Geistli-chen in Bayern* 58 (1933): 59–63.77–79, 60 f.
[35] Elert and Althaus, "Gutachten der Erlanger Theologischen Fakultät über die Zulassung der Christen jüdischer Herkunft zu den Ämtern der Deutschen Evangelischen Kirche (25/9/1933)," *JK* 1 (1933), 271–274 / *ChW* 47 (1933), 947–949 / *ThBl* 12 (1933), 321–323. See also Werner Elert, *Stand und Stände nach lutherischer Auffassung* (Berlin: Verlag des Evangelischen Bundes, 1940), 10 f.
[36] See Werner Elert, "Zur Frage eines neuen Bekenntnisses," *Luthertum* 45 (1934), 31–50.
[37] Werner Elert, *Bekenntnis, Blut und Boden: Drei theologische Vorträge* (Leipzig: Dörffling & Franke, 1934), 34 and 39.

Elert and Paul Althaus to oppose the Barmen *Theological Declaration*,[38] appeared on 11th June 1934. Elert implemented his long – pursued plan to elaborate the Lutheran confession by clarifying the term "law," thereby eliminating the gospel's claim to legitimacy in the political sphere. The *Führer* and the NS state are declared to be "pious and faithful magistrates," a "good government" "with discipline and honour" in the diction of the Small Catechism. Now "law and the gospel" became the watchword for Elert's political theological model.

2.6 The Transforming Power of Political Theology and the Unvarying Question of the Relation Between Christology and Political Theory

What made Elert's theology so plausible and amenable to his contemporaries was the mixture with modern *völkisch* political aspects. Its confessional form allowed it to be accepted after 1945 – cutting out its political aspects.[39]

Elert's confessional studies are erudite. His dogmatic position is incisive in its contrast to liberal theology and also to Barth. For this reason several attempts have been made in the last decades to cleanse his *Realdialektik* on law and gospel of its political implications so as to utilize it again. But Elert's theology is contextual and cannot be divorced from this. Notwithstanding his knowledgeable historical analyses and his dogmatic discernment, Elert's theology remains a concise paradigm of a Lutheran confessional type of political theology and its attendant problems.

It is this characteristic of his theology which causes us to ask how the connections between Christology and political theory which do indeed exist in Luther can be demonstrated more suitably: how could they become more fruitful for questions of political theory and ethics, without short-circuiting the relationship of God and man with political obedience?

---

38 In *Die Bekenntnisse und grundsätzlichen Äußerungen zur Kirchenfrage, vol. 2: Das Jahr 1934*, ed. Kurt Dietrich Schmidt (Göttingen: Vandenhoeck & Ruprecht, 1935), 102–104 (= *AELKZ* 67 (1934): 584–586).
39 See Assel, *Aporien*, 51: This ambiguity made "Elerts explizit politische Theologie des Gesetzes kompromisshaft und gerade darin repräsentativer als Hirschs antietatistische und antisemitische, radikal völkisch-politische Theologie."

3 Hans Joachim Iwand: Revisions of Lutheran Theology

While Elert represents the confessional political branch of the Luther Renaissance, Iwand, born 1899 in Silesia, stands for a second branch which was influenced by Rudolf Hermann's (1887–1962) research on Luther and his reception of Kant, but also by Martin Kähler's (1835–1912) biblical-eschatological theology.[40] Moreover Iwand belonged to a generation of young theologians such as Dietrich Bonhoeffer (1906–1945) and Ernst Wolf (1902–1971) who sought their position in a productive dispute with Karl Barth.

In 1923, Iwand became the 'inspector' of the Theological College (*Lutherheim*) in Königsberg. He was dismissed in 1934 and after two semesters in the Herder Institute in Riga he became the director of the Pastoral Seminary of the East Prussian Confessing Church in 1935. On 24 May 1937, a speech ban was imposed on him. He was arrested for the first time on 18 December 1937, and again at the end of November 1938. On the 4 March 1939 he was released after the St. Marien congregation, for whom he worked as a pastor in Dortmund, agreed to guarantee that the speech ban was respected.

3.1 Iwand's Studies on the Young Luther's (1920–24) Theology of the Cross

Iwand names his early source of inspiration precisely in a quotation from the 1930s: "We were gifted with a new start in the post-war years as we discovered Luther and the bible, as we succeeded in breaking out of liberalism and rediscovering the theology of the cross for which our fathers had suffered and fought."[41] The newly discovered *young Luther* is meant here – particularly his early disputations – but also the Christo-centric biblical theology of Martin Kähler. In Kähler Iwand found an approach near to Luther's theology of the cross

---

40 Iwand wrote in a letter to Rudolf Hermann (29/12/1920) in *Nachgelassene Werke vol. 6: Briefe am Rudolf Hermann*, ed. Helmut Gollwitzer, Walter Kreck, Karl Gerhard Steck, Ernst Wolf (Gütersloh: Chr. Kaiser, 2000²), 38: "Stange und Kähler, die ich noch immer eifrig lese, sind mir nun eigentlich diejenigen geworden, von denen ich lerne." While the influence of Carl Stange on Iwand soon decreased, the one of Martin Kähler remained unbroken.
41 Hans Joachim Iwand, *Nachgelassene Werke Neue Folge vol. 5: Predigten und Predigtlehre*, ed. Albrecht Grötzinger, Bertold Klappert, Rudolf Landau, and Jürgen Seim (Gütersloh: Chr. Kaiser/Gütersloher Verlagshaus, 2004), 439.

with emphasis on "the exclusivity of the knowledge of God transmitted by the cross, personal certainty of salvation and a *praxis pietatis* which formed and guided life,"[42] that was so characteristic for Iwand's own theological beginnings. His intensive examination of Luther's *theologia crucis*, in particular the *Heidelberg Disputation* (1518), informs his theological perception.

A comparison with Elert highlights the character of Iwand's beginnings. The war was a formative watershed for both of them, both belonged to a national-conservative milieu, both turned against historicism and liberalism, and found in Luther's texts a source of theological innovation. Iwand, too, read thinkers such as Oswald Spengler and Ernst Jünger and even took part in the reactionary *Kapp putsch* of 13 March 1920. But their theological development followed very different paths.

The young Luther's theology of the cross and Kähler's Christo-centrism led Iwand to a different track. It was above all the motif of hiddenness in the cross which led to a different understanding of dialectics, implying a different correlation of law and gospel, a different anthropology and ethics. Iwand sought the *hidden life in Christ* and not an experience of being under the law.[43] Based on the distinction between *theologia crucis* and *theologia gloriae* he asked critical questions about a false utilisation of the cross and the *Verweltanschaulichung* of theology.

3.2 Studies on Luther: Faith in Christ and the Doctrine of Justification (1924–33)

As early as 1921 Iwand expressed his intention to illuminate "the Christological foundation of justification"[44] – against Holl's justification theology of the religious conscience. To this end he studied Luther's Lectures on Romans very intensely. His habilitation thesis 1927 examined in what way *fides Jesu Christi* and *sola fide* belong together. The justifying belief in Christ is alone God's work in mankind, implying a critical anthropology which is summed up in the doctrine of the bondage of the will. But how does God's work come about? Around 1925 Iwand identified the promise (*promissio*), the linguistic form of announcement, as the place where the act of justification took place. It is open to dispute whether Barth was involved in this discovery – he held a lecture in Kö-

---

[42] Michael Korthaus, *Kreuzestheologie: Geschichte und Gehalt eines Programmbegriffs in der evangelischen Theologie* (Tübingen: Mohr Siebeck, 2007), 26–59, 33.
[43] See Iwand, *Nachgelassene Werke* vol. 6, 129 and 160.
[44] Iwand, *Nachgelassene Werke* vol. 6, 47.

nigsberg on 25 November 1924 about "the word of man and the word of God in the Christian sermon"[45] – or whether Martin Kähler along with Rudolf Hermann, Iwand's teacher and correspondent who discovered Richard Hönigswald's[46] philosophy of language in the same winter, had the greater influence. At any rate, theological doctrine was concentrated from then on constitutively on the sermon as situational religious speaking. A growing proximity to Barth was the result.[47]

3.3 Revisions of Lutheran Theology and Critical Debate with Barth (1933–45)

The events of the year 1933 exposed the long-existing faultlines within the theological renewal movements of the 1920s. For Iwand it marked the conclusion of an inner and an outer clarification process. The position he took in his last (!) letter to Erich Seeberg in 1935 is significant:

> In view of the general situation of theology I cannot close my eyes, all the less the longer I look, to the impression of what Barth and his reformed theology signify. Not as if I was a Barthian, my approach is quite different from his, but he is one of the few who are really theologians, and Lutherans have little to offer in reply. The fact that so many Lutherans went to the D[eutsche] C[hristen] was a last attempt to escape Barth. For exactly this reason he dominated the church as such more than ever.[48]

Iwand saw himself as a disciple of Luther. He now realized that little agreement existed within the Luther Renaissance with the path taken by the Confessing Church. Even before 1933, Iwand had not expected much from Hirsch and the Holl school, an understanding with Erlangen was a lost cause, at the very latest after the *Ansbach Ratschlag*.[49] Gogarten and Seeberg disappointed him deeply

---

45 Karl Barth, *Vorträge und kleinere Arbeiten 1922–1925*, Gesamtausgabe vol. 19, ed. Holger Finze (Zürich: Theologischer Verlag, 1990), 426–457.
46 See Assel, *Aufbruch*, 308. For Hermann's reception of Kähler see also 316 and 489.
47 See Hans-Joachim Kraus, "Martin Kähler," *TRE* 17 (1988), 514: "Es wird festzuhalten sein, daß die großen Themen, die in der Theologie Karl Barths hervortreten, bei Martin Kähler nicht nur anklangen, sondern in erstaunlich klarer Weise ausgeführt worden waren. Als um so bedauerlicher erscheint es, daß Barth sich nur selten und peripher auf Kähler bezogen und seine Versöhnungslehre überhaupt ignoriert hat."
48 Hans Joachim Iwand, letter to Erich Seeberg, 2/2/1935, Bundesarchiv Koblenz N 1248 E. Seeberg/14,68b.
49 See his letter to Rudolf Hermann, 20/9/1935, *Nachgelassene Werke* vol. 6, 282: "Ich werde auch allmählich dem Konfessionalismus gram, denn er ist wirklich weithin mit schuld an die-

and even with Hermann it was difficult to reach an understanding.⁵⁰ This did not mean that he came into line with Barth, on the contrary it meant that he had to revise what he had learnt from Luther, in contemporaneity to Barth. "It was not foremost Barth's theology, but rather his attitude, his theological existence in *Kirchenkampf*, which attracted Iwand."⁵¹ It is striking how emphatically Iwand referred to Luther's theology of the cross in his measures to unmask the nationalist theological heresy. He understood the *Barmen Declaration* as an updating of Luther's *Heidelberg Disputation* – and therefore he could affirm it unconditionally.⁵²

I shall divide the theological innovations which Iwand garnered from Luther through critical dispute with Barth into four aspects.

3.3.1 An independent Theology of the Word of God

God's creative word now became the focus of Iwand's theology.⁵³ The character of his theology of God's word differed significantly from Barth's. In his meticulous discussion of *Kirchliche Dogmatik I/1* Iwand payed tribute to Barth's theology and said that it proved to be "a mighty fortress… to which the church

---

sem Vorbeigehen an den uns heute aufgenötigten Entscheidungen. [...] Elerts Aufsatz über die Zukunft der Theologischen Fakultäten ist genau so gehalten. Das sind Grabgesänge."
50 On the other side, in the *Essen dialogues 1–3*, Iwand is 1936 still pleasant to arrange an understanding between the *Confessing Church* and the so called *Intakte lutherische Kirchen*. See Jürgen Seim, *Hans Joachim Iwand: Eine Biografie* (Gütersloh: Chr. Kaiser/Gütersloher Verlagshaus, 1999), 222–225.
51 Gerard den Hertog, "Annäherung und Entfremdung in der geteilten 'theologischen Existenz heute'. Das Verhältnis zwischen Hans Joachim Iwand und Karl Barth in der Zeit des Kirchenkampfes," in *Karl Barth im europäischen Zeitgeschehen (1935–1950) – Widerstand, Bewährung, Orientierung*, ed. Michael Beintker, Christian Link, and Michael Trowitzsch (Zürich: Theologischer Verlag, 2010), 333–354, 344.
52 See Hans Joachim Iwand, "Die 1. Barmer These und die Theologie Martin Luthers [1936]," *EvTh* 46 (1986): 222.
53 See Gerard den Hertog, *Befreiende Erkenntnis: Die Lehre vom unfreien Willen in der Theologie Hans Joachim Iwands* (Neukirchen-Vluyn: Neukirchener Verlag, 1994), 212: "Lange Zeit war es in der Theologie – sowohl in der Orthodoxie wie in der neuprotestantischen und konservativ-lutherischen Theologie – üblich, zunächst eine Anthropologie zu entwerfen, dann darzulegen, wie das Wort zum Menschen kommt und schließlich, wie der Mensch dieses Wort wiederum in die Tat umsetzt. Der Mensch ist dann der Angelpunkt, um den sich alles dreht. Dadurch fallen Theorie und Praxis, Dogmatik auf der einen Seite und praktische Theologie auf der anderen Seite auseinander. Bei Iwand hingegen ist das Wort der archimedische Punkt. Dieses Wort erschafft seine eigene Wirklichkeit."

can flee for salvation".⁵⁴ In the same breath he named three far reaching discrepancies in comparison with Barth:

- Iwand rejected Barth's teaching of the *one* word of God "beyond the law and the gospel." He feared that this teaching might distort the gospel into legalism and eliminate freedom. Iwand did not, on the other hand, intend to separate law and gospel as Elert did. Instead, in accordance with Chalcedonian dialectic, he intended to *differentiate* them in their unity and discrepancy.
- Iwand also intended a dialectic differentiation between God's word and man's word. He diagnosed a tendency towards separation in Barth. The *Kirchliche Dogmatik* should therefore be revised according to the logic of *communicatio idiomatum*, the participation of one in the other. "Where God talks to us *humanly*, he speaks to us as our God, otherwise we cannot endure him."⁵⁵ Beyond its actual proclamation, no word of God for mankind exists.⁵⁶
- The central point of Iwand's word-of-God-theology in the wake of his theology of the cross is this: God's word is "at the mercy of man;" man, however, is "at the mercy of his judgement. Both are God's doing."⁵⁷ The sovereignty of God's word is upheld not in a final hiddenness, but by being at the mercy of the word.

3.3.2 Preaching the Law – the New Approach in Ethics

Starting with the theology of the cross, Iwand began to revise the political ethics of Lutheranism. The readjustment in 1934 of the term *law* versus the doctrine of the people's *nomos* (*Volksnomoslehre*) was the first important step.

The law, according to Iwand in his significant paper *Preaching the Law*,⁵⁸ belongs to the sermon as God's public word which refers to both realms. It is wholesome and good because it points to Christ in whom the law is fulfilled.

---

54 Hans Joachim Iwand, "Jenseits von Gesetz und Evangelium? Eine kritische Besprechung der Lehre vom Wort Gottes in Karl Barths 'Prolegomena zur Kirchlichen Dogmatik' I/1," in *Um den rechten Glauben. Gesammelte Aufsätze*, ed. Karl Gerhard Steck (München: Chr. Kaiser, 1959): 87–109, 97.
55 Iwand, *Jenseits von Gesetz und Evangelium?*, 105.
56 See Edgar Thaidigsmann, "Der wirkliche Gott und der wirkliche Mensch. Iwands Verständnis der Theologie Luthers im Kontext der Lutherforschung," in *Die Provokation des Kreuzes. Entdeckungen in der Theologie Hans Joachim Iwands*, ed. Martin Hoffmann (Waltrop: Spenner, 1999): 81–101, 100 f.
57 Iwand, *Jenseits von Gesetz und Evangelium?*, 106.
58 Hans Joachim Iwand, "Die Predigt des Gesetzes," *EvTh* 1 (1934), 55–78.

Therefore, the law directs us to penance and not to ethics. A foundation for ethics is not possible from the law but only from the revelation of God's righteousness. It is, therefore, taken from the gospel in the sense of living in God's works: "God's righteousness signifies the *Lebensraum* which God's spirit wrested and reclaimed from the world, like dry land from water, so that mankind can live in it."[59]

That is, the starting point of ethics – and therefore also political ethics – is not obedience under the law, but God's creative righteousness.[60] Iwand criticized an understanding of the law which explained that mankind will be enabled to fulfil the law through mercy.[61] Theological ethics must instead begin with the *bondage of will*, the *resurrection of Jesus Christ* and the new "hidden life with Christ in God."[62]

Iwand attempted to walk the narrow path of protestant ethics between two alternatives which were ultimately nomological, a protestant legalism on the one hand and, on the other hand, a law which becomes independent from proclamation.[63]

3.4 *Simul* – Iwand's Chalcedonian Dialectic

Iwand's unique understanding of dialectics, which he gained from a Lutheran interpretation of the Chalcedonian Creed, the *communicatio idiomatum*, is of im-

---

[59] Hans Joachim Iwand, *Nachgelassene Werke vol. 4: Gesetz und Evangelium*, ed. Walter Kreck (Gütersloh: Chr. Kaiser/Gütersloher Verlagshaus, 2000²), 118.
[60] See Hans Joachim Iwand, *Predigtmeditationen [vol. 2]* (Neukirchen-Vluyn: Neukirchener Verlag, 1977), 16.
[61] See Bertold Klappert, "Die *Thora* ist in sich *immer geistlich*. Der Weg H. J. Iwands mit dem Thema 'Gesetz und Evangelium'," in *Aus der Umkehr leben. Hans Joachim Iwand 1899–1999*, ed. Bertold Klappert and Wolfgang Schulze (Neukirchen-Vluyn: Neukirchener Verlag, 2001), 129: "Was für Calvin ganz entscheidend war, daß von Golgatha die Linie zurück zum Sinaibund und Sinaigebot läuft, und was für Barth in seinem Kopenhagener Vortrag von 1933 ,Das erste Gebot als theologisches Axiom' essentiell ist, daß es eine gesamtbiblische Linie vom Sinai nach Golgatha gibt *und wieder zurück*, das wird hier von Iwand bestritten."
[62] Hans Joachim Iwand, *Ethik-Vorlesung* (1952), Kap 1, Die Aufgabe 8 (Bundesarchiv Koblenz, Iwand-Nachlass).
[63] See Hans Joachim Iwand, *Nachgelassene Werke vol. 2: Vorträge und Aufsätze*, ed. Dieter Schellong and Karl Gerhard Steck (Gütersloh: Chr. Kaiser/Gütersloher Verlagshaus, 2000²), 402f: "So wie Luther,Gesetz und Evangelium'sagte gegen eine spezifische Häresie, die aus der Umkehrung beider folgte [*theologia gloriae*], so sagt Barth: 'Evangelium und Gesetz' gegen eine ebenso handgreifliche Häresie, die aus der Ordnung 'Gesetz und Evangelium' hervorgegangen ist [*natürliche Theologie*]. "

mense significance. His whole thinking is orientated according to the *simul* of the theology of justification and of Christology. In this point Iwand's theology differs essentially from Werner Elert's *Realdialektik*, which tends towards a separation of law and the gospel and therefore of *peccator* and *iustus*. In my opinion it also differs from what Bruce McCormack called Barth's "real dialectic of veiling and unveiling"[64] which I would describe as God's abiding hiddenness, even in his revelation.

3.4.1 *Simul* of Revelation and Hiddenness: God's Hiddenness in the Cross

The character of Iwand's dialectic is seen in his dealing with the motif of hiddenness, in his differentiation between *God's* hiddenness *in maiestate* and his hiddenness *sub contrario* in the cross. The hidden God – beyond his word – is none of our business and above all cannot be associated with the law. "*Quae supra nos, nihil ad nos*"[65] applies here. God is present in all things, but we do not understand his presence. God's hiddenness in the cross is different: God wanted to be *recognized* here in faith, hidden in the juxtaposition of Jesus Christ's suffering and death, as one who loves and creates life. Therefore, God surrenders himself unconditionally to the grasp of man, becomes weak and vulnerable. Humans can only find themselves through understanding their role in these events, by seeing God's judgement upon them (*peccator*) and, in acknowledging this judgement, accepting for themselves God's hidden intent to save. Therefore "simultaneity [...] is the decisive category for the certainty of salvation."[66]

3.4.2 *Simul* of Righteous and Sinner

Hence, the *simul* of righteous and sinner is topical in God's judgement. This is the core of Iwand's anthropology. This "simultaneity" is not an expression of self-reflection in conscience, but the theological description of the person of a

---

[64] Bruce McCormack, *Theologische Dialektik und kritischer Realismus. Entstehung und Entwicklung von Karl Barths Theologie 1909–1936* (Zürich: Theologischer Verlag, 2006), 34 f. and 37–41.
[65] Hans Joachim Iwand, "Erläuterungen zu: Martin Luther, Vom unfreien Willen," in *Martin Luther, Ausgewählte Werke*, ed. Hans Heinrich Borcherdt and Georg Merz (München: Chr. Kaiser, 1939), 287–371, 346.
[66] Hans Joachim Iwand, *Rechtfertigungslehre und Christusglaube. Eine Untersuchung zur Systematik der Recht-fertigungslehre Luthers in ihren Anfängen* (Leipzig: C. Hinrichs, 1930), 100–111.

Christian as a new reality created by Jesus Christ on the cross. The events on the cross show that "Jesus Christ does not live *his*, but *my* godforsaken and cursed story, and that my story which is hidden in me is exposed in him, while I conversely am clothed in his righteousness and his life is the salvation which I was promised."[67] Unveiling and veiling are correlative occurrences which are not performed in the event of the cross but through its relevance for me. Iwand's anthropology, therefore, is rooted in a dialectic ontology of the sinner in his relation to Christ.[68]

3.4.3 Christ My Righteousness – and the Bondage of Will

Faith did not mean for Iwand – as it did for Elert – the reconstitution of a now truly free "I". On the contrary, the unfree will is an enduring sign of human creatureliness: "through that which we desire, the kingdom acquires the stature of the one to whom we belong, the kingdom of God in believers, the kingdom of Satan in the lost. [...] For in our volition we are people in the process of becoming – and in our becoming we are God's creature."[69] Therefore the doctrine of the bondage of will becomes the *shibboleth* of faith for Iwand. Christ is my righteousness enduringly *extra me* and *pro me*. In contrast to the old Adam and his will, he is a new man – with me *quasi una persona:* "It is no longer I who live, but Christ who lives in me" (Gal 2:20a).[70]

In my opinion this understanding of the person of Christ and of Christians, which relies specifically on the theology of justification, is Iwand's alternative model to the political Christology which we find in Elert. Christ is no longer the ideal of vicarious fulfilment of the law, whose dedication (on the cross) or whose rule (the one on high) is imitated or represented. Instead we should now ask how our new perception of human guilt, mediated by the cross, and of new life in God's righteousness lends human conduct a new direction. Iwand attempted to answer this question after 1945, by focussing on the political

---

67 Iwand, *Ethik* (1952), Kap 1, Die Aufgabe 9 (Bundesarchiv Koblenz, Iwand-Nachlass).
68 Because the old man has to die in his *concupiscentia spiritualis*, with which he also abuses the *faith* for himself, for Iwand the order *'law and gospel'* remains important despite Barth's critique.
69 Iwand, *Erläuterungen*, 301.
70 See Heinrich Assel, "'Nun lebt nicht mehr Ich ...' (Gal 2,20). Christomorphes Selbstbild und evangelisches Personverständnis," in *Beim Wort nehmen – Die Schrift als Zentrum kirchlichen Redens und Gestaltens, Festschrift für Friedrich Mildenberger zum 75 Geburtstag*, ed. Michael Krug, Ruth Lödel, and Johannes Rehm (Stuttgart: Kohlhammer, 2004), 13–23.

culpability which no-one desires to accept, and in a new explanation of theological ethics in God's creative righteousness, as outlined above.

3.5 The Eschatological Revelation of the Kingdom of God

In 1936, an estrangement between Iwand and Barth took place after Barth, in his doctrine of the power of the angels, based his fundamental principles for the state on reconciliation and not on creation. Iwand feared that a new form of political theology was being developed here, *alongside* a nationalist-*völkisch* one, in that it is now the *church* which lays down the law as an open demand – the theocratic "dream of every priest."[71]

As a counterpart, Iwand developed an eschatological interim concept of the state which confined politics to the area of rational human world-shaping, while at the same time remaining open, eschatologically, for the coming of God's kingdom. The eschatological revelation of God's kingdom in the events of Golgotha "outside the city gate" lies *beyond* the church and the state. But church and state are based on these events in a hidden manner, proclaimed by God's word.[72]

Iwand wrote to Julius Schniewind on 8 May 1939: "we must occupy the middle ground and should never forget that Christ's rule on earth remains under the cross until the end of time. Karl Barth always understood the doctrine of the two realms dualistically, but it is in fact meant as an interim. The regulations of the world 'still' pertain, but the forces of the future eon are already at work."[73]

---

[71] See Iwand, *Predigt des Gesetzes*, 57.
[72] See Iwand, *Nachgelassene Werke Neue Folge 5: Predigten und Predigtlehre*, 452 and Iwand, "Predigt [Hebr 13,12–14]. Ein Gruß an die Brüder und Gemeinden der Bekennenden Kirche in Ostpreußen," in *Das Wort sie sollen lassen stahn* (Eine Reihe von Einzelpredigten), gedruckt i. A. des Presbyteriums der evang.-reform. Gemeinde Barmen-Gemarke (Wuppertal-Elberfeld [1937]), 3 f.
[73] Quotes after Gerard den Hertog, "Stationen auf dem Weg des 'Denkens aus der Umkehr heraus.' Hans Joachim Iwands theologisches und politisches Umdenken in der Zeit des Dritten Reiches," in *Die Gemeinde als Ort von Theologie. Festschrift für Jürgen Seim zum 70. Geburtstag*, ed. Katja Kriener, Johann Schmidt, and Marion Obitz (Bonn: R. Habelt, 2002), 211–224, 220. After the war Iwand read Barth's writings on 'political worship' once again and much more positive. See his Barth-chapter in *Nachgelassene Werke Neue Folge 1: Kirche und Gesellschaft*, ed. Ekkehard Börsch (Gütersloh: Chr. Kaiser/Gütersloher Verlagshaus, 1998), 108–126.

3.6 After 1945

Another creative period began for Iwand after 1945. He strove to deepen his theological revision and to develop his thought further. Three themes were of particular concern:
- The renewal of the public political practice of preaching the law, to which ethical participation in the tasks of society also belonged. We should name the *Darmstädter Wort* in this context, Iwand's initiative for the *Göttinger Predigtmeditationen*, which had a sustaining impact on the practice of preaching in the *Federal Republic of Germany* and in the *German Democratic Republic*, and his commitment to reconciliation with the peoples of the East.
- The consequent renewal of political ethics along eschatological lines. In his lecture *Kirche und Gesellschaft* he amended the traditional doctrine of the two kingdoms by interpreting the church and society from the publicness of God's kingdom.
- His third theme was the renewal of dogmatic Christology which he now attempted to develop consequently according to the theology of justification, that is by defining the relation between Christ and sinners. "As the Son of God becomes man, he becomes a sinner and a righteous one at the same time."[74]. The core of his Christology is the exegesis of 2Cor 5:21: "God made him who knew no sin to be sin for us, so that in him we might become the righteousness of God."

Iwand had not produced any greater publications since 1930 (with the exception of *The righteousness of faith according to Luther* 1941). Therefore, his influence remained limited in Germany. But the posthumous publications and the second edition issued after 1999, offer plenty of material for future productive Iwand studies.

---

[74] Hans Joachim Iwand, *Nachgelassene Werke Neue Folge vol. 2: Christologie*, ed. Eberhard Lempp and Edgar Thaidigsmann (Gütersloh: Chr. Kaiser/Gütersloher Verlagshaus, 1999), 261.

Appendix

Rudolf Bultmanns unpublizierter Kommentar (1928) zu Friedrich Gogartens „*Ich glaube an den dreieinigen Gott*" (1926)

Ediert von Heinrich Assel

Editorische Einführung

Das insgesamt 27-seitige Typoskript der Rezension Rudolf Bultmanns entstammt der Nachlass-Bibliothek von Ernst Fuchs und befand sich in Ernst Fuchs' Privat-Exemplar von: Friedrich Gogarten, Ich glaube an den dreieinigen Gott. Eine Untersuchung über Glauben und Geschichte, Jena 1926. Dieses Buch wie das beiliegende Typoskript befinden sich im Privatbesitz des Editors. Das 27-seitige Typoskript der Rezension ist momentan das einzige vollständig erhaltene Exemplar dieses Textes von Rudolf Bultmann.[1]

Im Gogarten-Nachlass der Niedersächsischen Staats- und Universitätsbibliothek Göttingen befindet sich eine unvollständige 24-seitige Kopie des Typoskripts unter dem Archivstandort: COD.Ms.F.Gogarten 120: Beil.: Fr[iedrich] Gogarten: Ich glaube an den dreieinigen Gott ; [ausführliche Anmerkungen zur Buchveröffentlichung]/ Gerhard Krüger. – o.O., o.J. – Fragm.; Durchschl.: S. 1–6, 6b, 7–26 [Schluß fehlt] + 1 Bl. Erläuterungen zur Verfasserschaft von H.G. Göckeritz (1994) (Ts.: 1 S.).

Die mutmaßliche Zuweisung an *Gerhard Krüger* als Verfasser durch Hermann Götz Göckeritz, einem der besten Kenner des Nachlasses von Friedrich Gogarten, aus dem Jahr 1994 ist in diesem Fall unwahrscheinlich und zu korrigieren.[2] Der Autor ist *Rudolf Bultmann* selbst.

---

[1] Das Original-Manuskript und das Typoskript der Rezension zu F. Gogarten, Ich glaube an den dreieinigen Gott, befindet sich nicht im Nachlass Bultmann der Universitäts-Bibliothek Tübingen/ Abt. Handschriften/Alte Drucke (Briefliche Mitteilung Konrad Hammann, Münster an den Autor, 4. Mai 2018, bestätigt Universitäts-Bibliothek Tübingen am 8. Juni 2018). Es befindet sich auch nicht im Nachlass von Gerhard Krüger der Universitätsbibliothek Tübingen.

[2] So auch die Einschätzung von Konrad Hammann/Münster: „Die Vermutung einer Autorschaft Krügers wird durch den Bultmann-Krüger-Briefwechsel, den ich eigens für den Beitrag noch

Dies belegt schon das Exemplar aus dem Fuchs-Nachlass, das als Autor *Rudolf Bultmann* nennt: Über dem Namen „Fr. Gogarten" ist handschriftlich mit Bleistift notiert (sehr wahrscheinlich in der Handschrift Ernst Fuchs') „Bultmann" (n mit Geminationsstrich).³

Auch H.G. Göckeritz erwägt 1994 inhaltliche Gründe für eine Zuweisung des Typoskripts an Rudolf Bultmann. In seiner Erläuterung „Zu einem Typoskript über F. Gogarten ‚Ich glaube an den dreieinigen Gott', 24 Seiten auf Durchschlagpapier, ohne Verfasser" notiert er:

„Der Verfasser dieses Typoskriptes steht nach Begrifflichkeit und Stil seiner Argumentation Heidegger nahe: vgl. z. B. S. 5 unten, 6 oben S. 7 Mitte; S. 8 wird auf Heidegger (mit Angabe von Seitenzahlen, gemeint ist wohl „Sein u. Zeit") verwiesen. Der Vorschlag (S. 8), zwischen ‚Werk' und ‚Tat' zu unterscheiden, ist typisch für Bultmann. Nicht zuletzt das in dieser Kritik ausgeführte Verständnis des AT weist stark auf Bultmann – oder einen seiner Schüler?? – hin. Und vieles andere!

Die Kritik in diesem Text ist von großer Souveränität und begrifflicher Prägnanz, sie weist immer wieder unbeirrt auf Unklarheiten und Widersprüche hin und wird ruhig bestimmt, aber ganz emotionslos vorgetragen. Gleichwohl spricht der Verfasser gelegentlich per ‚ich', doch ohne sich zu erkennen zu geben. Die spärlichen handschriftlichen Korrekturen oder griechischen Wörter könnten vielleicht von Bultmann stammen (vgl. z. B. S. 7). [...] Ich wüßte nicht, wer Gogartens Buch so hätte besprechen können, wie es hier geschieht, wenn nicht Bultmann selbst."

Tatsächlich sprechen (neben den von Göckeritz erwogenen Gründen) folgende Gründe für die Autorschaft von Rudolf Bultmann.

1. Ernst Fuchs weist in seinem Exemplar des Typoskripts den Text Rudolf Bultmann zu.

2. Der Anlass für die Rezension von Gogartens Buch war mutmaßlich die zweite sog. „Arbeitswoche alter Marburger Theologen" vom 22.–24. Oktober 1928 in

---

einmal durchgesehen habe, nicht plausibilisiert." (Briefliche Mitteilung an den Autor, 4. Mai 2018).

3 „Die handschriftliche Notiz stammt m. E. nicht von Bultmann, der seinen Namen nie mit einem Geminationsstrich geschrieben hat" (Briefliche Mitteilung Konrad Hammann/Münster an den Autor, 4. Mai 2018). E. Fuchs verwendet den Geminationsstrich. Der Handschriftenvergleich spricht für Ernst Fuchs, nicht für Gerhard Krüger (Auskunft Ulrike Mehringer, Abteilung Handschriften/Historische Drucke Universitätsbibliothek Tübingen vom 6. Juni 2018).

Marburg, zu der auch F. Gogarten eingeladen war.⁴ Kurzfristig musste Gogarten am 19. Oktober 1928 seine Teilnahme absagen⁵ – zur Enttäuschung Bultmanns, der sicher mit seiner Anwesenheit rechnete: „Es war ein harter Schlag für uns, daß Sie nicht zu unserer Zusammenkunft im Oktober kommen konnten."⁶ Im selben Brief vom 4. November 1928 schreibt R. Bultmann an F. Gogarten weiter:⁷ „Über die Oktober-Zusammenkunft wird Ihnen [sc. Heinrich] Schlier wohl Genaueres berichten. Ich war nicht sehr befriedigt, hörte immerhin zu meiner Beruhigung, daß manche Teilnehmer sich befriedigt äußerten […] Auch Schlier und Frau trugen wenig bei. Am besten beteiligte sich Fuchs. – Ich hätte Ihnen gerne bei dieser Gelegenheit meine ziemlich umfangreichen Bemerkungen zu Ihrem Buch⁸ vorgetragen. Ich muß nun damit warten, bis Sie kommen, oder bis Frau Schlier, die meine Schrift mit den Abkürzungen lesen kann, Zeit findet, mein Manuskript in die Maschine zu tippen (ebenso wie den 2. Teil meiner Anmerkungen zu Barth)."

Die Autorschaft Rudolf Bultmanns und die Herstellung des maschinenschriftlichen Typoskripts sind damit identifiziert.

3. Das für die geplante Aussprache hergestellte, ausführliche Manuskript der Rezension wurde mutmaßlich nicht bei der „Arbeitswoche alter Marburger Theologen" 1928 selbst vorgetragen, aber im nachhinein maschinell verschriftlicht.⁹ Bultmann selbst trug die griechischen Phrasen handschriftlich ein.¹⁰

4. E. Fuchs als Teilnehmer der Arbeitswoche im Oktober 1928 konnte vom Manuskript Bultmanns Kenntnis haben und Empfänger einer Durchschrift des Typoskripts werden, das im Original nach dem Oktober 1928 durch Bultmann an Gogarten gesandt wurde. Dies ist umso wahrscheinlicher, als Fuchs und Bult-

---

4 Brief R. Bultmann an F. Gogarten vom 12. August 1928, in: Rudolf Bultmann und Friedrich Gogarten. Briefwechsel 1921–1967, hg. v. Hermann Götz Göckeritz, Tübingen: Mohr Siebeck, 2002, 137 Anm. 4.
5 Brief F. Gogarten an R. Bultmann, 19. Oktober 1928, a.a.O., 142.
6 Brief R. Bultmann an F. Gogarten, 4. November 1928, a.a.O., 142.
7 Brief R. Bultmann an F. Gogarten, 4. November 1928, a.a.O., 142.
8 Anmerkung durch den Herausgeber H.G. Göckeritz: „F. Gogarten: Ich glaube an den dreieinigen Gott. Eine Untersuchung über Glauben und Geschichte, Jena 1926."
9 Ein Programm oder eine Protokoll-Nachschrift der Tagung der Arbeitsgemeinschaft alter Marburger Theologen 22. – 24.10.1928 existiert nicht. Was wirklich das Thema dieser Tagung war, kann nicht mit Sicherheit gesagt werden, s. K. Hammann, Die Anfänge der „Alten Marburger", in: Christoph Landmesser/Doris Hiller (Hg.), Gerechtigkeit leben. Konkretionen des Glaubens in der gegenwärtigen Welt, Leipzig 2018, (127–140), besonders 129 und 138 mit Anm. 60. (Auskunft Konrad Hammann, Münster, 4. Mai 2018.)
10 Bultmanns Handschrift ist durch Konrad Hammann bestätigt (Auskunft, 17. Mai 2018).

mann sich zwischen Dezember 1926 und Oktober 1927 mehrfach intensiv über Gogartens Buch austauschten. Fuchs arbeitete gleichzeitig mit Bultmann an einer eigenen Brief-Rezension über Gogartens Buch, nachdem er mit 23 Jahren sein Theologie-Studium bei Rudolf Bultmann und Martin Heidegger im Frühjahr 1927 abgeschlossen hatte. Er sandte diese Brief-Rezension im Juli 1927 an Bultmann und dieser gab Fuchs' Brief-Rezension im Oktober 1927 an F. Gogarten weiter. Allerdings ist diese Brief-Rezension nicht identisch mit R. Bultmanns hier abgedruckter Rezension vom Oktober 1928.

Dies belegen Briefnotizen aus dem Briefwechsel zwischen R. Bultmann und E. Fuchs zwischen Dezember 1926 und Oktober 1927:[11]

R. Bultmann an E. Fuchs vom 6. Dezember 1926, während Bultmanns Erst-Lektüre von Gogartens Buch („eben jetzt, wo ich Gogartens neues Buch [...] lese): „Was werden Sie zu Gogartens Buch sagen?"

E. Fuchs an R. Bultmann, 7. April 1927: „Das Gogartenbuch las ich immer noch nicht ganz. Ich habe es mir nun für die nächste Zeit vorgenommen."

R. Bultmann an E. Fuchs 8. Mai 1927: „Ich freue mich auf Ihren Brief über Gogarten. Lassen Sie bald von sich hören."

E. Fuchs an R. Bultmann, 9. Mai 1927: Fuchs klagt über etwas zerrissene Arbeitszeit. „Darunter litt auch die Gogartenlektüre. Doch ich will versuchen, zu dem Stellung zu nehmen, was mich am meisten umtreibt – so gut es eben geht." Es folgen 4 ½ Seiten mit Bemerkungen zu Gogartens Buch. Diese Brief-Bemerkungen von E. Fuchs liegen im Archiv vor, decken sich aber weder im Ganzen noch in Einzelheiten mit der Rezension Bultmanns.

Offenbar arbeitete Fuchs zwischen Mai und Juli 1927 weiter daran, seine brieflichen Bemerkungen zu einer publikationsfähigen Rezension zu vervollständigen. Die Skizzen dazu sind erhalten unter Ernst Fuchs „Notizen zur Auseinandersetzung mit Gogartens Buch: Ich glaube an den dreieinigen Gott. Jena 1926", Datum: Oppenweiler 1927, Umfang 21 Blatt. Auf der Rückseite von Blatt 13 Teil eines Briefentwurfs an Rudolf Bultmann vom 29. Juni 1927, der aber nicht abgeschlossen und nicht abgesandt wurde.[12] Diese Notizen enthalten fragmentarische Exzerpte und Skizzen zu Gogartens Buch.

E. Fuchs an R. Bultmann, 19. Juli 1927: „Es hat lange gedauert mit dem Gogartenbrief. Ich habe mich Tag für Tag mit ihm herumgeschlagen. [...] Sollten Sie der Meinung sein, daß man G.[ogarten] diese Kritik schicken kann, freue ich mich recht darüber. Wenn Sie etwa selbst darauf eingehen, so freut mich's nochmal

---

[11] Die Briefe von R. Bultmann an E. Fuchs in: Universitätsbibliothek Tübingen Mn 22–531. Die Briefe von E. Fuchs an R. Bultmann in: Universitätsbibliothek Tübingen Mn 2–799.

[12] Universitätsbibliothek Tübingen, Ernst Fuchs Mn 22–364 und Mn 2–799. Ich danke Frau Ulrike Mehringer für die Bereitstellung von Scans dieser Archivalien.

mehr. Schade, daß ich nicht zwei Exemplare [sc. von Gogartens Buch] habe, sonst hätte ich Heidegger, mit dem ich auch über das Buch des öfteren gesprochen habe, eines geschickt. Aber ich habe die Zeit nicht zum nochmal schreiben. Er wird wohl finden, daß es ziemlich durcheinandergeht."

R. Bultmann an E. Fuchs 2. Oktober 1927: „So ist es gekommen, daß ich Ihren Brief u. Ihre Ausführungen über Gogartens Buch noch nicht beantwortet habe, u. nun stehe ich etwas beschämt vor Ihnen da. Ich bitte Sie, nicht zu zürnen! Ihre Kritik Gogartens finde sich sehr gut; ich habe sie an Gogarten geschickt und bin gespannt, was er sagen wird. Ich fürchte, daß ihm nicht alles verständlich sein kann (bei Ihrer Knappheit), wenn er nicht Heideggers Buch [sc. „Sein und Zeit"] schon gelesen hat."

F. Gogarten dankt in seinem Brief an R. Bultmann vom 12. Oktober 1927: „Für die Zusendung der Arbeit von Ihrem Schüler Fuchs danke ich Ihnen."[13]

Der Austausch zwischen E. Fuchs und R. Bultmann über Gogartens Buch reicht also ins Jahr 1927 zurück. Der Einfluss von Heidegger als Person auf diesen Austausch und von Heideggers Philosophie aus der Periode von „Sein und Zeit" wird greifbar und belegbar. Zugleich wird plausibel, warum Ernst Fuchs den Durchschlag des Typoskripts von Bultmanns Rezension nach dem Oktober 1928 erhielt und seinerseits mit Marginalien versah. Er legte die vollständige Durchschrift des Typoskripts seinem vollständig durchgearbeiteten Privat-Exemplar von Gogartens Buch bei.

Die Edition ist buchstabengenau, auch hinsichtlich orthographischer Eigenheiten und Tipp-Fehler sowie in Unterstreichungen und Abkürzungen. Offensichtliche Tippfehler und fehlende Satzzeichen werden jeweils mit Anmerkungen bzw. in Spitzklammern korrigiert.

* * *

Fr. Gogarten,
Ich glaube an den dreieinigen Gott.
Einleitung c.1

1–7 Die Antithese: Vernunftwahrheit bzw. allgemeine Wahrheit – zeitliches Ereignis. Dabei ist die Zweideutigkeit des Ereignisses nicht deutlich gemacht. Ist das Geschehnis vorhanden als innerzeitliches Geschehnis, als in der Vergangenheit vorhandenes Faktum, so ist die „Mitteilung" (die doch wohl von „Botschaft" streng zu unterscheiden wäre, cf. p. 2 unten) auch nur zufällige Wis-

---

[13] Universitätsbibliothek Tübingen Mn 2–842.

sensvermittlung wie die „Belehrung", wo es sich um allgemeine Wahrheiten handelt. Denn grundsätzlich sind alle vorhandenen Weltfakten dem[14] entdeckenden Forschen zugänglich, und nicht Botschaft, sondern Erkenntnis lässt des betreffenden Faktums inne werden. – Uebrigens konstituieren die Prinzipien (die als allgemeine Wahrheiten gewusst werden) und die Fakten <u>gemeinsam</u> die „Welt", und es gibt garnicht das Eine ohne das Andere. (Vgl. zu 5–7).

Zunächst ist also nur das Negative klar, dass es sich im Christentum nicht um allgemeine Wahrheiten handelt, nicht aber in welchem Sinne es sich um etwas handelt, was geschehen ist. Also auch nicht, inwiefern die „Botschaft" nicht einfach Mitteilung als Erzählung ist. In welchem Sinne kann es Botschaft von Ereignissen geben?

3–5: Frage an das Folgende: ist wirklich aufgedeckt, dass jener Irrtum uns „vom Mutterleibe her angeboren ist"? das würde doch heissen; ist gezeigt, wie die idealistische Weise, sich des Christentums zu bemächtigen, in einer bestimmten Weise des Daseins, sich selbst zu verstehen, begründet ist, und wie dies Missverständnis, – wenn es ein solches ist – ein Abgleiten von einem echten Verständnis ist, das von diesem aus begreiflich gemacht werden kann? /2/

5–7: Das S. 1–3 vermisste Problem meldet sich: das Geschehnis soll doch nicht als in der Vergangenheit vorhandenes Faktum verstanden werden; es „durchbricht die Grenzen seiner Zeit..." Aber das wird zunächst nicht positiv entwickelt, sondern eine falsche Interpretation dieser Möglichkeit wird vorgeführt: das Historische als Transparent des Ueberhistorischen. – Das dieser Interpretation zu Grunde liegende Daseinsverständnis wird S. 8 f. entwickelt (Geist-Natur).

9–11: die Sache (Entwertung des zeitlich-geschichtlichen Lebens durch den Idealismus) scheint mir zu einfach dargestellt zu sein. Zweifellos will der „Idealismus" Platons und Kants den καιρός[15] dringlich machen (cf Platons Verhältnis zum Staat oder etwa York an Dilthey S. 42 f.). (cf zu 24–29) Der Verfasser hat nur den romantischen Idealismus, wie es scheint, im Auge. – So ist auch bei aller Richtigkeit von 11–13 (Verkennung der Gottesfrage im Idealismus) unrichtig, dass die allgemeinen Wahrheiten ursprünglich keinen Bezug auf die zeitlich-geschichtliche Existenz haben.

13–15: Hier wäre wohl zu zeigen, wie die Fragen nach der Wesenseinheit die Abirrung der legitimen Frage des Menschen nach dem Verstehen seiner selbst ist. Dabei müsste geklärt werden, ob und inwieweit die „allgemeinen Wahrheiten"

---

14 Im Manuskript steht der Tippfehler „Weltfaktendem".
15 Sämtliche Worte in griechischen Buchstaben sind im Manuskript von Bultmann mit Tinte von Hand nachgetragen.

wirklich „Abstraktionen" (S. 7 ff.) sind. Der Mensch versteht sich z. B., wenn er das Gewissen hört, wenn er der Forderung der Wahrheit gehorcht usw. Die Verirrung ist die, dass er Gewissen und Wahrheit anders als in der Aktualität des Hörens zu verstehen meint und von da aus sich selbst als zeitloses in der Sphäre der Ideen eigentlich seiendes Wesen nimmt.

c.2

17–19: die Verwandlung des theologischen Problems in ein philosophisches ist darin begründet, dass ein zeitliches Geschehen nicht mehr in seiner Geschichtlichkeit, sondern als vorhandenes Weltfaktum verstanden ist. Der Begriff der Geschichtlichkeit, der dem Satz zu Grunde liegt, dass Offenbarung und Glaube selbst ein Geschehen (also nicht Geschehenes als /3/ vorliegendes Faktum) sind, muss geklärt werden. Es muss dabei aber nicht nur der heutige Geschichtsbegriff geklärt, sondern auch sein Verhältnis zum echten Begriff von Geschichte untersucht werden. 19–21 ist das Missverständnis nicht vermieden, als meine die Theologie das „Geschehnis" als in der Vergangenheit vorhandenes Einzelfaktum.

22–23: Es müsste deutlicher gesagt sein, dass es sich um den griechisch-ästhetischen Dualismus handelt, der Welt und Mensch unter den Kategorien Stoff und Form sieht (gut: „das bloss Materiale"!), der das Handeln als Herstellen der τέχνη auffasst und den Menschen als Kunstwerk sieht.

24–29: Müsste nicht gezeigt werden, wie durch den Begriff der Entwicklung erst das Geschehen seinen Wirklichkeitscharakter verliert? Das Verständnis des Geschehens nämlich unter dem Dualismus von Natur und Geist oder Erscheinung und Idee braucht das Geschehen noch nicht seines Charakters als begrenzt, aktuell und wirklich zu entkleiden. (cf zu 9–11.) Vielmehr soll offenbar bei Platon wie bei Kant dem Tun gerade dadurch sein Tatsachencharakter verliehen werden, dass es sich nicht als ein innerzeitlicher, ablaufender Vorgang (wie ein Naturvorgang) versteht, sondern als durch die Idee beansprucht und in der Möglichkeit, dem Anspruch zu hören oder zu verfehlen. Die Freiheit ist dabei vorausgesetzt, und sie wird durch den Entwicklungsgedanken vernichtet.

Dann müsste wohl die ganze Anlage anders werden. Die „verhängnisvolle Verwandlung" müsste als die Folge des Abgleitens des Idealismus von seinem eigentlichen Anliegen verstanden werden, und es müsste, nachdem in c.1 die gegenwärtige Situation dargelegt war, in c.2 zu ihrer Kritik zunächst das eigentliche Anliegen des Idealismus deutlich gemacht werden und darauf seine Verirrung gezeigt werden, die <er> in die gegenwärtige Situation hineingebracht hat. Es würde dann in 29–31 doch wohl gezeigt werden können, wie in den modernen

Menschen,[16] den Mythos oder die „Gestalt" zu zeichnen, sich das legitime Anliegen – freilich in unzulänglicher Weise – wieder geltend macht. Der Entwicklungsgedanke wird doch z. B. von Gundolf preisgege-/4/ben. Historisch wäre so zu differenzieren, dass romantische und naturwissenschaftliche Motive unterschieden würden. Uebrigens wäre dabei wohl auch an Nietzsche zu erinnern.

31–33: Ist vielleicht echtes und unechtes Verständnis des Dualismus von Geist und Natur so zu bezeichnen, dass man[17] sagt: ursprünglich (bzw. der Intention nach) bezeichnen Geist und Natur ein Sein, nämlich ein Sein des Daseins, das dessen Möglichkeit ist. Das Missverständnis läge darin, dass Geist und Natur je als ein Seiendes verstanden wurden? Das Missverständnis ist schon bei den Griechen angelegt, da die griechische Ontologie zwischen dem Sein und dem Seienden unterscheidet (Platon denkt die Idee als ein Seiendes, obwohl sie ihre Bedeutung darin hat, ein Wie des Seins zu sein.).

„Freiheit" ist von vorherein im Sinne des Natur-Geist-Dualismus verstanden. Es wäre aber zu fragen, ob das nicht ein Missverständnis eines ursprünglichen und geschichtlichen Freiheitsgedankens ist. Denn dem Begriff der Entscheidung korrespondiert allerdings ein Begriff von Freiheit, der mit dem zitierten Lutherwort nicht im Widerspruch steht.

Uebrigens ist der Gedanke von S. 32 nicht zu Ende geführt. Genau in der Mitte bricht er ab und mit dem Satz: „dieser Wunsch ist auch (!) insofern isoliert ..." setzt ein neuer Gedanke ein. Müsste nicht der Begriff der Entscheidung und damit die Zeitlichkeit des Daseins weiter analysiert werden, sodass dann erst der Begriff des Du gefunden würde? (Der Begriff des Jetzt als des „Augenblicks" wäre dabei zu erörtern.)

34–36: Ganz an Troeltsch bzw. am romantischen Geschichtsbegriff orientiert.

36: Es muss alles getan werden, damit klar wird, dass Ich und Du nicht als zwei „Subjekte", als zwei vorhandene Dinge, missverstanden werden, was ja auch die Absicht des Verf. ist, die schon darin klar wird, dass 36–38 das Wissen um das Du auf die Anerkennung[18] zurückgeführt wird. Aber die Abgrenzung könnte schärfer sein; die Charakterisierung des Du als des „zufälligen" ist missverständlich und wäre zu sichern durch Beziehung des Begriffs /5/ des Du auf den Begriff des Augenblicks. Und damit es nicht scheint, als sei zunächst ein „Ich" da, das dann „zufällig" ein „Du" findet, müsste gezeigt werden, wie durch das Du erst das Ich wird, und wie das Missverständnis des Ich und das des Du einander korrespondieren.

---

16 Ernst Fuchs bemerkt am Rand: Statt „Menschen" lies „Versuchen".
17 Im Manuskript steht der Tippfehler „amn".
18 Im Manuskript steht der Tippfehler „Annerkennung".

38 f.: Es dürfte nicht bestritten werden, dass die Besinnung von S. 1–38 eine philosophische und zwar ontologische ist (natürlich ist sie nicht eine „christlich"-philosophische). Nicht-philosophisch ist sie nur im Verhältnis zu einer untersuchenden. Uebrigens ist in ihr auch nicht von Gott die Rede, sondern sie führt nur zum Gottesgedanken, d. h. sie bleibt innerhalb der Sphäre des Menschlichen. – Es ist auch gar keine Besorgnis nötig, dass philosophische Besinnung unangemessen wäre, denn sie will ja nicht die christliche Botschaft begründen, und kann nur die christliche Theologie leiten, die sachgemässen Begriffe zu finden.

Erster Teil

c.3
Indem mit dem Gedanken der Schöpfung begonnen wird, wird jetzt von der christlichen Botschaft aus geredet. Man könnte fragen, ob nach 1–38 ein so abrupter Einsatz angemessen ist und nicht an die ontologische Besinnung angeknüpft werden sollte. Das ist nur scheinbar der Fall, wenn der Begriff der Zweiheitlichkeit aufgenommen wird; es ist ja nicht ohne weiteres deutlich, in welchem Verhältnis die Zweiheit von Ich und Du zu der Zweiheit von Geschöpf und Schöpfer steht. – Man könnte fragen, ob nicht die Erörterung des Schöpfungsgedankens anknüpfen sollte an den Begriff der „Geworfenheit" (Heidegger). Dafür wäre freilich Voraussetzung, dass in 1–38 der Gedanke der Zeitlichkeit und damit des Todes expliziert worden wäre.

43–45: Aehnlich wie 1–3 ist die Antithese einseitig! Es ist nicht nur das Missverständnis des Schöpfungsgedankens: Idee–Erscheinung, abzuwehren, sondern auch das: Hersteller und Hergestelltes. (Es folgt in gewisser Weise 45–47).

Uebrigens wäre doch zu sagen[19], dass „ordentliches Denken" im Fichteschen /6/ Sinne ein ganz bestimmtes Denken ist. In einem anderen Sinne kann man die Schöpfung sehr wohl „denken" (sonst könnte man ja nicht von ihr reden). Und es wäre wohl der Begriff des Denkens bzw. des Verstehens zu analysieren, was freilich in die anthropologische Besinnung der Einleitung gehörte (und zwar da, wo vom legitimen Anliegen des Idealismus und von seinem Abgleiten zu sprechen wäre): zum Dasein selbst gehört ein Verstehen (cf Heidegger). Natürlich wäre zu zeigen, dass zwischen Denken und Glauben kein Widerspruch besteht.

Die Interpretation von Rm 1,20 wäre doch zu erläutern, denn mit dem Gesagten wäre Platon und die Stoa wie Kant einverstanden, die ja auch nicht am „Sichtbaren" vorbeigehen wollen.

---

[19] Im Manuskript steht der Tippfehler „zusagen".

45–47: Abgrenzung gegen Otto (Kreaturgefühl!) wäre erwünscht.

Da man zweifellos die Zeit im Sinne von S. 46 auch philosophisch verstehen kann, erhebt sich auch hier die schwierige Frage nach dem Verhältnis der philosophischen und theologischen Analyse bzw. nach dem Verhältnis des „Vorverständnisses" und des christlichen Verständnisses des Daseins, (der revelatio generalis und specialis). Richtig ist (als theologischer Satz): „Glauben an Gott gibt es nur einer ganz bestimmten Situation gegenüber"; d. h. zugleich ich kann (echt theologisch) nur von Gott reden aus einem ganz bestimmten Verständnis von Zeit. Aber der Satz ist m. E. nicht umkehrbar, sodass ich nur aus dem Verständnis von Gott auch die Zeit verstehen könnte. Sonst bleibt man beim Gottes<u>gedanken</u>. – Man wird <u>wohl</u> sagen müssen: ich verstehe mein Jetzt je nur im Glauben. Aber was „Jetzt" überhaupt ist, d. h. den <u>Begriff</u> des Jetzt verstehe ich auch ohne den Glauben. Da aber um den Begriff des Jetzt zu verstehen, ich faktisch ja auch mein Jetzt verstehen muss (bzw. die Möglichkeit dazu habe, bzw. mein Jetzt mir verste<u>hbar</u> ist), lässt sich m. E. dem Satz nicht ausweichen, dass man das Glaubensverständnis auf ein „Vorverständnis" beziehen und theologisch von diesem aus klären muss.

Mir scheint nun, dass S. 46 f. vom christlichen Verständnis aus das vorchristliche Zeit-Verständnis beleuchtet ist. („es wird Zeit" oder „es ist /6b[20]/ Zeit" sagt ja nicht nur der Christ), dass also der christliche Gottes<u>gedanke</u> dem Vorverständnis deutlich gemacht wird (ich halte dies Verfahren für legitim). Dagegen ist noch nicht von dem Jetzt der Botschaft (2.Kor.6,2) die Rede, durch das jedes Jetzt qualifiziert und damit mir je mein Jetzt[21] wirklich erschlossen wird; es ist also auch noch nicht von <u>Gott</u> die Rede. M.A.W. es wird theologia naturalis entwickelt, – legitime, sofern sie vom Glauben aus entwickelt wird. – Aber sollte nicht die Methode der Analyse deutlich hervorgehoben werden?

48 f.: Es ist auch S. 45–47 nicht richtig zu sagen, dass der Glaube an die Schöpfung der Glaube an ein zeitliches Ereignis sei, zum mindesten ist es missverständlich, denn die Schöpfung ist nicht als zeitliches Ereignis gemeint, das in der Vergangenheit vorfindlich ist, sondern als die Tatsache, dass Gott mich je in mein Jetzt führt, dass mein Jetzt je von Gott geschaffen ist. – Dass sich ein Anfang „ereignete" dürfte also nicht gesagt werden, sondern „je ereignet".

49–51: Dass vom Glauben aus das vorchristliche Daseinsverständnis erläutert wird, findet seine Bestätigung. Dass dann die Zeit zwischen Anfang und Ende (Tod) unsere Wirklichkeit ist, ist auch vor dem Glauben zu sehen. Aber dass es die

---

[20] Wegen der irrtümlichen Doppelung der Seitenzahl 6 von Bultmann nachträglich von Hand mit „b" bezeichnet.
[21] Im Manuskript steht der Tippfehler „Jetzz".

Majestät Gottes ist, die in das Jetzt ruft und Halt gebietet, ist nur vom Glauben aus zu sehen.

Es wäre, wenn das so ist, deutlich die Frage zu stellen, wie denn diese, auch ohne den Glauben sichtbare, Wirklichkeit durch den Glauben qualifiziert ist, bzw. was Gott anderes[22] als ein mythologischer Name für den auch ohne ihn einsichtigen Sachverhalt ist. Dadurch könnte das eigentlich christliche Reden von Gott deutlich gemacht werden (was natürlich an dieser Stelle nur vorbereitet werden darf).

51f.: Auch hier zeigt sich: die Darstellung ist die christliche Interpretation des vorchristlichen Daseinsverständnisses. Denn nur für dieses gilt: „Von der Wirklichkeit des Schöpfers wissen wir nicht anders..." (S. 51). Es dabei[23] ja von der christlichen Botschaft abgesehen, die vom Schöpfer noch anders redet.

52f.: Dass das sichtbare Erscheinung des Unsichtbaren, das Vergängliche /7/ Gleichnis des Unvergänglichen ist, ist übrigens nicht griechisch (cf das Problem der μέθεξις), sondern neuplatonisch-orientalisch bzw. romantisch.

54f.: Im 2. Absatz S. 54 ist das Positive nicht ebenso klar gesagt wie das Negative! „Aber das heisst auf keinen Fall..." Ja! aber was heisst es positiv? Die Geschichtlichkeit des Daseins muss noch genau analysiert werden und zwar ist hier klar zu machen, dass Dasein nicht Vorhandensein ist, und dass der Fehler der abgewiesenen Meinung darin liegt, die Wirklichkeit unseres Lebens, in der wir Gott antreffen, als Vorhandenheit zu interpretieren. Und entsprechend ist die Zweiheit von Schöpfer und Geschöpf dem Missverständnis zu entreissen, als handle es sich um 2 vorhandene Wesen. (Vorhandenheit wird nicht anerkannt).

55–57: Hier wird die zu 54f. notierte Aufgabe ergriffen (die undialektische Sichtbarkeit des naturhaften Seins ist eben die Vorhandenheit). Sehr gut und entscheidend ist die hier (warum erst hier?) gegebene Daseinsinterpretation! Zur Klärung könnte dienen die Unterscheidung von Zeitlichkeit und Innerzeitlichkeit (cf Heidegger). Auch sollte über die verschiedene Weise, die Vergangenheit zu vergegenwärtigen, etwas gesagt sein!

Zur Terminologie: S. 56f. sollte nicht „verstehen" sondern „erklären" gesagt werden! Es muss gerade dagegen opponiert werden, als gäbe es nur ein Verstehen als ableitendes Erklären (als „Denken"). Entsprechend dürfte S. 57 nicht Anerkenntnis und Erkenntnis in Gegensatz gesetzt werden, sondern müsste die im Anerkennen fundierte Erkenntnis von der im „Betrachten" (θεωρία) fundierten unterschieden werden, und der θεωρία das Recht bestritten werden, allein von

---

22 Im Manuskript steht der Tippfehler „andere".
23 Ernst Fuchs notiert am Rand: „Es wird (?) dabei".

Erkenntnis reden zu können. – Ebenso mißverständlich[24] ist der Begriff des Gegenüber, das die θεωρία ja auch hat.

57–59: Wenn als einziger Inhalt des Glaubens der Schöpfer genannt wird, so wäre doch wohl ein Hinweis angebracht auf das Verhältnis von revelatio generalis und specialis.

Der Sprung zum Du geht mir zu schnell! Müsste nicht hier darauf rekurriert werden, dass meine Gebundenheit an das Geschöpf (in dem Gott mir allein begegnen kann) nicht bedeutet: mein Zusammen-vorhandensein mit anderen /8/ Vorhandenen? d. h. es müsste das Dasein als ein wirkliches Mit-Sein zuerst interpretiert werden, damit eine Gebundenheit in dem Sinne, um den es sich hier handelt, verstanden werden kann. Dass ich zu beliebigen Vorhandenen „Du" sage ist ja sinnlos. Andrerseits darf das Du nicht als ein zufällig mir unter anderm auch Begegnendes aufgefasst[25] werden, sondern als das, wodurch erst das Ich Ich ist, d. h. mein Sein muss in seiner primären Verbundenheit mit dem Du aufgedeckt werden. Dabei ist über die christliche Interpretation des Du-Ich-Verhältnisses noch nichts präjudiziert.

Ich könnte auch sagen: die beiden Sachverhalte, die das Dasein charakterisieren: das Sein vor dem Tode (bzw. zum Tode) und das Sein mit dem Du sind nicht in ihrer Einheitlichkeit deutlich gemacht. Daher auch der etwas abrupte Beginn mit dem Thema des Glaubens (S. 57).

60–62: Sehr gut und entscheidend! Terminologisch: ich würde „Werk" und „Tat" unterscheiden. Das „Werk" ist das „Getane", das hier[26] gerade nicht in Betracht kommen darf. Es muss zwischen dem Tun als „Herstellen" und dem reinen Tun (des Gehorsams) scharf unterschieden werden.

Sollte S. 62 überhaupt die Frage: „Entscheidung gegenüber der Vergangenheit" berührt werden, so musste m. E. das Problem exponiert werden. Dabei musste darauf Bezug genommen werden, dass Vergangenheit nach S. 56 nicht nur dem Charakter des durch die „Erinnerung" vergegenwärtigten Vergangenen zu haben braucht. – Die Frage durfte auch wohl nicht verschoben werden wegen S. 63 f; s. gleich[27].

63 f.: Hier ist doch wohl die Frage nach dem Ganzen (der Einheit) je meines Lebens und dem Ganzen der Welt zu unterscheiden. Das Letztere bleibt in „gedanklicher Undurchdringlichkeit". Aber das Erstere muss verständlich sein und ist es, wenn die Zeitlichkeit klargestellt ist, dazu gehört die Klärung des Begrif-

---

[24] Nachträglich von Bultmann handschriftlich aus „unverständlich" in „mißverständlich" geändert.
[25] Im Manuskript steht der Tippfehler „audgefasst".
[26] Im Manuskript steht der Tippfehler „heir".
[27] Im Manuskript steht der Tippfehler „glaich".

fes der Entscheidung (des Entschlusses in seinem Verhältnis zu Vergangenheit und Zukunft); im übrigen cf Heidegger S. 301–334 und besonders S. 389–392. /9/

c.4
Mir entsteht eine Schwierigkeit. In c.3 ist ein Daseinsverständnis unter dem Gesichtspunkt des Schöpfungsglaubens erläutert worden, das als solches nicht christlich ist (Faktisch war ja für ein solches Daseinsverständnis und von ihm aus der christliche Schöpfungsgedanke verständlich gemacht worden). Entsprechend wäre jetzt das Geschichtsverständnis, das im vorchristlichen Daseinsverständnis gegeben ist, vom Glauben aus zu erläutern. Faktisch geschieht das auch; d. h. es wird nicht der Begriff der Geschichte vom Glauben aus gewonnen, sondern vom Glauben aus gesagt, dass Gott der Schöpfer ist, der die Geschichte zur Geschichte macht. Da aber nicht streng unterschieden ist zwischen vorchristlichem und christlichem Geschichtsverständnis, tritt nicht hervor, was dieser Glaube selbst für das Geschichtsverständnis bedeutet. Bedeutet er überhaupt etwas für das Geschichts<u>verständnis</u> und nicht nur für die <u>Geschichte</u>? Bzw.: wieweit ist das Geschichtsverständnis vom Leben der Geschichte selbst abhängig? Es ist die gleiche Aporie wie in c.3 S. 45–47. Jedenfalls ist nicht oder nur halb richtig, dass man[28] ohne den Glauben an Gott die Geschichte nie als Geschichte verstehen kann. Man müsste dann schon in einem ursprünglichen vorchristlichen Daseinsverständnis eine fides implicita als Erfolg der revelatio generalis gelten lassen, – was wohl auch legitim wäre, aber das müsste geklärt werden.

65–67: dass es keine Geschichts<u>philosophie</u> gibt, ist natürlich wieder von jenem bestimmten Begriff der Philosophie aus gesprochen (S. 38f.). Eine philosophische Analyse der Geschichtlichkeit gibt es sehr wohl.

S. 66 usw. wäre statt „Perfektum" zu sagen „Präteritum", denn der griechische Begriff des Perfekts enthält gerade den Gegensatz gegen das Verständnis der Vergangenheit als Vergangenem und damit Erledigtem. – Zu klären wäre die Sache wieder durch Reflexion über den Modus der Vergegenwärtigung der Vergangenheit: Erinnerung oder Entscheidung.

Auf S. 67 vermischen sich Analyse und christliche Interpretation. Soll überhaupt von einer Einheit der Geschichte die Rede sein, die die des göttlichen Willens ist, so muss, damit dieser Satz nicht blosse Spekulation /10/ bleibt, gezeigt werden, wie diese Einheit im Dasein und für das Dasein fassbar ist, bzw. die, vielleicht nur im Glauben zu verwirklichende, <u>Möglichkeit</u> des Daseins ist. Dazu 63.f.!

---

[28] Im Manuskript steht der Tippfehler „amn".

68–71: Die Frage des Subjektivismus hätte längst erledigt sein müssen! – Es müsste wohl auch gesagt werden, dass in der subjektivistischen Interpretation des „Ich bin" der Fehler ist, dass das Ich als vorhandenes Ding (res cogitans!) gedacht wird. Auch S. 70 f. würde der Begriff des Vorhandenseins zur Klärung dienen.

71–73: Statt „verstehen (– im prägnanten Sinne –)" wäre wieder „erklären" zu sagen. Um der Klarheit willen wäre wohl zu unterscheiden: 1. Geschichtlichkeit; sie zu verstehen ist die philosophische Analyse da; 2. Geschichte im Sinne der Gesamtheit des Geschehens als in der Vergangenheit (evtl. auch in der Gegenwart cf Troeltsch) Vorhandenen; – sie erklären bzw. „deuten" will die abgewiesene „Geschichtsphilosophie"; 3. Geschichte im Sinne je meiner Geschichte; – sie versteht nur der Glaube. <u>Dass</u> sie nur der Glaube versteht, versteht ihrerseits die Theologie, aber nur, indem sie die Geschichtlichkeit versteht.

Dass ich von einem Vergangenem zur Entscheidung gerufen werden kann, ist zwar richtig, wenn auch missverständlich gesagt. Dass aber im Vergangenen ein Du begegnet, bzw. dass sich das Du als vergangenes und das Ich als gegenwärtiges begegnen, halte ich für falsch. Zum mindesten müsste der Begriff des Du geklärt sein. Aber ist dabei das Du nicht schlechthin anders verstanden als bisher?

73–75: Analyse des Begriffs Wahrheit ist notwendig!

75–78: Gut. 78 f. richtig, aber zum Negativen fehlt das Positive.

79–81: Seit S. 78 ist mir die Richtung der Untersuchung nicht deutlich. Es müsste durchsichtig gemacht werden, worauf es eigentlich hinausgeht (das S. 74 erreichte Problem steht doch wohl zur Debatte), und warum die Untersuchung auf diesen Wegen vorgeht: S. 79–81 erscheint als breite Wiederholung /11/ von schon Gesagtem, ebenso S. 81 f. Deutlicher wird[29] die Sache[30] erst 82–84. Hier könnte grössere Klarheit erreicht werden durch Auseinandersetzung mit Heidegger S. 372–404. Vor allem ist die Motivierung S. 83 („nur dasjenige Vergangene als Geschichte gegenwärtig, in dem mir ein Du begegnet") m. E. nicht ausreichend. Ich könnte (wenigstens zunächst) nur verstehen: nur dasjenige Vergangene, das mir durch ein gegenwärtiges Du aktuell gemacht wird.

Aber die Sachlage müsste viel umfassender geklärt werden: die <u>Motivierung</u> der Rückfrage nach der vergangenen Geschichte muss deutlich werden. Ebenso das Verhältnis der durch das Du vergegenwärtigten Vergangenheit zu der durch die Erinnerung vergegenwärtigten; denn jene kann diese ja nicht entbehren (und hierin ist das Abgleiten in die illegitime Geschichtswissenschaft begründet). –

---

29 Im Manuskript steht der Tippfehler „Deutlicherwird".
30 Im Manuskript steht der Tippfehler „Sach".

Vom Anspruch des gegenwärtigen Du aus muss der Anspruch des vergangenen Du (wenn man wirklich so sagen soll, s. o.!) deutlich werden.

Zweiter Teil

c.5
Jetzt muss offenbar vom Glauben aus geredet und zwar über die revelatio specialis geredet werden. Nur so kann die konkrete Frage, wie es mit Gottes Anspruch und unserer Verantwortung auf ihn steht, gestellt werden, die ja je mich fragt und deshalb von der philosophischen Analyse nicht mehr gestellt werden kann. Aber es fragt sich, ob die philosophische Analyse nicht auch hier noch zu berücksichtigen ist. Sie analysiert ja das vorchristliche Daseinsverständnis, und enthält nicht auch dieses das Wissen um Anspruch, Verantwortung und Schuld?

87 f: Weil früher nicht deutlich gezeigt ist, wie das vorchristliche Daseinsverständnis durch den Glauben qualifiziert ist, was also der Schöpfungsglaube über jenes Daseinsverständnis hinaus besagt, ist der Gedanke des Luther-Zitates nicht deutlich.

88–91: Ich glaube nicht, dass die S. 89 erwogene Möglichkeit richtig ist. Da der historische Entwicklungsgedanke ja nicht das Sichausleben der menschlichen Natur bedeutet, so sind für die Historie die Propheten so wenig als Störung verständlich wie Platon. – Im übrigen scheint mir S. 88–91 richtig wie 91 f., wo ich nur nicht verstehe, dass in den Urkunden des A.T. /12/ mir ein Du begegnen soll. Inwiefern denn? Damit das klar wird, sollte wohl auch 92–94 ausser Max Weber Nietzsche zu Worte kommen und die Frage aufgeworfen werden, ob überhaupt das Verhältnis zur vergangenen Geschichte für das Dasein notwendig ist, wenn es seine eigene Geschichtlichkeit nicht verfehlen soll. Man sollte doch erwarten, dass der traditionellen historischen Theologie gegenüber zunächst einmal gesagt würde: die Geschichte des israelitischen Volkes geht uns überhaupt nichts an, sondern nur das gegenwärtige A.T. Dessen Anspruch ist aber nicht einfach damit gegeben, dass es einfach da ist wie die platonischen Werke auch, sondern dadurch, dass jemand ihn erhebt bzw. vertritt – was dann nicht weiter ableitbar ist.

94–97: Denen, die Jesus in den Mythos verwandeln, wäre doch wohl nicht nur Deutungsmanie vorzuwerfen, sondern ebenso Vergewaltigung der historischen Fakten. In der Konsequenz des Historismus liegt ihr Verfahren nicht, da ja das Unternehmen der Deutung die zu deutenden Daten voraussetzt. Und ich glaube, es wäre besser, die Diskussion nur mit der anständigen Historie zu führen, wobei freilich gesagt werden kann, dass jene Mythologen eine auch für sie bestehende Gefahr signalisieren.

Ist in dem Satz, dass sich wirklich historische Tastsachen selbst bezeugen <,> an historischen Tatsachen der Vergangenheit gedacht, so kann doch nur gemeint sein, dass sie, wie es S. 91 hiess, gegenständlich vorhanden sind, nämlich in ihren Resten, den „Urkunden", also z. B. im A.T., aber auch im platonischen Schrifttum. Und was sollte sonst gemeint sein? Dann aber setzt dieser Satz noch nicht die Einsicht voraus, dass es kein Verstehen der Geschichte gibt ohne den Glauben an Gott den Schöpfer. Es müsste denn wieder die fides implicita gemeint sein; aber das ist im Zusammenhang doch wohl nicht möglich.

97–99: Die Frage des Uebersetzens aus der fremden Sprache scheint mir zu einfach genommen zu sein, weil jedes Uebersetzen ein Interpretieren ist. Es hätte wohl schon früher über die Möglichkeiten des Vergangenen und ihr gegenseitiges Verhältnis gesprochen werden müssen. /13/ Ist es richtig, dass weltanschauliche Voraussetzungslosigkeit der Geschichtsbefragung nur im Glauben an Gott den Schöpfer verwirklicht wird, so dürfte doch nicht verschwiegen werden, dass sie von vornherein eine Möglichkeit des Daseins ist, (wie sich daran zeigt, dass ich den Satz <u>verstehen</u> kann, ohne an Gott den Schöpfer zu glauben).

Da „Geschichte" als das in der Begegnung von Ich und Du sich vollziehende Geschehen bestimmt ist, kann man m. E. überhaupt nicht sagen, dass irgend ein vergangenes Geschehen „geschichtliche Qualität besitzt". Es <u>war</u> geschichtlich an seinem Ort in der Vergangenheit und ist als solches nicht mehr zu vergegenwärtigen. Soll meine gegenwärtige Begegnung mit einem vergangenen Geschehen selbst ein geschichtliches Geschehen sein, so ist nicht darüber zu präjudizieren, welches Geschehen der Vergangenheit dazu geeignet ist. Dass es nur ein Geschehen sein könne, „welches sich in der wahren zeitlichen Gegenwart eines konkreten, endlichen und darum die Unendlichkeit des Ich begrenzenden Du ereignet", lässt sich schon deshalb nicht sagen, weil sich <u>so</u> <u>alles</u> Geschehen der Vergangenheit ereignete; denn <u>nie</u> war ein Ich <u>nicht</u> durch ein Du begrenzt, aber der Unterschied ist, ob ein Ich diese Begrenzung <u>verstand</u> oder nicht. Darüber aber lässt sich von der Gegenwart aus nichts ausmachen; denn das Ereignis solchen Verstehens ist kein beobachtbarer Vorgang. Es lässt sich auch nicht sagen, dass es vom Glauben aus sichtbar werde; denn der Glaube ist in keinem Sinne θεωρία. – Die m. E. falsche Bestimmung verführt dann dazu von „wirklicher Geschichte" zu reden. Das mag einen guten Sinn haben; <u>hier</u> hat es ihn <u>nicht</u>. Es muss durchaus an dem Geschichtsbegriff festgehalten werden, der im 1. Teil aus dem natürlichen Daseinsverständnis entwickelt wurde, und es darf nicht der Geschichtsbegriff modifiziert werden, sondern nur gezeigt werden, dass die <u>Möglichkeit</u> des Daseins, eine echte Geschichte zu haben und nicht zu verfallen, nur im Glauben <u>verwirklicht</u> wird. – Im Zusammenhang kann m. E. nur gefragt werden, ob und wie das A.T. einen besonderen[31] Anspruch an die Gegenwart erhebt; wie die Begegnung mit dem A.T. eine geschichtliche ist. Ich zweifle, ob an die-/14/ser Stelle (ehe von der Begegnung mit der christlichen Botschaft die Rede war), von einem spezifischen[32] Anspruch des A.T. überhaupt geredet werden darf, und der Anspruch des A.T. nicht nur so motiviert werden darf, wie etwa der Anspruch Platons auch; denn auch für Platon usw. besteht ja die doppelte Möglichkeit, ihn nach Art der Historie unter dem Entwicklungsgedanken zu „betrachten", oder ihn zu mir reden zu lassen. – Es rächt sich, dass das Motiv der Rückwendung zur vergangenen Geschichte nicht ausdrücklich in den Blick gefasst ist (cf Nietzsche).

99–101: Die sehr treffenden Ausführungen scheinen mir hier nicht am Platz zu sein (wie denn überhaupt die Richtung der Untersuchung nicht durchsichtig gemacht ist). Sie müssten ihren Platz haben, wo über das Verhältnis des Vorverständnisses zum Glaubensverständnis ausdrücklich die Rede ist. Der allgemeine Gedanke von 99–101, dass es keine Universalgeschichte gibt, und dass Geschichte überhaupt nur vom Einzelgeschehen aus sichtbar wird, und zwar vom Einzelgeschehen aus, das sich zwischen Ich und Du vollzieht, ist vom vorchristlichen Daseinsverständnis aus durchaus schon zu vollziehen; und auch dieses vermag den allgemeinen Gedanken des Gegensatzes von Glauben und Schauen schon zu fassen. Was demgegenüber der Gedanke der Offenbarung sagt, ist nicht deutlich.

101f<.>: Hier wird jenes Verhältnis endlich zur Sprache gebracht und ausdrücklich zugestanden, dass dem vorchristlichen Daseinsverständnis die bisher vorgetragenen Gedanken vollziehbar sind. Aber die Konsequenzen sind m. E. nicht richtig gezogen. Dass nicht alles Geschehen schlechthin Offenbarung sein kann, darf m. E. nicht gesagt werden (die Möglichkeit hat es gerade!), sondern dass es das nicht ist. Das im Glauben an den Schöpfer geschehene Geschehen lässt sich (s.o.) nicht in dem Sinne als Offenbarung bezeichnen, als läge es nunmehr als Offenbarung vor (und die Frage ist doch die: was ist für die Gegenwart Offenbarung?), sondern nur in dem Sinne, dass damals in der Aktualität des Geschehens Gott offenbar war. War es so als Schöpfung qualifiziert, so bedeutet das nicht, dass es die Qualität der Schöpfung besitzt und in solcher Qualität sichtbar wäre. – Ich glaube, die Untersuchung /15/ hat sich verwirrt. Leitend ist doch die Frage, wie mir jetzt eine Vergangenheit Offenbarung werden kann, indem sie einen Anspruch an mich richtet, und so sich Geschichte zwischen dem gegenwärtigen Ich und einem vergangenen Geschehen vollzieht. Jetzt nach

---

31 Im Manuskript steht der Tippfehler „besondern".
32 Im Manuskript steht der Tippfehler „specifischen".

einem geschichtlichen Geschehen in der Vergangenheit zu fragen, scheint mir ein Abirren zu sein. Es darf m. E. nur aus dem Anspruch der Gegenwart motiviert werden, dass ich mich zur Vergangenheit wende, und dann sehe ich nicht in ihr ein vorliegendes Offenbarungs-Geschehen, sondern ihre Begegnung mit mir hat die Möglichkeit, jetzt Offenbarungsgeschehen zu sein.

108 f<.>: Richtig, aber nicht mit den eigentlichen Problem in Zusammenhang gebracht, der Frage, wie mir jetzt in der Vergangenheit ein Anspruch begegnen kann.

104–107: Erhebt das A.T., und nicht die hinter im liegende zu rekonstruierende Geschichte den Anspruch an die Gegenwart, so wird damit dem S. 97–99 und 101 f. Gesagten widersprochen. – Es müsste aber auch schon, damit ein spezieller Anspruch des A.T. sichtbar würde, auf die christliche Verkündigung hingewiesen werden, in der das A.T. mit seinem speziellen Anspruch begegnet.

107 f: Sehr gut. Nur hätte die erläuternde Ausführung über die „Inhaltlosigkeit" der Begegnung von Ich und Du viel früher gegeben werden müssen! Ebenso auch 108–110. Hier zeigt sich übrigens das oft gekennzeichnete Problem des Vorverständnisses in charakteristischer Form. Die „Begegnung" vollzieht sich in jedem Fall (so S. 109 f. mit Recht); sie soll aber (S. 110) nicht ohne Glauben und Offenbarung möglich sein. Man kann doch wohl nur sagen: dass sich das Ich echt versteht in der Begegnung, ist nicht ohne Glauben und Offenbarung möglich. – Gar nicht richtig scheint mir nun die Charakterisierung der qualifizierten Begegnung zu sein, die jedes Verstehen erst ermöglicht. Sie kann nicht die Begegnung mit einem Du sein, das an Gott den Schöpfer glaubt denn als Glaubendes kann mir das Du nie (auch im Glauben nicht) sichtbar werden. Und überdies ist schlechterdings nicht einzusehen, warum die Begegnung mit einem glaubenden Du eine qualifizierte sein soll. Mir scheint – um vorzugreifen – dass von „Begegnung mit dem Du" nur die Rede sein kann, wenn /16/ es sich um ein Du der Gegenwart handelt; kein Geschehen und keine Person der Vergangenheit kann mir je zum Du werden. Es lässt sich ausserhalb der christlichen Botschaft auch nicht davon reden, dass irgend ein Geschehen oder Sachverhalt sonst einen „Anspruch" auf mich erhebe, als eben ein Du; aller andere Anspruch ist immer nur durch ein Du vermittelt. Das eigentliche der christlichen Botschaft scheint mir dies zu sein, dass sie einen Anspruch erhebt, der nicht als Anspruch des Du verständlich ist, wie es denn auch den Glauben, den die Botschaft fordert, sonst nicht gibt. Die christliche Botschaft aber macht den Anspruch des Du, das mir jeweils begegnet, zu einem qualifizierten. Mit der rein formalen Analyse von Offenbarung 111–113 bin ich deshalb einverstanden: „Offenbarung ist nichts an-

deres....[33] als qualifiziertes Geschehen", d. h. sie ereignet sich da, wo das Ich die Qualifizierung der Begegnung mit dem Du durch das Wort der Verkündigung versteht. Dagegen sehe ich nicht ein, wie ich dadurch „vom Du unausweichlich als Ich gestellt werde", weil das Du an Gott als den[34] Schöpfer glaubt.

Die Darlegungen führen, wie 113–117 zu zeigen scheinen, noch in eine andere Schwierigkeit. Dass die bisherigen Erörterungen über die Offenbarung nur „prinzipielle, abstrakte Bedeutung" haben (113), kann doch nur bedeuten, dass sie den Offenbarungs-Gedanken so entwickeln, wie er für das „Vorverständnis" fassbar ist. Das scheint mir zwar eine legitime Aufgabe zu sein (die unter dem Titel der vom Glauben aus zu entwerfenden Lehre der revelatio generalis geleistet werden muss); aber kann dann die „Qualifizierung" der Begegnung (als welche die Offenbarung hier in der Tat bestimmt werden muss) anders verstanden werden als so, dass diejenige Begegnung eine qualifizierte ist, in der das Du als Du vom Ich verstanden (gehört) wird, wobei völlig dahingestellt bleibt: 1. ob solche qualifizierten Begegnungen wirklich sind, 2. wie das Du beschaffen sein muss, damit ich es als Du verstehen kann (sodass über seinen „Glauben" gar nicht zu reflektieren wäre).

Was das „wirkliche, aktuelle Sprechen von Offenbarung" (113) sein soll, ist mir dunkel. Wenn in ihm Offenbarung geschehen soll, so kann ich /17/ das nur so verstehen, dass es sich um ein Sprechen handelt, das in der Begegnung selbst geschieht, also um das Sprechen des Ich zum Du. Dies ist aber als Offenbarungsgeschehen doch nur innerhalb der Begegnung, d. h. für das Du verständlich; ein Bericht darüber an einen Dritten ist kein Offenbarungs-Geschehen mehr. – Davon abgesehen könnte „Sprechen von der Offenbarung" doch nur bedeuten: 1. eine formale Analyse des Offenbarungs-Begriffs, die natürlich kein Offenbarungs-Geschehen wäre, 2. die ganz besondere christliche Verkündigung; diese aber kommt hier ja nicht in Frage, und sie ist auch nicht in dem hier in Frage stehenden Sinne „Antwort, auf ein Gehörtwerden hin". Denn das Hören, um das es sich hier handelt, ist das Hören des Anspruchs des begegnenden Du. Das Wort der Verkündigung ist aber nicht der Anspruch eines je konkreten begegnenden Du, und die Weitergabe des Wortes ist nicht die Antwort auf das Du; sonst wäre ja die Konsequenz, dass die Wirksamkeit des Wortes vom Glauben des Verkündigers abhinge.

Mir scheint eben, dass der allgemeine und der specielle Offenbarungsbegriff nicht klar geschieden sind. Und dasselbe dürfte der der Fall sein, wenn als Träger der Offenbarung das Wort bezeichnet wird. Denn das ist zwar richtig, gilt aber für

---

33 Sic!
34 Im Manuskript steht der Tippfehler „alsden".

die allgemeine und die specielle Offenbarung in verschiedenem Sinn. Für jene gilt es, sofern mir das Du überhaupt immer im Wort begegnet und nur im Wort verständlich ist. Das Wort der speciellen Offenbarung aber ist ein ganz bestimmtes und zwar gar nicht direkt vom Du gesprochenes Wort. Die sehr richtigen Ausführungen über das Wort (die ja schon vom vorchristlichen Daseinsverständnis aus verständlich sind) S. 114–116 müssten schon in c.4 gegeben sein bei der Explikation von Geschichte.

Also kurz: S. 113–117 sind an sich sehr richtig es müsste nur deutlich sein, dass hier nicht über die christliche Offenbarung und das Wort der christlichen Verkündigung gesprochen, sondern für diese das Verständnis expliziert wird.

117 f<.>: Von dem entwickelten Vorverständnis aus ist garnicht klar zu machen, dass die „Zeugnisse der israelitischen Geschichte" dem Anspruch, Offenbarungs-/18/zeugnisse zu sein, erheben können, wie denn überhaupt der Begriff Offenbarungs-Zeugnis nach dem bisherigen garnicht verständlich ist. Der spezifische Anspruch des A.T. ist nur ein durch die christliche Botschaft vermittelter; ein allgemeiner Anspruch des A.T., der sich aber von dem Platons nicht unterscheidet, kann wohl behauptet werden und zwar vermittelt durch das Du, das mir in der Gegenwart begegnet. – (Uebrigens ist der letzte Ansatz S. 117 f. nicht sehr klar formuliert.)

118 f<.>: Unklar, solange der Begriff des Zeugnisses (den es nur im Christentum gibt) nicht geklärt ist. (Ausserhalb des Christentums kann „Zeugnis" nur Ausdruck des Ich bedeuten; dass solche israelitischen Zeugnisse, die zunächst auch nichts anderes sind, für uns Anrede sind, lässt sich meines Erachtens nur dadurch begründen, dass ihre Adressierung an uns autorisiert ist.)

119–122: Terminologisch: statt „Inhalt" würde ich „Charakter" sagen. So richtig im übrigen die Ausführungen sind,– was tun sie hier zur Sache?[35] Sollen sie zeigen, dass Israel den „Anspruch" erhob, geschichtlich zu sein? Ja, aber das ist doch nicht ein „Anspruch" in dem bisher in Frage stehenden Sinne! Die Ausführungen zeigen doch nur, dass im A.T. ein Daseinsverständnis sich ausspricht, das von dem modernen verschieden ist und als ein ursprüngliches bezeichnet werden darf. Sie sind rein historisch, freilich von einem nicht weltanschaulich gebundenen historischen Blick aus. Das gleiche gilt für 122–124.

124–126: Mittels des doppeldeutigen Terminus „Anspruch"[36] wird über das Problem weggesprungen. Die alttestamentlichen Aeusserungen[37] sind in Wahrheit vorher garnicht im eigentlichen Sinne als „Anspruch", sondern als Aus-

---

[35] Sic!
[36] Im Manuskript steht der Tippfehler „anspruch".
[37] Im Manuskript steht der Tippfehler „Aesserungen".

spruch, nämlich als sich Aussprechen eines bestimmten Daseinsverständnisses dargestellt. Inwiefern diese Aussprüche jetzt für uns einen Anspruch bedeuten, bleibt im Dunkel. – Nun kann man wohl sagen – wenn überhaupt die Rückwendung zur vergangenen Geschichte aus dem Dasein heraus motiviert ist –, (1) dass die Aussprüche der Vergangenheit einen Anspruch darstellen, insofern durch sie mein jeweiliges Daseinsverständnis gefragt ist. Aber ein spezifischer[38] An-/19/spruch des A.T. lässt sich von da aus nicht sichtbar machen. (2) (übrigens wäre S. 124 das Problem von Rm 2,14 f. zu berühren.)

----

(1) Eine solche Motivierung ist angedeutet in dem Satz: „wenn man an der Geschichte ... teil hat."

(2) S. 128 zeigt, dass das auch nicht beabsichtigt ist; aber der methodische Gang wäre von vorn herein klar zu machen!

Die Schlussfrage, die zum Folgenden überleitet, ist richtig; aber sie ist nach dem Vorhergegangenen nicht verständlich. Denn nach dem Vorhergegangenen ist „sich einer Situation anspruchslos und deutungslos stellen" und „der Glaube an Gott den Schöpfer" identisch (wie es auch innerhalb der revelatio generalis[39] sein muss). Aber jetzt soll der Glaube an Gott den Schöpfer als Voraussetzung jener Haltung gelten. Das ist an sich richtig; aber es kann doch wohl nur deutlich gemacht werden, wenn gezeigt ist, dass die revelatio generalis durch den Sündenfall verdunkelt ist, wenn die Möglichkeit des Glaubens an den Schöpfer als unmöglich erwiesen ist (was natürlich nur von der christlichen Verkündigung her geschehen kann). Dann nämlich kann gezeigt werden, dass die jeweilige Begegnung mit dem Du (und in ihr die Offenbarung) nur unter dem Lichte der Verkündigung echt verstanden werden kann. Die Erlösung schafft also den Schöpferglauben als die Voraussetzung jener Haltung.

c.6
127–129: Sehr richtig. Frühere Dunkelheiten werden jetzt geklärt; sie sollten freilich m. E. schon früher geklärt sein! Und auch jetzt müsste m. E. noch deutlicher gemacht werden, welchen Sinn die „Abstraktion" (S. 128 oben) eigentlich hat, dass es sich um das Verhältnis von revelatio generalis und specialis handelt.

130–132: Der Absatz 130 f. ist nicht ganz klar. Das echte Problem des „doppelten Evangeliums": Jesus als der Predigende und als der gepredigte, müsste doch wohl schon angezeigt werden.

---

38 Im Manuskript steht der Tippfehler „speziefischer".
39 Im Manuskript steht der Tippfehler „revelationgeneralis".

133–135: Die einzig mögliche Voraussetzung, unter der das Wort Jesu gehört werden kann, ist die, dass wir durch dieses Wort angesprochen sind. Gut. Aber inwiefern ist diese Voraussetzung gemacht? Wieder ist die doppelte /20/ Möglichkeit: 1.) sofern wir genötigt sind, uns zur Geschichte der Vergangenheit überhaupt zurückzuwenden und sie zu hören (Insofern steht uns also Jesus nicht anders gegenüber als Platon); 2.) sofern durch das gegenwärtige Wort der Predigt Jesu Wort vergegenwärtigt wird. Beides ist zu unterscheiden; das Erste scheint hier gemeint zu sein.

135–139: Richtig. Immerhin wäre der Doppelsinn von „Bekenntnis" zu berücksichtigen. Wie ist es zu verstehen, dass die „Confessio" ein „Symbolum" ist?

139–141: Einverstanden; doch enthält der letzte Satz ein Problem, das die Untersuchung weiter leiten müsste zu der 2. unter S. 133–135 genannten Möglichkeit; und in dieses Licht müsste 142 die Gleichung „Jesus ist das Wort" gerückt werden. Dagegen scheint mir der Satz „Weil dieses Wort ein von Anfang an verantwortliches Wort ist" irre zu führen.

142–145: Diese Analyse scheint mir wieder zu c.4 zu gehören. Uebrigens ist sie sehr gut und könnte etwa noch durch Hinweis auf den platonischen {}[40] und die griechische Auffassung des Verhältnisses von Ich und Du unter dem Gedanken der Erziehung bereichert werden.

145f<.>: Entscheidend für die Frage nach dem Verhältnis der revelatio generalis und specialis. Darum aber auch schon früher zu bringen! – Den letzten Satz freilich kann ich nicht anerkennen (s. o.).

146f<.>: Entsprechend der Beurteilung des letztens Satzes von 145f. kann ich nicht anerkennen, dass der Anspruch des A.T. an uns darin begründet sei, dass die Menschen des A.T. im Glauben an Gott den Schöpfer zu uns reden.

Entsprechend (s. auch zu 142) kann ich die Gleichung Jesus=[41] Wort Jesu nicht ohne weiteres vollziehen. 1.) die Gleichung Jesus = Wort kann m. E. nur bedeuten: Jesus ist als der gepredigte (nicht direkt als der Predigende) das Wort. 2.) Die Entscheidung, in die die Predigt Jesu stellt, ist nicht direkt: Jesus oder ich, sondern: Du (und zwar das jeweilige, konkrete, gegenwärtige Du) oder ich. Indem diese Entscheidung durch das Wort, das Jesum predigt, qualifiziert wird, ist die Entscheidung für das Du indirekt auch die Entscheidung für Jesus.

Nun würde ich auch sagen: die Propheten sind, was sie jetzt für uns sind, /21/ nur als Wort. Ihr Unterschied von Jesus ist nur der, dass sie nur durch ihn Wort für uns sind. Der Unterschied, dass sie aus der geforderten, nicht aus der erfüllten

---

[40] Im Manuskript steht eine längere Leerstelle, in die wahrscheinlich ein Wort mit griechischen Buchstaben per Hand nachgetragen werden sollte.

[41] Sic!

Beziehung sprechen, scheint mir nur für den historisierenden Blick vorzuliegen. Zu mir sprechen auch die Propheten aus der erfüllten Beziehung, da sie zu mir überhaupt nur sprechen, sofern sie durch ihn legitimiert sind. Deshalb scheint mir auch 148 f. künstlich spekulierend.

149 – 152: Diese entscheidenden[42] Ausführungen, die wieder das Verhältnis der revelatio specialis zur generalis betreffen, verstehe ich an diesem Platze nicht. Warum stehen sie nicht am Anfang des Kapitels?

152 f<.>: Fragwürdig; s. zu 146 f. Auch die Propheten, die aus der unerfüllten Beziehung reden, sind das Wort (und waren es auch für ihre Zeit, sie waren freilich ein anderes Wort). Auf diese Formel darf man den Unterschied m. E. nicht bringen. – Das „Wort der Liebe" redet andrerseits nicht der predigende Jesus, denn der predigt wie die Propheten das Gesetz und die Verheissung (so auch Luthers Meinung!), sondern der gepredigte Christus ist das Wort der Liebe. D. h. „Liebe" darf nur als Gottesliebe und nicht als der Vorgang eines Liebesaktes zwischen Ich und Du verstanden werden. Der „liebende" Jesus gehört in den Pietismus und in die liberale Theologie. – Das Problem des „doppelten Evangeliums" ist nicht zum Austrag gebracht!

153 – 156: Was „das Wort Jesu Christi" ist, ist nicht geklärt, da das Problem des „doppelten Evangeliums" nicht geklärt ist. Deshalb kann auch nicht deutlich werden, was „das Kreuz von Golgatha" ist, was es bedeutet, dass Jesus Christus die Sünde vergibt, indem er sie „auf sich nimmt". Inwiefern „weiss" er von meiner Sünde und „trägt" sie?

156: Es gilt das Gleiche; speziell ist der Begriff der Erfahrung am Schluss dunkel.

157: Hier könnte grössere Klarheit erreicht werden durch Beziehung auf die Eschatologie des N.T. (2. Kor.5,17; Gl.4,4; Joh. usw.!).

158: Richtig; aber müsste nicht der Begriff der Vergebung genauer analysiert sein?

159 f<.>:[43] /22/

159 f<.>: Unverständlich erscheint mir wieder, dass Jesus den Fluch des Gesetzes und den Zorn Gottes an seinem Leibe offenbare. Inwiefern? Das „deutungslose" Hören darf doch kein unverstehendes Hören sein; das Bekenntnis kein blindes: Auch bin ich bange, dass „Fluch des Gesetzes" und „Zorn Gottes" zu Deutungskategorien werden, wenn sie nicht in strenger Beziehung auf das Vorverständnis bezogen werden. Als was sind Fluch und Zorn in dem Dasein vor

---

42 Im Manuskript steht der Tippfehler „entscheidnenden".
43 Die Zeile bricht nach der Seitenzahl ab und setzt auf der nächsten Seite erneut mit der Seitenzahl an.

dem Glauben wirklich? als Angst und Hass. (Bei konsequenter Durchführung der revelatio generalis und specialis würde sich alles klarer sagen lassen.)

Dritter Teil

c.7
163 f<.>: Dass das Wort Jesu Christi (das ich wohl im Sinne des Verfassers als das Wort verstehe, das ihn predigt) das Einzige ist, was Geschichte schafft, muss m. E. mit Beziehung auf die Geschichtlichkeit, die das Dasein auch vor dem Glauben hat, interpretiert werden; d. h. wieder muss das Verhältnis von revelatio generalis und specialis geklärt werden.

Dass nur der Anspruch eines Du, der ein Bekenntnis zu Jesus Christus ist, zu einem wirklich geschichtlichen Wort werden kann, ist vorläufig völlig unklar; aber das Folgende soll ja Auskunft geben. – Das andere, dass es nur im Hören auf das Wort Jesu Christi eine Erkenntnis des Anderen gibt, ist dagegen deutlich.

164–167: Die reichlich deduktiv gehaltenen Ausführungen enthalten den durch alles Vorige vorbereiteten Gedanken, dass sich Gott in der Auferstehung Jesu Christi zu seiner Geschichte bekennt. Aber einiges ist mir bedenklich. 1.) Nicht vorbereitet ist die Aussage S. 164, dass es ausser im Hören auf das Wort Jesu Christi keinen Glauben an Gott den Schöpfer geben kann. Dieser Satz wird auch nicht zu begründen sein, sondern nur zu behaupten; d. h. es wäre wohl zu zeigen, dass dem natürlichen Daseinsverständnis kein Glaube an Gott als den Schöpfer möglich ist,– nicht als ob es den Sinn dieses Glaubens nicht verstehen könnte, aber ihm fehlt schlechthin das Recht zu diesem Glauben. Dies Recht gibt die christliche Verkündigung, dass nur sie es gibt ist kein Satz, an dem die Theologie Interesse hat, wenn nur sicher gestellt ist, /23/ dass das Dasein von sich aus dies Recht usurpiert. Sonst wird die Frage nach der „Absolutheit" des Christentums auf eine falsche Ebene gehoben.

2.) Dass die Auferstehung nicht am Anfang des Glaubens stehe, vermag ich nicht einzusehen. Denn ist das entscheidende Wort das, das Jesus Christus verkündigt, so kann es ihn doch nur als gekreuzigten und auferstandenen verkündigen. Oder: bekennt sich in der Auferstehung Gott zu seiner Geschichte, was kann der Glaube überhaupt anderes sein, als eben der Glaube, in der Geschichte Gottes zu stehen, καινὴ κτίσις im Glauben an Gott den Schöpfer zu sein? – Die Unterscheidung zwischen anfangendem und „reifem" Glauben verstehe ich nicht; umsoweniger, wenn nach 167–170 das Wort von der Auferstehung nicht nur das letzte, sondern auch das erste Wort der christlichen Verkündigung sein soll. Der Glaube ist doch von vornherein Glaube an die christliche Verkündigung. – Aber offenbar durchschaue ich das Motiv jener Unterscheidung nicht recht; denn im übrigen stimme ich S. 167–179 zu: Schöpfungsglauben gibt es für uns nur als <Auferstehungsglauben>[44], und dieser impliziert jenen.

70–172: Es ist mir fraglich, ob man das Wort von der Verkündigung als ein „verantwortliches" Wort bezeichnen darf. Verantwortlich können doch nur die Worte von Menschen sein (vom Ich zum Du), nicht das Wort Gottes. Sonst käme man ja zu der Konsequenz, dass die Verkündigung vom Glauben des Verkündigers abhinge. Anders steht es, wenn unter dem Wort der christlichen Verkündigung nicht ihr Inhalt sondern ihr Vollzug gemeint ist; das scheint im 2. Absatz der Fall zu sein, aber nicht im ersten! Im 2. Absatz aber scheint mir gesagt werden müssen, dass aus dem Glauben an die Kirche die Verantwortung des Verkündigers folgt.

172f<.>: Dass das Wort der Verkündigung nur das Wort der Gemeinde[45] sein kann, unterscheidet es 1.) von dem Wort, das nichts anderes als Aussprache eines Ich ist, 2.) von dem Wort der Anrede zwischen Ich und Du. Was das Wort der Gemeinde[46] positiv bedeutet müsste genauer geklärt werden, indem zunächst der Begriff der Gemeinde[47] geklärt wird. Sie wird konstituiert durch die Tradition. (cf 176–178!) Zum Wort der Verkündigung gehört konstitutiv, dass es gesprochen wird; also gehört das Faktum des Verkündigens zur Verkündigung selbst. /24/ Ich bin also je angewiesen auf den, der mir das Wort verkündigt hat (was ein anderes Angewiesensein auf den Anderen bedeutet als das im Mit-einander-sein von Ich und Du gegebene). So impliziert der Glaube an das Wort den Glauben an die Gemeinde, die also primär als Traditionsträgerin in Betracht kommt, nicht als glaubende[48] Gemeinschaft. – Von hier aus ist auch die Bedeutung Israels zu verstehen. – Ich glaube, dass ich die S. 172f. leitenden Gedanken damit treffe; doch scheint mir unerlässlich, das Moment der Tradition hier zur Geltung zu bringen und damit den Begriff der Heilsgeschichte einzuführen, die nicht aus der Geschichtlichkeit des Daseins allein[49] verständlich ist, sondern qualifizierte Geschichte ist, dadurch, dass das Wort, das nicht aus dem Dasein selbst herausgesprochen ist, sie bestimmt.

174–176: Entsprechend den früheren Bemerkungen kann ich auch hier nur z.T. zustimmen. Die Hauptthese, dass nur das Wort der Kirche ein wirkliches, geschichtliches Wort sein kann, müsste ich so modifizieren, dass nur durch das Wort der Kirche unsere Worte (vom Ich und Du) zu wirklichen, geschichtlichen Worten werden. Das Wort der Kirche ist „an sich" überhaupt kein „Wort" in dem

---

44 Im Manuskript steht irrtümlicherweise ein zweites Mal „Schöpfungsglauben".
45 Nachträglich von Bultmann handschriftlich aus „Gnade" in „Gemeinde" verändert.
46 Nachträglich von Bultmann handschriftlich aus „Gnade" in „Gemeinde" verändert.
47 Nachträglich von Bultmann handschriftlich aus „Gnade" in „Gemeinde" verändert.
48 Im Manuskript steht der Tippfehler „glaunende".
49 Im Manuskript steht der Tippfehler „allien".

Sinne, den „Wort" im menschlichen (und so auch im christlichen) Dasein hat; es ist ja das weitergegebene Gotteswort. Es ist auch gar nicht „an sich" verständlich, sondern nur in seiner Beziehung zu unsern menschlichen Worten, d. h. es wird nur da gehört[50], wo man sich durch das Wort der Verkündigung seine menschlichen Worte qualifizieren lässt.

Die Ausführungen über Kirche und Anstalt sind zutreffend; sie wären m. E. mit dem Traditionsbegriff zu verknüpfen.

Zu den beiden letzten Absätzen über die Verantwortung s. o. zu S. 170 – 172<.>

Es muss m. E. streng unterschieden werden, ob vom Hören oder vom Reden des Wortes der Verkündigung die Rede ist; bzw. es muss vom Reden dieses Wortes in doppelter Weise die Rede sein, nämlich 1.) sofern die Kirche redet, in dem sie die Tradition weitergibt. 2.) sofern auf die Verantwortung des Einzelnen Redenden reflektiert wird; diese geht niemanden etwas an ausser ihn selbst. Aber kann man in Bezug auf das Reden im 1. Sinne von Verantwortung reden? /25/

176 – 178: Dies sind die eigentlich entscheidenden Ausführungen; aber die hier gegebene Charakterisierung des Wortes muss am <u>Anfang</u> stehen; denn von hier aus ist alles andere (vor allem die Gedanken von Tradition und Kirche) erst verständlich.

Freilich scheint mir nun noch nicht völlige Klarheit erreicht zu sein. Denn wenn auch das „Wort" von einem Menschen zum andern gesprochen werden muss, so ist es doch missverständlich charakterisiert, wenn es als Beziehung zwischen Menschen bezeichnet wird. Die Bindung an den, der mir dieses Wort sagt, ist eine andere als die Bindung, die mich an ihn als den Nächsten bindet. Ich höre im Wort nicht den Anspruch dessen, der es mir sagt, sondern den Anspruch Gottes. Ich antworte sozusagen dem Wort der Verkündigung mit dem Glauben, dem Wort des Nächsten mit der Liebe. (Das Wort der Verkündigung kann mir z. B. von Luther gesagt werden; er ist für mich aber kein Du, dem ich in der Möglichkeit des Liebens oder Hassens gegenüberstehe.) Es kommt nun darauf an, dass die Beziehung der beiden Bindungen, des Wortes der Verkündigung und des Wortes des Du, die Einheit von Glauben und Liebe klargestellt wird.

179 – 181: Diese Ausführungen zeigen mir, dass wir in der Intention ganz einig sind.

c.8

182 – 185: Soll der Gedanke des Vorbildes Jesu klargestellt werden, so muss wohl gesagt werden, dass das „Tun Jesu" nicht das Verhalten des historischen Jesus ist, sondern Gottes Handeln in Christus.

---

50 Im Manuskript steht der Tippfehler „hehört".

Die Ausführungen über den verkehrten Anspruch des Menschen könnten vielleicht durch den Begriff der „Eigentlichkeit" geklärt werden. Ebenso könnte Klärung gegeben werden, durch Analyse des Begriffes „Handeln", indem Tun und Herstellen, Tat und Werk u. a. unterschieden werden. Endlich zeigt sich, dass im 2. Teil (Erlösung) von Schuld und Sünde genauer hätte geredet werden müssen.

185–188: Sehr richtig. Nur ist nach allem Vorangegangenen der Begriff des „Tuns Jesu Christi" noch ungeklärt.

188–190: Den Ausgangspunkt verstehe ich nicht; ist das Gesetz der Liebe nach dem Vorigen richtig verstanden, – was soll es dann heissen, dass es nur in /26/ einer gewissen Abstraktion, nur in der Isoliertheit und für die Isoliertheit besteht? Weil ich das nicht verstehe, verstehe ich offenbar auch nicht, was damit gesagt sein soll, dass Jesus Christus das Gesetz für mich erfüllt<.>

190–193: Dass mein Unverständnis gegenüber 188–190 nicht in einer sachlichen Differenz begründet ist, möchte ich daraus schliessen, dass ich hier (190–193) völlig zustimmen kann. – Notwendig und wohl hier am Platze wäre eine Erörterung des Begriffes Autonomie.

193–194: Nur Zustimmung; ebenso 194–196.

196–198: Ich bin völlig einig. Die Formulierung könnte m. E. noch deutlicher[51] werden. Es müsste wieder auf die Unterscheidung des Wortes der kirchlichen Verkündigung und des Wortes zwischen Ich und Du hingewiesen werden. Dieses höre ich anspruchslos nur, wenn ich jenes höre; und jenes höre ich nur, wenn ich dieses höre, d. h. wenn ich mir durch jenes dieses erschliessen lasse. Dem doppelten Wort (das aber nur in der strengen Bezogenheit des einen auf das andere das ist, was es ist) entspricht das doppelte Hören. Denn wie dieses und jenes Wort als innerzeitliches Ereignis auseinanderfallen so auch das Hören auf das Wort der Predigt und auf das Wort des Du. Genauer könnte die Sache geklärt werden durch die Unterscheidung von Innerzeitlichkeit und Zeitlichkeit.

198–200: Entsprechend lässt sich noch klarer sagen, was es heisst, dem Andern die Ohren für das Wort Jesu Christi zu öffnen: dies Wort ist ja auch ein doppeltes (in seiner Einheit zu verstehendes): 1.) das Wort der Predigt, 2.) das von mir zum Du gesprochene Wort, das je auf seinen Anspruch in der konkreten Situation antwortet.

200–202: sehr einverstanden; ebenso 202–204–206–209–211–212. Die Anknüpfung an das am Anfang über Schöpfung und Geschichte gesagte, könnte noch fester sein, sodass das Verhältnis von revelatio generalis und specialis noch einmal klar hervortreten würde<.>

---

51 Im Manuskript steht der Tippfehler „deutlucher".

Contributors

Heinrich Assel holds the chair in Systematic Theology at the University of Greifswald. He is editor of *Verkündigung und Forschung*, and co-editor of both the *Encyclopedia of the Bible and its Reception* and the *Berliner Theologische Zeitschrift*. He is the author of *Der andere Aufbruch: Die Lutherrenaissance – Ursprünge, Aporien und Wege: Karl Holl, Emanuel Hirsch, Rudolf Hermann (1910–1935)* (Vandenhoeck & Ruprecht, 1994); *Geheimnis und Sakrament: Die Theologie des göttlichen Namens bei Kant, Cohen und Rosenzweig* (Vandenhoeck & Ruprecht, 2001); *Beyond Biblical Theologies*, WUNT 295 co-editor (Mohr-Siebeck, 2012) and *Elementare Christologie, 3 Volumes* (forthcoming in 2020 from Gütersloher Verlagshaus).

David Congdon is the author of *The Mission of Demythologizing: Rudolf Bultmann's Dialectical Theology* (Fortress, 2015) for which he just received the Bultmann Prize for Hermeneutics from the University of Marburg; *Rudolf Bultmann: A Companion to his Theology* (Cascade, 2015); and *The God Who Saves: A Dogmatic Sketch* (Cascade, 2015). He is currently an acquisitions editor for the University of Kansas Press.

Hent De Vries is Paulette Goddard Professor of the Humanities at New York University (making him Professor of German, Religious Studies, Comparative Literature and Affiliated Professor of Philosophy). He is also Director of the School of Criticism and Theory at Cornell University and the *Titulaire de la Chaire de Métaphysique Etienne Gilson* at the Institute Catholique in Paris (2018). He will soon deliver the Gilson Lectures there. He is the author of *Minimal Theologies: Critiques of Secular Reason in Theodore W. Adorno and Emmanuel Levinas* (John Hopkins, 2005) and *Philosophy and the Turn to Religion* (John Hopkins, 1999).

Volker Leppin is Professor of Church History at the Eberhard-Karls-Universität, Tübingen. An internationally-acclaimed scholar, his books include: *Martin Luther* (2nd ed., Primus Verlag, 2010); *Geschichte des mittelalterischen Christentums* (Mohr-Siebeck, 2015); *Wilhelm von Ockham: Gelehrter, Streiter, Bettelmönch* (2nd ed., Primus Verlag, 2012); and *Die fremde Reformation: Luthers mystische Wurzeln* (C.H. Beck, 2016).

Bruce L. McCormack is the Charles Hodge Professor of Systematic Theology at Princeton Theological Seminary and Executive Director of its Center for Barth Studies. His books include *Karl Barth's Critically Realistic Dialectical Theology: Its Genesis and Development, 1909–1936* (Clarendon Press, 1995) and *Orthodox and Modern: Studies in the Theology of Karl Barth* (Baker Academic, 2008). As a past winner of the Karl Barth Prize (1998), he holds an honorary doctrine from the Friedrich-Schiller-Universität, Jena.

Jacqueline Mariña is Professor of Philosophy at Purdue University (Indiana). She is the author of *Transformation of the Self in the Thought of Friedrich Schleiermacher* (Oxford, 2008) and edited the *Cambridge Companion to Friedrich Schleiermacher* (Cambridge, 2003). She is currently working on a book on personal identity in Kant.

Christian Neddens was just appointed to a chair in systematic theology at the *Lutherischen Theologischen Hochschule* (LThH) Oberursel. He is the author of *Politische Theologie und*

Theologie des Kreuzes: Werner Elert and Hans Joachim Iwand (V&R, 2010); and co-editor of *Spektakel der Transcendenz: Kunst und Religion in der Gegenwart* (Neumann, 2016); and *Schalom Schabbat, Alexander!: Christlich-jüdische Begegnung in der Grundschule* (V&R, 2016).

Christine Svinth-Vaerge Pöder is Professor of Systematic Theology at the University of Copenhagen (Denmark). She is the author of *Doxologische Entzogenheit: Der Fundamentaltheologische Bedeutung des Gebets bei Karl Barth* (de Gruyter, 2009) and is the editor of *Mellem tiderne: fem dialektiske teologer* (Forlaget Anis, 2015).

Claire E. Sufrin is Associate Professor of Jewish Studies and Director of Jewish Studies at the Crown Family Center for Jewish and Israel Studies at Northwestern University. She is currently working on two books: *History and Hermeneutics: Martin Buber and the Jewish Bible* and *Story-Telling and Meaning-Making: Jewish Literature and Jewish Thought in America*.

Henning Theißen is Privatdozent at the Lehrstuhl for Systematic Theology at the Ruhr-Universität, Bochum. He is the author of *Die evangelische Eschatologie und das Judentum* (V&R, 2004) and *Die berufene Zeugin des Kreuzes Christi: Studien zur Grundlegen der evangelischen Theologie der Kirche* (Evangelische Verlagsanstalt, 2013).

Hartwig Wiedebach is Lecturer in Jewish Philsophy and Medical Ethics at the Swiss Federal Institute of Technology (ETH) in Zürich. He is also Director of the Hermann Cohen-Archiv in Zürich. He is the author of *Pathische Urteilskraft* (Herder, 2014) and is editor of *"Kreuz der Wirklichkeit" und "Stern der Erlösung": Die Glaubens-Metaphysik von Eugen Rosenstock-Heussy und Franz Rosenzweig* (Herder, 2016).

Index of Names

Albertini, Francesca 100
Almond, Philip C. 47
Alter, Robert 100
Althaus, Paul 4, 7f., 12, 15, 193, 214, 220f.
Askani, Hans-Christoph 150
Assel, Heinrich 1f., 5, 11, 13, 23, 30, 35, 66f., 69, 84, 86, 183, 193, 199, 213, 218, 221, 224, 229, 233
Aubry, Gwenaelle 156

Baasland, Ernst 6, 12
Barth, Karl 1–11, 13, 15–38, 57–64, 66, 68f., 71–73, 77–91, 110f., 123f., 159f., 165–167, 169, 171–177, 181, 183–191, 193–202, 205, 207f., 213, 216–219, 221–228, 230, 235
Baur, Ferdinand C. 5, 109f.
Beintker, Michael 11, 20, 28f., 38, 82, 194, 225
Bender, Kimlyn J. 89
Bergman, Hugo 98
Beyschlag, Karlmann 218
Bienenstock, Myriam 38
Bonhoeffer, Dietrich 7, 9, 15f., 79, 222
Bornhausen, Karl 10
Brody, Samuel H. 106
Brunner, Emil 110f., 123f., 159, 165, 169, 173f., 193, 219
Buber, Martin 38, 93, 95–108, 203, 210
Bultmann, Rudolf 1–3, 5–22, 149, 155–157, 163, 165–168, 193–195, 197f., 202–208, 210, 233–238, 242, 244, 257
Busch, Eberhard 33, 83, 184, 193, 208
Büttgen, Philippe 152

Calvin, Johannes 2, 6, 185, 216, 227
Chalamet, Christophe 1f., 150
Cohen, Hermann 19, 23–25, 27–31, 33–38, 96
Congdon, David W. 1, 16
Crowe, Benjamin D. 160

de Vries, Hent 150, 152
Degenhardt, Ingeborg 117f.
deJonge, Michael P. 7
den Hertog, Gerard C. 225, 230
Diem, Harald 5, 7, 16
Diem, Hermann 5, 9
Dierken, Jörg 30
Dietzel, Stefan 115
Dober, Hans M. 30, 38
Duensing, Friedrich 217

Ebeling, Gerhard 16, 79–87, 155, 219
Elert, Werner 1, 7–9, 11f., 15, 213–223, 225f., 229
Ellwein, Eduard 62f.

Ficker, Johannes 2, 64f., 84
Ford, David F. 90
Frei, Hans W. 89, 98
Friedländer, Saul 12
Fuchs, Ernst 193f., 204, 233–237, 240, 243

Gadamer, Hans-Georg 150–152, 157f.
Geiger, Abraham 93f.
Gens, Jean-Claude 152
Göckeritz, Hermann G. 3, 7, 10, 173, 177, 194f., 197, 233–235
Goering, D. Timothy 194, 202, 206
Gogarten, Friedrich 1–3, 5–12, 15, 165, 171, 173–186, 188–191, 193–211, 217, 219, 224, 233–237
Grabmann, Martin 114
Greisch, Jean 164
Grisebach, Eberhard 177f., 197, 203, 205, 210

Hadot, Pierre 158, 163
Hamm, Berndt 6, 86, 214
Hammann, Konrad 12, 157, 166f., 233–235
Härle, Wilfried 89
Harnack, Theodosius 64, 113, 115, 213, 215

Index of names

Hauber, Reinhard   214
Heidegger, Martin   2f., 12–15, 149–156, 158–169, 202f., 205f., 210, 234, 236f., 241, 243, 245f.
Heppe, Heinrich   185
Hermann, Rudolf   2–5, 7–10, 12f., 15, 19, 57–59, 64, 66–73, 77, 80, 84, 105, 118, 173, 197–199, 202, 218, 222, 224f., 233, 235
Hermle, Siegfried   12, 14
Herrmann, Wilhelm   1, 6, 14, 28, 33
Heschel, Susannah   94
Hirsch, Emanuel   1, 5–9, 11, 13f., 66f., 94, 96, 114, 119, 196f., 199, 216, 218f., 221, 224
Holl, Karl   2f., 5–7, 9, 14f., 57–59, 64–73, 77, 84, 111f., 119, 167, 199, 213, 218f., 223f.
Horwitz, Rivka   98f., 101
Hoskyns, Edwyn   57, 61–63, 72f.
Hunsinger, George   79–81, 89

Ibn Esra, Abraham   36, 38
Iwand, Hans J.   7, 9, 16, 198f., 202, 213, 217, 222–231

Jones, Hugh O.   89
Jüngel, Eberhard   1, 10, 21, 78, 89, 166

Kant, Immanuel   19–27, 29–31, 35f., 38–42, 47–55, 189, 198, 209, 217, 222, 238f., 241
Kaufmann, Thomas   6, 100, 117, 216–218
Klän, Werner   215
Klappert, Bertold   222, 227
Korsch, Dietrich   20
Korthaus, Michael   223
Kraus, Hans-Joachim   13, 224
Kuhlmann, Gerhardt   14
Künneth, Walter   7, 216

la Montagne, Paul   28
Lange, Dietz   5, 225
Lehmann, Hartmut   6
Leppin, Volker   6, 109, 111
Lévinas, Emmanuel   196, 203, 205
Liebing, Heinz   12

Lohmann, Johann F.   28, 185
Longuenesse, Beatrice   50
Luther, Martin   1–16, 18f., 21, 39–41, 45, 57–71, 73, 77–88, 90f., 102, 109–124, 149–153, 155–165, 167, 169, 171–174, 176, 180, 183, 187, 193–201, 205f., 209f., 213–228, 231, 247, 255, 258

Martyn, J. Louis   9
McCord-Adams, Marilyn   209
McCormack, Bruce L.   17, 28, 91, 171, 185, 228
McGrath, Sean J.   155
Mendes-Flohr, Paul   93, 95f.
Minney, Robin   41, 47
Mjaaland, Marius T.   160f.
Moxter, Michael   30
Müller, Alphons V.   6f., 10, 16, 111f., 120

Natorp, Paul   25, 28, 33, 150
Neddens, Christian   213, 217
Nielsen, Bent F.   38, 72
Nygren, Anders   5, 7, 9, 15

Oakes, Kenneth   20, 28, 30
Oelke, Harry   6, 117
Oepke, Albrecht   110f.
Ohst, Martin   119
Otto, Rudolf   6, 8, 39–50, 52–55, 115, 215, 242
Overbeck, Franz   16, 18, 150
Ozment, Steven E.   109, 121

Pedersen, Else M.W.   110, 113, 116
Pfleiderer, Georg   28
Põder, Christine Svinth-Værge   77
Pöggeler, Otto   155
Preger, Wilhelm   109f., 112

Rade, Martin   2f., 173
Rieger, Reinhold   78
Ritschl, Albrecht   110–113, 119, 123, 219
Ritschl, Dietrich   89
Rosenberg, Alfred   6, 117f., 122–124
Rosenzweig, Franz   23f., 38, 96f., 100–103, 106

Index of names

Safranski, Rüdiger 166
Sartre, Jean-Paul 196
Sauter, Gerhard 2, 5, 87, 184
Schleiermacher, Friedrich D. E. 15, 47–49, 67, 110, 155, 176, 213, 215
Scholder, Klaus 214
Seeberg, Erich 109, 115–118, 224
Seeberg, Reinhold 109, 113–115, 123 f.
Seim, Jürgen 222, 225, 230
Sheehan, Thomas 154
Slenczka, Notger 5, 217
Sommer, Christian 152
Stapel, Wilhelm 11, 13, 214
Stoevesandt, Hinrich 82, 190
Strohm, Christoph 9
Sufrin, Claire E. 93, 106

Thaidigsmann, Edgar 61, 63, 226, 231
Theißen, Henning 77, 91
Theunissen, Michael 196, 203, 205
Thierfelder, Jörg 12, 14
Thurneysen, Eduard 4, 15, 60 f., 165, 169, 173–176, 189, 193–197
Tietz, Christiane 83

Tolstaja, Katja 4, 57, 85
Trapp, Christian 112
Troeltsch, Ernst 2 f., 11, 78, 80, 203, 217, 240, 246

Van Buren, John 155
van der Kooi, Cornelis 4, 57, 85
Vogelsang, Erich 6, 109, 119–124, 196, 202
von Kirschbaum, Charlotte 82 f., 87, 193
von Rad, Gerhard 68

Waldenfels, Bernhard 209
Wallmann, Johannes 57
Ward, Graham 90, 150
Webb, Stephen H. 90
Wiedebach, Hartwig 19
Wolf, Ernst 7, 9 f., 16, 50, 158–160, 165–169, 222
Wolfe, Judith 152, 158

Zunz, Leopold 93, 102
zur Mühlen, Karl-Heinz 119

www.ingramcontent.com/pod-product-compliance
Lightning Source LLC
Chambersburg PA
CBHW030532230426
43665CB00010B/863